The English House

Also by Dan Cruickshank

Around the World in 80 Treasures

Dan Cruikshank's Adventures in Architecture

The Secret History of Georgian London

Bridges: Heroic Designs That Changed the World

*The Country House Revealed: A Secret History of the
British Ancestral Home*

Brick (with William Hall)

A History of Architecture in 100 Buildings

Spitalfields: The History of a Nation in a Handful of Streets

Skyscraper

Cruickshank's London: A Portrait of a City in 13 Walks

Built in Chelsea: Two Millennia of Architecture and Townscape

Soho: A Street Guide to Soho's History, Architecture and People

The English House

A History in Eight Buildings

DAN CRUICKSHANK

HUTCHINSON
HEINEMANN

HUTCHINSON HEINEMANN

UK | USA | Canada | Ireland | Australia
India | New Zealand | South Africa

Hutchinson Heinemann is part of the Penguin Random House group of companies
whose addresses can be found at global.penguinrandomhouse.com

Penguin Random House UK,
One Embassy Gardens, 8 Viaduct Gardens, London SW11 7BW

penguin.co.uk

Penguin
Random House
UK

First published 2025
001

Set in 11.5/15.5pt Adobe Caslon Pro
Typeset by Six Red Marbles UK, Thetford, Norfolk

Printed and bound in Great Britain by Clays Ltd, Elcograf S.p.A.

The authorised representative in the EEA is Penguin Random House Ireland,
Morrison Chambers, 32 Nassau Street, Dublin D02 YH68

A CIP catalogue record for this book is available from the British Library

ISBN: 978–1–529–15245–6

Penguin Random House is committed to a sustainable future
for our business, our readers and our planet. This book is made
from Forest Stewardship Council® certified paper.

MIX
Paper | Supporting
responsible forestry
FSC
www.fsc.org
FSC® C018179

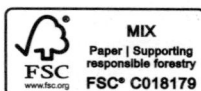

In memory of my friend Andrew Saint
November 1946 – July 2025

Contents

Preface   ix

Introduction   xi

1. ARCHITECTS AND PATRONS   I
Pallant House, Chichester (1712)

2. A HOME FOR IMMIGRANTS   33
19 Princelet Street, Spitalfields (1718)

3. A HOUSE BUILT BY CONNOISSEURS   79
Maister House, Hull (1743–c.1760)

4. A PIECE OF URBAN THEATRE   121
Heywood's House and Bank, Liverpool (1798–1800)

5. A QUESTION OF STYLE   155
Cragside, Northumberland (1869–95)

6. THE TWO-UP TWO-DOWN   205
Toxteth Bye-law Houses (c.1860–c.1890)

7. THE BIRTH OF THE COUNCIL FLAT   247
The Boundary Estate, Shoreditch (1890–1900)

8. THE FIRST 'MODERN' HOUSE   303
New Ways, Northampton (1925–6)

Afterword   347

Glossary   369

Notes   377

Picture Acknowledgements   439

Index   441

Preface

Thus book explores the manner in which buildings are made – the relationship between clients, surveyors, architects, building tradesmen and all involved in the architectural process. At the same time, it examines the ways in which buildings were used, and the social and aesthetic statements their creators intended them to make. The former ambition is not an easy one to realise, in part because contemporary documentation is often scanty, in part because the role of those involved in the process of design and construction varied from building to building and also evolved over time. The latter ambition also poses challenges of perception and interpretation. The task is nevertheless a rewarding one: delving beneath the veneer of style and fashion to unravel the story of how houses were conceived and built, combined with placing them fully in the context of their age, offers an opportunity for familiar buildings – or, at least, a familiar type of building – to be seen in a new way.

Many people have helped me tell this story. I cannot mention them all, but I must name a few:

Richard Harris for information about Bayleaf Farmstead, and for his drawing of its timber-frame structure; Simon Martin and, from Alan Baxter Limited, Richard Pollard, Vicky Simon and Heloise Palin for information and assistance on Pallant House; The Spitalfields Historic Buildings Trust and Rachel Lichtenstein for 19 Princelet Street; David Neave and the National Trust for Maister House, Hull; Andrew Saint for Norman Shaw and Cragside, and Gareth Carr for Toxteth and the Welsh Streets.

From the publishers, Nigel Wilcockson, who commissioned this book and has overseen its production – many thanks; and Joanna Taylor, Caroline Pretty and Hannah White-Steele for their great help in refining the text and gathering the images.

Introduction

ON STEEP HILL IN LINCOLN – a street of Roman origin[1] that leads up from the lower city to the spectacular eleventh- and twelfth-century cathedral – stands one of the oldest houses in England.[2]

The Steep Hill house is said to date from around 1170[3] and has long been known as the 'Jew's House'. Judging from what survives of the original front, it was clearly conceived not as a simple vernacular building but as a considered work of architecture. The house, while gnarled by age, remains very handsome. It is built of local limestone, cut into roughly squared blocks, with those forming the front laid smartly in horizontal courses that differ slightly from one another in depth. This gives the facade as a whole a sense of order, while also the charm that comes with gentle irregularity. Remnants of round arched windows set within larger semicircular relieving arches – all enriched with carved ornament – survive, as does a now-decayed, ornamented semicircular arch over the front door. Such motifs are typical of Romanesque or Norman architecture, familiar to us today in such grand buildings as cathedrals, churches and castles but perhaps slightly surprising to find on a house set within an informal terrace on an urban street.

The house is also remarkable in preserving on its facade a broad pier above the front door that contains a flue and that once terminated in a chimney stack. In the twelfth century it was usual for domestic buildings to have an open hearth placed towards the centre of the room they served. Here, by contrast, in the first-floor chamber that stood above a ground-floor hall or shop there would have been a fireplace set within a wall opening. Those whose houses contained open hearths would have had to endure the smoke that belched forth.

'The Jew's House', numbered 15 The Strait, Steep Hill, Lincoln, built *c.* 1170 and one of the oldest surviving continuously inhabited buildings in Britain. Note the robust masonry construction, the high-status Romanesque details including remains of semicircular arched windows, and the first-floor chimney breast set above the front door.

Those who lived in the Jew's House could have enjoyed the comfort of a fire's heat without the inconvenience of its smoke. The house was not only beautifully designed and crafted but also, in its incorporation of a fireplace and chimney, embraced a technical improvement that was then still a comparative novelty.

We do not know who created this house over 850 years ago, but the popular assumption is that it was originally occupied by a member of Lincoln's once relatively numerous and wealthy Jewish community. It is generally agreed that a Jewish presence in England was established – or at least greatly enlarged – at the time of the Norman Conquest in 1066 by William I, who valued the services of Jewish bankers when it came to securing much-needed loans. If the house on Steep Hill really was built by a well-to-do Jewish citizen of Lincoln (tradition associates it with the town's leading Jewish banker, Aaron, who died in 1186), that might explain both its authoritative appearance and the fact that it was built in a style closely associated with the newly established Norman state. It could also account for the reason why this small house was so substantially built – why, indeed, it almost resembles a small fortress. Any building associated with the Norman regime could have been a target for those long-established and disgruntled inhabitants of Lincoln whose fortunes and status had decreased in the years after the Conquest (the very fact that William I should have decided to build a castle and a cathedral side by side in the upper city suggests he was aware of the need to exert physical and spiritual control over his potentially troublesome new subjects). Any building associated with a Jewish banker who served the Norman king would have been doubly at risk, as was amply demonstrated by the events of 1190, when simmering resentment sparked by Crusader reversals in the Holy Land (including the loss of Jerusalem in 1187) turned to attacks on Lincoln's Jewish community.[4]

* * * * *

The Jew's House is a remarkable survival. It also neatly embodies several of the themes that this book explores: the technological innovations that have been incorporated into English domestic architecture; the ways in which houses were used; the – often complex – relationship between the person who commissioned them or who first lived there and those who actually built them; and, finally, the messages and meanings conveyed by the styles or forms that were chosen.

Technological innovations invariably involve introducing greater comfort and convenience into the home, but their progress has often been slow and uncertain. The Jew's House was, as I have just mentioned, one of the first surviving domestic buildings to feature a mural flue and fireplace. Nearly 180 years later, from 1348, each of the (originally) forty-four houses of the Vicar's Close in Wells, Somerset – two parallel rows of terrace houses facing each other across a cul-de-sac – was given a large, centrally placed chimney breast and towering chimney stack.[5] Yet even in the fifteenth century, many houses – for example, the oak-framed so-called Wealden hall houses that were once plentiful in the prosperous Weald of Kent (although by no means confined to that region) – were built with a large, double-height, centrally placed hall with an open hearth. The roof timbers of the magnificent hall at Bayleaf Farmstead, though probably originally painted, must quickly have become soot-blackened by the smoke rising from the open hearth and making its way out of the building via a louvre or gablet in the roof.[6]

Gradually, though, fireplaces became both standard features and important focal points. As we will see, at 19 Princelet Street in Spitalfields, the first known occupants, the Huguenot Ogier family, made their mark by installing a fine timber-made, French-style, mid eighteenth-century rococo fire surround (Chapter 2). Just over a century later the fireplace achieved what can be described as its grand apotheosis in the house of the Victorian industrialist William Armstrong at Cragside in Northumberland (Chapter 5). Other innovations – improved cooking facilities, for example, and sanitary arrangements – have similarly followed paths that have not always been strictly linear, not least because their adoption has invariably been bound up with questions of social status and relative affluence. At the time William Armstrong was installing kitchen ranges,

Vicar's Close, Wells, Somerset, dating from 1348 – the oldest coherently planned and continuously occupied uniform street to survive in Europe. The tall chimney stacks proclaim the pioneering domestic comfort of these small houses.

flushing lavatories and electrical lights in his grand house, many of his poorer countrymen would have been cooking over open fires, using a shared privy and lighting their houses with gas lamps or even still using oil lamps or candles (Chapter 6).

When it comes to the overall arrangement and usage of rooms within houses, the essential forces behind change were a combination of those that drove technological innovation – the desire for greater convenience and comfort – with those that served an increasing desire for privacy and those that expressed wealth, taste and social status. Sometimes, as with the Wealden hall houses, the last consideration might trump the other two. The owners of Bayleaf Farmstead went without the convenience of a fireplace set against a wall and supplied with a flue and stack. On the other hand, their double-height hall proclaimed their elevated position within the local feudal system. The hall was a grand affair, crowned by an impressive roof truss which incorporates a handsome crown post that supports a collar plate and collar-beam and which in turn rises from a stout and lightly orna-mented tie-beam, which is itself supported by massive arched braces.

This magnificent room would have been the heart of the home, a place of reception and entertainment, where meals were consumed and perhaps cooked (although there was probably a kitchen in a separate building as well), and where bedsteads for humble members of the household could be arranged at night. With its lofty dimen-sions and raised dais upon which the family and its honoured guests would, on festive days, dine in some state at the 'high table', it pro-claimed its owner's status. And while the house was, in some senses, quite old-fashioned for its time, it's worth noting that its first-floor 'solar', or upper chamber, probably serving as the family's private bedroom and sitting room, appears to have been supplied with the modern convenience of its own privy, projecting from the side eleva-tion of the main house and emptying into a cesspit below.

Grander medieval houses tended to follow a similar plan. Adjoin-ing the dais end of the hall would be a two-storey wing containing family rooms, including a ground-floor parlour and at first-floor level a solar that on occasion could project into the upper volume of the hall and hover above the high table, implying a canopy. There might also be a bedchamber for the head of the house. At the opposite end of the hall, beyond a cross-passage connecting front and rear doors that in larger halls might be concealed behind a screen, was typically a corresponding wing of equal size, reached usually via two or three doors from the hall. This was the service wing, with one door leading to a buttery, in which bottles of ale, cider or mead would be stored, and the other door leading to a pantry, used for food preparation and the storage of bread and flour. If there was a third door, it might lead to a separate kitchen (usually an innovation for slightly later hall houses of the larger kind), or to a ladder-like staircase to communal lodgings on the first floor.

By the early sixteenth century, the demand for comfort, convenience and privacy had increased markedly, and houses were being reconfigured accordingly. Typically, operations within the home became more streamlined, more efficient, and also more discrete, with fewer functions taking place in shared spaces such as the great hall and the solar. By the mid sixteenth century the double-height hall of the type to be found at Bayleaf Farmstead had mostly been superseded (often via the insertion of a new first-floor level), by a downstairs hall – reduced in function to serving largely as an arrival and reception area – and a more private and comfortable great chamber above. The new arrangement was made possible by the more general adoption of chimney stacks, which, of course, funnelled smoke away and heated rooms more efficiently and safely. To reach the upper-floor rooms, practical staircases were introduced, replacing the steep ladder-like affairs that had existed before. Often these early domestic staircases were of spiral form (like the larger staircases found in great medieval houses or castles) and placed within staircase towers. These frequently adjoined garderobe towers, which incorporated privies and which, to make life a little easier, were generally located near bedchambers.[7]

Grander houses of the Tudor period continued to make use of the courtyard arrangement popular in medieval times, but reined it in to achieve greater comfort. The standard pattern was four ranges around a central court entered by a gate of more or less symbolic grandeur.

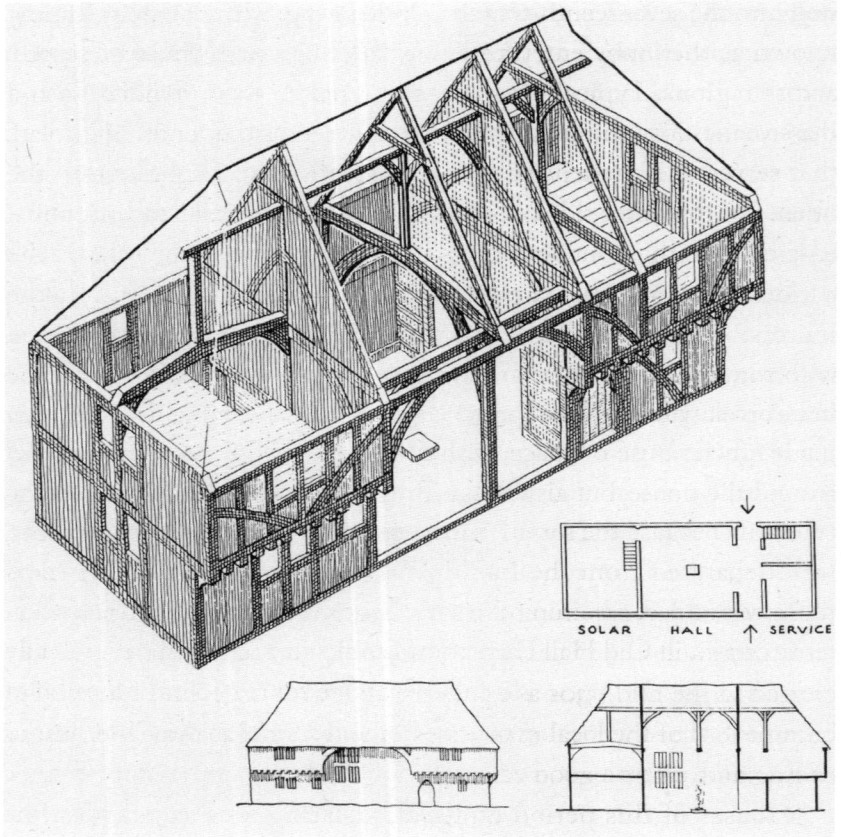

A typical fifteenth-century Wealden hall house, based on Bayleaf
Farmstead. In the centre is the full-height hall, with its crown post
roof truss and central open hearth. On the left are the family quarters,
including the solar, and on the right the service wing.

Hall and great chamber would typically sit within one range (usually facing the gate), with a service range including kitchen, pantry, buttery and lodgings, and a higher-status range for family and guests, perhaps including a first-floor long gallery for promenading and for the display of art and other treasures. Smaller houses from the 1530s or so until well into the seventeenth century often followed an arrangement now known as the lobby entry, though its precise form differed slightly across regions. Typically, a two-storey house was provided with a massive masonry chimney stack, located towards the centre of its plan, that served the kitchen/hall to one side of it and the parlour on the other. On the other sides of the chimney stack were placed a lobby – entered from the front door and giving entry to the kitchen and to the parlour – and a spiral staircase leading to first-floor bedrooms. The staircase could be entered from the kitchen or the parlour or indeed, with some ingenuity of planning, from both. This plan form, radical in its break with the cross-passage tradition of the hall house, not only made efficient use of space, with little required solely for movement around the house, but also offered increased convenience and privacy, primarily because the service functions of the house, and the servants, were separated from the family area of the parlour. Often a third room was added, adjoining the parlour or the kitchen. The brick-and-terracotta-built Old Hall Farm at Kneesall, Nottinghamshire, probably created in the mid 1530s as a hunting lodge for Sir John Hussey, who became lord of the local manor in 1522 and served as the Chief Butler of England, offers a good early example.[8]

Houses of this period built in England's ever-growing towns tended to adopt a different pattern, for the simple reason that because urban land was expensive and urban sites invariably constrained, more accommodation needed to be squeezed on to any given site. Some, it is true, continued to ape the approach of earlier houses: the ornately carved timber-framed Paycocke's House in Coggeshall, Essex, for example, which was built in about 1500 by a wool merchant named John Paycocke and extended in about 1510 by his son Thomas, incorporates the remains of an early fifteenth-century open hall house and cross-passage form of entry.[9] But the builders of other urban houses

Paycocke's House, Coggeshall, Essex, built at the very beginning of the sixteenth century for a wealthy cloth merchant, probably incorporating part of an earlier structure, and thoroughly but sensitively repaired and restored in the early twentieth century.

resorted to adding storeys or building more rear rooms or ranges to squeeze in as much as they could. Town houses built on so-called urban 'burgage' plots tended to be relatively narrow but deep, with rows of accommodation – tenements, workshops or warehouses but also some serving domestic functions – strung out behind the main house on the street and typically reached via narrow alleys. In ancient towns that had strong trade, manufacturing or port traditions, the pattern might be reversed, so that the street front contained a shop, and the rear range the house's 'hall' accessed by a narrow passageway. King's Lynn, on the wide River Ouse and once a major trading port, boasts a number of houses, set parallel to the town's river front, of roughly L-shaped plan where this disposition of uses applies.[10] Generally, the first floor of the street range would contain a private chamber, placed above the shop. Access to the rear was through a passage opening from the centre of the facade.[11] The combination of home with work or trading space remained a constant feature of urban houses. The owner of the magnificent Maister House in Hull (Chapter 3) would doubtless have met business clients there. At Heywood's in Liverpool (Chapter 5), we see a wealthy eighteenth-century dynasty of traders and financers creating a building that was both house and bank.

As for the materials from which such houses would have been constructed, this depended largely on what was most readily to hand and, in the case of humbler dwellings, what was cheapest.[12] Local stone was much used in the central portion of England, from south to north, in the West Country and in the south-east. The precise type of stone varied, of course, from area to area: Dorset offered Portland stone; oolitic limestone was to be found around Bath; Doulting limestone in the Mendip Hills; Barnack stone in Cambridgeshire and into Lincolnshire; sedimentary ironstone in Northampton; and around Derbyshire, Ashford 'Black Marble' (in fact a limestone). In Kent and along the south coast, the sedimentary Kentish ragstone, flint and chalk were all easily available and favoured. Flint – used as pebbles, or 'knapped' to present a sparking face – was common in East Anglia. To the north and north-east lay numerous types of sandstone as well as slate; to the west, igneous rock, notably granite. In areas where materials and money were scarce, there was always cob, which is essentially blocks of mud, bound with straw (and sometimes with a little lime added as a hardener), which could be used to build thick walls protected from the elements by regular coats of limewash. Clay was increasingly employed in south, east and central England from the thirteenth century to revive a brick-making industry dormant since Roman times. And over much of England there were forests of oak and elm that provided excellent and durable timber, mostly used to form frames, infilled with wattle and daub (woven twigs and mud mixed with straw) or later with laths and lime plaster or with brick.

Between the late twelfth and sixteenth centuries, such materials were employed to create traditional and native Gothic forms and details; thereafter foreign Renaissance influence became increasingly paramount. As the following chapters show, architectural style was often a matter for heated debate, notably in the nineteenth century when battle was joined between those who favoured Renaissance buildings and those who championed a return to the Gothic (Chapter 5). The use of local building materials, once a matter of convenience, similarly became a bone of contention, champions of the late nineteenth-century Arts and Crafts Movement arguing, for example, that domestic design and construction should be rooted in regional vernacular building traditions and utilise local materials. In the twentieth century, Continental influences once again came to the fore in the house that Wenman Joseph Bassett-Lowke had built for himself in Northampton and that he named New Ways (Chapter 8).

* * * * *

Until the mid seventeenth century, English houses were, for the most part, one room deep – or 'single pile'. This offered the advantage of making it easy to clear houses of smoke and allowing plenty of light to enter (particularly if the orientation of the house offered both morning and evening light). But because rooms were arranged in a linear fashion, like coaches on a train, it was often necessary to pass through one or several rooms to reach the one you wanted to be in. Various forms of lobbies were experimented with, but the lack of privacy remained an irritation and an inherent problem. The invention of the two-room-deep 'double-pile' house, served by a staircase, landings and passages, however, solved the conundrum. Early examples tend to be urban ones, like the square-plan Whitehall, in Monkmoor Road, Shrewsbury, which dates from 1578 to 1582.[13] Ultimately, architecturally conceived corridors (the word is first recorded in England in around 1600),[14] as opposed to humble passages, would become a standard feature of house design.[15] In his additions for Hampton Court Palace in the 1690s, for example, Sir Christopher Wren designed a sequence of eight connecting rooms for the King's Apartment (what is known as an enfilade plan), with doors aligned to offer a vista and a promenade of state from the guard room via presence chambers, dining room, throne room and state bedchamber to a small room where informal meetings could take place, termed 'a closet' or 'cabinet'. But he also created, running parallel to part of this route, a gallery that also functions as a corridor offering a route of service, via anterooms, to the state dining room and bedchamber.[16] One of the most stunning early double-pile houses is Hardwick Hall in Derbyshire, built for the Countess of Shrewsbury from 1590. Representing a possible evolution of the traditional H-shaped plan for such grand edifices, it uses passages to ease connections between its various rooms and to ensure convenience. The house is remarkable in other ways, too. In style it is a heady mix of Gothic tradition and boisterous Renaissance novelty. It contains the double-height hall that would have been familiar to the countess's ancestors, but this hall is set on an axis (i.e. on the main centre line through the building, not at right angles to the entrance), so creating the sense that it's a grand point of arrival through which one passes rather than a destination in which to linger; in a way it's more like a modern entrance hall than a medieval great hall. The best chambers are distinguished by their floor-to-ceiling heights and arranged in hierarchical manner, with the best (and tallest) ones at the top of the house, where the prospects of the surrounding estate are particularly enticing. This suggest a sense of functionalism that is, again, almost modern. One other unusual feature is that the wide and stately staircase is set to one side of the plan. It provides a grand route through the interiors – indeed something of an architectural promenade – its elemental scale and stone construction making it seem almost like a street, and its asymmetrical design offering a strong contrast with the dedication to the new-fangled Renaissance obsession for symmetry apparent in the rest of the house. And there is technological innovation, expressed best by the huge windows, demanding large amounts of glass that was an expensive luxury at the time, that allow daylight to flood into the best rooms. Perhaps most memorable is the house's sensational and romantic silhouette, with its tall cubic prospect towers that give it a fairy-tale quality – like an Elizabethan evocation of Camelot.

The outline plan of the Hall is also intriguing. It is formed by two squares of equal area separated by a pair of squares (each half the area of each of the large squares) that define the plan of the central great hall. Smaller squares, representing the Hall's six towers, are placed on or near the centres of the three outer faces of the large squares. Such use of squares and cubes suggests a familiarity with the Renaissance planning theories of Sebastiano Serlio and Andrea Palladio, for whom such forms were all-important.[17] But compositions incorporating ten squares, as is the case here, and implying 'ten squared', might also have been seen as a means of achieving mathematical and geometrical perfection, with square numbers – in this case 100, or 10 x 10 – representing harmony. If this ten-squared plan was a device, then it was fully in keeping with late Elizabethan thinking. This was an age fascinated by the witty or symbolic use of conceits, devices and emblems, of which the play of squares in the plan of Hardwick could be an expression.[18]

And this raises other – interrelated – themes that are pursued in the chapters that follow: the creative relationships that the patrons who commissioned houses had with their master masons, surveyors or architects, and with the building tradesmen they employed; the messages – touching on their status, beliefs, ambitions, loyalties and tastes – that patrons wished to convey through the architecture they commissioned; and the conundrum of establishing when the prime

Hardwick Hall, Derbyshire, built from 1590 for the Countess of Shrewsbury, probably in part, at least, to her design and to the design of the mason-architect she employed, Robert Smythson.

responsibility for the creation of a house passed from the client or occupant to the building professional responsible for its design and execution.[19]

To create Hardwick Hall, the Countess of Shrewsbury called on the services of Robert Smythson, a master mason and architect of prodigious talent, who had worked from 1568 at Longleat in Wiltshire and from 1580 at Wollaton Hall, Nottinghamshire.[20] His contribution at Hardwick Hall must have been of the greatest importance, although since no detailed plans of the Hall or correspondence between client and architect survive, it is hard to state this categorically. Such a gap in the historical record is as typical as it is perhaps extraordinary. Building a home is a personal and emotional affair that is well worth recording and discussing, yet relatively few contemporary or intimate documents – such as letters or diary entries – survive in significant number that chronicle the creation of historic houses, or at least those that are much more than a century old. What does survive, in large quantity, are building accounts that list names of tradesman, sums charged and dates on which bills were paid – the essential if somewhat arid evidence of once-tumultuous building projects. As it happens, these survive for Hardwick Hall and, if lacking in opinion or emotion, they do at least impart valuable if cryptic information about the creative process and the relationships between those involved. For example, they tell us that in March 1597, as the Hall was being completed, twenty shillings was paid to Smythson and ten shillings to his son, perhaps by way of token gifts from the countess, at the time of her house-warming, for services rendered.[21] That patron and designer worked well together seems to be confirmed by the fact that, even before Hardwick Hall was completed in 1597, the countess commissioned Smythson to design and build yet another new house – Oldcotes – nearby and for the use of her son William Cavendish.[22]

Whatever design and practical skills Smythson may have brought to bear at Hardwick, it's hard to believe that the countess was not herself closely involved. She was, after all, both a remarkable woman and an avid builder, whose several marriages generally had architectural consequences. In 1547 she married Sir William Cavendish, her second husband, who in 1549 she persuaded to buy the Chatsworth estate in Derbyshire. This presented her with the first great architectural opportunity: the building of a new house at Chatsworth, on an idyllic site near a river. Cavendish died in 1557, so she married again but death once again intervened, which led in 1568 to her fourth marriage – to the 6th Earl of Shrewsbury, one of the richest and most powerful men in England. This marriage proved deeply unhappy, and in 1584 the countess fled from Chatsworth – on which she had spent much of the earl's money – to her modest family manor house at Hardwick, which she had purchased from her impoverished brother the previous year. Here she put her heart and soul into the realisation of an architectural vision: to make the family home and estate at Hardwick an acceptable alternative to the renounced Chatsworth. First she built an almost entirely new house on the site of the manor, now known as Hardwick Old Hall, making it more convenient and fashionable. And then, thanks to the death in November 1590 of her estranged husband and the wealth that now came to her, Hardwick Hall itself. Begun within a month of the Earl of Shrewsbury's death, it constitutes a declaration of independence, of wealth, of advanced taste and of a determination, as the architectural historian Mark Girouard puts it, to create 'the perfect house'.[23]

Over the next centuries, as the following chapters show, the role of the designer of houses for more prosperous members of society would evolve and change. Number 19 Princelet Street in Spitalfields was planned and constructed in 1718 by a local carpenter and speculating builder named Samuel Worrall. Maister House in Hull, by contrast, while calling on the skills of the town's craftsmen, was in part overseen by one of the foremost arbiters of taste of the period, the 3rd Earl of Burlington, while in the following centuries Cragside in Northumberland and New Ways in Northampton were conceived by professional and widely acclaimed architects of national, indeed international, repute: Richard Norman Shaw at Cragside and Peter Behrens at New Ways.

As for the role of the patron, this varied enormously from project to project. At Pallant House, Elizabeth Peckham demonstrated that the Countess of Shrewsbury was not a lone female voice in English architectural history, even if she sadly lacked the power and authority the countess possessed to ensure that she was able to enjoy the house on which she lavished so much attention. The wealthy male patrons of Cragside and New Ways, on the other hand, were able not only to shape the projects they funded, but to depart from the architect's masterplan as and when they wanted. At Cragside, what had been a fruitful collaboration between patron and architect was ultimately damaged, at the very end of the project, by a niggling dispute over the detailed design of the 'Gilnockie' tower.

The messages such collaborations physically embody are fascinating to decode. The houses may simply reflect what was fashionable at the time, but they may also seek to present their creators as knowledgeable arbiters of what will come next. New Ways, for instance, was the brainchild of a wealthy businessman who proudly proclaimed it to be a 'Super-Modern Home' and 'a fore-runner of the house of the future'. The architectural styles these houses adopt may reflect a desire on the part of their creators to be regarded as people of considered taste and refinement, as the Palladian Maister House does. They may also reflect more general contemporary preoccupations and issues of the period. The Gothic elements of Cragside form part of a wider Victorian debate about appropriate national styles for architecture in an age of empire, industrialisation and radical change and about the ethical and moral symbolism of those styles.

The less well-off in society, of course, were never in a position to discuss the nature of the house they lived in with the person who designed it. They effectively had to accept what was on offer. But, as the chapters on 'two-up two-down' houses in Toxteth, built according to the standards imposed by local and national government byelaws, and the council flats of the Boundary Estate in Shoreditch, east London, show (Chapters 6 and 7), design principles were nevertheless on display in even the humblest of homes. The simplest, least ambitious of the houses in Toxteth display in the details of their brickwork the aspirations that those who created them entertained for those who lived in them. For its part, the Boundary Estate is the work of a highly talented and highly committed team of architects who were determined to create a paradise of 'sweetness and light' in an area that had until very recently been one of London's worst slum areas.

Each of the eight chapters that follows seeks to tell the story of the creation of a particular house or kind of house, from a grand Georgian town house to a Victorian country retreat, to a council-funded flat intended for the working poor. Each of these dwellings is also representative of an important moment or development in the history of the English house, while simultaneously offering a lens through which the wider history of the nation can be viewed and understood. Each, in other words, is individual but stands for something more than itself. Number 19 Princelet Street in Spitalfields is both an elegant early eighteenth-century terrace house and a physical record of successive waves of immigration, most dramatically so when it became a synagogue in 1870 for Jewish families escaping persecution in central and eastern Europe. Heywood's house and bank in Liverpool is a fascinating blend of home and institutional building and a window into the trading past of one of England's premier ports. The chapters covering the bye-law housing in Toxteth and the Boundary Estate in Shoreditch show how efforts were made in the late nineteenth century to replace desperate slums with decent homes for working people – in Toxteth through private and profit-orientated enterprise and in Shoreditch through a pioneering programme of public housing – where the ambition to provide hygienic accommodation was combined with a desire to achieve a certain beauty that would dignify and inspire those who would occupy these new homes. Each tale is individually remarkable. Each is also emblematic.

The entrance front of Pallant House, facing west onto North Pallant.
Built by Henry and Elizabeth Peckham in the early eighteenth
century in Chichester.

– 1 –

Architects and Patrons
Pallant House, Chichester
(1712)

MANY OLDER HOUSES ARE, in historical terms, fairly anonymous affairs. We may be fortunate enough to have a record of who commissioned them or had overall responsibility for their construction, or building accounts, tax or insurance documents may still survive. But beyond such information as these fragments might offer, we generally know little; and since so many of these houses were radically transformed by subsequent generations, even the surviving physical evidence they have to offer can be patchy and difficult to interpret. In the case of Pallant House in Chichester, West Sussex, however, not only does enough of the fabric of the original house remain to allow us to build up a good picture of how it was built, but thanks to a financial dispute between the husband and wife who commissioned it, we also know a lot about those involved in its genesis and about its first inhabitants.

The story of the house can be said to start in May 1711, when Henry Peckham married Elizabeth Albery (née Cutter) at the church of St Martin Outwich in the City of London. He was twenty-seven years of age, came from a well-established Chichester family with something of a turbulent financial history and appears to have been a merchant in the wine trade. She was a forty-year-old widow, the daughter of a clergyman and the sister of a Royal Navy officer. Her brother Vincent Cutter had died unmarried and childless in April 1710, and by the time of her marriage in 1711 Elizabeth was in possession of an inherited fortune of £10,000 and the lease of his six-window-wide house in London's Soho Square.[1]

Even before the marriage took place there were signs that all was not well. Elizabeth and her father had insisted that she should retain control over at least part of the £10,000 she would otherwise surrender to Henry on marriage, which Henry had resisted. So acrimonious did things become that at one point he 'did actually discontinue his address' – in other words, he stopped wooing Elizabeth.[2] Eventually a compromise was reached whereby he agreed to allow his future wife £50-a-year pin money to spend how she would, and the wedding went ahead.

The building project in Henry's home town seems to have been embarked upon soon after the marriage,[3] and, if the sworn evidence in the Court of Chancery case is to be believed, appears to have been Elizabeth's idea. A prominent site was selected,[4] before which lay a crossroads then dominated by the town's leather trade and marked by a timber-made market cross. The City Minute Books for the period record that Henry Peckham arranged for the 'Pallant', or space around the cross, to be 'altered to make the new building' – with his proposed house rising on a 'new foundation . . . square towards the South'.[5] Subsequently, in March 1714, Chichester Corporation agreed to Henry's request to demolish the cross itself, on the condition that he set up 'a convenient shed' elsewhere in St Martin's Lane to serve as a replacement market site.

Three years later, husband and wife were at legal loggerheads. According to the Court of Chancery Records of 1717, Elizabeth – the 'complainant' – argued that Henry – the 'Defendant' – had abused her financially and squandered much of her fortune on the new building project, and that he had sometimes operated in an underhand or fraudulent manner. Henry's defence was that his wife had known what was going on, and had been fully aware of the costs that had been incurred. Indeed, he claimed that she had run the operation, supervising and instructing the tradesmen and, through some of her actions, actually increasing the cost of the building project.[6]

That Elizabeth was very closely involved in the planning of the house seems unquestionable – and, for the time, perhaps unusual. Until the early twentieth century, there were (officially, at least) no female architects, and although women do appear to have been occasionally involved in the design of buildings – for example, Elizabeth, Lady Wilbraham, in the late seventeenth century – it's difficult to know what precise role they fulfilled. Even in the more refined areas of the arts, such as painting, famed female artists or decorators remained few and far between until well into the nineteenth century. The seventeenth century boasted the Rome-born Artemisia Gentileschi, the London-born Joan Carlile and Mary Beale, and Angelica Kauffman was active in the eighteenth century, but there was a minuscule number overall.[7]

When it came to the building trade, a few wives and widows did run tradesmen's offices (accounts for the construction from 1729 of the James Gibbs-designed ranges at St Bartholomew's Hospital in Smithfield, London, for example, record numerous payments to female members of the building trades.[8] But in general, just as women were denied the most basic civic rights (as the transfer of Elizabeth's fortune to her husband on marriage demonstrates), so any aspirations they might have nurtured for professional status or engagement were largely snuffed out. It's possible to identify only a small group of generally aristocratic female patrons of architecture and the arts: the Countess of Shrewsbury – 'Bess of Hardwick' – in the late sixteenth century (see p. xxi), Queen Mary II in the late seventeenth century and Sarah, Duchess of Marlborough, in the early eighteenth century. Thanks to the survival of the records of Elizabeth Peckham's legal dispute with her husband, we can add her name to that very short list.

* * * * *

The surviving court documents testify to Elizabeth's close involvement in the building of Pallant House. They also demonstrate that the term 'architect' – denoting someone with a professional ability and interest in building – lacked at that time a precise meaning that would have been universally agreed. Essentially, there were two types of building practitioners who fulfilled the role of architect, or, rather, the role of designer of buildings and overseer of their execution. One comprised educated gentlemen, like Sir Christopher Wren, for whom architecture was a civilised accomplishment, much like music, the classics, geometry, mathematics or natural philosophy. Such men were gifted dilettantes – in Wren's case, of course, exceptionally so. In early eighteenth-century England, talented gentlemen who did not gain high or public office but displayed architectural ability appear to have been called 'contrivers' of buildings – now a verb with a rather unflattering sound.[9] When Wren ultimately gained public architectural office, he was known by the rather grander title of 'surveyor'.[10]

Aspirant 'contrivers' at this time started out by serving as articled pupils, essentially as apprentices. They learned their craft within an established architectural office working under the auspices of a 'master'. A novice architect would be supervised closely, at least initially, to ensure they mastered the practical aspects of their profession: learning to draw and to set up perspective renderings of buildings, for example, and imbibing the language of architecture (notably the classical orders such as Doric, Ionic and Corinthian), structural theory and at least a little history. Increasingly, many would undertake grand tours, mostly to Italy, to acquire first-hand experience of antique exemplars of prime importance. James Gibbs, the Aberdeen-born designer of St Martin-in-the-Fields in Trafalgar Square, spent time in Rome in the very early eighteenth century, studying with the well-established baroque architect Carlo Fontana. Robert Adam, the son of a Scottish builder/architect, undertook a grand tour in the 1750s. John Soane, also the son of a bricklayer, followed suit in the late 1770s. In the usual course of events the young architect would become a principal assistant, a role many might retain for much of their career if their master was accommodating. The more ambitious would seek professional independence, and hope to gain the necessary distinction and expertise that would attract and please clients.

The other type of building practitioner – the one involved in designing and constructing the lion's share of England's buildings from the medieval age well into the eighteenth century – was populated by masters of the building profession itself. These were not 'gentlemen', nor were they necessarily highly educated in the classics or history. They were tradesmen, often members of dynasties of builders or quarry owners with strong regional connections. Typically, they had developed a strong empirical understanding of the structural and engineering aspects of architecture and had acquired knowledge about the qualities of building materials. When it came to planning buildings, however, they generally produced designs of a distinctly vernacular, traditional or regional character. For them, soundness of construction and functional requirements tended to be more impor-tant than style or the pursuit of current architectural fashions.

The princes of these tradesmen – often highly skilled and experienced – were masons.

From the early seventeenth century, masons might not have nec-essarily been commissioned to act as lead designer for high-profile, aristocratic or Royal Court projects (there are, of course, numerous notable exceptions), but they were the favoured choice as 'architect' for merchants, City of London institutions and the universities. Increas-ingly from the late seventeenth century, particular masons tended to develop close relationships with individual gentlemen surveyors. The latter did much to win commissions and supply designs with stylish erudition and a dash of beguiling fashion, while the mason, with access to a trusted body of tradesmen, was in a position to guarantee sound construction and detailing, and to provide knowledge about the acquisition of good building materials at competitive costs. The reconstruction of St Paul's Cathedral after the Great Fire of London in 1666 displays how fruitful and symbiotic this relationship could prove. In the course of its thirty-five-year gestation and construction the cathedral became almost a college for craftsmen and designers, including Nicholas Hawksmoor and Christopher Kempster. Such men, having drunk deep at the well of Wren's architectural knowl-edge, and having imbibed his design ethos, disseminated his inspired version of English baroque around the nation.

A number of the craftsmen involved in the building of Pallant House were called on by Henry to give sworn depositions in his defence, and so we know their names and the contribution they made.[11] Henry Smart, 'of the City of Chichester', who was by trade a mason, 'aged fforty years or thereabouts', was evidently the man Henry and Elizabeth Peckham had approached first to design and presumably to supervise the construction of their new house. Alongside him was Richard Clayton, 'of the City of Chichester . . . Carpenter . . . aged about Two and Thirty', together with 53-year-old John Page and 36-year-old John Chanell – also carpenters – and John Pryor, a local 30-year-old 'joyner'.

It is typical of a provincial town in the early eighteenth century that the Peckhams should have chosen a mason as their architect rather than an informed local gentleman, and Henry Smart appears to have been a mason who was capable of designing a sound building and who, through his trade connections, could supply contacts to the other tradesmen and craftsmen required, who would be employed independently. In 1712 this is how things were done in the building world: construction organised by a 'general contractor' – where one eminent tradesman took responsibility for all aspects of the building project – was still several decades in the future. It would only become a practical proposition from the 1770s under the inspired leadership of architect/speculators like the Adam brothers and from 1800 by builder/architects such as James Burton and the London-based builder Thomas Cubitt, who undertook the construction of entire urban quarters.

Certainly, from what we know of Smart, he appears to have been the epitome of a skilful, traditional master mason. In the course of his career he worked for the 2nd Duke of Richmond at Goodwood Park, near Chichester, and in about 1730 forged a relationship with the well-connected pioneering Palladian architect Roger Morris, who had been hired to redesign Goodwood's great hall. In around 1731 Morris won the commission to design the new Council House in Chichester – a remarkable Palladian project supported by the Duke of Richmond – and it seems likely that Smart was closely involved in the building that emerged. Ultimately, in 1751, at the age of about seventy-five, Henry Smart would become Mayor of Chichester, presumably as a reward for long and loyal service, and following in the steps of two of his patrons: the 2nd Duke of Richmond, who served in 1735, and Henry Peckham. Peckham was a committed Tory who served three terms, in 1722, in 1728 and in 1732, and so was presumably the first mayor to preside in glory at the new and very fashionable Council House.

From Smart's 1717 deposition it is clear that he had known both husband and wife 'many years' (Elizabeth was also originally from West Sussex) and that 'before the building of the House' he had been asked to 'make a fframe or modell thereof' that he then presented 'to the Complainant & Defendant Peckham'. As an experienced mason he was well able to do so, but it would appear that the design was not all the Peckhams had hoped for. Perhaps Smart's no doubt somewhat vernacular or provincial design wasn't ambitious enough for them, or perhaps their architectural aspirations evolved as construction drew near. Whatever the reason, it would appear they wanted something more dashingly up to the minute and metropolitan than the 'modell' offered.

Henry and Elizabeth Peckham now departed for London, and when they returned – Smart does not say how long they were away – Henry showed the mason 'a new Modell which was drawne at London' which Henry asked him to 'explain'. It seems a strange request, suggesting that Mr and Mrs Peckham were woefully ignorant and inexperienced when it came to reading architectural diagrams and anticipating the problems or costs realisation might involve. Of course, it's also possible that the design was very sketchy, and that it required interpretation or explanation by an experienced builder such as Smart. There is, sadly, no hint about the author of the 'Modell' or whether it was a sketch of an exemplary London house – or even a bespoke design drawn in London by an architect who was unnamed at the time, and who remains anonymous.

Smart's use of the word 'Modell' here is interesting. His deposition states that it was 'drawne', so it was not a three-dimensional model of a house in the modern sense. It can also be argued that the term 'Modell' confirms that the drawn design was modelled on a specific and exemplary London prototype that the Peckhams had seen and

admired, and, given that Smart had to 'explain the same modell to
them', that the 'drawne' design was no more than an amateur sketch
of an admired building that the husband and wife required Smart
to flesh out and to explain how it might be best built and detailed.[12]

It could also be that the Peckhams had in mind a design modelled
on the capital's way of doing things. Since 1667, domestic architecture in central London had been governed by Building Acts that were
framed to help ensure sound- and fireproof construction. These also
looked to relate the scale of a building to the site it occupied and,
in general terms, promoted brick or stone construction along with
simplicity of design and uniformity, and limited the external use of
timber and ornament. The use of potentially combustible external
timber details had become a particular issue, as revealed by the Buildings Acts of 1707 and 1709, which aimed to replace the use of timber
eaves cornices with brick or stone parapets and ordered that exposed
timber sash-window boxes be set back four inches – or the depth of
one brick – from the face of a building. At Pallant the boxes are not
recessed the London regulation four inches, though it's worth noting
that even in the Cities of London and Westminster, where the legal
rule of the Acts did apply, builders regularly set the boxes flush with
the facade well into the 1730s. There is, however, a brick parapet.

Whatever the precise details of the design that Smart explained to
his clients, he made it clear that in his opinion, 'the Modell brought
from London would be more expensive' than 'his Modell' and suggested that it would cost 'at least sixteen hundred pounds to build'.
This, he said, did not daunt Mrs Peckham. She 'liked best the London
Modell and upon her liking it' Mr Peckham 'proceeded and built the
said house according to the London Modell'.

If there's a single feature of the house that helps to explain why
'the London Modell' should have been so much more expensive than
the one initially proposed by Smart, it's the extraordinarily accom-
plished main staircase. Made of oak,[13] with bands of inlay, presumably in walnut, it was conceived and designed as if it were wrought
from stone, each of its treads shaped like a stone slab, one resting,
as it were, upon the slab below and supporting a slab above. The

Queen's House, Greenwich, designed in 1616 by Inigo Jones with construction continued to 1635. This could be one of the 'London Modells' admired and emulated by Mr and Mrs Peckham when commissioning Pallant House.

end of each slab-like tread presents a rectangular face carved with varied emblems and is combined with a delicately carved serpentine bracket that appears to help support the tread above. Seen from below, the treads have a strikingly sinuous form, echoing the profile of the carved brackets. Light, elegant, structurally daring and forward-looking in terms of style and construction, the staircase's two flights are linked by a half-landing and finish at a wide first-floor landing with a balustrade sitting on an architrave and carved frieze, and with a centrally placed arched window to light it – a standard design of the time.[14]

Not only does the staircase exhibit wonderful flair and a skilfully baroque concealment of its true construction, it also embraces a wealth of exquisite detail. The balusters, three to a tread, are thin and elegant, all composed of an urn sitting on a plain plinth and supporting a tablet upon which sits a Doric column rising to a block that helps to support the handrail. The columns are of barley-twist form (a popular late seventeenth-century detail): versions of the mythic columns that were thought to have graced Solomon's Temple in Jerusalem. The newels take the form of fluted Corinthian columns.

The emblems carved on the rectangular panels are impressively varied. One shows a pair of dragons emerging out of plant tendrils, which may possibly be a merely ornamental touch – chinoiserie was fashionable in the early eighteenth century – but could also relate specifically to Henry Peckham's role as a merchant (silk and porcelain had long been imported from China). There is a pair of what appear to be palm leaves, a familiar Christian symbol related to Easter and Palm Sunday; then a cornucopia, with flowers emerging out of a pair of shells seemingly implying the bounty and beauty of nature; a pair of crossed clay pipes from which issues smoke in the form of plant tendrils – presumably an emblem of the joy of tobacco and perhaps the profit of its trade; a scallop shell, which had long been a token of Roman Catholic pilgrimage to the shrine of St James of Compostela and to the Holy Land; and sprigs of oak leaves with acorns emerging out of what appears to be the stump of a tree. These could be a Stuart emblem inspired by Charles II's refuge in 1651 in an oak

The majestically formed and beautifully detailed staircase in Pallant House.

tree after the Battle of Worcester, or they could be connected with Freemasonry, which at that time had an interest in Druids and their associated oak-tree and acorn imagery. If so, then it's more than a matter of coincidence that acorn imagery should also appear among the little emblems that are carved or moulded on the bricks forming the centre of each lintel of the front house's facade. If Henry Peckham was indeed a Freemason, he was in good company. According to the seventeenth-century antiquarian John Aubrey, 'a great convention at St Paul's church of the Fraternity of the Adopted masons' was once held when Sir Christopher Wren was to be 'adopted a brother'.[15] And just a few decades later, in early 1750s Bath, John Wood the Elder, a very active Mason, or his son, would top the parapet of the Royal Circus not with familiar images of pineapples but with huge stone images of acorns, inspired by the Masonic embrace of Druids as 'men of oak'.

There is one other detail, physically related to the staircase but actually part of the panelling scheme of the hall, that appears to have something to say. The half-landing of the staircase sits on a shallow arch that leads to the house's back door, and in this arch is a keystone that is ornamented, in conventional manner, with a winged cherub's head. This was an immensely popular motif at the time, derived from Renaissance prototypes. Usually cherubs look happy, even ecstatic, or wear blank expressions implying contemplation of their divine duties – either as guardians of sacred places or as emblems of resurrection. But this one looks positively miserable, or at least very troubled. It's tempting to believe that it is a craftsmen's comment on the unhappy circumstances of the house's creation and of the acrimony and disputes that accompanied it.

* * * * *

Smart had explained to his clients at the outset that their 'London Modell' would prove expensive. As building work progressed, even his £1,600 budget first came under stress and was then rapidly exceeded. By the time the Peckhams' dispute had reached the courts, costs had multiplied almost twofold. For this, if the builders and craftsmen

The cherub keystone within the arch below the staircase half landing between ground and first floor. Cherubs usually look playful, ecstatic or contemplative but this one appears oddly peevish – even miserable and decidedly unhappy with its lot.

involved are to be believed, Elizabeth Peckham was very much responsible. Quite simply, according to them, she kept changing her mind, and her husband allowed her to do so.

Among the most expensive of Elizabeth's second thoughts was her decision to change the location of the kitchen. At the time that Pallant House was built, it was common practice in towns and cities – where land was expensive and generally in limited supply – to locate kitchens, along with pantries, sculleries, larders and washrooms, in the basement. But according to the carpenter John Page, Mr Peckham, having originally gone along with this standard approach, 'had altered his mind on account of his wife', who had objected that a basement kitchen would be 'too cold & damp for herself & servants'. Page's fellow carpenter, Richard Clayton, described the atmosphere in which this decision was made. Henry Peckham, he said, having given him orders 'to take down the kitchen and offices belonging to their dwelling house', had declared 'in the presence of the said Elizabeth that he had built the same to please her and it should be pulled down and rebuilt to please her'. He had then stated bluntly that 'he was going to London' and that he 'would not medle [sic] with it having had trouble enough about it already'.

It was a costly decision. Visitors to the house today might be tempted to assume that the large and substantial brick-vaulted cellars beneath the house were always intended to house Mr Peckham's stock of imported wines. In fact, the expensive brick vaulting was erected to make the basement largely fireproof and secure in the event of a cooking accident. It is not structurally necessary except, perhaps, beneath the stone-paved entrance hall. That the decision was made late on in proceedings is evident not only from the brick barrel vaults but from the large chimney breast with a deep fireplace opening necessary for cooking that is still in evidence.[16]

Clayton offered the court his opinion 'that the taking down and rebuilding such kitchen and Backhouses cost Threescore pounds or thereabouts' and that he 'verily believeth ... the whole Buildings of the House and Outhouses ... did cost the sum of three thousand pounds'.[17] In 1712 this was a large amount to pay for the construction

The ground-floor kitchen in Pallant House as reconstructed and presented after the house opened to the public in 1982. As a consequence of the construction of the gallery in 2006, this kitchen has been transformed into an anteroom, with a door cut into the wall (to the right of the dresser) linking the new building to Pallant House.

of a two-storey urban house, even one seven windows wide and two rooms deep. Just over forty years later Isaac Ware, in his *A Complete Body to Architecture,* asserted that the construction of a 'Common' London house – three storeys high above a basement, with a habitable garret and two rooms deep – was 'six or seven hundred pounds'.[18]

Smart concurred with Richard Clayton's assessment, asserting that 'the Backbuildings of the said house were taken down & rebuilt by the Complainant's order' and that he took up 'the pavement in the . . . Backbuildings', acting on Mrs Peckham's orders because Mr Peckham was 'then at London'. He also said that Mrs Peckham 'did consent to & approve the Building of the steps at the fforefront of the house', which Mr Peckham 'would not doe until she had ffirst given her Approbacon [*sic*] thereof' and that he followed Mrs Peckham's instruction 'to make and sett up two marble Chimneypieces out of two marble tables which were formerly Captaine Cutter's'. Finally, Smart, supporting evidence submitted by his fellow tradesmen, said that he had heard that Mr Peckham's later order to Smart to pave 'the passage from the house to the Washhouse' had been overruled by an order from Mrs Peckham, 'being also present', to 'pave the Washhouse first'. So far as the final cost of the works was concerned, Smart stated that 'he verily believeth that the Building of the said House & Outhouses cost Three Thousand Pounds' and he told the court that, as far as he was aware, Mrs Peckham 'did mightily approve of the Work'.[19]

Ultimately, Mrs Peckham changed her mind about the kitchen not once but twice. According to the deposition of the carpenter John Chanell, having ordered that it should be moved from the basement to a position against the 'Backside' of the house, she declared that she 'disliked' her new kitchen wing and issued instructions to have it 'pulled down & rebuilt'. Her husband, Chanell said, apparently merely ordered the 'workmen to doe' what his wife 'would have them do'. Today, the final kitchen that was built – largely within a rear ground-floor room of the main house with a scullery and storage in the adjoining wing – is devoid of interest beyond a few pieces of joinery (including the house's only original set of sashes). Originally, though, it would have housed a cooking range and spits within a large fireplace opening; a dresser for the storage and display of plates, and copper and pewter cooking and serving utensils; and food preparation surfaces, including a large, centrally placed kitchen table with a scrubbed timber top. There might also have been a stone sink and a water pump and lead cistern, although these were probably located in the scullery.[20]

Mrs Peckham's other significant intervention involved the 'private' chambers on the first floor. The joiner John Pryor described in his deposition that one day while he was 'wainscoting a Chamber in the dwelling house', Mrs Peckham came into the room where he was 'at worke and ordered a partition to be made & a door to be made in the Midle [*sic*] of the partition to make the Chamber more private'. The work was, stated Pryor, 'done accordingly'.

It is now generally agreed that the partition ordered by Mrs Peckham is the partition located on the first-floor staircase landing. This makes what was presumably originally intended to be a large lobby, at the centre of the first floor and open to the staircase landing, into an enclosed and private chamber. The partition does indeed have a central door and is a highly ornamental affair, framed by robustly detailed, fluted Corinthian pilasters and an elaborate cornice, even if, in its somewhat old-fashioned and slightly clumsy way, it suggests the work of a skilled provincial rather than that of the (presumably London-based) master craftsman who created the staircase. Nevertheless, the ornamental work here marks the chamber as probably the most important private or family room in the house,[21] functioning almost certainly as a meeting place for the occupants of the pairs of rooms to its north and its south and as an anteroom for both. In this, it followed the approach employed in great country houses of the time of creating a grand sequence of interconnected rooms. Mrs Peckham could not quite manage to create the full effect in the relatively compact Pallant House, but by adding this chamber she was at least able to increase the sequence of rooms.

The number of bedchambers and apartments served by this 'private chamber' or anteroom is debated. The convention of the time dictated that husbands and wives in the wealthier echelons of society had separate bedchamber apartments, often adjoining and sometimes sharing an anteroom, withdrawing chamber, closet/ cabinet or service staircase. It is therefore reasonable to assume that the pair of rooms each side of the anteroom served as apartments, including a bedchamber, one for Henry Peckham and the other for his wife, with the anteroom operating as their shared withdrawing room. The suggestion has been made that the smaller of the first-floor front rooms was in fact a 'study/sitting room' (though the term 'sitting room' is very unlikely to date from the eighteenth century).[22] That, however, doesn't explain why this room, if not originally a bed-chamber, retains a cupboard still fitted with original timber hooks on which to hang clothes, or a closet just large enough for a 'close stool', or lavatory, apparently connected to a cesspit in the basement below, with a door that still holds an early slide lock that can only be operated from within the closet. Clothes cupboards and close-stool closets are generally associated with bedchambers, not 'sitting rooms'. Even in an early eighteenth-century provincial city, to emerge from a small unventilated close-stool closet directly into a room of seated guests would have been a somewhat unhappy and disconcerting experience for all involved. It should also be noted that the location of the service staircase between the front and back rooms on the north side of the house is a favoured location when the stairs are adjoining the chambers they are intended to serve – in this case a bedchamber and its related cabinet or withdrawing room. The convenience of the staircase – both for private movement within the house and for facilitating services – would have been ample compensation for the relative smallness of this pair of rooms when compared with the pair on the south side of the house's first floor.

If this room in the north-west corner of the house was not a bed-chamber, the assumption has to be that Mr and Mrs Peckham defied the polite sleeping arrangements of the age and that rather than possessing their own separate apartments within their shared establishment, as all members of upper society at least aspired to do, were happy to spend the princely sum of £3,000 on a new, purpose-designed house that required them to 'pig' it together,[23] on a nightly basis, in the same bed in the same bedchamber. That this practice would have been known publicly would be guaranteed by gossiping servants. It is highly unlikely that the Peckhams would have invited this humiliation or risked the amusement and contempt of their local peers.

Of course, the other first-floor rear room, on the south side of the house, could have been used as a bedchamber, but this is unlikely. A rear room, overlooking outbuildings, a narrow lane and perhaps smelly stables, had a much lower status than a front room – as the relatively simpler decoration of the rear rooms in comparison to the front rooms makes clear. It would have been strange if husband or wife were obliged to occupy a bedchamber markedly lower in status than that of their spouse. If the two first-floor bedchambers did not occupy the two west-facing front rooms, then the whole convention of the floor containing two well-balanced apartments, each with bed-chamber and cabinet or withdrawing room of reasonably equal status, is called into question. Given the date and status of the house, this is most unlikely.

While Henry's bedchamber is lined with relatively simple panels (flat, not raised and fielded), Mrs Peckham's apartment, with its bed-chamber and cabinet or withdrawing-cum-dressing room, was more elegant. Such early panelling as survives – and a considerable amount does in the south-west room – is formed with raised and fielded panels set directly into frames embellished with ovolo, or quadrant, profile mouldings. In 1712 this would have been regarded as both elegant and fashionable, well suited to a lady's bedchamber.[24] The south-east room, which would have enjoyed morning sunlight, was most probably Mrs Peckham's cabinet or dressing room, and has been much altered. We know from the Chancery documents that it was originally wainscoted to match one of the best-quality rooms on the floor below.[25] In his evidence, James Burley, a 35-year-old joiner from Chichester, stated that Mr Peckham employed him 'to wainscot a Roome called [the] drawing Roome Chamber' on the ground floor and in his presence asked Mrs Peckham 'how it should be done'. Her response was most revealing: 'thereupon she went up stairs into her dressing roome' with her husband '& desired that the said drawing roome [should] be wainscoted like her dressing roome & it was done accordingly'. He also described how Mrs Peckham did not approve of the way her husband had ordered the dressing room's door hung, so she 'ordered the said door to be hung on the other side . . . and it was done accordingly'.

Why did Mrs Peckham want her door re-hung? The way a door is hung is significant: if the door opening is located in the corner of a room (which is generally the case in Pallant House) and if the hinges of the door are fixed to the post within the corner, then when the door is opened an immediate view is offered of the room and all in it. If the door is hung from the outer post, then the prospect is not revealed immediately to the person entering the room and those in the room see and hear the door opening and, while still screened, have a moment or two to prepare themselves for their visitor. Perhaps Mr Peckham had preferred the more ostentatious and baroque manner of entry, while his wife had deemed that a degree of initial concealment would be better for a lady's dressing room.

* * * * *

The outline plan of Pallant House is roughly 3:2 (or a square and a half) in area, and it contains a number of rooms that are similarly roughly square in plan, or those permutations of a square – notably the 2:1 (double square) and 3:2 proportions – that were favoured by the Italian architect Andrea Palladio, expressed through his mid sixteenth-century north Italian villa and palazzo designs, and made available through his *I quattro libri dell'architettura* of 1570. There is nothing surprising in this, since Palladio had been a major influence in Britain from the early seventeenth century and his rational architecture – in particular his harmonically related system of proportions – had by 1712 long been an important part of the British classical design tradition. As for the disposition of rooms, the house takes the double-pile form that had become usual for houses designed in Britain from the mid seventeenth century onwards: two rooms deep, with corridor-like landings and halls used as circulation space. Previously, it had been necessary to pass through one room to get to the next. Now each room had its own discrete form of access. The former approach offered a certain sense of baroque drama, opening up vistas throughout a house and giving a sense of grand progress. The latter was more private, and arguably more convenient. The arrangement of the Peckhams' private apartments suggests a certain theatricality, but for the most part not much baroque planning was attempted at Pallant House, beside aligning doors of the rooms at ground-floor and first-floor levels behind the west facade.[26] Of course, it's possible that later alterations to the house, in particular to its main reception rooms on the ground floor, swept away layouts that were originally more dramatic.[27]

The overall plan of Pallant House, then, is eminently sensible and functional. The central entrance hall, large and impressive, divides the ground floor into two zones – the north one more utilitarian and with smaller rooms than the rather grander south one – and contains the staircase. By 1712 it was well established that such an entrance hall should be treated in the Renaissance tradition as a tough or semi-outdoor space, in the manner of a Venetian palazzo, ideally with a marble or stone floor (as at Pallant House), and walls that were at least part lime-plastered or stone-faced, rather than being fully clad with delicately detailed timber panelling. This suggests that the plaster would originally have been painted a convincing stone colour, or even have been painted in imitation of marble. The hall panelling at Pallant is not quite of the grandest type used elsewhere in the house – in keeping with the conceit of the hall being a semi-outdoor space – though the area of plaster between the top of the timber panelling and the ceiling itself perhaps expresses a memory of the arrangement found in medieval and Tudor great halls, where it would have been used for family portraits or other objects for display, such as pewter and tin-glaze plates and chargers or implements of defence.[28]

There's also one element inside the house that seems a throwback to an earlier time: the keystone in the centre of the arch in the first-floor partition that Elizabeth Peckham insisted upon. It is embellished with a most peculiar, grotesque face of a type that was the standard stock-in-trade for wood and stone carvers in the Middle

Detail of the screen separating the staircase landing on the first floor from the adjoining chamber. Ornate Corinthian pilasters frame an arch with a curious keystone embellished with what appears to be the visage of a ferocious long-eared bat or a clawed and fanged feline creature of the night.

Ages and that on occasion, as here, still found expression in the late seventeenth and early eighteenth centuries. Presumably carvers were following a long-established tradition stretching back to the mid twelfth-century Sheela-na-Gig carvings on Kilpeck Church, Hereford-shire, which include smiling naked women gleefully exposing their genitals, the bare-bottomed and bare-chested male and female 'hunky punks' on the chapter house of York Minster, and medieval gargoyles generally. Relevant later examples include the grotesque faces on the keystones of the arcade around Sir Christopher Wren's Fountain Court at Hampton Court Palace of the early 1690s; and the window keystones of c.1705 in Queen Anne's Gate, Westminster. The faces on these buildings include imps, long-eared elves, green men and diverse goggle-eyed oddities. But none is quite like that placed on the first-floor partition in Pallant House. It seems demonic, perhaps the snarling face of a long-eared bat or a malign feline, with long fangs and claws. It is possible that it was, like medieval hunky punks and gargoyles, intended to function as a protective spirit, fierce and frightening-looking to keep evil at bay. This was still an age – just – in which 'witch bottles', containing nail clippings and urine, were installed above door lintels to keep witches out, and dead cats and old shoes were put under floorboards to bring good luck. If a token to repel evil, then the one at Pallant House conveyed a slightly odd message to guests as they swept up the staircase to the anteroom. Or perhaps the ferocious face is Pryor's comment upon Elizabeth Peckham. Did she haunt the building site by night – like a wicked cat or bat – in quest of details to change or poor workmanship to condemn? Whatever its meaning, it must have had, at least in part, a benign aspect because Mrs Peckham would, of course, have been one of the first to see the keystone and it would surely not have survived if she thought it a contemptuous or humorous tradesman's comment about her conduct.

* * * * *

While in early eighteenth-century English houses some rooms had particular, dedicated functions, many didn't. Kitchens, sculleries, pantries, butteries and washrooms all had specialised furniture, fire-places, ranges and ovens, water pumps, sinks and other fixtures. But a room could be transformed into a bedroom simply by the introduc-tion of a truckle bed, a once common item of readily movable furni-ture. A parlour could be converted into a dining room, if circumstance demanded, simply by opening up a gate-leg table.

Pallant's own dining parlour (the ground-floor north-west room), which, according to the survey made in 1905, connected directly and conveniently to the kitchen via the adjoining landing of the service staircase, contains a pair of arched recesses each side of the fireplace. These were usual in dining parlours of the time and were intended to contain small-scale buffets – sideboards or tables, usually marble- or oak-topped – on which food and drink would be placed.[29] The fact that the room is relatively small, and that its panelling, although rich, is not as sophisticated as on, for example, the first-floor screen,[30] suggests that the room was intended for family or intimate dining, and that larger, more formal dinners were held elsewhere, perhaps in a ground-floor room to the south. Dining chambers tended to be regarded as masculine rooms, and were perhaps intentionally a trifle old-fashioned and simple in their decoration, probably to suggest the family's ancient pedigree and to imply that it had no need to enhance its standing through ornate display. Such rooms were places where family portraits and heirlooms might be on display, and a too rich or too fashionable appearance might be thought not only inappropriate but also at odds with the room's male ethos as a place where men would gather to drink and talk of politics or hunting, after food had been eaten and the women had removed themselves to the more elegant 'drawing Roome Chamber'. Unfortunately, the 'drawing Roome Chamber' and its adjoining room on the south side of the house were severely altered in the nineteenth century – probably between 1830 and 1840 – so while these rooms contain rea-sonably high-quality early to mid nineteenth-century-style details, the original look has been lost.

The surviving panelling in the dining parlour, though, serves as a reminder of the subtle and complex messages that the various rooms in a house such as Pallant House were designed to send. 'Public' rooms and spaces tended to be grander – to remind visitors of the status and aspirations of those who lived there. 'Private' rooms, not intended for show, could afford to be simpler. At Pallant House, the basic scheme of panelling is of the bolection – or raised moulding – type that dominated fashionable interiors in England from around the 1660s into the early eighteenth century. It encompasses a wide range of panelling, differing considerably in complexity and grandeur. Panels might be flat, or, in more important rooms, raised and fielded – that is, with a flat central area raised above a slightly bevelled edge. At its grandest, the elegance of the design and manufacture of the finest panelling reveal the refined sophistication of joiners and carpenters, such as John Pryor and John Chanell. How and where these humble men achieved and honed their not inconsiderable skills remain something of a mystery. Architectural pattern books were available, but rare and expensive until the 1730s, which saw a rapid increase in the publication of builders' guides offering information about design, proportion and the classical orders as well as construction. Prior to this, the only practical and generally accessible source of information was the contemporary exemplary buildings – churches, country houses and civic buildings – constructed near where a building craftsman might be based. There were a number of expensive publications available in the very early eighteenth century, but these would generally have been inaccessible to humble tradesmen – and too costly to readily purchase.

As for the original colour scheme that would have been employed at Pallant House, this would have been relatively muted and far less exotic than the colour schemes incorporating marbling and graining that had been popular only a few decades earlier. The simpler scheme at Pallant House no doubt incorporated 'Common Colours', made with pigments chosen because they were economical and relatively stable. Earth colours, such as yellow ochre and umber, were particularly popular and were used as the basis of a variety of stone colours. Imported indigo leaves were used to achieve a strong blue that when mixed with ochre or lamp black produced an olive green or lead colour. Also popular were verditer (a copper carbonate producing blue and green) and mahogany, walnut and oak colours. The softwood panelling of the type fitted at Pallant House would have been coated with white lead paint ground in linseed oil, coloured with one of these pigments. The overall effect would have been one of elegance, simplicity – and richness (see also page 48).

* * * * *

In the attic, or garret, within the roof space at Pallant House is a short and narrow central corridor that links the top landing of the secondary staircase at the north end of the floor plan with central rooms and the large room at the south end of the garret. As most have well-lit dormer windows, one has a fireplace, and all enjoy a degree of privacy, thanks to the corridor, these rooms were probably considered 'too good' for servants. Certainly, the more common servants would have occupied truckle beds at different locations around the house, often in the kitchen. The one heated room might have been for a superior servant or a guest, or for children if the couple had ever had any.[31]

As it turned out, children at Pallant were never a realistic prospect. The Peckhams' marriage lasted just five years. The lawsuit, which got under way in 1717, dragged on until 1720. The precise terms of settlement are unknown, but it seems that Henry Peckham remained in occupation of the house that had been built largely using his wife's money, and for which she had, to some degree at least, acted as designer, certainly as far as internal arrangements and decoration are concerned. So Pallant House, conceived of as a family home of fashionable design and built to a high standard, was not lived in initially as planned, and when Henry died in 1764, he was still childless.

Reading the 1717 depositions, it's tempting to feel that as the building of Pallant House progressed there was a conspiracy against Elizabeth Peckham, founded on deep-rooted misogyny that was orchestrated by Henry Peckham and supported by tradesmen willing to present him as the long-suffering man beset by a wilful wife. One can easily imagine the carpenter Chanell, looking at the all-male members of the court – some of them actual or potential clients – as he delivered his evidence, and rolling his eyes ruefully as if to say, *Women will be women*. English men during most of the eighteenth century generally had a patronising view of the opposite sex: they were 'only children ... of larger growth', Lord Chesterfield told his son in 1748; individuals with 'an entertaining tattle, and sometimes wit', he acknowledged, 'but for solid reasoning, good sense, I never knew in my life one that had it, or who reasoned or acted consequentially for four-and-twenty hours together'.[32] In such a world, it is scarcely surprising that women were generally excluded from architecture and house design, and it says much for Elizabeth's determined nature that she carved out a role for herself.

Her ideas and innovations are to be seen everywhere in the house today, from its overall layout to the details of individual rooms. And surely she must have had a hand, along with her husband, in one of Pallant House's most intriguing and mysterious details – the little emblems that are carved or moulded on the bricks forming the centre of each lintel of the front facade (and, on the lintels of the three first-floor centre windows, not on individual bricks but on large terracotta blocks). They include a rose for England (and the houses of York, Lancaster and Tudor); a thistle (for Scotland); a harp (for Ireland), a fleur-de-lys (House of Plantagenet, but also in its H shape possibly a reference to Henry Peckham or Henry Smart); an oak sprig (House of Stuart); a tulip (House of Orange); and another as yet unidentified. The large arched window in the rear elevation – lighting the staircase – also has a carved keystone, in this case showing three tulips in a pot.

The authors of *Pallant House: Its Architecture, History and Owners* (1993) state that most are 'armorial devices representing the royal families and realms of Britain', which seems a reasonable assessment. But what is their message? Presumably, one of patriotic loyalty and unity. The years around 1712 were turbulent: the wayward and wilful Catholic monarch James II had been obliged to flee Britain twenty-four years earlier, after a reign of just three and a half years, in the face of an invasion by William, the Prince of Orange, invited by a group of leading English Protestant aristocrats (the 'Immortal Seven').

William then ruled with Mary – the Stuart daughter of James II –
until his death in 1702, and was succeeded by Queen Anne, another
of James's daughters. Although Stuarts, Mary and Anne were Protestants, and the Jacobite Catholic cause, although apparently defeated
at the Battle of the Boyne in 1690, flared back into violent life in
1715, after the accession of the Protestant Hanoverians to the British
throne on Anne's death the year before.

Quite where Henry and Elizabeth Peckham stood in this
mounting maelstrom is uncertain. Henry is said to have been a Tory,
which may have meant his opposition to the 1714 arrival of the Hanoverians, which was very much a Whig Protestant project. Given
their accession only became an issue two years after the facade at
Pallant House was completed, the unity that is perhaps alluded to in
the house's stone emblems is the official Union of the English and
Scottish thrones that took place in 1707 and that saw the creation of
Great Britain. There may also be other, parallel, meanings to at least
some of these emblems. Possibly the union suggested is to do with
unity through trade (Peckham was, after all, a wine merchant), or, as
suggested earlier, emblems of Freemasonry are on show.

A puzzling additional element to this story is presented by the
pair of gate piers which frame the prospect of the doorcase. These
are each topped by a large, stone-carved approximation of an uncertain but large-limbed bird. They have previously been assumed to
be representations of dodos (a strange choice for 1712), but are in
fact intended to be ostriches. Henry Peckham had selected as his
emblem and informal family crest these birds, which since Roman
times had been symbols of strength and resilience, owing to their
mythical ability to eat iron and glass. More intriguing is the symbol's
association with the Roman Catholic Church, in which the ostrich
egg represents the immaculate conception of the Virgin Mary. This
raises the prospect of the Tory Peckham as a closet Catholic, and a
potential Jacobite supporting a Catholic pretender to the throne, who
in 1712 was in enforced exile in the French court. The Jacobites used
many furtive symbols, and indeed communicated by them in secret
manner to avoid prosecution, and an ostrich could well have been

Details on the entrance front of Pallant House. Above: the ostriches that stand on the gate piers that frame the main door. Below: one of the carved or moulded brick details on a ground-floor window lintel. It depicts a thistle, a symbol of Scotland.

one of them. If this was the case, then placing a pair of ostentatious ostriches outside one's front door was a bold statement. In 1712 – three years before the Jacobite uprising in 1715 – this was not nearly as perilous as such actions, if Jacobite by association, were to become.

Pallant House led a quiet existence as a family home between Henry Peckham's death in 1764 and its acquisition in 1919 by the local council to serve as its offices.[33] Its fortunes took a dramatic turn when in 1977 Walter Hussey, the Dean of Chichester Cathedral, donated his important collection of British twentieth-century art to the city on the condition that it was housed in the Peckhams' former abode; and in 1982, accordingly, the house became an art gallery of national importance. The Hussey collection has been greatly augmented since, and given a more cosmopolitan character through the acquisition of works by Continental artists such as Paul Cézanne. But the biggest change came in 2006 when, on a site adjoining the house, a large gallery space was added, designed by Colin St John Wilson (the architect of the British Library) with his wife M. J. Long, in partnership with Rolfe Kentish. This new space, incorporating the architects' twentieth-century prints and drawings, is contemporary in character but brick-faced to help it harmonise with Pallant House, and is described as a wing of the house. It would be more accurate to say that, owing to its size and facilities, it has transformed Pallant House, to which it is physically connected, into a wing of the art gallery. This is not necessarily a bad thing, for it takes pressure off the house, leaving it, with its splendid interior, now freer to display its character and tell its own fascinating story.

Part of the north side of Princelet Street, Spitalfields, looking west. The door surround on the right serves number 21, built in c.1705. Left of 21 is 19 Princelet Street, built in 1718, with a synagogue created within its lower three floors in 1870. The stucco ground floor, with the three arched openings, is an alteration of c.1892/3.

– 2 –

A Home for Immigrants
19 Princelet Street, Spitalfields
(1718)

P ALLANT HOUSE WAS A specially commissioned home. Number 19 Princelet Street (originally number 18 Princes Street) in Spitalfields, which was built just a few years later, is representative of a different building tradition then common in English towns and cities: the speculative build.[1] Where Pallant House was the result of constant consultation between builder and client, 19 Princelet Street, though a fine building in many ways, is less individual; a house built for profit and first inhabited by people who had little or no say in the details of its construction.

At the time the house was constructed in 1718, Spitalfields – on the north-east edge of the City of London – was in the grip of a building boom. After the Great Fire of London in 1666, charred remains of the old city had been taken beyond its immediate boundary and dumped in a manner that significantly raised and levelled the ground in the north-west portion of the Spitalfields area, so both facilitating drainage and largely burying the ruins of a scattering of older buildings on the site. This operation allowed new houses to be swiftly erected by investors and speculating builders, some to accommodate those displaced by the Fire, others to house new arrivals, in particular Huguenots – French Protestants of Calvinist persuasion – escaping persecution in their native land. Pre-eminent among those speculators active in the area was Nicholas Barbon, who in the early 1680s played a key role in the post-Fire rebuilding of the City and who in Spitalfields developed the former Artillery Ground, on the City boundary. A ruthless businessman, he was known to employ distinctly strong-arm and intimidatory tactics to get his way and so make his profit. He and his like were greedy and seemingly unprincipled. Even so, aided by the 1667 Building Act that governed the reconstruction and in part the replanning of the City, the houses that they built, if sometimes far from structurally sound, were at least architecturally handsome and appropriate for the functions they were designed to fulfil.

Princelet Street started life in about 1705 as a small court off Brick Lane that lay on the east edge of an estate that had been acquired and was then developed during the second and third decades of the eighteenth century by two lawyers, Charles Wood and Simon Michell.[2] The court itself was extended in around 1717 to form a thoroughfare (initially named Princes Street) to a new north–south street called Wood (now Wilkes) Street, while in the mid 1720s Church Street (now Fournier Street), which runs parallel to it, became built up with large and handsome terrace houses of diverse design. At around the time that Princelet Street was extended, the north side was divided into building plots, several of which were leased and a few sold freehold to a speculating builder and local worthy named Samuel Worrall, who, with his fellow speculators Marmaduke Smith and William Tayler, lived on the Wood-Michell estate in houses that they designed and built for themselves and that still survive.[3]

Number 19 Princelet Street was built as a pair with number 17 (on which a bricklayer, Samuel Phipps, worked in collaboration with Worrall). The layout of both is typical of the period: each is one room wide, two rooms deep and three storeys high above a basement kitchen, pantry and scullery. Number 19 would also have had a third-floor garret, as is apparent from the fact that the 1718 staircase rises to third-floor level. The original garret probably occupied only the rear portion of the house, so the existing garret is almost certainly, at least in part, an addition from the later eighteenth century, although evidently incorporating some fabric from its first incarnation. Doubtless, the top-floor room was originally intended for use as a small workshop or counting house for the merchant class for whom the house was envisaged.[4]

The house, while sturdily constructed with thick pairs of pine beams spanning from party wall to party wall at each level,[5] was clearly built to a strict budget. Samuel Worrall, like most early eighteenth-century speculating builders operating in Spitalfields, was economical with time and materials. He built the pair of houses as a single operation, and rather than construct three party walls (one at each end of the pair and one separating them), he opted to erect just two, burrowing into the flank wall of the existing number 21 (built in 1705 by the Brick Lane brewer Joseph Truman) to provide footings for the beams he needed to install at the east end of his development.[6] It was a far from ideal solution, and could have proved structurally unsound, but it was not a particularly unusual procedure at the time for speculators seeking to maximise their profits. One assumes that Worrall must have come to an understanding with Joseph Truman or whoever was then occupying number 21 while this noisy work was under way. Whatever the origin of this constructional arrangement, it has stood the test of time.

The internal details of 19 Princelet Street are in many respects standard products of Samuel Worrall and his workshop. The full-height painted pine panelling that still survives on the first floor is relatively plain, with flat panels and unmoulded frames, and ornament largely confined to the Doric profile of the box cornices. The staircase, which, typically for medium-sized early eighteenth-century Spital-fields houses of the better sort, rises in compact dog-leg form in the rear corner of the plan, allows some display but is essentially a space-saving solution in which alternate flights abut and run parallel to each other and are connected by landings or winders. The staircase is nevertheless finely constructed, including balusters – full-bellied and boldly profiled – set over urns; and while the newel posts in the upper floors are square in section, that at first-floor level takes the form of a particularly large and curvaceous baluster rising from an equally large urn. The staircase in the adjoining number 17, built at the same time and evidently by Worrall's team of tradesmen, has a matching

The staircase at first-floor level, dating from 1718. The newel, formed by a bulbous baluster set over an equally bulbous urn, is particularly impressive. The evident wear and tear reflects the building's intense occupation.

staircase, but otherwise ostentatious baluster newels of this type are very rare in Spitalfields. Significantly, such details are more ornamental than Worrall's work of only a few years later – for example, the staircase of his own house opposite of *c.*1722 – and show how he rapidly refined and reduced ornament, presumably to save money. It's also interesting to note that while at Pallant House the simplest and most rustic form of internal partition (comprising planks and short stiles, the latter known as muntins) was confined to the attic storey, at 19 Princelet Street it's to be found at second-floor level, which would originally have been the location of the best bedchambers. A surviving decorative *trompe l'œil* scheme, in the rear room at this level, shows an attempt to disguise the rustic structure, with a more 'polite' painted panelling scheme, created using a dark brown paint shadowed with grey, laid over a pale yellow stone-colour ground.[7]

In one – legal – respect, 19 Princelet Street was slightly unusual for the time. In the seventeenth and eighteenth centuries, houses were generally built as speculations on leasehold land (usually on 61- or 99-year leases). Wood and Mitchell, however, decided to dispose of the site of 19 Princelet Street freehold. Purchasing it seems to have caused some cashflow problems for Samuel Worrall, for in 1721/22 he sought to raise money, probably in the form of a mortgage, by conveying the ground to a consortium comprising a 'drugster, a draper and a glover', who were subsequently joined by a 'needleworker'.[8] It could well have been from this consortium that the house was purchased by its first inhabitant, a Huguenot master weaver named Peter Abraham Ogier.

* * * * *

The French Huguenots who settled in Spitalfields in significant numbers from the early 1680s had long been ill-treated in their native land. The first wave of persecution against them had reached a bloody crisis in 1572, during the wedding in Paris of the Huguenot prince Henry of Navarre. Catholics, perhaps with the support of King Charles IX, had launched what became known as the St Bartholomew's Day massacre, slaughtering leading Protestants who had gathered for the wedding and then over the next weeks extending

their murderous onslaught beyond Paris (as many as 30,000 Huguenots may have been killed). That period of persecution came to an
end when Henry of Navarre, who had narrowly escaped assassination
himself, and who inherited the throne in 1589 as Henry IV, approved
the Edict of Nantes in 1598, which granted official toleration of the
practice of the Protestant religion in France. Henry, meanwhile, had
converted to Roman Catholicism in an attempt to achieve civil unity.

During the seventeenth century, persecution of Protestants in
France and its colonies gradually increased, coming to a head in 1681
when Louis XIV authorised the quartering of dragoons (the *dragonnades*) in Huguenot communities to suppress the Protestant faith
through terror and intimidation, and to induce conversion to Catholicism. Initially, many French Protestants chose to remain in their
homeland, hoping that the persecution would pass. When it became
clear that it was only really possible to stay put if they renounced their
faith, large numbers chose to emigrate. It was an extremely risky path
to take. To leave France without permission was illegal. If caught,
Huguenots risked loss of property, imprisonment, enslavement in the
king's galleys or even summary execution.

Huguenots nevertheless fled in their tens of thousands to Protestant
nations such as England, as well as to territories under English control
such as Ireland and colonies in America. A committee established in
London in early 1687, charged with distributing charitable funds to
distressed Huguenot refugees, estimated that by December 1687 13,050
French Calvinists had settled in the capital, mostly in Spitalfields.[9] By
1710 it's possible that as many as 50,000 had settled in the British Isles,
half of them in London, and many of those in Spitalfields.[10]

The attraction of Spitalfields to these new arrivals was due, in part,
to its proximity to the long-established French Protestant church in
Threadneedle Street in the City,[11] and in part to trade. The eastern
parishes and liberties of London had long been home to weavers
working with wool and then from the mid seventeenth century producing silk ribbon.[12] Silk was hugely popular with the English, but
the native silk industry before the arrival of large numbers of Huguenots was unable to manufacture the more complex or wider fabrics

required for much-sought-after high-quality silk dresses, waistcoats and coats.

The newly arrived refugees from France, many of whom possessed skills in the silk trade, therefore saw a business opportunity: they could create a new, high-quality French-style silk industry in an area of London where French Protestants could feel at home, and which possessed associations with the embryonic native silk-weaving industry.[13] It helped, too, that the area had so much new and attractive housing to offer as a result of the financial stimulus – and speculative model – offered by the speedy and successful rebuilding of much of the City.

Official attitudes to these new arrivals were ambiguous and shifting. Charles II, the reigning monarch during the early 1680s – one of the major initial periods of migration – had occasionally opposed Louis XIV of France in the early years of his reign. By the time of the 'secret' Treaty of Dover of 1670, however, Charles was hoping for a rapprochement in order to secure financial aid from the French that would free him from dependence on Parliament for funds. He was also reaching a personal reconciliation with Catholicism. On the other hand, he was a tolerant man who disliked the notion of religious persecution and, as an exile himself in earlier life, clearly felt sympathy for the new refugees.[14] In 1681, therefore, he issued a document to be read in churches around the country that was designed to raise funds to relieve the more distressed of the newly arrived immigrants.

Four years later, in 1685, Louis XIV outlawed the Protestant faith in France altogether when he revoked the Edict of Nantes that had previously protected it, so prompting a further mass exodus. England's new king, James II, who had succeeded his brother in February of that year, was rather less sympathetic to the Huguenot refugees than his predecessor. As a pro-French Catholic, he did not want to encourage their arrival, but as sovereign over a Protestant people, he knew he had to tread carefully. He therefore followed a two-faced policy. He contrived to appear to be continuing Charles II's sympathetic policies in order to appease the Protestant sensibilities of the majority of his subjects, while simultaneously making life sufficiently difficult for Huguenots in England that some might leave and few would feel inclined to choose it as a place of refuge.

It was not until the Glorious Revolution of November 1688, when the Protestant William of Orange and his wife Mary (the daughter of James II) were invited by an establishment increasingly hostile to the king to 'invade' England and drive James out, that life became less complex and more certain for the French religious exiles in England. Indeed, the joint monarchs supported a 'Royal Bounty' paid from the 'Privy Purse' to aid distressed Huguenots. (James II had offered financial aid only to those who 'conformed' to Anglicanism.) The 'Bounty' remained in operation until 1804. Even after 1688 there were fears among the Anglican authorities about the religious beliefs and practices of the Calvinist Huguenots who were, in the end, yet one more Dissenting Protestant sect outside the authority of the established Anglican Church and who jealously guarded their right to worship in their own churches, or 'temples'. It was the Anglican Church's determination to assert its authority, as the state religion headed by the monarch, that in large part led to the passing in 1711 of an Act of Parliament to build fifty new churches in London.[15] Spitalfields was an obvious candidate for one of the fifty, and so, from 1714 to 1729, Nicholas Hawksmoor's impressive Christ Church slowly took form in the heart of the area, on what is now Commercial Street.

Popular British attitudes to the Huguenots varied and vacillated, too. As a rule the English Protestant middle class and aristocracy welcomed the arrival of their co-religionists. There was political capital to be made from offering refuge to Protestant Frenchmen fleeing persecution in their own land that simultaneously showed the autocratic monarchy of Catholic France in such a poor light. And, after all, the upper echelons of English society had little to lose and much to gain from the arrival of French craftsmen. But working people, notably journeymen weavers and smiths involved in the precious-metal trade (in which the Huguenots also showed themselves masters), feared that they had much to lose. For them

the newcomers represented a potential or actual threat to their livelihoods, perhaps undercutting established wage structures and introducing new work practices.

Ultimately, a pragmatic acceptance set in. Many realised that, in
comparison with France, England suffered from antiquated trade and
manufacturing traditions and was unable to compete with the high-
quality luxury artefacts of fashion being made on the other side of the
Channel. Now it had in its midst skilled workers who could level the
playing field.[16] In a 1719 pamphlet, Daniel Defoe stressed the economic
importance of the Huguenots' contribution to national well-being and
emphasised the fact that the 'Silk Manufactures of this Kingdom' were,
with the wool industry, 'the Staple of our Trade and the most considerable and essential part of our Wealth, the Fund of our Exportation,
the Support of our Navigation, and the only Means we have for the
Employing and Subsisting our Poor'.[17] A year later, John Strype, in his
Survey of the Cities of London and Westminster, wrote of the new arrivals
in Spitalfields in the following admiring terms:

> The North west Parts of this Parish (Spittle Fields and Parts
> adjacent), of later Times became a great Harbour for Poor
> Protestant Strangers, Waloons and French: Who as in former
> Days, so of late, have been forced to become Exiles from their
> own Country for their Religion, and for the avoiding cruel
> Persecution. Here they have found Quiet and Security, and
> settled themselves in their several Trades and Occupations;
> Weavers especially . . . [and] a great Advantage hath accrued to
> the whole Nation, by the rich Manufactures of weaving Silks
> and Stuffs and Camlets: Which Art they brought along with
> them. And this Benefit also to the Neighbourhood; that these
> Strangers may serve for Patterns of Thrift, Honesty, Industry,
> and Sobriety, as well.[18]

* * * * *

To understand the nature of the Huguenot community in London,
and the speed with which it successfully established itself, it is

necessary to remember that, because for decades these French Calvinists had been an isolated and persecuted minority within their own
homeland, they had had to develop powerful traditions of self-reliance
and mutual support. Family was all-important. Survival mechanisms
became well honed. In London, they soon formed a tightly knit
community – families and neighbours uniting in a common purpose,
intermarrying, and, because the rearing of large numbers of children
was regarded as a necessary consequence of holy matrimony, creating
thriving dynasties. A perusal of the register of the Huguenot church
of La Patente, which by the mid century occupied a still surviving, if
much altered, building in Hanbury Street (formerly Brown's Lane),[19]
shows that many of the Huguenots who attended the church were
already silk weavers or members of the silk trade when they arrived
in London and that a large number came from just two cities in
France – Lyon and Tours – so they probably already knew each other
before they arrived in Spitalfields.[20]

By the time construction began on the Anglican Christ Church, at
the west end of what is now Fournier Street, the Huguenots had been
established in large numbers in Spitalfields for around thirty years,
and by the time the church was completed, in 1729, the Huguenots
were, essentially, Spitalfields. Huguenot families were the families
that mattered, economically and culturally. They were the significant
merchants and entrepreneurs and occupied many of the area's largest
and grandest houses. They were a respected part of London society,
with many rising high in the professions and the Weavers' Company.
They had command of Spitalfields' wealth and most of its wealth-
generating industries and, although not members of the established
Anglican Church, effectively ran the area through the vestries and
parish administration.

They retained their distinct identity, invariably forging business
partnerships within Huguenot society and preserving their stern Calvinist faith. Where their Anglican neighbours generally believed that
conduct in the course of life determined reward or punishment after
death, Huguenots believed that by virtue of being born into the Calvinist faith they had already been predestined by God for eternal

salvation, that they were a 'chosen people'. While it may perhaps seem a little paradoxical that such an austere Calvinist group – in many ways Puritanical in its outlook – should have sought to devote their working lives to the production of visually seductive luxury consumer goods and the building of personal wealth, Huguenots took the view that wealth earned with a good heart and honest toil was godly, and that even the reasonable display of wealth amassed through righteous labour was 'not ostentation'.[21]

* * * * *

This was the context within which the Ogiers settled in Spital-fields in the late 1690s. Peter Abraham Ogier was born Pierre Abraham in 1690 at Chassais l'Eglise near Sigournais in Bas-Poitou in western France. He was one of fourteen children, of whom at least ten lived beyond babyhood. His parents, Pierre and Jeanne Ogier, had chosen to remain in France after the Edict of Nantes was repealed in 1685. But in around 1697 Jeanne, by then recently widowed, found herself in trouble for attending Prot-estant *assemblées* and, despite being heavily pregnant, decided to flee to England. She brought with her perhaps eight of her children, leaving two sons behind in France. One, Daniel (born 1683), remained as a Catholic while the other, Pierre (born 1680), struggled as a merchant at Moncoutant until 1730, when he left for England. (Peter was a popular name in the extended Ogier family in London and so Pierre is now generally known as Peter II.) Whether or not Jeanne immediately took up residence in Spi-talfields is not known, but given how swiftly the area was being developed at that time, it is perfectly possible.[22]

Jeanne evidently recognised that the silk industry offered the prospects of wealth and security for her family (the Ogiers had not been notable silk weavers or merchants in France) and used some of her money to apprentice Peter Abraham to Samuel Brule, a foreign master. Peter Abraham became a successful master weaver, a freeman of the Weavers' Company in 1716, and a liveryman in 1741,[23] as well as an elder of the church of La Patente. His success is reflected in the fact that in 1745 he was able to offer twenty-eight men to serve the Crown to help ward off the threat of a Catholic monarch – in the shape of the 'Old Pretender', James Francis Edward Stuart, or his son 'Bonnie Prince Charlie' – returning to the throne of Britain. Overall, the Ogier dynasty and their six companies volunteered a force of 164 workmen.[24]

In 1712 Peter Abraham married a Frenchwoman, Esther Dubois (Duboc), from Normandy at St Dunstan's, Stepney (the parish church that served much of central and east Spitalfields until the creation in 1729 of the parish of Christ Church, Spitalfields). The couple went on to have twelve children (seven of whom died young), and by the 1740s, if not significantly earlier, he, his family and his servants were living at 19 Princelet Street.[25] His son, also called Peter (now distinguished as Peter IV, who was born in 1716 and died in 1754) was also to become a weaver. He married Elizabeth Cadet and they had five children – but all died young. Peter Abraham's second son, Abraham (1717–84), who had eight children (of whom five died young) with his first wife, Martha Tarquand, later became a notary who lived over his business premises in Pope's Head Alley, opposite the Royal Exchange, in the City.

Over the course of Peter Abraham's life in Spitalfields, he became a key member of a closely entwined network of family and business associates, many of whom lived nearby. The Land Tax returns of 1743 reveal that David Godin, a partner in the silk-weaving firm of Godin and Ogier, by 1759 lived at nearby 24 Hanbury Street (which still survives, although much altered internally). In nearby Red Lion Street (now subsumed into Commercial Street) lived John Ogier, probably Peter Abraham Ogier's younger brother.[26] In Fournier (Church) Street, probably in the now-lost numbers 24 or 26 at the south-east end, there lived 'Thomas Tryquett', who was in all likelihood involved in the silk manufacturing firm of Ogier, Vansommer and Triquet based in Spital Square.[27] Crucially for Peter Abraham Ogier, a near neighbour from 1728 at what is now 2 Princelet Street was Anna Maria Garthwaite, the acclaimed textile designer employed by many of the leading masters of Spitalfields – including Peter

Abraham. The building was Garthwaite's home and workplace until her death in 1763.

By the time Peter Abraham moved to Princelet Street, the house had in likelihood been standing for some time, so it is scarcely surprising that it betrays little evidence of the Ogier family's tastes. The layout of rooms remained as originally planned and is typical for Spitalfields, with the exception of a cupboard door in the second-floor front room that conceals a private connection or passage between back and front rooms. If these were originally intended to serve as bedchambers, as is most likely, this short passage provided a private route between them so that the occupants could move from one to the other without being observed by the servants (which could have been the case if they had been obliged to cross the staircase landing). The kitchen and scullery were in the basement. The ground floor contained the more public rooms of the house, where, in Peter Abraham's time, meetings with suppliers, designers, weavers and mercers could have taken place. Perhaps one was the dining chamber in which some meals would have been taken, although now that this pair of ground-floor rooms no longer exist in their original form it's impossible to tell for sure. Perhaps Ogier occasionally displayed his latest products in one of these rooms, in the same way, at roughly the same time, that George Frideric Handel sold his sheet music from one of the ground-floor rooms of his comparable house in Brook Street, Mayfair.

On the first floor were the main reception rooms – the drawing room and parlour – above those the bedrooms, and at the top the garret room that may well have served as the Ogier's counting house. Although Peter Ogier was no doubt a skilled weaver and had worked as one in his youth, he was now a successful businessman: this house was his home and not a place of noisy industry, passed through by working weavers and carters. In Ogier's time the actual weaving process would have been undertaken elsewhere, by journeymen weavers in their wide-windowed workshop homes, on the Bethnal Green and Shoreditch edge of Spitalfields, or in courts and in smaller houses and in more modest streets in central Spitalfields.

Today, only a fine timber-made French-style rococo fire surround of *c.*1745–50, which the family must have added in the last years of Peter Abraham Ogier's life, survives to bear witness to the personal stamp that the Ogiers placed on their house. The fire surround, located in the first-floor front room – almost certainly once the house's finest room – was stolen in the early 1980s but was later recovered and is awaiting repair and reinstatement. For the rest, there are sadly no records of life in 19 Princelet Street during the occupation of Peter Abraham Ogier and his family, or indeed detailed records of the daily and domestic lives of any Spitalfields Huguenot families at the time.

It is nevertheless possible to attempt a portrait of 19 Princelet Street in its early days from such physical evidence as survives and from circumstantial documentary evidence. One thing we know for sure is that the Huguenots made and admired fine silver ornaments, clocks, furniture and beautiful silks. Since their Calvinist principles did not inhibit them in the display of riches honestly earned, they would have laboured hard to make the interiors of their houses beautiful. Many certainly had the money to spend on fine luxury items. The master weaver Peter Bourdon of 27 Fournier Street, in his will of 1732, left all his 'household goods [and] all [his] plate' to his 'beloved wife' Margaret, along with 'linen, rings and jewels' and the then vast sum of £3,500 in 'lawful money', the total value of his bequests being £6,880 (around £1,250,000 today).[28] The Land Tax returns of 1743 indicate that the inhabitants of Princelet Street were almost all prosperous individuals – and that Peter Abraham Ogier, who was assessed at £14, owned not only a house here but one in Hanbury Street – probably the one that, since rebuilt, backed on to 19 Princelet Street.[29] We can fairly safely assume, then, that 19 Princelet Street was handsomely appointed during the time that the Ogiers lived there.

Archaeological investigation of the house, and of comparable and contemporary houses in Spitalfields, suggests that the panelled interior was painted in soft and simple stone colours – light ochres and pale blue/green greys, known as 'drab' – all realised through the

The first-floor front room of 19 Princelet Street in early 2025.
Above: the panelling dates from 1718, and the cupboard doors from the
later nineteenth century. Below: the mid eighteenth-century rococo fire
surround before its theft from the first-floor room in the early 1980s.
It was soon recovered and will be repaired and reinstated.

mixing of earth pigments such as 'Oxford Ochre' and umber, indigo organic dye, soot (called 'lamp black') or copper carbonates with white lead ground in linseed oil. Strong, darker colours could also be achieved with these pigments ('lead' colour, for example, olive green, 'wainscot' (oak) colour, and blue or green verditer), but these seem to have been used rarely in primary rooms in the 1720s to 1740s, with verditer being reserved for very occasional use only in kitchens or workshops, on plaster as well as timber.[30] The main rooms of Ogier's house would probably have been painted in the lighter stone-hued 'Common Colours' (see page 25), with most principal rooms painted in similar manner. There is, however, some evidence that while the first-floor front room, the principal room of the house, was initially painted a stone colour, it was then given a darker, grey-blue look. Pale or dark stone schemes would have been uniform – mouldings or panels were not picked out in different colours – and must have acted as splendid foils for the rich oak, walnut (and latterly mahogany) furniture, strongly coloured silk or needlework upholstery, sparkling silver and burnished brass, and prints or family portraits. Analysis of the surviving early paint on the rococo fire surround in the first-floor front room of 19 Princelet Street suggests that it was originally painted a pale stone, almost cream, and coated with a clear resin lacquer or shellac glaze. This would have been highly fashionable in the 1750s, displaying a chinoiserie influence and emphasising the surround's playful rococo character.[31]

The house had, for Spitalfields, an unusually large rear garden.[32] This would no doubt have contained a 'house of office', or privy, set over a cesspit, into which the contents of chamber pots from close stools would have been emptied by servants. The garden would also have served other practical purposes, such as a location for fuel and water storage. However, it was large enough to have been ornamental as well and, since Huguenots included gardening among their many cultural attributes, would probably have been laid out with flower beds and plants set between gravel paths. The plants, including varieties of roses and jasmine, would presumably have come from the Shoreditch and Hoxton market gardens of flower-men and nurserymen such as Thomas Fairchild, the author of *The City Gardener* (1722). As for the 'house of office', this might well have been disguised as a plant-veiled pavilion, with roses, perhaps, twined around or in front of it. This was not unusual in the eighteenth century, hence the euphemism for going to the lavatory, to 'go pluck a rose', as in the verse by Jonathan Swift:

> The bashful Maid, to hide her Blush;
> Shall creep no more behind a Bush;
> Here unobserv'd, she boldly goes,
> As who should say, to Pluck a Rose.[33]

* * * * *

Peter Abraham Ogier died in 1757.[34] By then the Ogiers were extraordinarily rich and powerful members of the French merchant community in London. They had also become an extensive family: just three members – Peter Abraham, Peter II and Peter III – had twenty-nine children between them, most of whom lived to adulthood, many occupying houses in virtually adjoining streets. They made strong and long-lasting alliances. Louisa Perina, for example – who was the daughter of Peter Abraham's brother Peter II (born in 1680, who had stayed in France when the family originally emigrated and had then followed in 1730) and Catherine Rabaud – married Samuel Courtauld, a Huguenot goldsmith, in 1749.[35] She was a remarkable character. Alleged to have been smuggled out of France in 1730 at the age of one in a sack of potatoes when her father belatedly decided to flee to England, Louisa prospered, no doubt partly because in 1740 he left her £2,560 in his will. When her husband died in 1765, Louisa – by then the mother of eight children – oversaw the growth of the Courtauld precious metals business from a goldsmith's shop in Cornhill and laid the foundations for the Courtauld commercial empire that had expanded to include fabrics. Louisa had a home in Essex, where she lived the life of a country gentlewoman, and latterly in Clapton, where her will was addressed and dated. For her burial, though, she wanted to return to what had been the Ogier family's

London power base and its place of identity. In 1807 Louisa Perina's earthly remains were returned to Spitalfields to be interred in the vault beneath Christ Church. Here she rested until the mid 1980s, when her skeleton – and around 2,000 others interred between 1729 and 1851 – was removed and archaeologically investigated.[36]

As for 19 Princelet Street, its fortunes in the years immediately after Peter Abraham Ogier's death remain uncertain. We do know, however, that in the 1770s and 1780s number 17 was occupied by Samuel Ireland junior, a weaver,[37] and it was almost certainly around this time that most of the weaving garret as we see it today, with a long row of mullioned windows to admit as much light as possible, was added to number 19. Sand was placed between the joists of the garret and the ceiling beneath to insulate and deaden the noise of looms in motion, and it may well have been the weight of the sand, combined with the burden on the structure of the house imposed by the additional garret room and the equipment it housed, that was responsible for the bulging panelled partition that is now evident at first-floor level. The house was now a workshop as well as a home.

It's possible, too, that as with other similar houses in Spital-fields at this time, 19 Princelet Street was divided to form a multi-occupied tenement in mixed use. The last decades of the eighteenth century witnessed a dramatic change in the area's fortunes, as the once-prosperous silk industry began a precipitous decline. The 1760s proved a tumultuous time of unrest and riot: journeymen weavers, facing uncertain futures as their work and rates of pay decreased, took direct and often violent action in an attempt to secure their futures. Their suffering was briefly ameliorated by the Spitalfields Acts, passed from 1773, which sought to guarantee wages and protect the industry from foreign competition, but such recovery as there was proved piecemeal and short term. When the Acts were repealed in 1824, as part of free trade reform, the demise of the industry became inevitable and Spitalfields degenerated rapidly into a district defined by poverty, unemployment, decay and discontent. Charles Dickens offered a dismal portrait of the area in April 1851, when in his pub-lication *Household Words* he asked his 'dear readers' if they had 'any distinct idea of Spitalfields'. He answered his own question: 'A general one, no doubt . . . an impression that there are certain squalid streets, lying like narrow black trenches, far below the steeples, somewhere about London – towards the East End perhaps – where sallow, unshorn weavers who have nothing to do, prowl languidly about, or lean against posts, or sit brooding on doorsteps . . .'[38] The dire nature of Spitalfields was, in Dickens's forlorn opinion, the result of 'de-regulation' by Free Traders and the resulting ruthless competition with cheaper foreign goods. It was, for him, 'the grave of modern manufacturing London'.

By the time of the 1851 census, the once-powerful Ogier family appears to have disappeared from Spitalfields altogether,[39] and 19 Princelet Street (then still 18 Princes Street) was occupied by two households. One was headed by John Broadbridge, a 'Surveyor' who lived with his wife, Sarah, born in 'America'. The second household comprised, on the day of the census at least, Elizabeth Carter, aged seventy, the 'House Proprietor', born in East Elm, Essex. It was a far cry from 19 Princelet Street's glory days, even if it represented a low density of occupation for mid nineteenth-century Spitalfields. By contrast, nearby 23 Princelet (16 Princes) Street, which was built around 1705 and was roughly the same size as number 19, was occupied by five households and contained eighteen people on the day of the census, including Edward Hall, a 30-year-old 'Vullum binder' (vellum binder, or bookbinder), and his 37-year-old wife; William Frost, a 'Foreman salesman', his wife, two children and mother; and Sarah Anne Spraggs, a 42-year-old widow and 'silk winder' and her 'errand boy' son. The immediate neighbour – 17 Princelet (former 19 Princes) Street – was occupied by thirteen people in three households, among whom was the 96-year-old former parish beadle Thomas Hart.[40]

* * * * *

But all was soon to change for 19 Princelet Street. In 1862 Ashkenazi Jewish, Yiddish-speaking immigrants – Polish or Lithuanian in origin and escaping persecution by Russian Tsarist authorities – established the Chevras Nidvat Chain ('Loyal United Friends Friendly Society') in a rented building in 46 New Court, Fashion Street, off Brick Lane and close to Princelet Street.[41] Then, in 1870, it took out a twenty-year lease[42] on the now-empty four-storey 19 Princelet Street, and on the workshop that had at some point been constructed in its former garden.[43]

What followed was a radical programme of building and change of function. The society offered, in return for a small weekly contribution, financial assistance to its members in times of need. It also functioned as an Orthodox synagogue. It therefore required a building that could both host meetings and social events and function as a centre of worship. According to Samuel Melnick, who wrote a comprehensive chronicle of 19 Princelet Street's time as a centre of east London Jewish life, 'the conversion consisted of excavating the garden to provide a basement-level general-purpose meeting hall and a ground-level synagogue with a gallery at first-floor level for ladies.'[44] At the same time, the rear part of the eighteenth-century house was altered, and much of its rear wall removed at the three lower levels, to accommodate the new synagogue and its related functions. According to Melnick, the cost of the conversion was £1,100, 'paid for in part by the membership and the remainder by means of a public appeal for £500'. The architect employed was a 'Mr Hudson' and 'the builder was Mr Langmead'.[45] Work completed, the synagogue was consecrated on Sunday, 4 September 1870.[46]

The impoverished circumstances of many of the synagogue's congregation is suggested by the fact that in its early years it became a favoured venue for cut-price and semi-communal marriages (a move approved by the United Synagogue, which had been founded in 1870 with Nathan Rothschild as its first president, to govern the affairs of British Orthodox synagogues). The first marriage – costing ten shillings and sixpence (or a half-guinea), rather than the usual three guineas – took place in August 1877, and on any given approved day there might be as many as eight or nine.[47] Wedding parties were held in the basement hall and often spilled on to the street. Festivities could be riotous and sometimes veered out of control. On one occasion, when a fight broke out following an officiating minister's

The synagogue, built in 1870 on the former garden of 19 Princelet Street, looking from the 'ladies' gallery' to the ark. The bimah and benches that stood on the floor of the synagogue are currently in store and will be reinstated.

attempt to charge a groom an additional half-crown (two shillings
and sixpence), a bride's dress and veil were torn in the affray. Perhaps
not surprisingly, therefore, cut-price marriages were discontinued at
Princelet Street in 1890.[48]

This termination of cheap and rowdy marriages seems to have
been part of a more general drive to imbue the synagogue with a
greater aura of respectability, no doubt in part because those responsible for running it were acutely aware that the lease was shortly to
expire. It also came at a time when members of the wider Jewish
community were scrutinising the smaller Orthodox synagogues and
chevras, or religious societies, that had sprung up in east London, predominantly to serve poor refugees from Tsarist Russia and its empire.
In October 1887 the Federation of Minor Synagogues was established, its first meeting, held in the Spital Square Synagogue, presided
over by Samuel Montagu, a prosperous banker and, since 1885, MP
for Whitechapel. Representatives from sixteen synagogues, including from 19 Princelet Street, were present, and from this point on the
Princelet Street synagogue determined to operate under the auspices
of what became known as the Federation of Synagogues (the word
'Minor' being dropped).[49]

In late 1889 a new lease for fifty years was obtained from the free-
holder, Henry Bawtree, and plans were put in hand for the renovation
of the building. The federation's Honorary Architect, Lewis Solomon,
was commissioned to produce a survey – identifying defects and suggesting repairs and improvements – and this was produced in mid
1892. He estimated the cost of works would be £600. Raising funds
now became a matter of priority. In November 1892, at a meeting
held in the synagogue, it was resolved to borrow £200 from the Loyal
United Friends Friendly Society funds (to be repaid at £20 per annum
with 3 per cent interest) and to launch an appeal for the remaining £400.[50] A document was duly circulated, in a neat copperplate
hand, entitled 'An Appeal for Funds for the Partial Re-Building of
the Princes Street Synagogue'.[51] It explained that the synagogue was
'situated in a densely populated locality of the poorest Jewish inhabitants and is always well attended', and that its 'Provident Society'

helped its 'Members in Sickness and Shiva [mourning], and pays for the burial of Members and relieves them in distress'. In appealing for 'about £500', it pointed out that 'many structural alterations' had become 'necessary', that 'the Hon. Architect to the Federation, Mr. L. Solomons [sic]', who had been instructed to report on the condition of the current building, had 'condemned . . . several portions', and that the scheme he had come up with would offer visible improvements, including better access and ventilation – and some added architectural grandeur.[52] The pamphlet was signed, and the appeal validated, by the Rev. Dr Adler, Chief Rabbi, and Samuel Montagu MP, along with J. Davidson Esq, of 16 Princes (now 15 Princelet) Street, the 'President of the Princes St Synagogue'.

The appeal was successful, thanks in part to a donation of £50 from Lord Rothschild and thirty guineas from Samuel Montagu (whose generous actions are still commemorated on a panel set within the synagogue's gallery), and soon repair and improvement work was under way. The entrance passage from the street was widened, the hall was paved with stone flags supported on iron girders, and the staircase from the basement to the first-floor half-landing was rebuilt in stone with an iron balustrade. The ground-floor frontage of the building was also redesigned and rebuilt, with three wide arched openings – one serving as a door and the others as windows – set in a single-storey stucco elevation and embellished with bold voussoir, or wedge-shaped, ornament. The intention seems to have been to give a synagogue that was housed within a converted home something of the more elevated status of a public or institutional building. On Sunday, 26 March 1893, the synagogue was formally reopened, Samuel Montagu performing the opening ceremony and Dr Adler solemnising the consecration.[53]

The architect for the early 1890s works to the synagogue, Lewis Solomon, was a significant member of London's late Victorian building world. Born in 1848, he was apprenticed in the early 1860s to the eminent architect Sir Matthew Digby Wyatt, who worked for the government and for fabulously rich and influential private clients such as the Rothschilds. It was Wyatt who, in 1866, designed the exotic circular, domed, column-clad Rothschild Mausoleum in the West Ham Jewish Cemetery, commissioned by the banker Baron Ferdinand James de Rothschild for his wife, Evelina, who had died in childbirth, aged twenty-seven. Solomon rose to become Wyatt's Clerk of Works, and may have worked on the Rothschild project, but in 1872 he left this safe haven to set up on his own. It seems that his aim was primarily to serve London's increasingly prosperous Jewish community, and his work on the synagogue at 19 Princelet Street was an early endeavour. In 1902 he designed the 'Soup Kitchen for the Jewish Poor' in Brune (originally Butler) Street, Spitalfields, which he furnished with a buff-coloured terracotta ground-floor facade of elaborate design and, at third-floor level, with a large lunette set within a gable pediment. A couple of years later he undertook alterations to the Sandys Row Ashkenazi synagogue, before going on to design the still existing synagogues on Commercial Street and Nelson Street in Whitechapel.[54]

By the time Solomon worked at Princelet Street, the synagogue had become an important location within Spitalfields's Jewish community, which by then was thriving. Its early marriage records confirm that the majority of its congregation in the late nineteenth century lived nearby – many in multi-occupied houses in Princelet Street – and worked in the tailoring and cabinet-making trades, which flourished in Spitalfields and a little further to the north in Bethnal Green. Around it, as the writer Rachel Lichtenstein describes, was 'a chaotic fusion of religious and secular life – boasting bustling Jewish commercial and trades centres, social and entertainment hubs, and a complex network of self-supporting interconnected Jewish societies, youth, political and literary clubs, theatres, schools and institutions'. Street signs, she records, were written in Yiddish, 'kosher food was available to buy in shops, market stalls, kosher dairies and eateries, slaughterhouses and poulterers'. There were also 'multiple newspapers and journals, literary groups and societies, cinemas, dance halls and many active political groups', including 'anarchists, Zionists, Bundists [the Jewish secular socialist labour movement] and communists who met on street corners as well as in purpose-built places like the Workers

Circle'.[55] And, in addition, there were four Yiddish theatres, the first being in Princelet Street.

The Princelet Street theatre carries its own – tragic – story. Founded in 1885 by Jacob Adler and David Smith, and located at the south-west end of Princelet Street, the theatre had a compact music-hall form, complete with proscenium arch and galleries. It proved extremely popular. On the evening of 18 January 1887, packed with an audience of 600 or so watching an escapist production called *The Spanish Gypsy Girl*, there was a sudden sense of alarm within the building. Cries of 'fire!' and the dousing of gas lamps that followed provoked the audience to panic, and in the rush to escape seventeen people, including five children, died – most crushed to death. The scene in Princelet Street in the immediate aftermath was, as the *Daily News* recorded, grim indeed: 'women who had lost their children, men who had lost their wives . . . walking, weeping and lamenting through the crowd', who 'refused to be comforted'. As Melnick records, 'prayers were said for the dead and injured on the following Sabbath in the synagogue'.[56] Since members of the synagogue would have been among the dead, it must have been a sombre and emotional occasion. The alarm, incidentally, turned out to have been a false one.

When the philanthropist and social reformer Charles Booth, accompanied by his secretary George H. Duckworth and a police guide named Sergeant French, surveyed Spitalfields street by street in 1886 and 1898, they found pockets of affluence – Duckworth noted that Fournier Street, for example, contained the homes of 'well-to-do Jews' who 'keep servants' – but also houses and streets where deprivation and overcrowding were obvious.[57] Booth had devised a crude colour-coded system of grading what he saw, ranging from black ('Lowest class. Vicious, semi-criminal') to gold or yellow ('Upper-middle and Upper classes'), the other gradings being dark blue ('Very poor, casual. Chronic want'); light blue ('Poor'); purple ('Mixed. Some comfortable, others poor'); pink ('Fairly comfortable. Good ordinary earnings'); and red ('Middle class. Well-to-do'). When he first surveyed Princelet Street in 1886 a number of the houses, including those flanking the synagogue, were classified as pink (the synagogue as a public building went ungraded). In his 1898/9 survey he reclassified the houses to the east of the synagogue, and the synagogue itself, as black. A map of the same period (1899), purporting to trace the pattern of occupation of 'Jewish East London', suggests that the street at the time was 75 to 95 per cent Jewish.

Given that the houses Booth colour-coded black included a pair of buildings on the south-east corner of Princelet Street and Brick Lane (titled 'Lodging House' in Charles E. Goade's insurance map from the 1890s) that were known to be owned by the distinctly unsavoury John Cooney (another of whose establishments, at 55 Flower and Dean Street, had been linked ten years earlier with one of Jack the Ripper's victims, Catherine Eddowes), a black rating is not necessarily so surprising. And perhaps some of the houses in Princelet Street did indeed shelter 'Vicious, semi-criminal' people. But the overwhelming impression to be gained from the 1891 census is that the people of Princelet Street, while they might have been from the 'Lowest class', were far from 'Vicious'. They were, however, clearly having to cope with appalling conditions. Number 17 Princes Street (now 21 Princelet Street, and downgraded to black in 1898) – a five-storey, ten- or eleven-room house built between 1705 and 1706 – contained on the day of the 1891 census an astonishing forty-eight people, organised as eight family groups. They included Henry Prollius, a 44-year-old cabinetmaker born in Germany who lived there with his 12-year-old daughter, Elizabeth; Isaac Newman, a 35-year-old 'Hebrew book seller' born in Russia, and his Russian wife and eight children; Barnet Cohen, a 45-year-old 'Boot finisher' from Germany, his Polish wife and three children; William Germantis, a 30-year-old Polish-born 'Tailor's Presser', his wife, son and five Polish male lodgers – aged 18 to 25 – who were tailors, table makers and a 'skin dresser'; and Philip Swartz, a 20-year-old tailor from 'Russia Poland', his 19-year-old wife and his daughter.[58] Water would have been supplied only to the basement and perhaps to a couple of landings, and the lavatories – perhaps two – would probably only have been in the backyard.

As for 19 Princelet Street (renumbered from 18 in the early 1890s), those rooms not occupied by the synagogue were in 1891 home to thirteen people in three family groups, living in four or five rooms. One family comprised the 77-year-old Harris Levy – one of the founders of the synagogue in the 1860s – along with his wife and cousin. He is described in the census as the 'synagogue Beadle', but a more accurate description of his role would be salaried sexton or 'Shammash', whose tasks included assisting the cantor and under-taking secretarial work. Another of the families in number 19 con-sisted of the widowed 53-year-old Polish-born Leah Lichenstein and her five grown sons, who worked as tailors and bootmakers. It is probable that the Levy family occupied the second-floor rooms and the Lichensteins the top two rooms.

* * * * *

The synagogue in 19 Princelet Street continued to prosper and serve a large congregation into the 1930s, even if by this time its domi-nance in the local community had been usurped by the Spitalfields Great Synagogue that had been founded in 1891 (by mostly Lithua-nian Jews) within a former Huguenot temple of 1743 on the corner of Brick Lane and Fournier Street.[59] In 1921 Princelet Street Syna-gogue was once again renovated – perhaps this is when electric lights were installed – with a 'Re-opening' service held on Sunday, 17 April 1921. The ceremony involved a formal opening by Sir Stuart Montagu Samuel, the nephew of Samuel Montagu and until 1916 the MP for Whitechapel – a man who, like his uncle, took a keen philanthropic interest in the Jewish population of east London.[60]

Over the next few decades, decline gradually set in. The Jewish population began to abandon Spitalfields soon after the start of the Second World War, choosing to move from a well-known Jewish area in case a successful Nazi invasion took place, which, for a few months after the fall of France in June 1940, seemed more likely than not. After the war the dispersal of the community continued, largely because less dense urban areas, unmarred by decades of sordid slum depravation and untainted by sad memories of suffering, became

available for increasingly prosperous and mobile members of the
community.

The last entry in the synagogue's account book is dated 26
February 1962. Soon after this, according to Melnick, 'the synagogue officers faced with the ... impossibility of obtaining a *minyan*
[a group of at least ten men] for its Shabbat services decided to
accept the inevitable and abandoned the building.'[61] Even then, the
building was not left entirely empty. In 1961, when Myer Reback, a
long-time supporter of the synagogue, died, his daughter took up residence in the second-floor rooms that were probably once occupied
by Harris Levy and his family to serve as caretaker. Above her, in
the garret, lived David Rodinsky, a hermit scholar of languages and
Jewish lore, who had moved into the building as a child in around
1929 with his mother and sister and who stayed on for the next forty
years or so, living in conditions of increasingly eccentric squalor, until,
as Melnick puts it, he left one day in 1969 'not to return, having collapsed in the street and died a few days later in hospital'. For the
following decade Rodinsky's possessions, including his collection of
books and notepads, remained in his garret behind locked doors, with
his writings and newspapers spread upon his table and clothes and
folded sheets still in his cupboard.[62]

In 1970 the synagogue formally merged with the Bethnal Green
Great Synagogue, although, according to Melnick, some activities –
such as winter *mincha*, or afternoon prayers – continued to take
place in Princelet Street.[63] Ten years later, the Federation of Synagogues, which had acquired the lease of the building (no doubt
due to the loans it had made) exercised its right to buy the freehold
of the building for £35,000 and then immediately sold it to the
newly formed Spitalfields Historic Buildings Trust for the same
amount.[64]

The first members of the trust to cross the threshold in 1980 were
astonished by the state of the abandoned building. Books and fabrics
were scattered around, as if – in Melnick's words – the synagogue
had been 'abandoned in some sudden emergency'. Dust from disinte-
grating plasterwork lay everywhere. Rain damage was all too evident.

When the doors to Rodinsky's rooms at the top of the house were opened, those present were confronted by heaps of what appeared to be abandoned junk. Amid the chaos there could nevertheless be perceived a sense of order and also poignant reminders that this had once been someone's home. In the front room a bed was squeezed into a far corner, next to the chimney breast; an upright piano stood nearby; and a centrally placed Victorian table, evidently a place of work, was laden with projects in hand with a gas light fixed in the ceiling above.[65]

The sacred atmosphere of the building still lingered. Melnick asserts that the synagogue's Sefer Torah, or handwritten scrolls containing the first five books of the Old Testament, once housed in their shrine in the Holy Ark, had been removed by the federation before the sale. But the scrolls' richly decorated covers – dating from the early twentieth century and made of white silk, blue velvet and embroidered with sacred imagery, including the Lion of Judah and the Star of David – remained. Some bore the name of the person who had given them. Sacred books from Poland, Lithuania, Russia, Germany and elsewhere, bearing testimony to the range and richness of the Ashkenazi Jewish heritage, lay scattered around. According to Jewish tradition, those found to be seriously damaged have to receive special treatment, because their display can cause dismay at their abuse or neglect. One course of action is to bury them, another is to seal them within a Genizah – a sacred hiding place in a synagogue, usually located in the attic or the basement. Such a small and seemingly mysterious cupboard exists in the garret of number 19, perched above the staircase. Perhaps this was the Genizah, but, if so, this cupboard has long been bare, with its doors smashed. It remains one of the many mysteries of the building, but would be an eminently suitable resting place for the synagogue's damaged sacred texts.[66]

What immediately became clear to all those who visited this deserted building in the early 1980s was that this was not a place that would be appropriate to convert into a private home. It was too complex and too sacred for that. It needed to be preserved, much as found, to tell its story – indeed, the story of a now-lost world – and to serve, in some public way, the reinvigorated community of Spitalfields.

*****

Much remains to be discovered about the building, its contents and people and the life of the synagogue, but tantalising details are constantly emerging. We are, for example, slowly finding out more about the members of the Jewish community who worshipped in and looked after the building – people such as Abraham Heisar, a bead maker and glass merchant from Prussia, who was the secretary of the Loyal United Friends Friendly Society from the inception of the synagogue in 1869/70;[67] and Ahron Haim Schwartz, who was born in 1883 and came to London before 1914, serving as rabbi in the late 1920s.

Schwartz is a particularly interesting figure. A pamphlet recently discovered in the synagogue relating to the 'Society for Chanting Psalms & Visiting the Sick', addressed from the 'Princes St Synagogue' and dating from 1893, lists an 'A. Schwartz' as one of the 'Officers' of the synagogue, or schul, along with 'H. Levy'.[68] Schwartz would ultimately go on to become the rabbi of Birmingham's New Synagogue in the 1920s (and later a rabbi in Ohio),[69] and while at Princelet Street he was clearly an active member of the community. During these years he forged a friendship with Rabbi Abraham Isaac Kook, who had been born in the Russian Empire but by 1915 or 1916 lived just a few doors down at 9 Princelet Street, and this connection provides a fascinating linking thread between the Princelet Street synagogue of the early 1900s and the nascent Zionist movement that would prove so key to the foundation of the modern state of Israel.

Before moving to London after the outbreak of the First World War, Kook had been Chief Rabbi of Jaffa and the Colonies of Palestine when they were under Ottoman rule. Classed by the Turks as an 'enemy alien' during a visit to Europe in 1914 and refused readmission to Palestine, he gravitated to the Anglo-Jewish heartland of Spitalfields, becoming Rabbi of Machzike Hadath, on the corner of Brick Lane and Fournier Street, in about 1916.[70] Here, it may be assumed, Rabbi Kook sought to encourage the Jewish population of Spitalfields to help fulfil a divine prophecy and emigrate to Palestine – or at least donate funds for Jewish settlement – to contribute to the establishment of a homeland that had, according to the Torah, been promised by God to his 'chosen people'.[71] The creation of this homeland, most Jews believed, was the essential prelude for the arrival of the Messiah – the one anointed by God and descended from King David who would deliver the Jews from worldly oppression. Such a vision must, in the early twentieth century, have been most attractive for poor Jewish families living and working in the overcrowded and decaying buildings of Spitalfields and was apparently achievable if sufficient of them contributed – through emigration or donation. Many poor Jewish residents of Spitalfields no doubt believed they had little to lose and much to gain by helping the Zionist movement.

Melnick confirms that the congregation of 19 Princelet Street did, indeed, do its bit to make the vision reality. When the Balfour Declaration was published in November 1917, stating that the British government was in favour of the 'establishment of a national home for the Jewish people in Palestine', the synagogue at 19 Princelet Street 'was represented at ... a "Great Thanksgiving Meeting" at the London Royal Opera House', with 'the meeting ... chaired by Lord Rothschild, to whom the Declaration had been addressed'. This meeting encouraged many small meetings in support of Zionist organisations and to raise funds, 'and the Princelet Street synagogue hosted its fair share of them', raising 'considerable sums of money ... in support of the settlements being established in the Holy Land'.[72]

Rabbi Kook himself stayed in Princelet Street until 1919, when he returned to Palestine as Chief Rabbi of Jerusalem and then, in 1921, of Palestine itself – then under British Mandate rule – before his death in 1935.[73] In one of the surviving letters between Rabbi Kook and Rabbi Schwartz, written in the early 1920s and addressed from 73 Belgrave Road, Birmingham, Schwartz refers to the funds he had raised from his congregation to support the Jewish settlement of Palestine.[74] The problem, of course, was that the Promised Land was already inhabited by a people – Muslim and Christian Palestinian Arabs – who had their own dreams of founding an independent sovereign state in the region.

* * * * *

To step inside 19 Princelet Street today is to enter a building that openly bears its scars but is rich in both atmosphere and memory. Within its walls the past exists, layer upon layer, each evoking the generations that have lived, prayed, strived (and on occasion thrived) within its walls. Sometimes this layering is literal, as in the rear garret room where a wide weavers' window has been partly boarded up, marking a change from workshop to home. The boards are covered with fragmentary layers of playfully patterned wallpaper that reflect changing fashions and, perhaps, the hopes and dreams of the poor occupant of the room who might have had nothing beyond the ability to purchase a few scraps of gaudy ornament to enliven their bleak home and express their aspirations towards a more affluent and fashionable late Victorian domestic comfort. Over part of the boarding is another, later piece of board – perhaps a repair – and this bears its own mosaic of old wallpapers. And so it goes with this house: its deeper and darker corners preserve such minuscule episodes of social history, each precious, fascinating and informative and now so fragile that you feel, even by just gazing too hard, all might fragment.

On the ground floor there is a small washbasin, tap and fixings for a roller towel located at the threshold to the synagogue, adjoining the head of the stone stairs to the basement. It is customary to undertake a ritual cleansing (usually no more than a washing of the hands) before prayer (*Netilat Yadayim*) and before offering a priestly blessing. The flight of stairs next to it, with its simple iron balustrade and handsome cast-iron newel, clearly became so worn over time that at some point they were resurfaced with a thick layer of cast concrete – the concrete surface shows the paw prints of the synagogue cat that, like so many of the former inhabitants of the building, continues in its way to be present still. Those signs of heavy wear

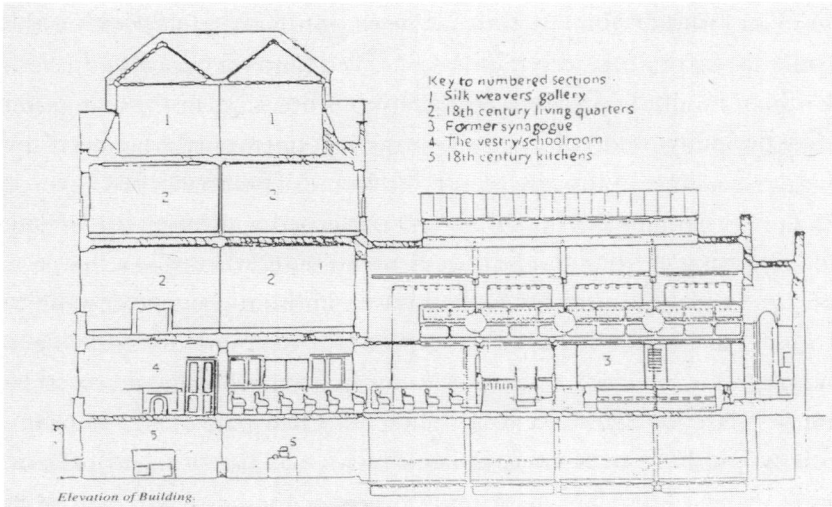

Elevation of Building.

Cross-section, looking west, of 19 Princelet Street. That the top floor was a 'silk weavers' gallery' is likely but speculative, and it is probable that the well-lit workshops were added in the late eighteenth century, replacing an existing rear room and a front garret formed within the roof space and lit by dormers. The basement room below the synagogue was used to conduct the business of the Friendly Society, for public meetings and for celebrations, often related to weddings in the synagogue above.

confirm that the basement was once a hive of activity, containing as it did the meeting room of the Friendly Society that offered help to the poorest members of the congregation, as well as a place for parties after weddings and bar and bat mitzvahs. The current still- ness of the room is haunting: once so full of life; now, for decades, sunk in silence. It takes only a little imagination to fill its shadowy corners with spectres, and it's hard not to strain to hear the voices of the long dead.

The front basement room is now gaunt, with exposed brick walls that were formerly plastered. This once served as the Ogiers' kitchen, and indeed there is still, in one corner, a large stone sink that they probably used.[75] The rear basement room would have been the Ogiers' scullery. In the nineteenth century, the room was fitted with a 'copper' – a large cauldron set over a small stove and used for boiling and cleaning clothes and fabrics. A metal pipe, serving as a flue, was at some point cut into the arched recess in the room, presumably to connect to the flue serving the fireplace above. When the synagogue was established in 1870, these two rooms would have continued to serve as kitchens, but, in accordance with the practices of Judaism, one would have been used to cook meat, and the other to prepare milk dishes. There are no windows serving the large hall excavated below the former garden, but there are narrow grilles set in the floor of the synagogue above to allow some light to enter. The grilles must also have been intended to provide ventilation: to each of the base- ment's cast-iron columns, installed when the synagogue was created, remains attached a fitting for a gas lamp, and the fumes emitted by coal gas would have been both dense and very unpleasant.

The long and large table that once stood in the large basement rear room, below the synagogue hall and around which members of the Friendly Society and the synagogue's committee would have gathered to conduct business, is still to be found in the house, as is a framed board that hung above it that commemorates donations and gifts to the society. Headed, in ornamental lettering in English and in Hebrew, the 'Loyal United Friends Friendly Society . . . the Princes Street Synagogue' and dated September 1870 (5630 in the Jewish calendar), it states that 'the following Gentlemen have kindly presented the above synagogue with the undermentioned gifts'. Unfortunately, years of damp have taken their toll, so that many of the names and gifts are now difficult to read. However, some words can still be made out. For example, 'S. Salmon' is thanked for the gift of a ewer and basin; 'L. Harris' (perhaps Harris Levy, one of the founders of the synagogue and an inhabitant of the house), for a 'cover mantle'; 'M. Hollander' for three velvet cushions, 'J. Adler' for carpets, 'M. Cohen' for 'a pair of silver . . .' (alas, we do not know because the word is indecipherable). The name of the first president of the society, 'J. Davidson', can be discerned, too.

The double-height ground-floor synagogue hall that dominates the building, dusty and forlorn though it now is, still retains a sense of the sacred. It is top-lit by a roof lantern, or a pitched glazed roof, and opening side-lights that sit below the ceiling, itself formed of large sheets of colour-tinted glass (Melnick mentions these as having been present in 1870). These sheets were presumably intended to screen the upper portion of the lantern roof, which would otherwise have looked depressingly industrial. The coloured glass, even though long dirty and with some panes cracked, looks becoming. Perhaps it was acquired by the synagogue's first secretary, Abraham Heiser, who operated as a glass merchant.

The cast-iron columns that support the synagogue's galleries are narrow, elegant and ornamental, with spiral shafts. They were probably bought off-the-peg, because similar columns can be found in other contemporary public buildings and music halls,[76] but their spiral form evokes a memory of popular depictions of the columns Jachin and Boaz, which stood at the portal of Solomon's Temple in Jerusalem, and so their selection may well not have been coincidental. The perimeter walls of the synagogue are strengthened by shallow piers that carry trusses supporting the roof structure, strengthened by minimal metal tie-bars from which three metal chandeliers hang.

Many of the original fittings of the synagogue are still to be found in the building, although long ago moved out of context. The Ark, however, which contained the synagogue's Torah scrolls, remains firmly in place, crowned with a pair of painted tablets that bear the Ten Commandments written in Hebrew. Melnick describes how the ceiling above the Ark was 'painted azure with gold stars', evidently to conjure celestial associations. Daylight came from the roof lantern, tinted by passing through the ceiling of coloured glass, but artificial light was provided by gas lamps and two 'sun burners'. These were circles of gas lamps used in public buildings to light and, by generating an updraught, to help ventilate a large interior.[77]

Stacked away now, but once taking pride of place in the centre of the synagogue, was the reading desk (or bimah), with pews placed sideways on either side, and those behind the bimah facing forwards. Many of the pews appear home-made and are rough-and-ready affairs, serving as reminders of the humble and intensely personal atmosphere of this small synagogue where people from widely diverse places came together in a strange land. Other pews look like salvage from Christian chapels. The former location of these various fittings is hinted at by traces and shadows on the floor. A section of patterned linoleum that has been pounded into the floorboards by generations of worshippers carrying the Torah scrolls between the Ark and the bimah marks the location of the short aisle between the benches facing sideways.

On the ground and first floors, there are glazed partitions between the old house and the later synagogue that can be folded back. On the ground floor the partitions open into the rear room, so that it could serve as seating space on busy occasions, and into the front room that once perhaps served as the Ogiers' dining room. In 1870 it was stripped of its panelling to form what Melnick describes as the 'vestry/school room'.[78] Small folding benches are still fixed to the walls for the use of the local children attending Sabbath school. The first-floor rear room of the original house, still with its 1718 panelling but open at its east end, served the synagogue as an extension to the ladies' gallery and also perhaps as a retiring room for both women and men. Although the segregation of the sexes for worship was standard in Orthodox synagogues, men and women could gather after services.

On the front of the gallery, faded painted inscriptions testify to the support the synagogue once received from eminent Jewish families and, quietly, record its demise. 'N. M. Rothschild & Co.' gave £50 in around 1892; the MP Samuel Montagu donated £31 10s 6d, F. D. Mocatta £10, and Leopold de Rothschild, who in 1874 had become head of the London branch of the family's banking business and was treasurer of the London Board of Jewish Deputies, gave £5. Among the later inscriptions is one from April 1953, which records £7 given by the children of 'the late Fanny Rinkoff', who must surely have been a member of the family that from 1911 owned famed bakeries around Spitalfields and Whitechapel (two small branches survive today in Valance Road and Jubilee Street). The last dated donation still legible is on behalf of a Mrs R. Cousins, who died on 21 September 1956.

As you make your way up the house, from the world of the nineteenth-century synagogue into the eighteenth-century home of the Ogiers, the bruises incurred through the years of multiple occupation, mixed use and neglect multiply. Floorboards, many of which seem to be of considerable age, are worn and patched, and the painted and wallpapered surfaces of walls are flaked and peeling. There are constant reminders of later adaptations. One of the two doors that leads from the first-floor landing to the front room is a nineteenth-century addition, behind which a lavatory was installed for the convenience of the tenants occupying the upper floors.[79] On the left-hand doorpost of the original door is a 'mezuzah' – a small box inside which is a scroll containing two prayers from the Book of Deuteronomy – which would have been touched by the Jewish people who lived in the house long after the Ogiers' time, and by their visitors, as a token of prayer and as a reminder that the home and family are sacred. Mezuzahs are found fixed to the front door of every Jewish household, and in devout households on most internal doors, too. Theoretically, they should be fixed to the doorpost that is on your right-hand side as you enter the room. Here, for some reason, the mezuzah is fixed to the inner rather than the outer face of the post.[80]

Yet even here much of the fabric of the early eighteenth-century house survives. With the inserted lavatory removed, the first-floor front room must look much as it did when occupied by the Ogier family. The panelling is intact; the carved timber, rococo fire surround that was presumably added by Peter Abraham Ogier towards the end of his life merely awaits reinstalment. Next door, there is a handsome mid nineteenth-century cast-iron grate, but there is also early eighteenth-century panelling furnished with a moulded dado rail and topped with a Doric-style timber-made box cornice decorating the three walls that survived when the house was merged with the synagogue gallery in 1870.

The second floor, although quite seriously damaged, is essentially intact and retains an authentic pair of early interiors that reveal much about merchant life in Spitalfields in the opening years of the eighteenth century. The front room resembles a late seventeenth-century cottage in its simplicity and lack of detail. The timber partition that divides it from the staircase and from the rear room takes the form of wide vertical planks framed into slightly narrower timber stiles, or muntins – a robust rather than elegant approach, arrived at in part because this system could be load-bearing and so form part of the building's structural system. The partition is pierced by three doors, two of which connect it to the staircase landing, while the third is for the cupboard/passage, mentioned earlier, that connects back and front rooms. The two doors between front room and landing are original, with one serving the close-stool closet located on the landing.

The door in the rear room to the cupboard/passage is, in its way, an unconscious work of art. Its inner face remains plastered with layers of wallpaper, each, as in the garret above, telling its own small story about the changing fortunes of the house and of those that occupied these rooms. This archaeological evidence is fragile in the extreme. One good spring-clean and it would be gone. The cupboard itself still bears the evidence of the various usages to which it was first put. Set against the party wall are remains of simple panelling that suggest its use once as a closet housing a close-stool. Later ad hoc shelves make it clear that, when the house was multi-occupied and space in short supply, the cupboard was used for storage. Early wallpapers on the door look mid to late nineteenth century, while a top layer – featuring a jaunty abstract, cubist mosaic – could date from anywhere between the late 1930s and 1950s.

Additional evidence of the later life of the house at second-floor level are the fixings and damage caused by a sink that was fitted on the landing, at the junction of closet and party wall, with a drainage pipe cut through the riser of one of the steps. There might have been sinks on each landing, supplied with cold-water taps, to serve families residing in adjoining rooms. Perhaps most poignant of all is a mid to late nineteenth-century range that contains an open grate flanked by a small oven, set into the original fireplace in the front room. On this range one of the families that occupied the house in 1891 would have cooked their food and boiled their water – probably Harris Levy, his wife and cousin, who likely occupied these two rooms. Once, long before, this room had almost certainly been the house's best bed-chamber. If these room were the Levy family's home, then Leah Lichenstein and her five sons, as mentioned previously, must have occupied the floor above.

The staircase that leads up to David Rodinsky's former home, its treads and landing floor, are worn and grimy through decades of heavy use and minimal maintenance, while the panelled partition, painted a weathered ethereal green and patched in an ad hoc manner, is much as it was when Rodinsky left the house for the last time. The door to the rear room is a very early two-panel affair, still with one early eighteenth-century wrought-iron and hand-forged strap hinge. There is a pair of small round 'porthole' windows cut into the top of the upper panels – to improve ventilation, possibly – but, if so, also rather strangely allowing either those in the room to keep an eye on those outside the room or those coming up the stairs to glance inside. The paint evidence makes it clear that they were once sealed, long ago, by panels fixed internally. On the left doorpost, seen from within the room, is evidence of a now-removed mezuzah.

The partition doors dividing this rear garret room from the front room appear to have been assembled from a collection of early joinery, including a pair of double doors. It's possible they once opened to unite both rooms, so creating a larger, practical space for the weaving garret or workshop that may have been constructed here in the late eighteenth century. The walls in the rear room retain the fragments of wallpaper already mentioned, some laid over boards that partly block what was, perhaps, a wide workshop window.

As for the front garret room, perhaps added in the late eighteenth century and which appears to have served as David Rodinsky's living quarters, this has been made watertight in recent years and its wide weavers' window heavily repaired, but otherwise remains much as it was when I first saw it in 1980. One somewhat curated photograph taken back then shows Rodinsky's table in the foreground loaded with items – open books and notebooks, a newspaper titled *Israel Reborn*, a beer bottle and a print of a painting by the mid nineteenth-century French realist painter Gustave Courbet, who operated as a political radical during the 1871 Paris Commune. A larger print of the same painting is placed upon the shrouded shelf above the fireplace. It appears to have been a Rodinsky favourite.

Today the movable items recorded in the photograph have been packed and stored, but the overall view remains largely unchanged. The fireplace is still there, with its sinuous shelf, even if the rotting and peeling paper or fabric covering the overmantel has gone, revealing in the process an ad hoc cladding of horizontal boards and wide stiles, suggesting the chimney breast was cobbled together when the garret was added. The fixed cupboard survives, with its two-panel door, pegged joints and strap hinges suggesting an early eighteenth-century origin. The party wall is plastered and painted with pale-coloured distemper or limewash, while the ceiling, like that of the adjoining room, is boarded.

Against the room's east wall is a partitioned corridor that once formed an escape route in case of fire. This was probably constructed in 1870 and is a not uncommon feature of Spitalfields houses that became multi-occupied during the late nineteenth or early twenti-eth centuries. It leads to a narrow door that opens on to the parapet gutter, leaving would-be escapees with no choice but to scramble over the parapets to neighbouring houses. At the facing end of the corridor is a small cupboard closed with a door, which projects over

The top-floor room at the front of number 19. The 'weavers' window', with its mullions and casement, is a scholarly re-creation from the late 1980s, based largely on surviving fragments and archaeological evidence. Until 1969 the room was occupied by the enigmatic scholar David Rodinsky.

the head of the staircase. At one time this cupboard, in fact a small cell-like room, perhaps contained a window that, probably many years ago, was then closed with boards and lath and plaster. Wallpaper survives on some of the surfaces. What this cell was used for is uncertain. Perhaps it was simply for storage or served as a bedroom for a child in a crowded house. Or it could have been the synagogue's Genizah – its hidden room for the preservation of decayed sacred texts.

Fixed to the door frame adjoining the escape corridor and in part framing the door to the front room, is a mezuzah, presumably belonging to the Rodinsky family. Engraved on its cover is an image of a palm tree and Rachel's Tomb in Bethlehem. The tomb of the matriarch is revered by Jews, Muslims and Christians and in the 1840s was repaired by Sir Moses Haim Montefiore – banker, philanthropist and one-time Sheriff of the City of London. If this choice of imagery of Rachel's Tomb was David Rodinsky's then it suggests an interest in the theological beliefs linking, rather than dividing, the three religions of the book. It also perhaps confirms a scholastic curiosity, and a consequent tolerance, implied by his notebooks. These make it clear, for example, that he had a wide interest in distant and ancient languages, including those of ancient Assyria – Akkadian and Aramaic – the latter being the language of Christ.

When the Spitalfields Trust started repairing and cleaning the building in the early 1980s, objects of interest, missed in the first wave of collecting and cataloguing, would turn up, often most unexpectedly, under floorboards, behind furniture, beneath debris or stuffed into cracks or crevices. One item is particularly evocative: a handsome leather-bound book printed in Hebrew that shows evidence of much hard and regular usage. The title page bears the date 1864 and proclaims, in ornamental Hebrew letters printed in red and black ink, that the book is a volume of prayers and commentaries – a machzor – related to Rosh Hashanah (the Jewish New Year, which includes a ten-day period of 'awe' and penitence that culminates with Yom Kippur). Rosh Hashanah is the holiest day in Judaism, a time for reflection, confession and atonement, and terminates with a blast of the shofar, an instrument usually made from a ram's horn, which – symbolically, at least – clears the air.

The place of origin of the book of prayers confirms where part, at least, of the synagogue's early congregation came from. It was printed in Vilnius, in what is now Lithuania, and in the 1860s was part of the Tsarist Russian Empire. By the late nineteenth century, Vilnius was the centre of a large and active Jewish community and was regarded as the spiritual and cultural heart of eastern European Jewry.[81] There were over a hundred synagogues and prayer houses in the city, which boasted six daily Jewish newspapers, most in Yiddish. In the late nineteenth century, Vilnius was also the centre of the Jewish Labour Movement, led by the Bund, or socialist party, that, among its many tasks, was to secure civil and political rights for Jews within the Tsarist Empire, and to improve housing conditions. But, as the Russian pogroms intensified, many Lithuanian Jews chose to migrate in an attempt to escape persecution and to find freedom and opportunity in foreign lands. The squalor and poverty they encountered in 1880s Spitalfields was no doubt a bitter blow, but ultimately the community did integrate and thrive, even if it took several generations to do so. It is salutary and important not to forget the fate of the Jewish population that did not flee. After 1941 an estimated 90 per cent of the Jewish population of Lithuania was murdered by the Nazis and their collaborators. Today the Jewish population of Vilnius is no more than 5,000, and just one synagogue in the city still fulfils its original function.

That surviving leather-bound book in 19 Princelet Street helps bear testimony to the fact that in the late nineteenth century some of Vilnius's Jewish population found their way to Spitalfields. It adds to the inescapable sense of almost overwhelming pathos that the house possesses. Yet such fragile items as this also give the dead a tangible presence. At the very least, 19 Princelet Street is a shrine to long-lost people who deserve not to be forgotten. It's a monument to waves of immigrants, from the late seventeenth century and into the mid twentieth century – including in the 1960s Bengali Muslims from East Pakistan – that passed through the portal of Spitalfields in their quest for better and safer lives for themselves and their families. Most arrived in desperate circumstances and most did find refuge and, in the fullness of time, prospered and moved on.

This is the story the building tells through its rooms and its surviving artefacts. Most are gnarled in appearance and require little in the way of supporting material or 'characters' to tell the tale. Some rooms could be gently recreated, as, for example, the first-floor front room where the rococo fire surround must be put back to evoke more accurately the domestic world of Peter Abraham Ogier and the Huguenots. The fittings of the synagogue should be taken out of store and reinstated. But, in simple terms, the building is the story, telling the tales of the lives of generations of diverse but ordinary people who, eventually and collectively, made London a great world city. All it requires is the opportunity to speak.[82]

Maister House in Kingston-upon-Hull, viewed from the High Street. A grand merchant home of extraordinary architectural ambition, its proportional power, in part due to strict symmetry, and its majestic presence, are immediately apparent.

– 3 –

A House Built by Connoisseurs
Maister House, Hull
(1743–*c*.1760)

AS 19 PRINCELET STREET demonstrates, it was usual in the early eighteenth century to design and build homes without the direct involvement of an architect, or 'surveyor'. Houses were usually not only executed by building tradesmen and crafts- men but designed by them as well. Even the architecturally exqui- site Pallant House – perhaps based on a London 'Modell' supplied by an architect – supplanted a design made by a mason who subse- quently undertook the construction of the design that was selected. The client might well be involved, as was clearly the case with Pallant House, but invariably much design and detailed planning, as well as construction, was undertaken by the team of building tradesmen. In the case of Pallant House, this team seems to have been led by the mason Henry Smart; in the instance of 19 Princelet Street, the car- penter and building entrepreneur Samuel Worrall appears to have been in charge. Only the very wealthiest in society would have con- templated engaging an architect, and even then much of the detailed work would have been conceived and carried out by the masons, car- penters and plasterers on site.

Maister House in the High Street of Kingston-upon-Hull, however, represents a significantly different approach. Here, we have a grand merchant home, dating from the 1740s and of extraordinary architectural ambition, that displays the hand of at least one, perhaps two, leading British architects of the age. While the precise extent of

their involvement in the design of Maister House cannot be established with certainty, it is evident that this building is a product of the
most refined and sophisticated architectural thinking.

At the time the house was built, Kingston-upon-Hull, in the East
Riding of Yorkshire, was one of the country's major trading ports
and a town of considerable magnificence. Established by Edward
I in 1299 by royal charter because of the existing port's importance
in the local wool trade, its high status was confirmed by the Hull
Minster, which was begun in 1300 and which remains the largest
parish church, measured by floor area, in the country.[1] The Minster is
a dominant feature in Wenceslaus Hollar's superb copperplate bird's-
eye map of the port, engraved in about 1642, which also shows the
serpentine High Street packed with the bristling gables of tall buildings and the adjoining quays or wharfs along the banks of the River
Hull. The long, narrow and winding High Street itself, which closely
follows the course of the River Hull and the 'Old Harbour' only a few
metres to its east, became the location of individual buildings, and
sequences of buildings, of outstanding architectural interest, some
of which survived wartime bombing and unsympathetic post-war
redevelopment.

One or two of those that still stand are mid seventeenth century,
including Wilberforce House, which boasts such flamboyant Jacobean
details as lozenge-embellished stone blocks embedded in brick-
built rusticated pilasters – a constructional and decorative technique
employed since the Roman period to express solidity by emphasising
the joints between masonry blocks – as well as a sensational rococo
staircase hall that dates from around 1760.[2] Most of the best surviving High Street buildings are Georgian. Blaydes House is a superb
example of a mid eighteenth-century merchant's house in which the
grand and the practical dwell side by side. Probably started in around
1740 for, and occupied by, the Blaydes family, leading merchants and
shipbuilders who had an abiding interest in local politics, it still
bears the monogram in the ceiling of its entrance hall of Alderman
Benjamin Blaydes, who in 1738 served as Hull's civic chamberlain
and in 1768 as its sheriff. The front, domestic portion of the house,

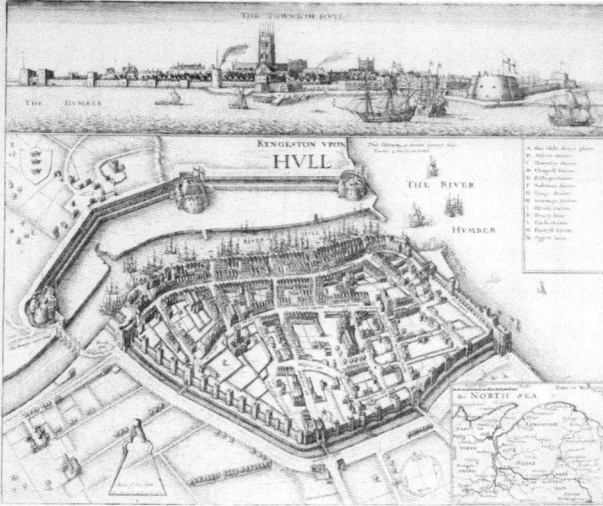

Above: copper plate of a bird's-eye view of Hull executed by Wenceslaus
Hollar in about 1642. The gently serpentine High Street, with its closely
packed bristling gables, runs north (left) to south roughly parallel to
the River Hull with its wharfs and staiths. Below: Blaydes House,
on the High Street, is a merchant's house dating from perhaps 1740;
its front was remodelled in around 1760.

entered from the High Street, is distinguished by the use of stone corner quoins to embellish the ground floor. The rear portion of the house – lower in height, extending towards the river and perhaps originally entered by a side door from Blaides Staithe – was in trade use, probably serving as a counting house. (In the north and east of England, 'staithe' is the name given to a landing place or quay on a riverbank.) The family's shipbuilding yards and warehouse lay further towards the river, also facing on to Blaides Staithe. These have now gone, but the surviving riverside warehouses constructed by Joseph Pease in the mid eighteenth century are a sublime reminder that it was Hull's success as a port that led to its merchants and their building tradesmen becoming pioneers in the design of bold, industrial architecture.[3] Such a juxtaposition of grand living with water-borne trade is also to be found at King's Lynn in Norfolk, which, like Hull, was a member of the Hanseatic League, a trade confederation that, since the thirteenth century, had linked numerous ports and cities in northern Europe and had done much to forge close commercial and cultural connections between distant and superficially disparate locations.

And then, at 160 High Street, there is Maister House, built between approximately 1743 and 1760, and externally and internally one of the finest terrace houses in England.

*****

The man who built and owned Maister House, Henry Maister, was an important figure in eighteenth-century Hull: both a leading merchant and a politician of local and national significance. He was Sheriff of Hull in 1729, and Member of Parliament for Hull between 1734 and 1741, when, as a Whig by conviction, he voted regularly in support of Sir Robert Walpole's government.

Eighteenth-century Hull merchants were not directly involved in the slave trade. England's slaving ports (with the exception of London) were located on the west coast, where there was easier access to the Atlantic and thus to Africa, the Caribbean and the Americas (see page 126). Rather, these merchants developed and sustained maritime connections with Hanseatic and Baltic ports in north Europe, and with inland cities reached readily by rivers such as the Elbe. A daybook in the Maister family archives[4] shows that Henry and his younger brother Nathaniel imported and exported a number of goods, including wine and seed (Hull developed a large seed-crushing industry), and that their most important import was iron from Stockholm (including cannonballs, which were melted down); this they then sold on to Hull manufacturers.[5] A typical cargo was worth between £1,000 and £2,000 and was insured through companies in London or Amsterdam. It's clear that the Maisters also did business with some of the wealthiest local landed families, including members of the East Riding aristocracy, the Hothams and the Sykes, and that they bought into government stocks. Over time they added to the family property they already possessed through the purchase of Patrington Manor in 1739 and Winestead Old Hall, in the East Riding. [6]

Henry Maister was a highly successful man, but he was also one whose life was stalked by misfortune. His first wife, Mary Tymperon, died of smallpox in May 1725, less than twelve months after their wedding. Three years later he married Mary Cayley, daughter of Arthur Cayley, the 3rd Baronet of Brompton, and the couple went on to have nine children, seven of whom were boys. But then tragedy struck again. In April 1743, fire broke out in the predecessor to 160 High Street. Henry managed to escape, as did Mary, but when she realised her infant son was still in the house she went back to get him. Mother and son, along with two maidservants, all perished.[7]

Maister must have been devastated by his wife's death and he would surely have felt guilt over the circumstances in which she met her end. Perhaps he agreed she should return to the burning house; certainly he failed to prevent her or to go in her stead. His response, though, was not self-pity or all-consuming remorse but – as befitted an eighteenth-century Hull merchant whose family had, for generations, risked all on the vagaries of perilous maritime trade – was to be constructive. Almost immediately he started work on a bigger, better and far more fireproof building. It was almost as if, in responding to the tragedy by creating something beautiful, enduring and exemplary, he believed that his wife, son and loyal servants had not died in vain. And to achieve beauty – and to ensure that his house was of more than just provincial significance – Maister turned for assistance, at some point in 1743 or in early 1744, to Richard Boyle, the 3rd Earl of Burlington, the nation's then-premier arbiter of architectural taste and also a local landowner with strong links to Hull's merchant community.[8]

Since the early years of the century, Burlington had made it his goal to promote the north Italian, mid sixteenth-century architecture of Andrea Palladio and, as far as possible, establish it as the British national style and the tangible cultural expression of Whig political convictions and power. Palladio's architecture – rational, bold, dependent on a mathematically coherent and harmonically unified system of proportion steeped in the ethos of classical antiquity – was perceived by its adherents to be in stark contrast to the wilful, subjective baroque school of classicism. So, while baroque had been favoured and promoted by the culturally influential but autocratic Roman Catholic France of Louis XIV, the English Whigs embraced its artistic opposite – Palladian design – to represent Protestant, parliamentary or constitutional monarchy, as expressed since 1714 by the Hanoverians.

The embrace of Palladio by the Protestant English elite gave precise architectural expression to theories floated in 1712 by the Whig 3rd Earl of Shaftesbury in a 'Letter Concerning the Art, or Science of Design' that was published in timely manner in 1714 to coincide with the ascent to the throne of a new Whig-supported Hanoverian royal dynasty. In the letter, Shaftesbury asserted that 'our genius, I am persuaded, will carry us ... to that higher, more serious and noble part of imitation, which relates to history, human nature, and the chief degree or order of beauty.' So imitation of ancient architectural models was fine – the question was: which models to imitate? Shaftesbury provided some guidance. The beauty he referred to is that found in nature and that reflects 'the *rational* life'. This alone, he argued, could form the correct basis for the formation of '*a National taste*'. The rational approach Shaftesbury promoted tallied, of course, with the new Palladian desire for an architecture based on apparently immutable 'natural' and logical laws such as those governing geometry, building construction and music.[9]

Lord Burlington, aged twenty, had made a grand tour to Italy in the year Shaftesbury's plea was published – 1714 – but, although he passed through the Veneto region, Palladio's architecture does not seem to have attracted his particular interest. Things, however, were changing rapidly and dramatically. From 1715 to 1720, Giacomo Leoni published the first English-language edition of Palladio's highly influential *I quattro libri dell'architettura* of 1570, and, also in 1715, Colen Campbell published the first volume of his seminal *Vitruvius Britannicus*. This publication popularised designs inspired by Palladio, while attacking baroque architects because they attempted 'to debauch mankind' with their 'odd and chimerical Beauties'. *Vitruvius Britannicus* also nominated Inigo Jones, who a hundred years earlier had pioneered Palladian architecture in England, as the 'great master' who 'had outdone all that went before' and who had proved that 'in most we equal, and in some Things surpass, our neighbours'. Campbell's flight of patriotic fancy was not, apparently, in any way disturbed by the fact that Jones had been court architect to autocratic Stuart monarchs whose central belief in rule by divine right had been such a significant cause of the civil war that broke out in 1642. As well as promoting Palladio, 'whose ingenious Labours' had rivalled 'most of the Ancients', Campbell presented a selection of contemporary Palladio-inspired architecture, including those of his own design, notably for Wanstead House in Essex, which he had designed in 1713, and on which construction started in 1715.

The publications of these two works seem to have awakened Burlington's architectural sensibilities, while the association between Whig patriotism and Palladian design perhaps chimed with his political allegiances. These appear to have been confirmed in 1715 when George I and the Whig government of Lord Townsend, Lord Stanhope and Lord Sunderland (the position of prime minister was not created until 1721) appointed Burlington Lord Treasurer of Ireland

and Lord Lieutenant of the East and West Ridings of Yorkshire. In addition, in 1729 George II appointed him to the Privy Council and the following year a Knight of the Garter.

Burlington's enthusiasm had been made clear in 1719 when he returned to Italy in August to indulge his still-nascent passion for Palladio and to study his architecture first hand, in Vicenza and Venice. During this visit Burlington made a point of finding and purchasing drawings by Palladio, some recording designs that had not been included in *I quattro libri*, including, in particular, Palladio's drawings of Roman baths.

A possible twist to this tale is that Burlington, while accepting Whig and Hanoverian honours and apparently using art and architecture to promote the cause of both, may have been a secret supporter of James Francis Edward Stuart ('the Old Pretender'), the son of the last of the Stuart kings, James II, who had been ousted in 1688 and died in exile in 1701. In other words, that Burlington was a Jacobite. Admittedly, there is only circumstantial evidence to support this speculation. Given that Inigo Jones's Palladio-inspired architecture became in the early seventeenth century the 'house style' of the Stuart court, it is reasonable to wonder if, at a time when architecture was charged with a political message, Burlington's Palladio obsession was an expression of Stuart sympathies. Times were complicated and nothing is proven, but this possible intrigue adds another dimension to the Palladian revival, suggesting it could, on occasion, be a secret act of homage to the Stuart cause and to the 'king across the water'. In which case were Burlington's trips to Italy to see Renaissance and antique architecture in fact, in part at least, a cover for meeting the Stuart court in exile, based in Rome?

Whatever the motives might have been for his passion for Palladio, things started to move fast just before Burlington's second pilgrimage to north Italy. He began to use his position and fortune to become a leading architectural patron and connoisseur, with the clear aim, as the architectural historian Howard Colvin puts it, of returning 'Palladian architecture to the position it had held in England in the time of Inigo Jones'.[10] To achieve this, Burlington developed his professional relationship with Colen Campbell and, when possible, helped to secure him commissions within the Whig aristocracy and government. Burlington himself had employed Campbell in 1718 to complete Burlington House, on Piccadilly, as a Palladio show-piece. He also engaged Campbell as a collaborator in the design of a number of palatial terrace houses on the Burlington estate to the north of Piccadilly. These houses, built between 1718 and 1724, were intended to demonstrate the application of Palladian principles to urban domestic architecture. Notable was a four-house group in Old Burlington Street; only two – numbers 31 and 32 – survive, but they confirm the influential nature of Campbell and Burlington's collab-oration. The houses have simple brick facades that, like the plans of the houses and of the rooms within, are a worked example of Pallad-io's theories about harmonically related proportions. In his *I quattro libri* he published his seven ideal proportions for rooms, and these are, broadly, permutations of the square or cube, which are extended rationally to create, for example, the 2:3 proportion (square and a half) and 2:1 proportion (double square). Consequently, the facades of these Old Burlington Street houses are a homage to the square and its ratios, and these define window proportion and spacing and the areas of wall between windows. As such, they are clearly harbin-gers of architecture to come, foreshadowing such designs as that of Maister House.

It is important to understand that for Palladio and his disciples, such as Burlington, this system of related proportions was not just a way of achieving pleasing integrated designs in which plans, ele-vations and details possessed a harmonic relationship. It was also a means by which to arrive at a system of mathematical relationships that were perceived as being rooted in nature and so divine in origin. This is partly why Palladianism was embraced by Protestant Whigs. They saw it not only as rational but also as God-given. Fundamental to this theory was the conviction that certain systems of proportion – applied in architecture, art and music – not only reflected immutable laws of beauty but possessed an innate harmony that was expressed through number. The authority for this was no less a book than the

Bible, and in particular the passage in the Wisdom of Solomon in the Septuagint where God is venerated because 'thou hast ordered all things in measure and number and weight'[11] and which underpinned much sixteenth-century architectural theory. Daniele Barbaro, the Venetian commentator, architect and client of Palladio, echoed it when, in reflecting on the written works of the Roman first-century architect Vitruvius, he declared it as self-evident that 'proportion is general and universal in all things given to measure, weight and number'.[12] It was a position that echoed writings from the ancient world, notably by Plato, who, referring to the sixth-century BC philosopher Pythagoras, explained in his *Timaeus* dialogue, which explored the creation of the universe, that cosmic order and harmony are contained in certain numbers. The Italian architect Leon Battista Alberti, in his *De re aedificatoria*, written from 1443 and published in 1485, 'affirmed' that Pythagoras was correct 'that Nature is wholly consistent' and confirmed the connection between music and the visual arts: 'the very same numbers that cause sounds to have *concinnitas*, pleasing to the ears,' he wrote, 'can also fill the eyes and mind with wondrous delight.'[13] *Concinnitas* is to compose a work of art – building, music or painting – in parts that are distinct from one another but that, through the application of 'definite number, outline, and position', achieve beauty. Or, as Alberti put it, '*Concinnitas* [is] the absolute and fundamental rule of Nature ... and the source of her dignity, charm, authority and worth.'[14]

Palladio was not as direct as Alberti in pressing the analogy between musical harmony and visual proportion, but he did write, when giving his opinion on a model of the cathedral proposed for Brescia in 1567, that 'just as the proportions of voices are harmony to the ears, so those of measurement are harmony to the eyes' but 'without it being known why'.[15] For Alberti's compatriot and near contemporary Leonardo da Vinci, music was the sister of painting: music conveys harmony by its chords, painting by its proportions, all derived from the same numerical ratios. Perspective in painting, developed in the early fifteenth century by the Florentine architect Filippo Brunelleschi, in part achieved by geometrically defined foreshortening and vanishing points, was the consequence of 'harmonic' progression. For his part, Giovanni Paolo Lomazzo in his *Idea del tempio della pittura* of 1590 expressed the Renaissance conviction that all elements of creation were connected by number and proportion: 'the human body itself is built according to musical harmonies. This microcosm created by the Lord in his own image contains all numbers, measures, weights, motions and elements. Therefore all the buildings in the world together with all their parts follow its norm.'

Lord Burlington had, by the early 1740s, long abandoned any overt political ambitions he might have entertained, having resigned all his government appointments in 1733. Instead, he devoted his wealth and position to the promotion of architecture and music, the works of George Frideric Handel (who from 1712 to 1714 had been his house guest in London) becoming a particular passion of his. In the process, Burlington amassed a large chorus of acolytes – including painters, building tradesmen and architects such as William Kent and Henry Flitcroft – and polemicists for the Palladian cause such as Robert Morris, kinsman of Roger Morris (see page 6). Robert Morris, who worked with Burlington on the design of the now-demolished Kirby Hall, North Yorkshire (1747–55),[16] had become well known following the publication of his *Essay in Defence of Ancient Architecture* (1728), in which he nailed his colours to the mast by referring to a contemporary baroque design as a 'Lump of Deformity, which has neither Judgement, Order, nor Beauty' because it was not 'founded upon natural Reason'.[17] He developed his theories in his *Lectures on Architecture*, published in 1734, in which he asserts that just as 'Nature had taught Mankind in Musick certain Rules for Proportion of Sounds', so 'Architecture has its Rules dependent on those Proportions, or at least such Proportions as are Arithmetical harmony; and those I take to be dependent on Nature.'

Foremost among Morris's rules was that 'the Square in Geometry, the Unison or Circle in Musick, and the Cube in Building, have all an inseparable Proportion; the Parts being equal, and the Sides, and Angles etc give the Eye and ear an agreeable Pleasure.' This led him to propose a system of nine strictly proportioned forms through which architectural 'Harmony' could be achieved. The system is clearly derived from Palladio's seven 'ideal' proportions, because the first five of Morris's proportions (starting with the cube and ending with the double cube) follow the Palladio pattern. But the following four 'ratios', as he terms them, are a rational extension of Palladio's double cube, being the closely related ratios of 3:2:1; 4:3:2; 5:4:3 and 6:4:3.[18] Morris's theories, promoted and codified by Burlington's followers, can be interpreted to suggest the artistic, indeed philosophical, principles upon which Maister House was designed.

Precisely when and how Maister and Burlington first encountered one another is unknown. Given their overlapping social circles in merchant Hull, though, it is not surprising that they should have become acquainted or that, as he set about the construction of his new house, Maister would have thought to seek the advice of England's most prominent arbiter of architectural taste. He was scarcely unique in doing so. Around the time that work on Maister House was beginning, Lord Malton, a fellow Yorkshire Whig politician, had for nearly ten years engaged Burlington as consultant and architectural advisor on the design of the east-facing portion of Wentworth Woodhouse, near Sheffield. Wentworth Woodhouse is a stupendous 600-foot-long composition of seven distinct but harmonious parts that are the epitome of the Renaissance theory of *concinnitas*.[19] It is also surely significant that Henry Maister, along with fellow Hull merchant George Crowle, was a 'subscriber' to the fund for building the York Assembly Rooms (completed in 1735), designed by Lord Burlington and based in turn on designs by Palladio and on sketches of Roman bathhouses. By this time, Burlington had been working for a number of years with his protégé William Kent, whom Burlington had first met in Italy in 1719 during his grand tour. He had collaborated with him on the interior of Burlington House in London and the proto-Palladian Chiswick House, completed in 1729. The York Assembly Rooms display, as does Chiswick House, in spectacular antique manner the bold brand of Palladian interior design that Kent had perfected. Maister donated £25 to the project.[20]

A few years later, in 1744, Maister and Crowle would be among the

The east front of Wentworth Woodhouse, South Yorkshire, designed in the early 1730s by Ralph Tunnicliffe. Its design was amended and extended from *c.*1734 under the direction of Lord Burlington and his London-based protégé Henry Flitcroft.

recipients of a gift of venison sent by Burlington from Londesborough, his country seat near Hull, to forty-five Hull residents and merchants for their annual 'Trinity feast'.[21] Burlington's relationship with Crowle seems to have been particularly close. He was a regular guest at Londesborough, and on at least one occasion entertained Burlington at his county retreat at Springhead, just to the west of Hull.[22] Since Crowle was also Maister's fellow MP for Hull, he provides another possible link through which Maister met Burlington.

Burlington's architectural theories and ideals, enshrined in Morris's writings in large part, were by the 1740s starting to become part of the stock-in-trade of Hull's building community and of the affluent architectural patrons of the city and its environs. These men – and, no doubt, women – would also have been informed and inspired by other recent architectural publications packed with theory, advice and plates of relevant and authoritative ornament, notably William Kent's lavish *Designs of Inigo Jones,* published in 1727 in collaboration with Lord Burlington; James Gibbs's *Book of Architecture* published in 1728, and Isaac Ware's 1738 translation of Palladio's *Four Books of Architecture.*[23] That Burlington was happy to advise Lord Malton, or that a few years earlier, in about 1730, was on hand, along with Kent, as Sir William Strickland sought to classicise his sixteenth- and seventeenth-century home, Boynton Hall in the East Riding, no doubt further encouraged Maister to ask Burlington for help.

*****

Surviving letters written in November and December 1744 to Henry Maister by his brother Nathaniel include references not just to the building of the new house in the High Street but to those who worked on it. They included Joseph Page, a bricklayer and plasterer who at the outset of the project was in his early twenties and who after the house was completed in 1745 would lay claim to the title of master builder and architect.[24] Then there was Samuel Spencer, a Hull house carpenter by trade who by 1743 had over thirty years' experience in the building trade.[25] Henry Towns, whose name crops up in in other contemporary Yorkshire building accounts, worked as a glazier on the project,[26] while Robert Bakewell, who had, earlier in life, made the rood screen and entrance gates for All Saints, Derby (now Derby Cathedral), completed in 1725 to the designs of James Gibbs, supplied ironwork for both the main and the back stairs.

Perhaps the most intriguing of the names mentioned in the letters is that of 'Musgrave'. He may possibly have been one or either of the 'housecarpenters' named Thomas and Michael Musgrave known to have been active in early eighteenth-century Hull.[27] But it seems more likely that the man Nathaniel refers to was Henry Musgrave, an illegitimate son of William Constable, 4th Viscount Dunbar of Burton Constable, and a man with indirect family links to Lord Burlington.[28] A letter from Nathaniel to his brother Henry, dated 5 December 1744 but apparently an addition to an earlier letter of 13 November, certainly seems to suggest that at the time that Maister House was being built the role Musgrave had established for himself was rather different from that of a skilled craftsman. 'I am told,' Nathaniel wrote, '[that] Musgrave has agreed with Mr Perrott [a Hull merchant], about building him a house [at 22 High Street]. That S[amuel] Spencer is to build it, and that he intends after Christmas to take off most of the best hands from your house to set them to work in making the sashes & for Mus[grave] . . . I have not seen Sam[uel] since I heard it, to know the truth of this report.'[29] It's tempting to infer from this that at Maister House, Musgrave was operating as some sort of overseer and go-between connecting Henry Maister and Lord Burlington, with Samuel Spencer being the main contractor.

The exact relationship between Lord Burlington, Henry Maister and those involved on a day-to-day basis will probably never be fully known, but it seems likely that the client and his aristocratic advisor drew up a brief, no doubt with some details and proportional systems specified by Burlington, and that the tradesmen gave physical form to the vision. Nor is it clear precisely how involved Lord Burlington was in the design work, although the letter from Nathaniel to Henry dated 7 November 1744 suggests that at the very least Burlington was keeping an eye on the internal decoration of the house as it neared completion. In the letter, Nathaniel informs Henry that 'Musgrave says My Ld. Burlington don't approve of the Cornice you had pitched upon, he says it must be a plain one' and that he has 'promised ... w[he]n he gets to town to send a draught of one that will be suitable'.

That updates on progress should have been passing from Nathaniel to Henry rather than the other way round suggests that Henry was quite frequently absent from Hull, and indeed that was the case. The letter which Nathaniel sent on 7 November 1744 is addressed to 'Mrs Rawlinson's, A Toy Shop, In Bedford Street, Covent Garden, London'. Given both Covent Garden's dubious reputation at the time as London's primary sex quarter, and the fact that children's toy shops are not thought to have existed in London until 1760, when William Hamley opened 'Noah's Ark' in Holborn, it seems not unlikely that the toys available at Mrs Rawlinson's were of a distinctly adult nature: in nearby Half-Moon Street (the south extension of Bedford Street connecting to the Strand) in 1740, in Constantia Phillips's shop, the 'Green Cannister', condoms and dildos of exceptional quality were sold.[30] Whatever the precise truth of the matter, it would seem that Henry, now forty-five and twice a widower, was perhaps intent on enjoying some recreation that would lift his spirits and improve his health, while retaining a keen interest in progress on his new house.[31]

Subsequent letters in November and early December 1744 add a little more information about that progress and, by implication, about the role played by Burlington.[32] On 12 November 1744, Nathaniel told Henry that 'I shall let Page know wt. you say about the Cornish [cornice].' Five days later, on 17 November, Nathaniel wrote again to Henry, to keep him abreast of the High Street project: 'The Inclosed from Mus. Should have gone last Post but he was too late.' The 'Inclosed' was presumably Burlington's suggested design for the cornice. Frustratingly, it has been lost.[33]

A week later, on 24 November, Nathaniel informed his brother that 'I don't see any great progress ye workmen makes at ye h[ouse]. The stone cutters are working the pavings and Page is finishing the gallery. [Henry] Towns has put in all the glazing in ye front windows, but I think has not [served? (word missing from edge of page)] you well. A great many of the Squares being curled ... one cannot see an object distinctly through 'em.' The 'Squares' were the panes of 'crown' glass, a type of glass blown into a sphere, then flattened and spun as it cooled. The consequence of this process was that the panes could contain small air bubbles, concentric circles and be slightly bowed rather than flat. They could also contain a 'bull's eye' where the blowing tube joined the sphere. These slight imperfections could add character, but taken to extremes were clearly frowned upon. Nathaniel also noted that 'Thorpe of Malton called yesterday wth. his note [a list of materials, including nails, and their prices] for the post & rails, a copy of which you have here under', and that he was waiting to hear from 'Bakewell about the iron work for the Back stairs'. This is an important reference because it confirms Robert Bakewell's involvement in the construction of Maister House.

By the end of December 1744 the house was largely complete, with the main exception being probably the decoration of the first-floor front rooms. The building must have created quite a stir among the merchants of Hull. It is certainly a visually arresting conception: refined and simple, its five-window-wide and three-storey-high facade, set back slightly from neighbouring buildings, exudes a massive, solemn and brooding quality.[34] Its beauty comes almost entirely from the high-quality craftsmanship of its brick construction, its erudite stone-made Ionic pedimented door surround and, importantly, from its finely considered and harmoniously related system of proportions. This raises the elevation from being merely a well-wrought brick wall punctuated by openings, to a piece of culturally attuned architecture in which restraint is the prime expression of artistic sophistication.

Palladian principles are everywhere apparent. The brick-built facade, rising above a low-ceilinged basement or cellar, is divided into two horizontal portions – of roughly equal area – by a stone sill course set below the first-floor windows. The area of facade above this sill course, stretching up to the somewhat peculiar stone-wrought frieze and cornice set above the second-floor windows, is roughly a double square in area, thus relating to Palladio and Robert Morris's sets of ideal proportions. Within this portion of the facade the first-floor windows are each double square in area (when the sill is included) and the second-floor windows are each square and so read like the attic windows of Roman and Renaissance architecture.

The brick piers between the windows are equal to the windows' width, and the area between first-floor window heads and second-floor sills is roughly a square and a half, or 3:2 in proportion – again ratios favoured by Palladio and Morris. The extra height is due to the fact that the first-floor rooms were the house's *piano nobile*, or lofty main rooms, of Renaissance tradition, and required, for artistic reasons, generous floor-to-ceiling heights.

The ground-floor portion of the facade – between the soffit, or underside, of the first-floor sill course to ground level – is also strictly regulated to present an area of double-square proportion and is similar in height to the portion above, as far as the soffit of the stone frieze. This means that the sill course marks what is roughly the centre horizontal line of the composition, with the surface area of the entire facade – from flank to flank and from ground level to the top of the cornice – defining a perfect square. This is yet one more example of the Palladian obsession with the square as a proportioning device, uniting all elements of the composition. A good early eighteenth-century example is 31 Old Burlington Street in Mayfair, London, designed in 1718 by Colen Campbell for Lord Burlington's estate, which has a facade that is square in area with first-floor windows double square in proportion.

The square-area elevation of Maister House is also a direct reference to a seminal Burlington project. In 1727 he designed a three-window-wide house, two storeys high over a raised basement, for a site in Round Coppice, Buckinghamshire. This house, now long demolished, had a square ground plan, a square front elevation, a centrally placed front door, double-square and square windows, and a sill course and cornice with a deep frieze. Clearly it embodied much of the detail and proportion to be later deployed at Maister House. Was this Buckinghamshire design the basic model Burlington provided, leaving Henry Maister's tradesmen to adapt to fit the site and brief while respecting its essential qualities?

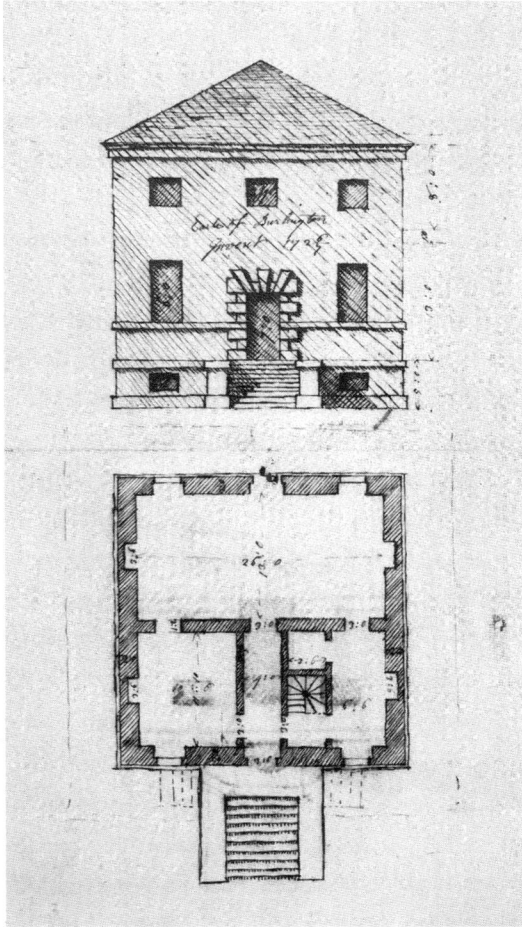

Lord Burlington's design of 1726/7 for Round Coppice, Iver Heath,
Buckinghamshire. The house, commissioned for Lord Bruce,
was demolished in 1954.

At Maister House the ground-floor windows are, like those
on the first floor, of double-square proportion – a slightly unusual
feature for such a hierarchically conceived Palladian composition.
It is more common, in three-storey compositions, for the lower
status of the ground floor to be confirmed by its windows being of
a less elongated proportion than the first-floor windows. Presumably the desire here was that the portion of the facade most visible to
passing citizens should not in any sense appear mean or curtailed
but proclaim, through generous proportion, the magnificence of the
Maister dynasty.

One would normally expect to find cellar or basement windows,
but there are none. This is perhaps a practical recognition of the fact
that the water-table here is high due to the proximity of the river,
making basements along the High Street damp and liable to flooding
and so limited in their utility. But it also gives the lower half of the
facade the appearance of the sort of podium that supports the main
elevation of a Roman temple, with the associations with pedigree,
authority and solemnity that that brings. Treating the ground floor
like a podium is appropriate in its meaning because, within the hierarchy of classical composition, the podium is inferior in its function
to the floor above. This was indeed the case with Maister House,
because it was at ground level that the counting house was located,
with splendid *piano noble* rooms above.

The centrally placed ground-floor front door is embellished
by the stone-made door surround previously noted, comprising
Roman Ionic pilasters that are set over, and slightly to the side of,
vertical slivers of Ionic half-pilasters, and with, at the top, a triangular pediment. The design, mildly baroque in manner due to the
theatrical overlapping of the pilasters, seems to be based on a design
included by James Gibbs (who had trained in Rome as an architect
from 1703 to 1708 and subsequently forged an idiosyncratic fusion
of the baroque and the Palladian) in his highly influential *Book of
Architecture*, published in 1728.[35] The choice of Ionic would appear to
have been carefully considered. In his *Lectures*, Robert Morris notes
that while the Doric order is appropriate for 'grave and solemn uses'

The stone-made Ionic pedimented door surround to Maister House.
It would appear to be based on a published design of 1728 by James Gibbs.

of masculine or martial character, Ionic is for more feminine 'Riant uses'[36] – that is to say, that Ionic displays mirth and pleasure, and expresses a sense of welcome; all appropriate emotions to evoke at the entrance to a house.[37]

Enter through the Ionic door surround and in front of you is a quite narrow entrance passage that leads to the large and generous staircase hall. The house is two rooms deep and two rooms wide, which coalesce to form the square outline plan that is the standard Palladian solution. It was a design solution seen as applicable by Palladians to both free-standing houses and terrace houses with windows only on two sides.[38]

The main staircase hall is the largest volume in the house, and in plan is of Palladio's ideal square-and-a-third proportion. The front rooms on each side of the entrance passage are also of a square and a third in proportion, but slightly smaller in scale. The rear room, adjoining the staircase volume, is almost square in plan and virtually cubic in volume. So in the design of the house's front elevation and ground-floor plan it is possible to see, in the repetition of the square and its permutations, the disposition of harmoniously related proportions in action. The resultant proportions are all those favoured by both Palladio and Morris.

The threshold between the entrance hall and the magnificent staircase hall is marked not on the floor but on the ceiling, where a beam, located at the junction of passage and hall, is embellished with rich plaster-made decoration, no doubt executed by Joseph Page, who was almost certainly responsible for the execution of the house's exceptionally fine plaster decoration. The degree to which he also designed it is uncertain. Nathaniel's letter of 12 November to Henry, in which he undertakes to 'let Page know wt. you say about the Cornish [cornice]' supplied by Burlington, suggests that Page's role in the project was to execute designs by others. As a highly skilled tradesman, however, he was also, no doubt, allowed creative freedom when appropriate. The decoration on this beam is probably an example of Page design. The central motif in the composition is a C-shaped leaf, and all is loosely asymmetric, so this is tentative rococo, a somewhat wilful classical style recently in vogue in the early 1740s, and not quite Burlington's taste.[39] The plaster ceiling below the first-floor landing is, along with the flanking motifs, more firmly Palladian in the William Kent and Burlington manner. The beam at the edge of the ceiling is embellished with a dentil cornice (formed, as the name implies, with small, teeth-like cubes) and large-scale and boldly detailed Greek-key moulding set along its lower face. This is a most striking motif for the mid 1740s, but one favoured by Burlington and Kent and probably derived from Palladio.[40] It could have been the initial design of this visually prominent cornice that Burlington did not 'approve of' and that Nathaniel mentioned in his letter. Perhaps, like the beam with the C-shaped leaf, it was too rococo and asymmetrical for Burlington – and this is the more abstract, geometric, antique and 'plain' solution he sent from town.

If this was the case, then the visual character of the rejected design is further suggested by the existing plasterwork on the ceiling adjoining the entrance passage. Tendril motifs fill the four corners of the oblong ceiling and stretch along its length, blossoming into acanthus forms, to reach a central moulded square, with semicircles bursting from its four sides. Within the square is a sunburst, at the centre of which is the head of a long-haired and beardless youth – Apollo. The attributes of the sun god are many, but why Henry Maister chose his image for this key location, at the start of the procession through the house, must remain a matter of speculation. Apollo embraced the arts but was also a god of crops and a protector: perhaps Henry thought his inclusion on the ceiling appropriate for the house of a merchant in seeds and corn. He may also have considered that while Apollo was a god of life he was also, as are all gods that preside over the cycles of creation, a god of death, and that a motif that suggested both life and death was fitting for a house that arose from despair but was created with joy and beauty in mind.

The staircase that arises beyond Apollo's head is one of exquisite geometric form and beauty, bathed in light. It rises against the walls of the stairwell in three flights that allow it to turn back on itself to reach a wide first-floor landing that is paved with large lozenge-shaped slabs of stone. The ground floor of the staircase hall is also stone-paved, reinforcing the idea that the entrance passage and hall are semi-outdoor spaces. Each tread is a slab of stone, with its underside fully exposed to create – as the stairs rise – a sculptural, stepped composition. Usually in such eighteenth-century stone-built staircases the lower corner of each tread is furnished with a rebate to help it lock into the tread below to prevent turning or movement. But here each tread is a simple slab topped with a torus moulding of semicircular profile that simply supports the tread above. It is much like the staircases illustrated by Palladio in his *I quattro libri* of 1570.[41]

The stairs are furnished with a delicately made wrought-iron balustrade of complex design, incorporating tall, lyre-profile panels on each tread, linked by arched, bow-like flourishes of wrought-iron tendrils. This balustrade, as Nathaniel Maister's correspondence makes clear, was the work of Derby-based Robert Bakewell, and since Apollo's attributes were a bow to symbolise terror and death, and a lyre to represent joy through music, dance and poetry, it's tempting to think that a reference is being made to him here, too. Of course, the various design elements on show may well have been staple ones for Bakewell (he did, after all, make very similar balusters in 1748 for Okeover Hall, East Staffordshire), though, given the order in which the two houses were built, it's always possible that Maister House's Apollo theme pointed the way for him.[42]

Who could have designed this staircase – a faultless piece of work as clever and functional as it is beautiful in its forms? Much of its beauty comes from its erudite display of large-scale Palladian detail and its theatricality. This stems in part from the visual drama offered by the play of moving daylight, in this case supplied by generous top-lighting achieved by means of a tall octagon fitted with large windows.

Here we enter the realm of speculation, but it's tempting to see in this masterly work the hand of Burlington's protégé William Kent. Between 1740 and 1744 he was working on the design of two London houses, each with a staircase that can be compared with that being built at roughly the same time in Maister House. One

Detail of the staircase hall in Maister House, showing the underside of the gallery serving the second-floor rooms and the cove and lantern set above the hall.

was 44 Berkeley Square, which still survives. The other, very slightly earlier, is 22 Arlington Street, off Piccadilly.[43] Built for a future prime minister, Henry Pelham, it also survives, although greatly altered, extended and restored. Both houses have three-storey and three-window-wide brick-built front facades of very similar design to each other – notably with square second-floor windows, balustrades below first-floor windows, and corner quoins at ground-floor level.

Kent located the staircase at 22 Arlington Street in the centre of the deep-plan terrace house, and to get some daylight into its heart he top-lit the staircase by means of a 'circular skielight', rather in the manner of a Roman atrium. The stairs were organised to rise in three flights separated by landings, around three sides of a square-plan well to reach a broad first-floor landing.[44] The slightly later staircase at 44 Berkeley Square is an astonishing bravura act that, simultaneously, assumes a massive Palladian presence while also possessing a baroque theatricality calculated to surprise, even baffle, visitors, causing the politician, writer and antiquarian Horace Walpole to say in the 1780s that it 'is as beautiful a piece of scenery and . . . art as can be imagined'.[45] It rises from ground level as a flight of free-standing stone steps, through the central opening in a somewhat simplified Roman-style triumphal arch. This first straight flight leads to a half-landing, where the staircase turns back on itself to rise as two flights to reach the first-floor landing. The first-floor landing is wide and deep with, at the end opposite the stairs a semi-elliptical colonnade formed by four tall free-standing Ionic columns supporting a full entablature and flanked by pedimented door surrounds. This is Renaissance architecture of the type one might find in a piazza or church in Rome or Venice (indeed there is something similar framing the altar in Palladio's Il Redentore on the Giudecca) but surprising to confront, secreted, in an upper level of a London terrace house little more than thirty feet wide.[46] Beyond the colonnade, a gently curving elliptical staircase rises to second-floor level, where a gallery serves the upper rooms. The visual integration of the secondary staircase so creatively into the main scheme is a tremendous artistic and compositional improvement of the approach followed at 22 Arlington Street and Maister House, where in both houses the secondary staircase is isolated, out of sight, in its own compartment.[47]

The client for the extraordinary creation at 44 Berkeley Square was a significant figure within the Lord Burlington–William Kent circle. Lady Isabella Finch (Lady Bell), the daughter of the Earl of Nottingham – who had set her a stimulating architectural precedent by designing, from 1694 and with great panache, the family home of Burley-on-the-Hill in Rutland – was also the sister-in-law of Lord Malton (the future Marquess of Rockingham), who during the 1730s and 1740s transformed, with Burlington's advice, Wentworth Wood-house in South Yorkshire into a huge and supremely Palladian palace. She knew Lord Burlington and his wife well (a lengthy correspond-ence with the latter – Dorothy Boyle and, in fact, her half-niece – survives in the archives at Chatsworth House), and she was also a close friend of William Kent.[48] The fact that Kent had lived for ten years in Italy – the fountainhead of so much of the art and archi-tecture admired in early eighteenth-century England – evidently impressed her: she started to refer to him as the 'Signor' in her letters to Lady Burlington, not with a sense of irony or mockery but clearly out of admiration.

Lady Isabella's surviving correspondence shows her to have been obsessed with her house ('I grudge every hour yet lost of the fine weather for building,' she wrote to Lord Malton on 1 September 1742).[49] Though expressing a concern in August 1744 that costs were rising (the final bill for the house was £7,000), she remained deter-mined that 'ye Staircase' will 'be completely adorned and beautified according to ye Signor's plan without regard to expense'.[50] She also scrutinised all tradesmen's invoices personally.[51] Lady Isabella moved into 44 Berkeley Square in May 1745, then aged forty-five, and evi-dently greatly enjoyed the spatial gymnastics she and Kent had con-trived within her new home. The sublime scale and complex form of the staircase of course defied the expectations of most visitors to the terrace house, but so did the first-floor 'great saloon' to which it led. From external appearances this promised to be a relatively modest room lit by only three (generously large) windows. In fact, the three

The staircase in number 44 Berkeley Square, London, constructed in 1743/4 to the design of William Kent. The illustration was made for Sir John Soane, who included it in his Royal Academy 'Lectures on Architecture', delivered between 1809 and 1836.

square second-floor windows are fakes, so that the great saloon rises
into the second-floor volume. As she wrote, somewhat triumphantly,
to Lord Rockingham on 31 December 1748, 'My House begins Now
to Shew out to ye Admiration of all who see it who could not com-
prehend ye plan ... Now they begin to find out the joke.'[52] The one
sour note was that by the time Lady Bell wrote her letter to Rockingham, Kent had been dead eight months.[53]

* * * * *

Apart from the handful of letters from Nathaniel Maister to Henry,
written towards the end of the project, there is none of the documentary wealth of evidence for Maister House that survives for 44
Berkeley Square. But much can be inferred from the fabric of the
house. The front door, with its pedimented door surround, opens on
to a passage that is stone paved, as is the staircase hall beyond. The
story this tells is of solidity and endurance – and a desire to make
the house more fireproof. It's tempting to assume that Henry wanted
to learn from history, that he was determined his new home would
escape the tragedy that had engulfed his previous one. The old house
would have been constructed principally of timber and plaster. The
new house was of brick and stone. The current owners of Maister
House, the National Trust, have painted this entrance passage and
the staircase hall beyond in a simple pale stone colour and off-white,
with the panelled dado (made of pine, as is virtually all the panelling
within the house) a lighter hue than the plastered, stone-coloured
walls above – a choice of colours that fits in with the Palladian conceit
of treating entrance spaces somewhat like exterior spaces.[54]

At the far end of the entrance passage, just before the staircase hall is reached, a pair of doors face each other. The creation
of vistas through interiors by the alignment of doors is a Palladio
planning principle much imitated by British Palladians, and is a
device found throughout the house, although its compact plan means
the visual potential and drama of door alignments is limited. In this
case, each door is formed with six raised and fielded panels and is
painted in a mahogany colour, an accurate reflection of early to mid

eighteenth-century Palladian taste. The door surrounds are grandly imposing, topped with richly decorated entablatures that incorporate convex friezes embellished with sheaves of oak leaves, a standard Palladian design much used by Kent.[55] As at Pallant House (see page 12), it's tempting to link the display of oak leaves with Freemasonry.

On the ground floor, to the left on entry, is the former counting house, or office. It is panelled in a simple manner, reflecting its commercial or utilitarian function.[56] The room opposite – to the north – must have been intended for family use as a parlour of some sort. Significantly superior to its neighbour, it is lined from floor to ceiling with fine panelling. It also boasts a cornice-like dado rail with a projecting flat-topped moulding, a box cornice embellished with a dentil course and a door architrave with carved mouldings. The chimney breast is particularly impressive, with an overmantel formed by a large-scale quadrant, or ovolo, moulding within which is set a more delicately moulded frame. This was no doubt intended to enclose a painting. The fire surround itself is very handsome indeed, incorporating figured white marble slips, or narrow slabs, that define the fireplace opening, and these are framed by a large ovolo ornamented with a deeply carved egg-and-dart motif. Above is a plain frieze topped by a richly carved cornice. Such details are part of the standard Palladian design vocabulary used by Burlington and Kent in other houses.

Above the middle flight of stairs, leading from the ground floor to the first-floor landing in Maister House, is a niche flanked by two ornate brackets. On the brackets are antique-style busts and within the niche is a statue of Ceres, Roman goddess of grain crops and fertility. Above is a garland of plaster-made shells. Again, all are appropriate motifs for a merchant who dealt in grain and whose commerce was water-borne. The sculpted figure was made by the eminent London-based Henry Cheere, who in 1743 had been appointed 'Carver' to Westminster Abbey.[57] It was not actually put in place by Henry Maister himself, but some years after his death by his 24-year-old eldest son, also called Henry, who in 1754 wrote to a local friend, John Grimston, to explain that he had been at Cheere's and had 'by his advice fixt upon an Antique Flora for the nitch on my Stair case. He saies it will fill it better than a Venus, & show the attitude [posture] not so liable to be broke.'[58] Clearly Henry the younger was not aware of the difference between Flora – the Roman fertility goddess of flowers, spring and youth – and Ceres, the Roman goddess of agriculture.

The visual delight that rises above Ceres is primarily architectural and spatial, with layers of landings and a tall octagonal lantern – a luminescent beacon of light in daytime – rising above a boldly coved ceiling. The whole spectacle offers a surprising sense of expansive volume, the large scale of the details serving to seemingly magnify the space and imagery in a manner very reminiscent of Kent's artfulness at 44 Berkeley Square, and with elements that recall Palladio – for example, the roses on the underside of the second-floor landings that were no doubt inspired by illustrations in his *I quattro libri*.[59] They are almost certainly the work of Joseph Page, whose standard price-list for decorative plasterwork states '18 inch . . . Roses . . . 16 s – For 2 foot & half Roses £1.1. s.'[60]

The main staircase terminates at the broad, stone-paved first-floor landing, off which lead five doors of matching design – two to the front rooms, two to the rear room and one to the closet wing that contains the 'back stairs'. This staircase is stone-built with simple iron rails, minimal and beautiful. It provides the sole route to the floor above. The door surrounds on the landing are like those on the ground floor, with pulvinated, or cushion-shaped, friezes embellished with oak leaves. These are probably of carved wood, but Page offered a price for rendering this detail in plaster: 'Frizes adorned with Oakes & Acorns 4 p [a] foot.'[61]

The principal point of decorative interest on this landing is the roundel set between the doors to the rear room and 'suspended' by plaster-made ribbons hanging from a lion mask and framed by festoons of plaster shells, similar to those above Ceres. It contains the profile image of a man in classical attire, which is claimed to be John Locke, who died in 1704.[62] It has to be said that it doesn't particularly resemble existing portraits of the great philosopher, but if it is, then it's tempting to assume that Henry Maister elected to display a representation of him for the simple reason that at the time the house was built Locke was regarded as a great Englishman and in many ways the epitome of the English character. Famed as an empiricist, Locke held that useful knowledge comes primarily through experience. He was thus a practical fellow, quite unlike such theoretical Continental exponents of the art of philosophy as the Frenchman René Descartes. It is perhaps significant in the context of Maister House that the 3rd Earl of Shaftesbury – who wrote the letter in 1712 that set out a logical philosophical basis for Palladianism – had been Locke's pupil, and that Kent had already incorporated images of Locke in royal interiors. Whatever the reason for the presence of his image on the landing, at the very least it says much about the virtues and values of Hull's mid eighteenth-century merchant fraternity.

More personages, far more ambiguous in their identity and meaning, occupy the second-floor staircase gallery, with its large-scale cove that suggests a dome when viewed from far below. Such large coves were a device favoured by Kent, but while his are usually coffered, the coves here are peopled with varied busts, three per side, framed by swirling plaster-made acanthus leaves and separated by large concave scrolls. The curved form combined with its height above ground make this vault seem celestial, in which case its occupants should be angelic. Some could be cherubs but most look too aged and worldly-wise for that role. Perhaps they're gods or immortals. One female, who wears a crown, might possibly be Hera, the queen of the gods on Olympus, or Venus, who on occasion is shown wearing a diadem. The centre bust in each group is placed upon a bracket and looks a somewhat generic rendering of a youth – conceivably Apollo, though the garb and absence of attributes suggest not. More unusual are the faces of bearded men, who might possibly be philosophers and part of the staircase theme that starts with Locke. On one side images are more explicit: the profile busts with laurel-leaf coronets that face each other are surely Roman emperors.

* * * * *

The quality of the design and execution of the fabric of Maister House, particularly the interior, begs the question: how were local

Detail of the plasterwork in the cove above the staircase hall
in Maister House.

builders, craftsmen and tradesmen able to build and fabricate, and on occasion design, to such a high standard? How did they learn, and how were they able to apply with such dexterity the details and compositional language of the high game of classicism?

In particular, how were they able so successfully to adapt the formal rules of classical composition to often awkward vernacular or irregular forms?

There are various answers. At Maister House, of course, they were able to make use of Lord Burlington's expertise. Undoubtedly they would also have consulted published pattern books and design guides. In addition, there were inspirational houses and public buildings they could have visited to discover how others had executed and adapted the ideals of classical composition to particular locations. The Earl of Malton's home at Wentworth Woodhouse – a sensational combination of quantity and high-quality details – was from the late 1730s starting to be a source of architectural information for curious and artistically ambitious tradesmen. It's also fair to assume that in the course of their lengthy apprenticeships, young tradesmen would have been introduced to the 'mysteries' of their craft, and have learned not only the language of classical architecture but also the principles of sound construction.

What is certain is that working on a building like Maister House would have proved beneficial to all those involved. For Lord Burlington it would have presented a splendid opportunity to promote his architectural convictions; for Henry Musgrave a pleasant diversion from collecting revenue and a chance to indulge any architectural aspirations he might have entertained and, of course, a pleasing way to exploit his tenuous aristocratic and highly influential connections. For Henry Maister it would have been a chance to display prince-like patronage in his home city, to express his wealth and taste, and perhaps help divert him from dwelling upon his recent tragedy. For the craftsmen and tradesmen who toiled on the building, it would not only have provided a living but enabled them to enhance their skills and their reputation. It's interesting to note in this context that the 25-year-old Joseph Page, who executed the house's exquisite plasterwork, built for himself such a reputation that in time the entire design of the house was credited to him.[63] It certainly marked the beginnings of an extraordinarily successful career, because Page went on to apply Palladian principles to Blaydes House on the High Street, probably as the designer at least of its facade.[64] In around 1771, acting as architect and speculating builder, he created a splendid set of buildings on King Street that incorporates a central building with a wide ground-level arch framed by voussoirs and keystone, that leads to the narrow and curving Prince Street.[65] This most attractive specimen of Palladian urban design – a belated homage to the enduring influence of Burlington that creates a beguiling piece of townscape – was one of Page's last architectural forays; within five years he was dead. The epitaph on his gravestone at St Peter's Church, Barton-upon-Humber, states that he was: 'Architect and master builder, of an extensive genius in the liberal arts superior to many and excell'd by few.' That encomium – which he may well have written himself – refers to his professional status over thirty years after the start of Maister House.

* * * * *

The owner of Maister House, meanwhile, had died many years before. The last of the surviving letters from Nathaniel to his brother is addressed to Henry Maister 'at Mr Davis upon ye Parade, Bath' – a suitably Palladian terrace composition for a man of Henry Maister's tastes. That he was staying in the spa town suggests that he was taking the waters, for the sake of his health. If so, they proved ineffective. That last letter is dated 5 December 1744. Henry died on 15 December, and was buried at Bath. As M. Edward Ingram reflects, he had long been far from well and 'perhaps . . . had never fully recovered from his wife's death'.[66] The construction of Maister House was, perhaps, a form of therapy for the ailing Henry. It seems he was not quite the stoic merchant it's tempting to assume such men must have been, but more a man of volatile emotions. Though it appears he could not bear to be in Hull – the scene of such a terrible family tragedy – he was obsessed with the project, craving regular progress

Prince Street, Hull, seen through the arch leading from King Street.
Both these streets were designed and developed as speculations
by Joseph Page in about 1771.

reports from his brother on the creation of this enduring monument to his bereavement.

It is probable that work on the interior stopped in December 1744, or at least slowed down considerably, and the house does not appear to have been completed until at least the late 1750s.[67] It must be assumed that Nathaniel oversaw works when they recommenced, perhaps still with Musgrave involved, but if works did extend until that date then they were undertaken without Lord Burlington's advice, because he died in London in early December 1753. The first occupant of the house was probably Nathaniel, since Henry Maister's eldest son, Henry the younger, was only fourteen or fifteen when his father died.

* * * * *

The plans of the upper floors of the house were probably resolved before Henry's death and are unexceptional, delivering little spatially or decoratively to compete with 44 Berkeley Square or with the staircase of Maister House.[68] Executed probably around 1760, they demonstrate, though, how polite taste evolved during the intervening decade. In what was once the larger of the first-floor front rooms (now knocked into one) overlooking the High Street is, for example, an exceptionally fine fire surround and overmantel, whose rococo playfulness and slight asymmetry in the detailing suggest a distinct move away from Burlington's influence. The relative lightness of the design and execution also suggests that Page was not involved, and that it was the work of Samuel Spencer's team of tradesmen, perhaps with a joiner referring to published designs, for example from one of Batty Langley's popular pattern books, such *The City and Country Builder's and Workmen's Treasury of Designs* of 1745, or from Isaac Ware's *A Complete Body of Architecture* of 1756.[69]

The date for the completion of this room and the installation of the overmantel – if not necessarily the fire surround – is suggested by Henry Maister the younger's marriage in 1760 to Margaret Warton. Such a momentous event would certainly have called for some redecoration, and the main first-floor room would have been a suitable location for the introduction of fashionable, festive and feminine rococo ornament, rendered in a delicate manner, while the vine decoration complete with bunches of grapes entwined round the architrave that frames the overmantel proclaims the convivial function of the room – almost certainly intended as the drawing room or perhaps, on occasion, used a dining room, where wine would have been consumed and friendship and companionship celebrated. That the overmantel was part of a redecoration scheme prompted by the marriage is seemingly confirmed by a letter Nathaniel Maister wrote on 13 December 1760 to John Grimston, who had evidently been consulted about the acquisition of an appropriate painting to hang within the overmantel's tabernacle frame. Grimston was 'in Town' and Nathaniel sent him the dimensions, noted that the painting would be lit from the 'left hand side' and, in addition, requested that he order a bust from Cheere the 'same as that he sent to Kilnwick', which was the Grimston home near Hull. A week later, in a second letter, Nathaniel confirmed the painting was for 'Harry's room above Stairs'. In May 1761 Nathaniel wrote again to Grimston to inform him that 'Cheere has sent down a Bust of Faustina for Harry by your order.'[70] That the bust was intended for the overmantel, to be placed within the open swan-neck pediment, is confirmed by a description of the room included in Tindall Wildridge's *Old and New Hull*, published in 1885.[71]

The character represented by the bust – Faustina – is a revealing choice as a focus for a room decorated to celebrate a marriage. Antoninus Pius, the second century AD Roman emperor, had a wife and a daughter both named Faustina. The wife has something of a mixed character and shaded reputation, but Antoninus loved her and their marriage, which produced four children, ended only with her death in AD 140, after which her husband deified her, built a temple in her honour on the Forum in Rome, and founded a charity in her name to assist high-born but destitute girls. The daughter married her adoptive brother and future emperor Marcus Aurelius, and the relationship endured for thirty years. Like her mother, she was given divine status by her husband after her death and charity schools for orphan girls were opened in her name. Faustina the Younger had fourteen children with her husband and her role as a mother was glorified, though, as often in Rome, her enemies did their best to undermine her. Rumours were circulated, and persist, that she was involved in a revolt against her husband and had a proclivity for assignations with sailors and gladiators. Presumably, if Henry knew a little more about the Faustinas than he seemingly did about Ceres, it was their reputations as long-serving wives and fruitful mothers that prompted him to raise a bust to their honour in his marriage room. Henry and Margaret seem to have had a good marriage, or at least they stayed together, but they failed to emulate the Faustinas and their husbands in dynasty-building and the Maisters had no children. This was the key reason for the gradual abandonment of Maister House to commercial use after Henry's death in 1812.

A curious feature of the smaller adjoining rear room is a door next to the fire surround and its overmantel, which appears to be a cupboard door but in fact leads via a lobby and staircase to the narrow alley separating Maister House from its neighbour. If the connection is original, this alley would have allowed discreet and direct entry into this first-floor room, a convenient route for the disposal of rubbish and an escape route in case of fire. Another possibility is that this room doubled as a grand place of business – like a boardroom – with this door allowing it to be reached directly from the street without imposing upon the splendid repose of the main staircase.

The second floor was originally organised in a standard manner to, potentially, form three bedchambers of fairly similar size, but with the one above the first-floor drawing room probably furnished with a small closet lit by the central second-floor window. This chamber and closet could have been occupied by Henry and Margaret, and might have been linked to the rear room to form the sort of three-room apartment found in near-contemporary Palladian country houses – such as Houghton Hall in Norfolk – in which a private drawing room joined the bedchamber and closet. This seems likely because this three-room apartment would have enjoyed the convenience of direct access to the gallery landing and to the back stairs, and to a curious little timber-made newel staircase leading to a flat lead roof. Located next to the tall lantern roof – which with a bold dentil cornice looks like an octagonal temple – this little terrace must once have offered charming prospects over the town and the river and have provided Henry with a vantage point to observe shipping and the coming and going of his merchandise.

The spirit of Henry Maister senior is almost entirely absent from these upper rooms. But it makes a reappearance in the rear wing – in several ways a miniature building in its own right. This contains the secondary staircase that not only serves the main house but also links the tiers of room in the wing in a very convenient manner. Its vaulted basement, as mentioned earlier, lacks both windows and ventilation and so would have served as a cellar and storage area for the house, rather than as the kitchen one would normally expect to find below ground level in an eighteenth-century urban house (the kitchen would, instead, probably have been on the ground floor of the wing).[72] And then on the rear wing's first floor, beyond the utilitarian but extremely handsome back stairs, is an elaborately panelled room of the highest quality, almost certainly a 'cabinet' in which Henry Maister senior no doubt intended to receive guests (who could have reached the room privately if desired by means of the back stairs that originally rose from the ground floor).[73] The room appears to have been designed in the early 1740s and has a distinctly masculine nature, with its robust detailing and hearth framed with a simple stone architrave.[74] It's tempting to think that Henry planned it as a retreat from the world, where he could entertain his most valued male friends in an intimate manner, perhaps over a pipe, a bowl of punch and – as at Lord Burlington's Londesborough Hall – a hand of 'Whisk' (or whist), a card game very popular at the time.[75]

The room on the floor above comes as a surprise. It is lined with early seventeenth-century square panelling, now painted white but probably made of oak, and with upper frieze panels and a cornice, all of which clearly predate the house. Yet it surely can't be part of an earlier structure that somehow survived the fire, because the wing is faced with bricks that match those of the main house. The assumption has to be, then, that the panelling is reused salvage. The 1720s-style timber-made staircase leading to the roof terrace also appears to be salvage. Whether all this came from the earlier fire-ravaged house on the site is unknown. If it did, then perhaps there was a now-forgotten sentimental reason, beyond simple economics, for saving these details and, despite the fact that they were no longer in fashion, incorporating them in the new house.

The surprise of this top-floor closet wing comes not only from its Jacobean panelling but from its plan. To one side of the chimney breast is a narrow two-panel door hanging on early strap hinges. This looks like an early eighteenth-century cupboard door, but it doesn't lead to a cupboard. Instead, the door opens on to a narrow staircase that winds around and over the breast to serve a room in the garret. Opposite this narrow door is a second early door hanging on strap hinges. This opens into a small room, or closet, lit by one window and inserted into the volume at the top of the back stairs. It appears to be a compact apartment, secreted at the most distant part of the house, comprising a garret bedchamber, a quaint old-fashioned panelled drawing room and a closet that, more likely than not, contained a close stool. Who could it have been for? Perhaps a faithful retainer or clerk, possibly the mysterious Thorley who evidently lobbied Nathaniel Maister in late 1744 to have a 'partition made in his garratt'.[76] If so, then perhaps Thorley was a loyal scrivener or clerk who toiled below by day and watched in this apartment by night to ensure that the house of Maister would never again be consumed by nocturnal fire.

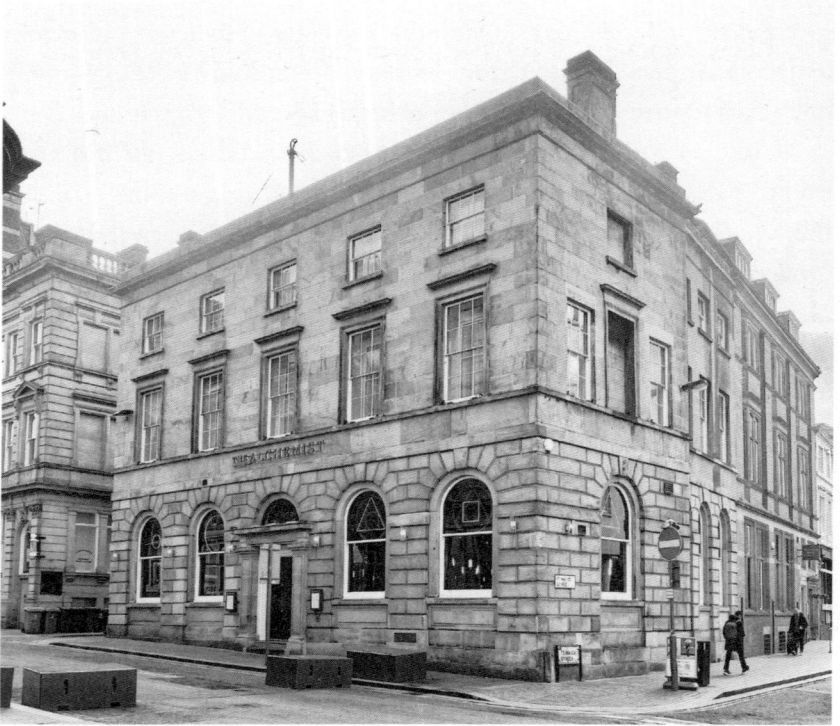

Heywood's house and bank, built in *c*.1800 on the corner of Brunswick Street and Fenwick Street (right). The architect was probably John Foster senior and the building combined banking hall, office and spacious accommodation.

– 4 –

A Piece of Urban Theatre
Heywood's House and Bank, Liverpool
(1798–1800)

MAISTER HOUSE HAD BEEN intended to serve as a place of business as well as a home, but in outward appearance it followed all the conventions of contemporary domestic architecture, albeit domestic architecture on a grand scale. When, half a century later, the Heywood family – probably in the persons of Arthur Heywood the younger and his brother Richard – decided to build themselves a new house in Liverpool, they took a different approach. The edifice that went up on the corner of Brunswick Street and Fenwick Street between 1798 and 1800 was designed to provide spacious accommodation, but it also included a banking hall and offices for the family's company, Heywood's Bank. Maister House concealed its use as an office. The building the Heywoods erected was not so reticent about its dual function.

It is hard to believe that the men behind the bank would not have thought long and hard about the message they wanted to convey through its architecture. They needed a building that embodied solidity, reliability and longevity – one that invoked the virtues of trust, propriety and honesty appropriate for a bastion of financial security. Earlier, in the 1790s, Sir John Soane had created top-lit and vaulted banking halls of incredibly abstract sophistication for the Bank of England in the City of London. But these were a series of internal spaces screened externally by a tall, solemn and virtually windowless rusticated wall that bore little relation to the spaces behind it. For the Brunswick Street site, by contrast, the Heywoods needed a bank with a more public face: one that would both inspire confidence and, of course, attract passers-by.

In this ambition they were surely successful. As John Booker puts it in his seminal 1991 book *Temples of Mammon: The Architecture of Banking*, the design of the Brunswick Street building – by an 'unknown' architect (but probably by John Foster Sr) – is 'too grand for a shop or office', but simultaneously 'under-embellished for a public building, and in the wrong place for a town-house'. The fruits of the brothers' pondering was, arguably, the emergence of a distinct type of building. Speculating how a Liverpudlian of 1800 would have reacted to it, John Booker suggests that 'perhaps for the first time in Britain the word bank came spontaneously to the mind'.[1]

Booker's description of the bank as expressing a 'feeling of reserve and serenity without losing the quality of strength' neatly encapsulates the impression it makes. Although its carcass is constructed of brick, the building is mostly stone-faced – perhaps with Storeton sandstone from Bebington in the Wirral, or with the same Toxteth Park sandstone that was used on the mid eighteenth-century exchange and town hall that stands nearby. The stone blocks are mostly of a mellow yellow buff colour, but with some a pale dusty pink. All have edges that are cut very straight, are tightly jointed, and the courses they form are of matching depth. These are so well related to the overall design of the facade that details such as the top of the first-floor window cornices and the window sills relate precisely to the coursing of the stone. The excellence of the material and of the workmanship does much to bestow the relatively small building with a character that is both restful and monumental.

The fact that the residential portion of the composition is architecturally subservient to the office and banking hall is perhaps ironic, for the architectural ancestry of the building as a whole lies very much within the traditions of domestic design rather than of imposing public edifice. In this it follows in the steps of London's Somerset House – constructed from the late 1770s to the design of Sir William

Chambers – which was built as offices and exhibition space but is reminiscent of uniform and splendid stone-fronted terrace houses.

In fact, the Heywood's building tantalisingly appears to hover between different worlds. Is it a private building or a public one? Is it a home or an institution? Either way, it is very much of its age, and indeed in both its slight ambiguity and its imposing nature it anticipates coming architectural events. Unified grand schemes of the Heywood's variety – embodying an almost visionary approach to urban planning – had been attempted early in the eighteenth century, and sometimes achieved, as with John Wood the Elder's Queen Square in Bath, started in 1729, and the Adam brothers' Portland Place in Marylebone, constructed during the 1780s. But it was really the turn of the century that saw the evolution of what might be termed urban theatre, by which whole quarters of towns or cities were transformed into fantastical streets of seeming palaces. The developments around Regent's Park in London, and the creation of Regent Street – initiated in 1811 on Crown-owned land to a master plan by John Nash – which include single houses in private occupation organised to form monumental palatial compositions, are notable examples. Others include the schemes undertaken in Devonport and Plymouth from 1811 under the direction of the architect John Foulston; and Eldon Square and the magnificent Grey Street in Newcastle upon Tyne, designed and built by architect John Dobson and builder Richard Grainger from the 1820s. Fundamental to the fantasy of these theatrical urban stages was that the buildings that constituted them should be given substance by having stone-built facades, as is the case in Newcastle and with the Heywood's building, or by being faced with stucco treated to look like stone, as with Nash's and Foulston's projects. Such facades were part of the architectural vocabulary by which single houses were successfully unified to create visually powerful and convincing palatial compositions and, like Heywood's, assume some of the architectural significance of public buildings.

* * * * *

The brothers responsible for the project were the grandsons of a merchant, Benjamin Heywood, who was born around 1687 in

The Quadrant Regent Street and the column-clad County Fire Office of 1819 seen from Piccadilly Circus, London. The quadrant was designed by John Nash and built between 1818 and 1820. The buildings were rendered with stucco to give them a stone-built appearance and the quadrants were originally furnished with ground-floor colonnades. This mid nineteenth-century image shows the quadrant's denuded form after the colonnades were removed in 1848. All has since been rebuilt.

Ormskirk, Lancashire, established a business in Drogheda, County Louth (where in 1707 he married Ann Graham), and died in 1725.[2] His oldest son, Arthur – essentially the founder of the business dynasty that was eventually to be housed in Brunswick Street – left Drogheda for Liverpool in 1731, aged fourteen, to serve as an apprentice in the counting house of John Hardman, the MP for Liverpool. Soon an entrepreneur in his own right, he became a town burgess in 1736. Three years later he married a local heiress, Sarah Ogden.[3] In 1741 Arthur's brother Benjamin, who was about five years younger than him, joined him in Liverpool, where he completed an apprenticeship with James Crosby, an eminent merchant and in 1753 Mayor of Liverpool. Thereafter Benjamin went into business partnership with his brother. During the Seven Years War of 1756–63 the two men thrived as merchants and entrepreneurs, initially trading with the Baltic and the Mediterranean, and in Irish linen, but soon expanding their interests to include the 'Africa trade' – predominantly ivory and slaves. Over time they became very wealthy men.

The Seven Years War was global in extent, involved numerous belligerents and led to fighting between Britain and France in India and North America. For Britain, it concluded with a limited victory. For British merchants, the war's course and its aftermath provided glorious business opportunities, particularly in the highly profitable North American market once French goods and competition had effectively been eliminated from France's former possessions in Canada.

The Heywood brothers exploited the war in a robustly aggressive manner, taking full advantage of the lawlessness that the prolonged international conflict inevitably generated by engaging in privateering. The official letters of marque they acquired meant, in essence, that they could, with full government approval, invest in private warships operating for profit that could legally plunder any craft belonging to a country identified as an enemy. Such licensed buccaneering served both national and private interest, combining as it were patriotism with profit. Of course, given that enemy privateers operated in the same waters, it also involved considerable risk. For the Heywoods, these must have been extraordinary times. Any day might bring news of giddying profits or crippling losses.

In 1773 Arthur Heywood, with his eldest son Richard (who had been born in Liverpool in 1751) and his brother Benjamin, formed Arthur Heywood, Sons and Co., trading from a pair of adjoining purpose-designed buildings in Hanover Street (sadly now long demolished).[4] They also extended their commercial activities to include banking, which presumably took the form of holding other merchants' money and investing it in their enterprises in return for a healthy percentage profit. Much of their business involved slaving. Indeed, it has been estimated that the Heywood family invested in 133 slaving voyages between 1745 and 1789.[5]

* * * * *

That the Heywoods' business interests should have included the buying and selling of slaves is scarcely surprising, for this appalling but lucrative trade drove so much of Liverpool's economic success in the eighteenth century and contributed to its quick-paced trans-formation. By 1740, it has been suggested, the town had become one of the chief ports in Europe for slaving expeditions. Between 1761 and 1790 Liverpool-based merchants and investors were responsi-ble for 1,871 – or 70 per cent – of the 2,220 slave expeditions that sailed from Britain's three leading slaving ports – the other two being Bristol and London. Between 1791 and 1807 Liverpool dispatched 1,700 slaving voyages, representing nearly 80 per cent of the trade.[6] Overall, according to Liverpool's Maritime Museum, around 1.5 million Africans were transported across the Atlantic between 1700 and 1800 in ships from the Lancastrian port. The destination of most of those ships was the islands of the Caribbean.[7]

The town benefited materially and visually from the trade. As early as the 1720s, Daniel Defoe had described it as 'one of the wonders of Britain', arguing that 'there is no town in England, London excepted, that can equal Liverpoole for the fineness of the streets, and the beauty of the buildings'.[8] He would have been par-ticularly impressed by the town's new 'Wet Dock', completed in 1715, after five years' work, and encompassing three and a half acres of an enlarged tidal pool off the River Mersey, from which it was sealed off by lock gates. Surrounded by quays, warehouses and a substantial wall,[9] its non-tidal nature ensured that ships could be loaded and unloaded more efficiently, more safely and more securely.[10] Its chief promoter, Sir Thomas Johnson, who, as MP for Liverpool, steered the required bill for its construction through Parliament, and who is generally regarded as the founder of modern Liverpool, was also to a significant degree the man who cemented Liverpool's role as a world centre for the notorious 'triangular' slave trade that involved bartering cargoes for slaves in Africa, transplanting the slaves in the ships' now-empty holds to the American colonies (until the revolution) and the Caribbean, and then stocking those ships with such cargoes as rum, sugar, tobacco and mahogany for the homeward journey.

For men such as Arthur and Benjamin Heywood – as for so many eighteenth-century merchants and men of commerce – making money through the slave trade appears to have presented no moral or ethical issues. They must have known its bloody and brutal reality – families torn apart, people held in chains on a hellish journey from Africa into slavery, sold, held in bondage in perpetuity, as were their children, beaten and on occasion slaughtered or worked to death. But, as far as we now know, the Heywoods were not shocked by the business in which they were involved, or at least certainly not to the extent that they ever appear to have considered abandoning it. For them it was simply too valuable a trade to ignore.

At one point, the brothers – or, rather, the Heywood family – operated businesses in three towns: Lancaster, Manchester and Liverpool. Their Lancaster-based firm – initially named Parke & Heywood and Parke, then Heywood & Conway – was dissolved in May 1785, probably because investment in slaving started to decline following the loss in 1783 of the American colonies.[11] Their Manchester business was opened, probably by Arthur Heywood's son Richard, in 1784. It lasted for just two years, before being ultimately replaced in 1788 by a separate banking partnership, established by Benjamin with his two sons Benjamin Arthur (the eldest son) and Nathaniel, that was named Benjamin Heywood Sons & Co. Benjamin and his sons took bills of exchange from the Liverpool bank to help launch the Manchester business, but it operated independently of the Liverpool bank, which from 1788 was controlled solely by Arthur Heywood.

The family's involvement in the slave trade persisted into the 1790s, notably through a company named Robinson and Heywood that supplied textiles for barter to James Rogers of the Bristol-based James Rogers & Company. Rogers was a key figure in the late eighteenth-century British slave trade. Between 1774 and 1793 he organised fifty-six voyages to Africa to collect slaves, becoming in the process one of Britain's most active slave dealers and 'the second largest Bristol slave merchant in the decade after 1785'.[12] He himself was rarely the sole investor in these expeditions but, as was the usual practice, operated as part of a syndicate, working with an ad hoc group of partners, usually assembled for each specific voyage, with which he shared the expenses, risks and profits. Even this reasonably cautious approach, however, did not save him during the financial crisis that overtook Britain in 1793 following the outbreak of war with Revolutionary France. As war loomed, financial uncertainty escalated and credit rapidly contracted. Rogers was evidently, at the time, operating as a financial speculator, borrowing to finance his expeditions in the expectation of substantial profits. But the sudden credit squeeze meant it all went wrong and in 1793 he was declared bankrupt. Precisely what role Heywood's Bank played in the collapse of Rogers' enterprise is not known. That the Heywood brothers were unaffected by it, however, is clear from the fact that even as it was unfolding – or, possibly, as early as 1789, when unpredictable revolutionary chaos was starting to engulf France – they most probably decided to pursue their ambitious Brunswick Street building project, although building works would not start for nearly a decade.[13]

* * * * *

The profits from the slave trade that helped fund Heywood's house and bank serve as an important reminder that while individual buildings reflect the tastes and the lives of those who lived in them, they are also intricately bound up with wider economic and social trends. The early history of 19 Princelet Street, Spitalfields (see page 33), was shaped by Huguenot refugees promoting a vibrant, greatly revitalised trade in silk. Maister House (see page 79) was made possible by Kingston upon Hull's bustling trade with the Hanseatic and Baltic ports of northern Europe. Heywood's house and bank arose in an era when Liverpool's merchants thrived on the 'triangular' trade. It should come as no surprise, then, that what is true of the Heywoods' building enterprise holds more generally for the urban context in which it was placed.

As Daniel Defoe's description of early eighteenth-century Liverpool suggests, this century of affluence for the city was also one of considerable architectural expansion and ambition. The traveller and writer Celia Fiennes had observed in 1698 that Liverpool was comprised of twenty-four streets. By 1725, according to James Chadwick's 'Map of all the streets, lanes and alleys within the town of Liverpool', these had expanded considerably. The urban spine, running roughly west to east at right angles to the River Mersey, comprised Water Street and Dale Street with, at their junction, Castle Street running south towards Derby Square. This was the historic nodal point, which marked the site of the long-lost early thirteenth-century Liverpool Castle, and, from 1726, of St George's Church,[14] promoted by Johnson, and designed by the civil engineer Thomas Steers whose other projects included not only the Wet Dock but also central Liverpool's oldest surviving building: the splendid Blue Coat School of 1718 on School Lane. A monumental edifice organised in three ranges around a court, whose design owed much to the work of Sir Christopher Wren and Andrea Palladio, the school was built to serve 280 orphaned or 'fatherless' boys and girls and for children whose parents were in 'indigent circumstances'.[15]

Where the line of Water Street and Dale Street – the main axis of the town's plan – met Castle Street coming from the south and High Street heading north, a dominant central site was defined. In the 1740s this was duly selected as the location for another public building – probably the most important built in eighteenth-century

Liverpool. The Merchants' Exchange, which was built from 1749 and which is now known as the town hall, was intended to fulfil a dual function, serving both trade and local government, with an exchange and council room on the ground floor and additional public offices above. Its designer was not a Liverpool man but the Bath-based architect John Wood the Elder, who was responsible for a variety of public and private buildings and developments in his home city, and also from 1741 for the Exchange in Bristol.

That the town authorities should have chosen an architect with a national reputation, and not turned merely to a local man, is arguably a reflection of Liverpool's growing sense of self-importance, civic confidence and economic power. Interestingly, the commission came about thanks to the remarkable local businesswoman, industrialist and mine owner Sarah Clayton, who, like so many people of means at that time, was in the habit of visiting Bath in due season to take the waters and enjoy its pleasures and who was clearly impressed by what she saw. In June 1749 she wrote from Bath to Thomas Shaw, then the Mayor of Liverpool and a member of the committee to select a design for the town hall, recommending John Wood, who, she said, 'is agreed to be a great genius' (she cited the recently completed Palladio-inspired Queen Square and North and South Parades in Bath as particularly impressive works).[16] Her endorsement was sufficient. Wood embarked on the Liverpool Exchange project the same year.

Sarah Clayton's admiration for Wood did not stop with this act of patronage. In 1752, as the town hall was nearing completion (under the control of Wood's son, John Wood the Younger), she initiated the construction in Liverpool of her own mini-Bath: Clayton Square, with its simple three-storey, three-window-wide, brick-built houses, and adjoining streets.[17] The largest of the houses in the square was purpose-designed for Sarah Clayton's occupation, and it was here that she lived until her death in 1779, barely a year after her business ventures had failed and she had been declared bankrupt. The square itself survived two world wars but its houses – by now mostly much altered and in commercial use – were demolished by 1986, after which

The grand medieval country house: Haddon Hall in Derbyshire. Two large adjoining courtyards are separated by a range containing the great hall, flanked on one side by a buttery, pantry and kitchen and on the other by a parlour set below a great chamber. This view shows the porch leading to the screens passage and great hall, with the parlour and great chamber on the right.

The great hall at Haddon Hall, constructed *c.* 1370, with additional timber screen and gallery from *c.* 1450. Improved communication and domestic comfort came from the second gallery added in 1600. The current roof structure dates from 1925.

An uncommon survival of a relatively modest urban building in mixed use: the Medieval Merchant's House in Southampton. Dating from around 1300, it has a ground-floor shop, with a bedroom above, and a great hall and kitchen in the rear wing.

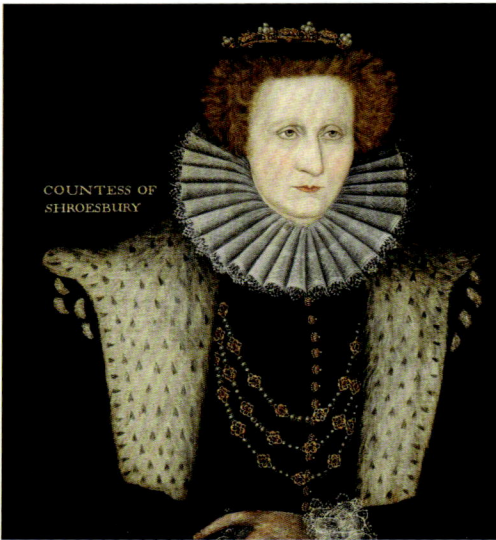

'Bess of Hardwick', the Countess of Shrewsbury. A rare example of a female architectural patron. The portrait dates from around 1580.

Henry Maister was the moving genius behind one of the great mid eighteenth-century town houses, Maister House in Hull, but died before it was completed. This portrait shows his son, Henry Maister the younger, who completed the first-floor interior in around 1760.

The early nineteenth century saw the creation of imposing buildings designed for both domestic and commercial use. Heywood's house and bank in Brunswick Street, Liverpool, was commissioned by Arthur Heywood the younger (shown here) and his brother Richard.

Among the leading architects of the seventeenth and eighteenth centuries, Sir Christopher Wren was pre-eminent. His buildings, which included colleges, palaces, churches and, of course, St Paul's Cathedral, offered inspirational models that many designers followed.

James Gibbs, born in Scotland, trained as an architect in Rome, and from 1714 became a highly influential figure in the British building world.

Richard Boyle, the 3rd Earl of Burlington, who from about 1716 established himself as an arbiter of architectural taste in Britain and a powerful promoter of the Palladian school of design.

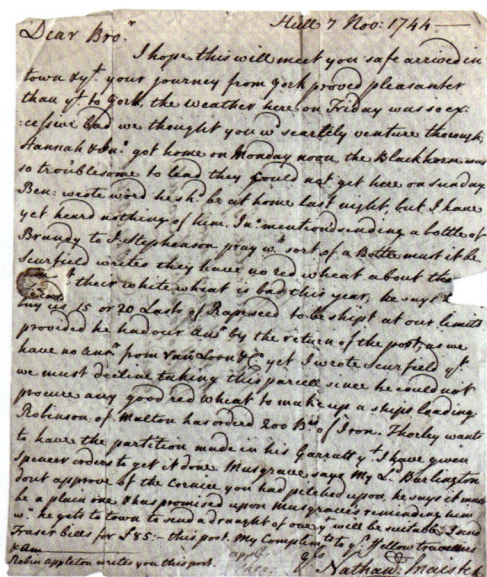

Patrons and architects. A letter, dated 7 November 1744, from Nathaniel Maister to his brother Henry – the client of Maister House in Hull – detailing the advice on detail offered by 'My L. Burlington.'

English baroque: Marlborough House, St James's Park, London, completed in 1711 to the design of Sir Christopher Wren and his son Christopher.

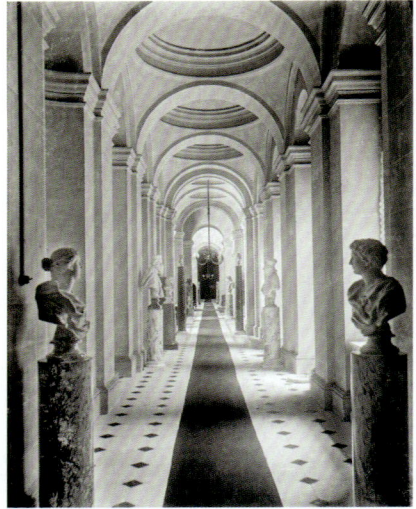

Baroque architecture's theatricality is on display in a corridor in Blenheim Palace, Oxfordshire, designed from 1705 by Sir John Vanbrugh.

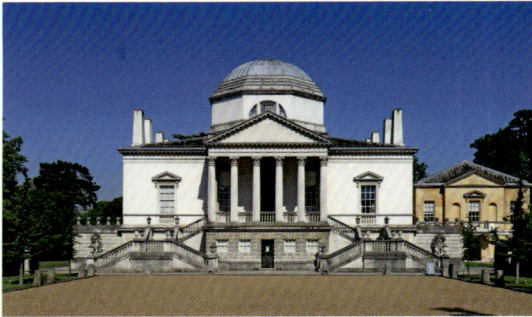

Palladian architecture: Chiswick House, London, inspired by antique Roman architecture and that of the sixteenth-century Italian Andrea Palladio. It was built from 1723 to 1729 and its architects were Lord Burlington and – for interiors – William Kent.

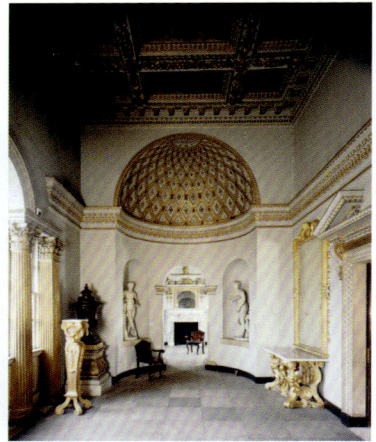

The gallery inside Chiswick House, with an apse and coffered hemispherical vault inspired by the type of Roman architecture – often found in bathhouses and basilicas – promoted by Palladio.

Neo-classical architecture: Bedford Square, London, built between 1776 and 1783, reflects the Georgian urban ideal – as later expressed by Park Square East – within which individual houses were designed to form a single palatial composition, usually (as here) organised around a central pediment and framed by baluster-topped pavilions.

London's Park Square East looking north from Park Crescent, built from 1823 to 1824, and part of a visionary scheme, conceived by John Nash, that included the creation of palatial terraces of heroic design that combine Greek and Roman forms and details.

A neoclassical interior: the library at Kenwood House, Hampstead, completed in 1770 to the design of Robert Adam as part of his 1764 remodelling of the house for Lord Mansfield, and inspired by new discoveries about authentic Roman domestic design.

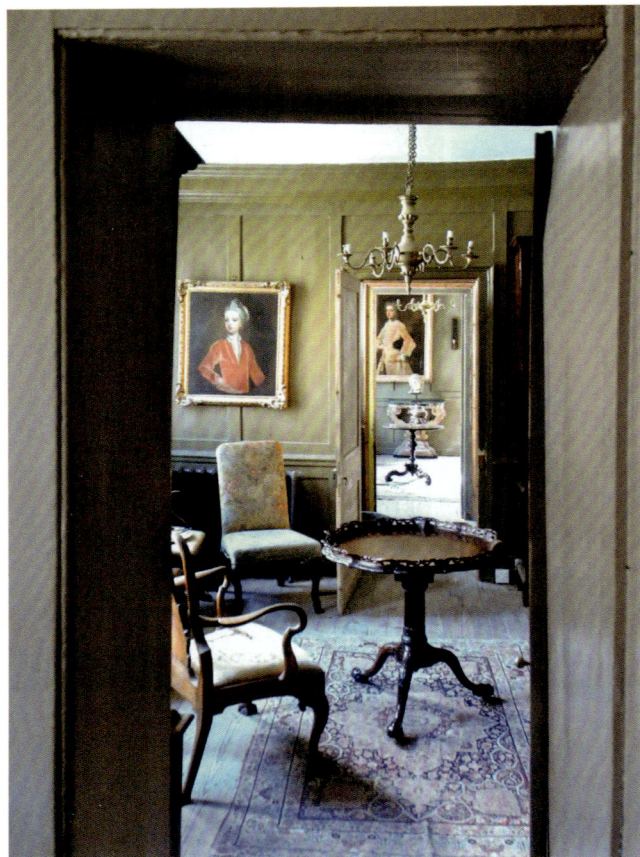

Domestic interiors in relatively small houses of the mid to late 1720s in Elder Street, Spitalfields, London. Left: a miniature first-floor enfilade through four spaces – from a closet, across a parlour or possibly a bed-chamber, to a staircase landing with a withdrawing room beyond. Below: a first-floor front room. Although compact, there is some grandeur in its detailing, with panelling set in moulded frames and topped by a generous Doric box cornice.

Detail of the staircase of 1712 in Pallant House, Chichester. Made of oak, the tread ends are carved with various emblems. This one shows a pair of cornucopia – horns of plenty and symbols of abundance and prosperity – from which flowers issue.

Eighteenth-century interior design: detail of a plaster decoration in Maister House, Hull, Yorkshire, almost certainly executed by Joseph Page in 1744. This shows the head of Apollo – the sun god – set within a sunburst and framed by foliage, including stylised acanthus leaves.

Detail of a first-floor room in a Bedford Square house. Dating from around 1780, the interior features, above its fireplace, a pair of figures in antique dress, rendered in plaster.

Houses in their original form: the east side of Elder Street, Spitalfields, London, which was constructed from 1725 to 1727 by various speculating builders. The houses are little altered externally, most retaining timber-made doorcases with ground-floor facades still brick-faced, as originally intended.

Houses remodelled: the north side of Princelet Street, Spitalfields. The earliest house shown, number 21, one bay of which is visible with a blue replacement doorcase, was built in about 1705. To its west (left) is number 19 Princelet Street, built in 1718, with its ground floor altered and rendered in c.1892.

Above: The Exchange and Town Hall, Liverpool, built in 1749 to the designs of John Wood the elder. Below: A detail of the frieze on the town hall displaying the heads of an African and an elephant. These represent the 'Africa Trade' on which the fortunes of Liverpool largely depended.

the dismal Clayton Square shopping centre was constructed across most of the site.

If the public buildings of eighteenth-century Liverpool increasingly expressed a sense of civic pride, many of its buildings were also touched in some way by the city's merchant ethos in general and the slave trade in particular. It was no act of chance that the frieze that runs round the exterior of the Exchange/town hall should have been embellished with the carved heads of an elephant, an African and a lioness flanked by barrels, presumably representing the riches of the Africa trade in ivory, slaves and other valuables. Sarah Clayton herself had a connection with slavery, via her nephew and business collaborator Thomas Case; so too did many of the town's leading citizens. Indeed, a study of Liverpool merchants between 1774 and 1795 suggests that over a third were involved in 'slaving' – most of them operating in partnerships. One such was John Dobson, chairman of the Liverpool Chamber of Commerce between 1774 and 1777, who was a major merchant and corn dealer with interests in the European, West Indian and African markets, in whaling, and in slaving in partnership with Thomas Case.[18] The ambitious complex at the junction of Parr Street and Colquitt Street, which was going up at roughly the same time (*c.*1799) as the Heywoods were building their new house and bank, owed its inception in part to the profits that its owner, the merchant Thomas Parr, was gaining from the slave trade (his own ship, named the *Parr*, was purpose-built in Liverpool in 1797 as a slave ship capable of transporting 700 slaves at a time; he also specialised in iron-made goods that no doubt included the shackles used to subdue abducted Africans).[19] The buildings that he erected comprise a five-storey brick-built warehouse (57 Parr Street) – solemn in appearance but with a large gable pediment and a few characterful neoclassical details including a stone cornice – and beside it, his solid-looking mansion. It is three storeys high and flanked by large cubical wings, one of which served as a counting house.

According to the contemporary slave-trade apologist William Moss, author of *The Liverpool Guide*, 'from the year 1783 to 1793 . . . the value of Slaves imported into the West Indies in Liverpool vessels,

The group of buildings at the junction of Parr Street and Colquitt Street, central Liverpool, constructed in about 1799 for Thomas Parr to serve as his mansion, counting house and warehouse.

amounts to £15,186,850'.[20] This reflects the profits of the trade as reconfigured following the loss of the American colonies and the replacement of an American slave market with one solely in the West Indies. After 'deductions', Moss estimated that 'on the average of the 11 years', £1,117,647 was 'annually remitted' to Liverpool, of which 'the clear annual profit . . . after deducting all other expences, will be to the merchant £214,677. 15s. 1d.'.[21] This was a huge sum. To put it in context, the money raised nationally by income tax in 1799 – the first year of this particular tax's existence – was just over £5 million.

* * * * *

By the time that the builders were at work on the Heywoods' new project, though, the slave trade was coming in for considerable criticism. Even William Moss, who was at such pains to defend its economic benefits, acknowledged that 'the merits of this Trade, in a moral and political light, have long been the subject of earnest contention by the legislature and individuals of this country'. His conclusion was that from the 'political point of view, every thing favours it', but 'as a simple moral question, considered in the abstract, it can meet with no countenance'.[22] A couple of decades earlier, in 1779, William Bagshaw Stevens – the poet, cleric and one-time headmaster of Repton School in Derbyshire – had bluntly noted of Liverpool in his journal that 'through-out this large-built town every brick is cemented to its fellow brick by the blood and sweat of Negroes'.[23]

Apologists for the trade, such as Moss, not only defended it on economic grounds but also – tendentiously – sought to find religious sanction for it. After all, they pointed out, in the very first book of the Old Testament – the Book of Genesis – where the patriarch Noah curses Ham's son Canaan and states that 'a servant of servants shall he be to his brethren', slavery appears to be accepted as a natural condition of mankind, condoned by God.[24] The Book of Leviticus, champions of the trade contended, similarly defended the institution of slavery, in its declaration that while slaves could not be seized from one's own people, they could be taken from among nations that are cursed, like the descendants of Canaan; that have been defeated in war; or that are composed of non-believers.[25]

James Boswell, the somewhat sycophantic biographer of one of the literary giants of the age, Samuel Johnson, was not untypical of those who supported slavery in not only advancing theological justification for its continuation ('a *status*, which in all ages God has sanctioned, and man has continued'), but suggesting that its abolition would 'be *robbery* to an innumerable class of our fellow-subjects'. To add insult to injury, he also argued, in an exquisite perversion of common sense, that the abolition of slavery 'would be an extreme cruelty to the African Savages, a portion of whom it saves from massacre, or intolerable bondage in their own country, and introduces into a much happier state of life'. Bondage in a Christian world, he held, was far preferable to what would be experienced in a heathen one. 'To abolish that trade would', he argued, quoting Thomas Gray's 'Elegy in a Country Churchyard', "– shut the gates of mercy on mankind."[26]

By the time Boswell was writing, however, not only were the ranks of those opposed to the slave trade growing but a number of court cases had seemingly confirmed the argument for ending it. One that proved to be an important milestone on the road to abolition involved a man named Joseph Knight, who had been born free in Africa but abducted in circumstances that are unknown and carried as a slave to Jamaica. Here he was sold to a Scottish planter and landowner named John Wedderburn of Ballindean. In 1769 Wedderburn returned with Knight to Scotland, where it was assumed he would continue his life of slavery. But Knight soon took the view that in Britain – with its Bill of Rights of 1689 outlawing 'cruel and excessive punishments', its case law, and its assumption that freedom is an inherent human right – there was an opportunity to escape perpetual bondage. His hopes must have risen in 1772 when in a not dissimilar case involving James Somerset, a slave who escaped from America to England, the Chief Justice of the King's Bench, the Earl of Mansfield, while not condemning slavery as an institution (though he described it as 'odious'), ruled that it was illegal to transport a slave out of England against their will.[27] (It's interesting to note that Mansfield had had his great-niece Dido Elizabeth Belle living with his household at Kenwood in Hampstead since 1765, where he treated her as a loved member of the family and later supported her financially. Dido's father was Mansfield's nephew Sir John Lindsay – a Royal Navy officer; her mother was Maria Belle, an African slave in the British West Indies.)

At one level, Mansfield's ruling merely sustained the long-established legal principle and popular notion that freedom in England was so deep-rooted, and the practice of slavery within its boundaries and within its laws so alien, that effectively any slave that set foot in England, or was confined in England, became, by being in England, free. But it also marked a sea change because until the Somerset ruling the slaving centres of England – London, Lancashire around Liverpool and Lancaster, and Bristol – were, it seems, in their own regard laws unto themselves. A 1766 edition of the weekly *Williamson's Liverpool Advertiser*, for example, includes a notice headed: 'To be sold at the Exchange Coffee-house in Water Lane This day the 12th inst. September at One O'clock precisely Eleven Negroes imposted per the Angola', with the 'broker' being one George Drinkwater. It is just possible that the 'Negroes' themselves were absent, but given that the usual practice was to display those being sold so that they could be physically inspected by potential purchasers, this seems unlikely.[28] Two other contemporary advertisements would appear to confirm the suggestion that enslaved people were sold in the flesh in Liverpool. One, also dated 1766, is for an auction at George's Coffee House, Castle Street, where a 'very fine negro girl about 8 years of age, very healthy' that 'hath been some time from the Coast' was offered to those 'willing to purchase', who were invited to 'apply to Captain Robert Syers and Mr Bartley Hodgetts, Mercer and Draper, near the Exchange, where she may be seen until the time of the sale'.[29] The other advertisement, again from *Williamson's Liverpool Advertiser* and dated 27 November 1767, states that 'One Negro Man, and Two Boys' were 'To be Sold by Auction at Richard Robinson's office in High-street near the Exchange'. Those interested were informed that all three 'will be brought up to the Place of Sale, to be view'd'.

Joseph Knight's tribulations did not end with the Mansfield ruling in the Somerset case. After the verdict he decided that he should be treated as a free man and be paid for his work. Wedderburn refused, and in 1774 in response Knight chose to leave his service. Wedderburn had him arrested, exactly on what charge is not clear, and at a hearing before a Justice of the Peace at Perth, Wedderburn's actions were sustained. The JP was not a legal expert, simply a local gentleman who predictably supported another local gentleman having trouble with his servant, and who proceeded on the basis that Scottish law and English law were not one and the same. Although no doubt dismayed by the JP's decision, Knight was not bowed. He appealed to a higher, and far more able, legal authority, the Sheriff of Perth. The sheriff found in Knight's favour, on grounds similar to those utilised by English judges. As he put it, 'the state of slavery is not recognised by the laws of this kingdom, and is inconsistent with the principles thereof' and emphasised that 'the regulations in Jamaica, concerning slaves, do not extend to this kingdom'.[30]

This was still not the end of the matter. Wedderburn appealed the verdict to the Court of Session in Edinburgh on the grounds that Knight owed perpetual service until discharged, like an indentured servant, and should be sent by force back to the slave-culture of Jamaica. The case was heard in 1777 in front of a full panel of judges, including Lord Kames, an advocate, philosopher, pivotal figure in the Scottish Enlightenment and patron of David Hume and Adam Smith. The trial was clearly going to be a most elevated affair.

It was at this point that James Boswell's hero Samuel Johnson became involved – on Knight's side. Johnson had long been an opponent of the slave trade, and had himself effectively adopted a former slave from Jamaica, Joseph Barber, in 1752, subsequently employing him as an assistant on the production of his *Dictionary of the English Language*, and leaving him an annuity of £70 per year in his will – roughly equal at the time to the annual wage in London for a skilled artisan. Now Johnson helped Knight's legal team to prepare the case and offered the court an opinion on the powerful issues of natural justice the case touched upon, and on the inherent human right to freedom. He could not simply attack the institution of slavery, which was, after all, still legal. Instead, while recognising that 'it must be agreed that in most ages many countries have had part of their inhabitants in a state of slavery', he suggested that 'it is impossible not to conceive that men in their original state were equal; and very difficult to imagine how one would be subjected to another but by violent compulsion.' 'An individual may, indeed, forfeit his liberty by a crime,' he went on, 'but he cannot by that crime forfeit the liberty of his children.'

Johnson's carefully nuanced advocacy helped win the day.[31] Webberburn's appeal was rejected. Lord Kames, with his fellow justices, ruled that 'the dominion assumed over this Negro, under the law of Jamaica, being unjust, could not be supported in this country' and that the 'defender had no right to the Negro's service for any space of time, nor to send him out of the country against his consent'.

If the intellectual and legal case against slavery was gradually gaining ground, a series of scandals served to strengthen the resolve of the abolitionists. Just four years after the Knight case, in August 1781, the Liverpool-registered slave ship the *Zong*, while on the 'middle passage' from Accra to Jamaica, became lost due to astonishingly incompetent navigation and mismanagement. To lighten the load, the captain, Luke Collingwood, ordered that 132 enslaved people, including women and children, should be thrown overboard.[32] The ensuing legal debate focused on the insurance claim for the lives lost, made by members of the Liverpool-based Gregson syndicate who had masterminded the venture. The accompanying moral furore focused on the callous and wilful destruction of life. Then, in 1792, just a few years after the Slave Trade Act of 1788 (also known as Dolben's Act) was passed to regulate the slave trade and mitigate its horrors by limiting the number of enslaved people that could be carried on a ship, a further *cause célèbre* arose when Captain John Kimber, the master of the *Recovery*, a slaver out of Bristol, was tried for murder having, it was alleged, whipped a teenage female slave to death, while she was suspended by one leg, because she had refused to dance for the entertainment of the ship's crew. (He was acquitted.)

Abolition of the slave trade (if not of slavery) in the British Empire would eventually come in 1807. By that time, the Society for Effecting the Abolition of the Slave Trade had been established for two decades, its founders including Thomas Clarkson and Granville Sharp, with the MP William Wilberforce soon recruited to lead the campaign in Parliament. The anti-slavery medallion created in 1787 by the potter Josiah Wedgwood – on which the image of a kneeling and shackled black man is combined with the motto 'Am I Not a Man and a Brother' – soon become a popular emblem. And biblical texts that had been called on to support the institution of slavery were countered, not least by the former slave Ottobah Cugoano, the title page of whose 1787 work *Thoughts and Sentiments on the Evil and Wicked Traffic of the Slavery and Commerce of the Human Species* bears a text entitled the 'Law of God': 'He that stealeth a man, and selleth him, or maketh merchandize of him, or if he be found in his hand: then that thief shall die.' The text is from Exodus 21:16, although the quote direct from the King James Bible is a little, but not significantly, different.

* * * * *

The Heywood brothers' building project, then, comes at a significant turning point in the history of the town in which it was situated. It was part funded by a trade that was now controversial and would soon be banned. But it was erected by a generation of men who were unashamed of the way in which they had made so much of their money. Heywood's house and bank is a confident, unapologetic architectural statement. It proclaims the success of 'one of the ... most respectable merchants in Liverpool', as Arthur Heywood was described in an obituary that appeared shortly after his death in 1795, and the durability of the dynasty he had founded in the persons of Arthur Heywood the younger (who had joined the bank as a partner)[33] and his brother Richard. These two men, presumably, were the driving force behind the design and construction of the new bank and family home in Brunswick Street.

It is not known for sure who the architect of the building was, but it seems likely that he was John Foster, a former joiner and builder and the son of a builder. Over time, he became surveyor to the Corporation of Liverpool and the docks, oversaw the construction of Prince's Dock from 1810, and ultimately became, in the words of one scholar, 'a dominant figure in the architectural affairs of Liverpool'.[34] Other architectural projects that he undertook included the Atheneum, completed in 1799; the New Exchange, started in 1809; and the Corn Exchange, dating from 1807 (all three buildings have long since been demolished). Foster also worked on the remodelling of the Exchange/town hall in 1788 with the London architect James Wyatt and again after the interior was seriously damaged by fire in 1795. If he did indeed design Heywood's house and bank, it would have been one of his earlier projects.[35] His son (now known as John Foster Jr), who trained at his father's office, also became a successful architect, and a highly gifted one, responsible among other works for the magnificent, domed and porticoed Liverpool Custom House constructed on the site of the city's Old Dock, which was completed in 1835, badly bomb-damaged in 1940–41 and, rather than being lovingly restored, was heartlessly swept away in 1948.[36]

The design of the bank and house in Brunswick Street can be viewed in the heroic context of a line of architecturally related family works that possess stylistic continuity and that reached their climax with the Custom House. Like the Custom House, the bank is a solemn neoclassical affair that displays a fine feel for the antique. Its main facade is based on the then accepted classical precepts of proportion and composition, with a ground floor treated as a podium that's faced with rustication to express solidity and windows with semicircular tops to suggest an arcade, like the town hall. The first-floor windows are near double square in proportion and framed by architraves and a cornice, second-floor windows are square, and all is topped by a finely detailed and very masculine Doric cornice.

A similar approach is followed in the two shallow side elevations of the main building, both of which are three windows deep, though the upper-floor windows of both are placed closer together. In both side elevations only the centre first-floor windows have architraves and cornices, but the most notable feature is that on both side elevations all the first- and second-floor centre windows are blanks – filled with recessed masonry panels, not sashes. The reason for this oddity is easy to discover. Above the centre of each side elevation rises a chimney stack, so behind these blank windows are chimney breasts and fireplaces. Either the first floor was formed of two rooms, or perhaps, given the business function of the building, it housed a single very large room with a fireplace at each end, forming a splendid banking hall of roughly double-square plan.

The domestic elements of the building, which are set back slightly from each of the side elevations of the bank, are rather more modest. The facade that faces on to Lower Castle Street – formed of two parts of contrasting scale and design – is brick-built.[37] The one that fronts on to Fenwick Street speaks essentially the same architectural language as the bank building, with ground-floor rustication, arched windows and string and sill courses. But embellishments are reduced, the windows of its three-bay elevation are more closely spaced, the first-floor windows lack the monumental detailing (in terms of architraves or entablatures) of the front facade, and the upper portion of the elevation is rendered and patterned with false pointing, rather than being faced with stone. It's possible that the house was originally entered by a front door on this elevation, but early twentieth-century remodelling means that it is now impossible to be sure.

So radically has the interior of the house and bank been altered over the years that it is very difficult to tell precisely how it would have looked when its first owners lived and worked there.[38] Indeed, it's not even clear today how bank and house related to one another. Clearly, the banking hall would have occupied the ground floor. It's hard to believe that it would, in its architecture, have resembled Sir John's Soane's near-contemporary but very personally idiosyncratic banking halls for the Bank of England in the City of London, which were not only top-lit but also mostly without lower windows. However, its layout was no doubt similar: long mahogany counters with tiers of drawers beneath, set near side walls and behind which staff would have been ranged and in front of which customers would have gathered. There would also probably have been tall bookcases fitted with doors, set against the walls. It's tempting to think that the Heywoods would have taken a leaf out of Soane's book by making use of one particular recent innovation he adopted both in his banking halls and in his house in Lincoln's Inn Fields: Argand lamps. Invented in around 1780 by a Swiss chemist named Aimé Argand, these were relatively safe and efficient oil lamps with an improved wick and fuelled by gravity-fed viscous rapeseed oil. They yielded a light equal in strength to that of about six candles. They would have given the bank – and the house more generally – much-needed brightness in the evenings and during the winter months.

The main business of the bank would, of course, have been conducted on the ground floor, but the presence of a row of giant fluted columns on the first floor, stretching from the rear (southern) corners of the main building's side elevations, suggests that it, too, was pressed into bank service. The columns themselves appear relatively new, but it's hard not to think that they form, in essence, an original feature of the building. The fact that the top part of each one disappears into the ceiling could possibly be taken as evidence that the original room was imposingly double height. Given their scale, though, it seems more likely that all that has happened is that the ceiling above has at some point been lowered.[39] On balance, it seems likely that this part of the first floor was originally a grand meeting or reception room, with doors that opened into rooms to its south and so to the domestic part of the building.

If the Heywoods made use of Argand lamps, they also doubtless incorporated two other recent technical improvements in their new house. One was the simple but effective heating innovation introduced by an American loyalist named Benjamin Thompson, who had been obliged to flee his nation at the end of the American Revolutionary War, settling first in London and then in Bavaria, where,

A top-lit banking hall – the Old Colonial or 5% Office – designed in the early nineteenth century by Sir John Soane for the Bank of England in the City of London.

in royal service, he acquired the title of Count Rumford. While in London he had noted how poorly fireplaces functioned – producing lots of smoke and little heat with, in reverse of preference, much of the smoke entering the room while most of the heat went up the flue. Being of a scientific and analytical turn of mind, Thompson rede-signed the traditional coal-burning fireplace and caused quite a stir when he published his recommendations in 1796 and 1798. They were sensible and relatively easy to implement: essentially he suggested the insertion of bricks into the fireplace opening to reduce its size, and thus increase the updraught, with those bricks forming the sides being angled to help reflect heat into the room. This simple adapta-tion worked and caught on rapidly, becoming common practice by the late 1790s. The other innovation the Heywoods may well have taken advantage of was a water-flushed lavatory (see Chapter 5), made a ready possibility from the late 1770s as the manufacturing advances of the Industrial Revolution led to the replacement of leaky water pipes made from elm with robust cast-iron pipes and to the improvement of sewage systems.

As for the decoration of the interior of the Heywoods' home – certainly of its grander rooms – it's tempting to think that they might have shared some of the richness to be found in Sir John Soane's houses, architectural office and museum (the first two houses created between 1792 and 1812) in Lincoln's Inn Fields, even if, again, his taste was probably too idiosyncratic to serve as a direct model. But perhaps Soane's preference for strong colours – particularly Pompei-ian red combined with bronze green for the dining room and library; and bright chrome yellow for the drawing room – might have been echoed in the interior of the Heywoods' Liverpool house. Closer to home, they could have found inspiration in the neoclassical build-ings and interiors on which their probable architect John Foster Sr had worked. His collaboration with James Wyatt on the rebuilding of the interior of the nearby town hall, particularly after the gutting of much of the original building by fire in 1795, yielded a Wyatt-designed dining room. Although later in date than the Heywood inter-iors, it perhaps reflects the taste that inspired them. Here walls are embellished with giant Corinthian pilasters of yellow artificial marble that support a coved ceiling; and there are large painted roundels and a coloured frieze with scrolls and urns and crouching dogs.

A recreated merchant house of the period – though in Bristol rather than Liverpool – offers a few further clues as to the likely appearance of the Heywoods' home. In 1789, John Pretor Pinney, who had made his fortune in the sugar plantations he had run in Nevis in the West Indies,[40] commissioned the architect William Paty to build him what is now number 7 Great George Street (and, since 1937, a museum run by Bristol City Council).[41] The design of the grand but simple exterior of the house, which is faced in limestone, with a rusticated ground floor and with minimal classical detail, does not appear to have been specified by Pinney; it simply follows the pattern of much late eighteenth-century Bristol architecture. But the interior is much more individual. Below stairs there is a housekeeper's room – originally occupied by the freed slave Frances Coker, who had been Mrs Pinney's maid in Nevis – a kitchen, laundry and a cold-water plunge bath. Above are elegant, almost aristocratic, rooms that include an eating room, a drawing room, Pinney's study (which retains his bureau/bookcase), a ladies' withdrawing room and a library. In 1789 a library was still something of a novelty in an urban terrace house. So, too, was the fitted plunge bath in the basement. Representing the twin virtues of culture and cleanliness, they would have placed the original occupants of 7 Great George Street at the forefront of fashion and modernity.

The decorative scheme that has been created inside Pinney's house is typical of the time: tasteful, almost neutral. The dining room and the drawing room are each painted in hues of pale blue and green, with the lower portion of the walls (that below the dado rail) different in tone than that above, and with joinery, cornice, frieze and ceiling painted off-white. The library and study have pale pea-green walls with off-white dado panels, joinery and plasterwork, while the kitchen has walls painted the mid-blue verditer that was usual in the eighteenth century for the decoration of utilitarian rooms and that was made by adding copper nitrate to limewash. We will never know

A bedroom and the drawing room in 7 Great George Street, Bristol,
built in 1789 for West Indies plantation and slave owner, and sugar merchant
John Pretor Pinney.

whether, in their Liverpool house, the Heywoods chose to be merely tasteful, as Pinney was, or adventurous in the way Soane was. The stone-clad and solemn neo-antique exterior of Heywood's house and bank surely suggest the latter.

A further sense of richness in the Brunswick Street house would have been introduced by the extensive use of dark-hued mahogany (also used in Pinney's Bristol home for the mahogany-made pediment-topped bookcases that line the library). The import into England from the Caribbean of this handsome, durable and fine-grained hardwood had started during the late seventeenth century. By the early eighteenth century it had started to be used by cabinetmakers for furniture and from the early 1720s for architectural interiors.[42] Initially, it was imported into England primarily from Jamaica (which at first supplied around 90 per cent) and Cuba. By the early 1760s, however, it was arriving from Honduras as well, and the overall quantities being imported were increasing. In 1750, 3,688 tons of mahogany arrived in England. By 1788 this had increased to 30,000 tons.[43] Much would have found its way into the country via Liverpool and Lancaster, where Robert Gillow, a former ship's carpenter who had sailed to Jamaica in 1720 and returned with samples of mahogany, founded 'Gillows of Lancaster' a decade later – a high-quality furniture and furnishing business that exploited the West India trade, importing rum, sugar and mahogany and exporting mahogany-made furniture back to the West Indies.

One has, then, to imagine the Heywoods' new house decorated in the height of contemporary fashion: either coolly neoclassical as Pinney's interior is now presented – with pale blues, greens and stone colours – or robustly neo-antique like Soane's house, with Pompeiian red walls, *trompe l'œil* frescoes and marbling. But, whichever style was chosen, the house would surely have been filled with exquisite furniture, and with a rich array of silverware and gilt picture frames that would have glinted in the light from the Argand lamps. Perhaps the overall scheme followed the theory of 'distribution of colours in the various parts' of a domestic interior published by a London architect named James Peacock in 1785, according to which a 'close study of

nature in several select landscapes' revealed that 'in the ceiling should
prevail, the light, cool and delicately softened azure of the sky [as is
the case with several Soane interiors], the walls should partake the
middle hue, and the floor a deeper die ... All strong and vivid tints
must be very sparingly used; the glory of the sun is too powerful for
mortal sight.'[44]

* * * * *

Although the long-term prospects for Liverpool's slave-based
economy were uncertain when the Heywoods' building in Brunswick
Street was completed around 1800, the grandeur of this structure
suggests that those making money through the slave trade lacked
neither funds nor confidence. But then the Heywoods had long been
diversifying their business activities. Although much of their profit in
1800 presumably came from their own slave-related business interests
or from investors who were slavers, the brothers – as bankers – did
have wealth-creating activities and interests beyond the slave trade. In
any case, even when the trade was finally outlawed in 1807 for British
merchants and ships, many of the commodities that had formed part
of its complicated web – such as sugar, molasses and rum from the
Caribbean – continued to be imported and to be profited from. They
were simply paid for in different ways.

In their bid to diversify after 1807, owners and captains of Liverpool's former slave ships used their West Africa contacts to establish a monopoly on the import of palm oil, which became a valuable
trade, as did the import of raw cotton from the southern states of
America. Liverpool had overtaken London in 1795 as the leading
cotton importer in Britain, largely because of the popularity of short-
staple American cotton and Liverpool's long-established trade links
with the southern states. In 1802 the quantity of cotton imported into
Liverpool from America for the first time exceeded that imported
from the West Indies, and this America trade expanded rapidly after
1807. Mahogany, increasing in demand and use, was another com-
modity that was imported in ever greater quantity after the eclipse of
the slave trade, helped by the collapse of French and Spanish power

in the Caribbean and the subsequent opening up of ports that had previously been closed to British traders and ships – notably the formerly French-controlled Saint-Domingue (from 1804 the independent republic of Haiti) and Santo Domingo (a Spanish possession again after 1809). Such staples, of course, simultaneously funded the Liverpool merchants and furnished their houses and made their lives more comfortable. Mahogany was employed for a huge number of domestic items, even in more humble homes, from furniture to doors of fitted cupboards and staircase handrails. And cotton now took the place of duck feathers, horsehair, straw or wool for mattresses, replaced linen for durable sheets, curtains and tablecloths, and well-made, stylish and easy-to-wash cotton garments firmly established themselves as a very practical alternative to those made of expensive silk.

What the Heywoods thought of this changed world is unknown. To some of their neighbours – even those who had supported the continuation of the slave trade for economic reasons – it's possible that abolition may have come as something of a relief. By the 1790s the 'Africa trade' was viewed by most Liverpudlian merchants not as a source of pride but as a necessary evil. Even William Moss, apologist for Liverpool's slave trade though he was, took issue in his *Liverpool Guide* of 1796 with some of the emblems that had in the 1750s been included in the stone frieze of the town hall. Among those he found most irksome were, no doubt, the carved head of the African and the elephant that commemorated the profitable Africa trade. The offending emblems he considered 'childish and ridiculous ornaments . . . which the chisel would remove'.[45]

Inevitably not all Liverpool's wealthy trading families proved as long-lasting as the Heywoods. Thomas Parr, for example, who in 1798 followed the example set by the Heywoods in securing a letter of marque from the government for his eponymous ship, managed to lose the craft in the same year. Having gathered a cargo of slaves at Bonny Island, in the Niger Delta, his ship was sailing along the coast of Africa en route to the West Indies when it caught fire and exploded – presumably it was carrying a cargo of gunpowder.

Whether or not it was carrying its full 'cargo' of enslaved Africans at the time is unknown. All we can be reasonably sure of is that 29 of her crew and around 200 of its prisoners were saved – at least, according to some reports.[46] By 1805, Parr had left his new Liverpool mansion and, aged only thirty-six, had retired from merchant life, and probably from the slave trade. He settled at Lythwood Hall in Shropshire, where he sought to assume the role of an English country gentleman. In this ambition he appears to have met with no great success, because in 1840 Charles Darwin described him as 'an old miserly squire'.[47]

By an ironic twist of fate, Parr's mansion, built at least in part from the profits of slavery, in 1822 became the home of the Liverpool Royal Institution. At the time it was headed by William Roscoe, a banker, attorney, politician and also one of the nation's leading abolitionists. In 1806, as an MP, he had supported William Wilberforce's motion in Parliament that led in 1807 to the end of Britain's involvement in the slave trade. Roscoe died in June 1831, just two years before his life's work – the abolition of slavery throughout the British Empire – came to pass.

Even after this final act of abolition Liverpool continued to benefit from slavery, at least indirectly, thanks to its strong links with the slave-operated cotton plantations of the southern states of America. By the 1860s, indeed, the cotton that served the textile mills of Lancashire was Liverpool's most important cargo. The outbreak of the American Civil War in 1861 led to a reduction in the quantity imported, thanks to the naval blockade imposed by the Union north on the Confederate slave-owning south, but in some ways it strengthened the links between the English port and the Confederacy since the cash generated by the trade helped to fund the Confederacy's war effort. For a period, Liverpool became the unofficial capital abroad for the Confederacy – with 19 Abercromby Square (with the palmetto tree of South Carolina a symbol of defiance painted on the ceiling of its entrance vestibule) forming its 'White House' in exile. Liverpool also served as the Confederacy's primary – if illicit – shipbuilding resource and arsenal. Britain adopted a neutral stance during the

Civil War, but many Liverpool merchants and manufacturers did what they could to thwart embargoes and aid the Confederate cause. At its Birkenhead shipyard, for example, John Laird undertook the 'secret' construction of the swift 'commerce raider' that was subsequently named the CSS *Alabama*, and that in the two years after it slipped out of Liverpool in July 1862 with a largely Liverpudlian crew captured or burned sixty-five Union merchant ships. And Liverpool's support for the Confederacy was further demonstrated after the Civil War ended in 1865, when the commerce raider CSS *Shenandoah*, which had been fitted out in Liverpool a year earlier and whose crew had not learned of the south's defeat until four months after its surrender, crossed the Atlantic in order to avoid being charged with the capital crime of piracy, and sailed up the Mersey with its Confederate battle ensign flying, moored next to a Royal Navy warship and then dispatched a party ashore, including the ship's captain, who offered his formal surrender at the town hall. The crew of the *Shenandoah* was not disappointed in its hope of Liverpool's support and hospitality. No arrests were made and no charges levelled.

This surrender of the last cog of the Confederate apparatus of war marked – symbolically at least – the end of slavery in America and – by extension – of Liverpool's connection with goods produced through slave labour. This was the moment many Liverpool men of business had dreaded for decades. But the economy of Liverpool did not collapse. As had happened after 1833, trades in goods not related to slave labour increased, including all manner of maritime commerce, as did industry, notably shipbuilding, with Liverpool's prosperity waxing rather than waning. Britain was, in any case, remaking itself. As the historian James Walvin suggests, it had gradually become impossible to reconcile social and political reforms – notably the Reform Act of 1832 that extended the franchise in Britain – with the continuation of the ancient and barbaric institution of slavery.[48]

And what of the Heywood's building in Brunswick Street? The end of slavery did not destroy its fortunes. It remained a bank in Heywood ownership until 1883, when the family sold the building and business to the Bank of Liverpool for the enormous sum of £400,000.

The Bank of Liverpool was absorbed into Martins Bank, which in turn became part of Barclays. But the building on Brunswick Street is not now part of this banking conglomerate. Since the early twenty-first century this former financial powerhouse has been a hotel and bar. Where transactions were once hammered out is now a very contemporary and convivial interior with a long and sparkling bar, and much chatter and music. And the vaults where the bank's funds were held are now the bar's lavatories and staff offices. The shades of Liverpool's past have been obscured, if not forgotten.

Cragside, Northumberland, enlarged between 1870 and the mid 1880s to the designs of Richard Norman Shaw for Sir William Armstrong and his wife Margaret. Above: Cragside seen from the west. The library, lit by large windows in a tall bay topped by battlements and a faceted conical roof, was completed in 1872. Below: the entrance on the south front.

– 5 –
A Question of Style
Cragside, Northumberland
(1869–95)

I N THE COURSE OF the eighteenth century, out of the various
roles of surveyor, engineer or speculating builder to be seen at
work in the Liverpool of the Heywoods' time, there emerged
with ever greater clarity the profession of architect. In 1600, as the
architectural historian Howard Colvin puts it, 'there were no architects in the sense in which we understand the term today', but by
1840, 'there was an established architectural profession, based on a
regular system of pupillage and held together by the newly founded
Institute of British Architects.'[1]

The Institute of British Architects was not the first such organisation initiated by members of Britain's building fraternity. The Society
of Civil Engineers had been founded in London in 1771, the Surveyors' Club in 1792, followed in 1818 by the Institution of Civil Engineers, which evolved out of the 1771 society. Even so, for architects,
the establishment of their institute in 1834 marks a seminal moment
in the development of their vocation in Britain, because it helped
confirm the status of the architect as a professional and as a gentleman. The institute ensured that architects were governed by codes of
conduct, bye-laws and regulations expressing principled considera-
tions. It demanded of them to be not just competent in their trade
but also in possession of a broader social conscience, and to take an
almost moral attitude towards architecture and the people it served.
Many, in consequence, came to promote particular architectural styles

not only on an artistic basis, but on an ethical one, too. The evolution of the institute was rapid and reflects the speedy rise of the profession's status. It received a royal charter in 1837, and in 1848 Queen Victoria allowed it to present annually a royal gold medal to architects that met its exacting standards of professional behaviour and architectural achievement. Architects did not have to be a member of the Royal Institute of British Architects to practise, but the institute increasingly served as an invaluable reference for clients who were wondering which architect to engage.

In parallel with the foundation of the RIBA was the establishment of dedicated architectural schools (as opposed to art schools – such as that at the Royal Academy Schools, established in 1769 – that taught aspects of architecture). An early example was the Architectural Association in London, founded in 1847 and still flourishing as an independent school. Such new schools were professionally orientated and practical; they were essentially part of the early nineteenth-century Mechanics' Institute movement that offered education to aspirational working men setting out on the path to self-improvement and better employment prospects.

All these early professional institutes took the sometimes contradictory form of being part learned society – often complete with library, gentlemen's club with coffee room and restaurant – and part livery company, or trade association, dedicated to safeguarding the interests of the members. The RIBA's founding articles of 1834 make it clear that while on the one hand it was there to serve the 'general advancement of Architecture', and to promote and facilitate 'the acquirement of the knowledge of the various arts and sciences connected therewith', it also existed to champion its members and the work they wished to undertake.

Among those to rise through the architectural ranks in the decades that followed, Richard Norman Shaw was, without a doubt, one of the most outstanding. Born in Edinburgh in 1831, just when the architectural profession was starting to be regulated, his early years were somewhat peripatetic. His father, an Irish Protestant army officer, died when Shaw was barely two, leaving his mother, a member of a large and successful Edinburgh-based legal family, having to look after six children. Shaw started school in Edinburgh and then spent some time in Newcastle, where, after a brief spell of formal education, he was home-schooled by his older sister, Janet. In 1846 he and the rest of his family joined his older brother Robert, who worked for a City shipping company in London, settling in Middleton Road in the lower-middle-class suburb of Dalston. Shortly afterwards he was articled to an architect, whose identity remains unknown. In about 1849 he transferred to the London office of the Edinburgh-born architect William Burn. Aged sixty at the time, Burn had moved into the shadowland of fashion, but he had secured a good reputation as a designer of country houses, working typically in the eclectic mix of styles characteristic of the very early nineteenth century, but also becoming something of a master in what came to be known as the Scottish Baronial Revival, which mixed elements of regional domestic late Gothic with some Renaissance details in a generally idiosyncratic manner. While Burn's architecture was not particularly inspiring, in the late 1840s he did possess valuable experience and connections, and a good list of clients. A post with him, presumably secured through family connections, was a useful one to acquire, even if not particularly exciting. For inspiration and excitement, Shaw looked elsewhere.

This was the era of Samuel Smiles's *Self-Help*, a guide to the attainment of 'sound character' and the virtues of self-reliance, self-education and thrift.[2] It is not surprising, therefore, that a man such as Shaw should have anticipated Smiles's way of thinking and have sought to widen his education by taking himself off to evening lectures, notably those given at the Royal Academy of Arts by Charles Robert Cockerell, the then much-admired and committed classical architect. Cockerell had travelled widely in Greece and Italy while on a seven-year grand tour, during which he was involved in important archaeological discoveries, including those made with John Foster Jr in 1811 at the Temple of Apollo Epicurius at Bassae in Arcadia in the central Peloponnese. After Cockerell's return to England in 1817 he had become the architect for many of the most impressive classical buildings of mid nineteenth-century Britain, notably the

158 THE ENGLISH HOUSE

Cambridge University Library of 1837–4, the Ashmolean Museum and the Taylor Institution in Oxford (1841–5), and branch offices of the Bank of England in Bristol and Liverpool (1844–7). Cockerell had strong views on selecting what he regarded as the correct historical precedents for particular types of buildings. 'I am sure', he wrote, 'that the grave & solemn arch[itectur]e of Temples were never adopted to Houses', and he was scathing of those who presumed to 'stick a slice of an anc[ien]t Greek Temple to a Barn'.[3] For him, great public or institutional buildings required the solemn grandeur and cultural pedigree of classicism. Although Cockerell was ready to question which historic style might be appropriate for different types of modern buildings, he was not ready to question the role of historic styles or conceive of a modern architecture that was entirely liberated from cultural and decorative references to the past. This assumption about the creative role of history seems not to have been lost on the young Norman Shaw.

From 1854 to 1856, thanks to a Royal Academy scholarship, Shaw undertook an architectural and sketching tour through Europe. On his return to London he secured a position, in around 1856, in the office of Burn's younger contemporary George Edmund Street, then advancing rapidly as a church architect, and who in 1868 was to secure a major commission when he won the competition to build the Royal Courts of Justice (now the Law Courts) in the Strand in London. Shaw spent a number of years with Street, perfecting his drafting skills and learning the practicalities of his profession: how 'to conceive of volume and space in architecture'. Later he would say that 'he learnt all he knew about architecture that was worth knowing in this period' while working at Street's architectural practice.[4] While there he worked briefly with Philip Webb, who would soon leave to work with another of Street's apprentices, William Morris, and who, like Morris, would become a major figure in the world of late Victorian design and architecture.

In 1863 Shaw left Street to set up practice with his close friend, the architect William Eden Nesfield, whom he had met in Burn's office. Together they developed what became known as the 'Old

English style', promoted from the early 1850s by the architect George Devey, and largely inspired by picturesque vernacular domestic architecture built between the Middle Ages and the seventeenth century. Shaw's projects at this time were relatively few. Even so, he established enough of a reputation to be invited in 1869 by the industrialist William Armstrong and his wife, Margaret, to view a small shooting lodge the couple had built in the Northumberland countryside in the early 1860s that they wished to alter and extend. Gradually, the clients and Shaw would transform it into a completely new house that would become known as Cragside.

The setting chosen for such a project could not have been more dramatic. Cragside sits in secluded splendour upon steeply rising land in what was once a rough and undulating heath, about thirty miles north from Newcastle upon Tyne at Rothbury, just inland from Alnwick on the east edge of what is now the Northumberland National Park. The project itself promised to be both an exciting and rewarding one, for Shaw's patron, the second generation in a family of self-made men, had both the money and ambition to create something truly exceptional.

William Armstrong's father was a corn merchant who rose from trading on the Newcastle quayside to a position of great wealth and political power, becoming the town's mayor in 1850. Armstrong himself, born in 1810, was trained for the law but his dominant interest was engineering, technological innovation and invention. This is hardly surprising. In the 1830s Newcastle and the surrounding northeast was one of the nation's great powerhouses and, rich in natural resources such as coal, a centre of manufacturing and industry. Iron, coal and steam became the region's lifeblood, with railways, bridge- and shipbuilding and the improvement of the means of maritime commerce the focus of its heavy industry. In all these enterprises the quest for better ways of doing things – ways that were faster, stronger, more economic – became critical, and were almost invariably based on a new mastery of materials coupled with audacious innovation and emerging technology. The early nineteenth-century phase of Britain's Industrial Revolution threw up such men (often of pure genius) in remarkable number: the mining engineer Richard Trevithick, who from 1801 pioneered steam-powered road and rail engines; mechanical engineer George Stephenson, who in 1825 launched the proposition of passenger-carrying, steam-powered railways; and Isambard Kingdom Brunel, who took these ideas and from the early 1830s forged the modern world of long-range, integrated steam-powered and iron-built transport, with a system stretching from London via Bristol to New York. And, of course, there was Armstrong. All these men were, in their sensibilities, powers of invention and single-minded strength of imagination, artists as much as engineers and technocrats. They were able to imagine the future and, having seen it in their mind's eye, possessed the ability, confidence and commitment to find the physical means to make the dream a reality.

While still a teenager, Armstrong's feeling for engineering had drawn him to William Ramshaw's engineering works, located near his grammar school in Bishop Auckland, County Durham. Here Armstrong met Ramshaw's daughter Margaret. She was six years his senior and a very eligible young woman, being the daughter of a successful professional engineer and businessman. When they met, Armstrong was little more than sixteen and still at school. It was almost inevitable that Margaret would, initially at least, have been the dominant partner in this relationship, and was probably one of the key forces in Armstrong's subsequent rise to engineering prominence. He went on to study law in London, and in 1835, two years after he had returned to Newcastle to practise as a solicitor, the couple was married. Armstrong pursued a career as a solicitor for fourteen years, indulging his passion for mechanics and engineering in his spare time. While pursuing this hobby he devised in 1843 a 'hydraulic machine' that generated electricity by friction, and in 1847 founded W. G. Armstrong and Co. at Elswick, Newcastle, to manufacture hydraulic machinery capable of operating cranes and mobile bridges. Inspired by the extraordinary range of cutting-edge technology on show at the Great Exhibition in London in 1851, and motivated by the outbreak of the Crimean War in October 1852 to help Britain's war effort, he then developed a new passion: artillery. He rapidly devised a novel weapon that was breech-loading, and with a barrel that was rifled and reinforced with 'sleeves' of wrought iron, all of which enabled Armstrong's weapon to fire a dynamically superior conical shot faster, further and with greater accuracy and power than any of its rivals. At a stroke he revolutionised the design and manufacture of ordnance that soon made Elswick the centre of a huge international arms market. In 1887 he would be raised to the peerage as a baron, largely as a result of his wide range of engineering achievements and his pre-eminence as an arms manufacturer and pioneer.

By the time Armstrong and his wife had decided to expand their lodge at Cragside, they had more than sufficient funds to indulge a vision that would become ever more ambitious. The question was: what architectural style should they, in consultation with Norman Shaw, adopt for their grand new house?

* * * * *

The middle decades of the nineteenth century were ones of tumultuous change in Britain. Rapid industrialisation and an accompanying expansion of towns were transforming the lives of millions, sometimes for the better, but often – certainly in the short term – for the worse. Skilled craftsmen found themselves replaced by machines. Those who elected to move from the countryside to the town in search of work often ended up having to endure appalling conditions in decaying slums. For men such as Karl Marx's friend and collaborator Friedrich Engels, Britain had become a profit-driven land in which entrepreneurs and industrialists had forged a selfish, materialistic and heartless society, where the poor, if deemed unproductive, were suffered to starve in despair. Engels described how in the capital of Britain's empire, London, it was not unusual to find 'a man, his wife, four or five children, and, sometimes, both grandparents' all living in a single room 'of ten to twelve feet square'. In his *The Condition of the Working Class in England*, first published in 1845, he quoted an article from *The Times* that in October 1843 observed of London 'that within the most courtly precincts of the richest city of God's earth, there may be found, night after night ... Women – young in years – old in sin and suffering – outcasts from society – ROTTING FROM FAMINE, FILTH and DISEASE'.[5]

The political response to the challenges of this new Britain was varied and complex. Some defended a laissez-faire capitalism that rewarded a fair few and left others to fend for themselves. Others argued for a degree of state intervention to mitigate the worst effects of rural and urban poverty. At a popular level, the Chartist movement sought to remedy inequality through a demand for constitutional reform that, among other things, would open the franchise much wider than the Reform Act of 1832 had done by extending the vote beyond the property-owning middle class to working men. Chartism ultimately fizzled out in 1848 – a year of revolution elsewhere in Europe. Thereafter, working-class political energies were devoted to trade-union activity.

The uncertainties of the era were, to an extent, reflected in the arts, and particularly in architecture. In a rapidly changing world, the set forms of the immediate past were called into question. At a time when England was in a state of flux, debates were had about what style, if any, could be deemed quintessentially 'English'. At the same time a new, almost spiritual, dimension was perceived. Architectural style or taste, it seemed, was now a moral as well as an aesthetic issue.

For the previous nearly 300 years Britain had been gripped by the Continental Renaissance and its championing of the classical world. The pagan architecture of Rome and then of Greece had inspired all manner of building types, from cathedrals and churches to palaces, houses, inns, banks and town halls. Combined with this general architectural tendency was another that, at times, could appear to be contradictory: a desire for variety, and a willingness to choose a style to capture a mood or evoke romance and pleasing nostalgia. All was playful and changeful, and the approach eclectic, expressed for example in the mid eighteenth century by non-scholarly and far from authentic 'Gothick' or rococo chinoiserie architecture.

While classical styles were in the ascendancy, the authentic Gothic architecture of the medieval period languished. But by the last decades of the eighteenth century that judgement was being re-examined, and an appreciation of medieval architecture, along with an admiration for its engineering excellence, was becoming apparent. In the mid 1770s the London-based stone carver and illustrator John Carter published carefully observed drawings of Gothic buildings in the *Builders' Magazine*. These promoted an archaeologically correct approach to the design of modern Gothic architecture that he argued was the natural style for ecclesiastical structures. Carter became embroiled in the battle to save authentic Gothic architecture from the hands of the ignorant or insensitive who were set on illiterate or conjectural restorations. In his *Ancient Architecture of England*, published from 1795 to 1814, he not only offered a highly informed and sensitive representation of Gothic architecture (which he termed 'pointed architecture' after its most distinct and crucial use of the strong and highly abatable pointed arch), but also suggested a chronological development in distinct phases. The architect and antiquary Thomas Rickman developed aspects of Carter's work when in 1817 he published the first attempt to establish a chronological evolution and terminology for Gothic architecture, much of it based on a close and personal observation of key details such as window tracery, shafts, ribs and vaults. His book, *An Attempt to Discriminate the Styles of English Architecture*, introduced the classifications, based on evidence of a style evolving through time, that are still in use: 'Early English', 'Decorated Gothic' and 'Perpendicular'. The key point he established was that Gothic was not chaotic but had developed in a coherent manner within a distinct and admirable discipline.

Carter and Rickman established that Gothic was as sophisticated and ordered in design as classical architecture, and certainly not the 'barbarous' style without rules that had previously been assumed. For his part, Augustus Welby Northmore Pugin took the argument to a new level in the mid 1830s when he suggested that it embodied a moral sensibility and a constructional excellence beyond classical architecture. Born in 1812 to a French émigré, Pugin had learned his architecture in the old way, partly coached by his father, Auguste Pugin, who worked as an architectural draughtsman and book illustrator, and partly learning from study tours he undertook in France. For a while he worked as a furniture and theatre designer, before entering the architectural profession with gusto in the late 1830s. Swiftly establishing himself as the epitome of the architect with a moral conscience, he entertained dogmatic views of the wrong and the right ways to design and build, not just for the client but for the spiritual benefit of society. Wrong was the continuation of the classical tradition, in which the spark of creativity was long dead. Right was to revive Gothic, or pointed, architecture, because it had greater structural potential and honesty in its relationship between materials and modes of construction, was Christian not pagan in origin, and was, in some senses, native to the British soil. Pugin therefore not only raised the Gothic as a potent contender to the long-dominant classical tradition, but also positioned the architect as a moral arbiter of taste.

Pugin's views were expressed forcefully in his illustrated books *Contrasts*, published in 1836, and *The True Principles of Pointed or Christian Architecture*, published in 1841. The polemical nature of the former was embodied in its subtitle: 'Or, a Parallel between Noble Edifices of the Middle Ages, and Corresponding Buildings of the Present Day, Shewing the Present Decay of Taste'. The missionary zeal of the latter was expressed in a series of punchy aphorisms that attempted to identify the principles that the best ancient Gothic architecture expressed and that new Gothic should emulate. According to him, 'the two great rules for design are ... 1st, that there should be no features about a building which are not necessary for convenience, construction, or propriety; 2nd, that all ornament should consist of enrichment of the essential construction of a building.'

The first rule echoes one of the ancient strictures seeking to define the qualities of good architecture. As early as the first century BC, the Roman architect and theorist Vitruvius had in his *De architectura* (*On Architecture*) stated that architecture should possess '*firmitas*', '*utilitas*' and '*venustas*': strength, utility, and delight or beauty. The first two qualities were self-evident. The third, essentially the refinement of utility by the addition of non-functional but beautiful details, was what, for the Romans, raised building to the lofty realm of architecture. Pugin's thinking follows essentially the same lines, although, instead of '*venustas*' he uses the word 'propriety'.

As for his second rule, he contrasted most contemporary architecture – where 'ornaments are actually constructed' – with an ideal approach where ornaments form 'the decoration of construction, to which in good taste they should be always subservient'. He also argued that in 'pure architecture the smallest detail should have a meaning or serve a purpose' and that 'the construction itself should vary with the material employed, and the designs should be adapted to the material in which they are executed.' That by 'pure architecture' Pugin meant Gothic is made clear in his assertion that 'strange as it may appear . . . it is in pointed architecture alone that these great principles have been carried out.'[6] To reinforce this argument, Pugin praised the engineering and structural superiority of ideal Gothic architecture as superior to classical architecture, especially as regards masonry construction: 'A pointed church is the masterpiece of masonry. It is essentially a stone building; its pillars, its arches, its vaults, its intricate intersections, its ramified tracery are all peculiar to stone, and could not be consistently executed in any other material.'[7] The result, he argued, is engineered elegance, with strength achieved in a minimal and skeletal manner through skilful design and construction. Overall, his second rule implies that there is a rational discipline underpinning Gothic architecture – akin to the governing orders of classical architecture – that would, for most casual observers, have been a novelty in the early 1840s.

Pugin was disparaging of classical architecture. For him, 'Grecian architecture is essentially wooden in its construction', and he expressed surprise and contempt 'that when the Greeks commenced building in stone, the properties of this material did not suggest to them some different and improved mode of construction'. In his view, 'the finest temple of the Greeks is constructed on the same principles as a large wooden cabin.' That such classical buildings should have been 'held up as the standard of architectural excellence, and the types from which our present buildings are to be formed, is a monstrous absurdity, which has originated in the blind admiration . . . for everything Pagan, to the prejudice and overthrow of Christian art and propriety'.[8]

Pugin's morality revolved around the principle, ancient in origin, that truth and beauty (by which he meant 'pure' as opposed to 'decadent' beauty) are intertwined. 'Pointed architecture', he declared, 'does not conceal her construction, but beautifies it', while 'classic architecture seeks to conceal instead of decorating it.'[9] So the honest expression of the materials and means of construction – a virtue of the best of Gothic architecture, according to Pugin – was a fundamental architectural issue. It is perhaps telling that, when it came to truth, honesty and beauty, Pugin revealed that he perceived elegant Gothic as feminine. For most mid Victorian males, truth, honesty and beauty were the ideal female attributes.

Pugin's life was in many ways a difficult one. His first wife died in childbirth in 1832 (he went on to have two more wives and ultimately eight children), and his decision to convert to Roman Catholicism, in a Protestant country that had granted Catholics full civil rights only in 1829 and continued to regard them with a degree of hostility, was met with suspicion. He tried to forge an architectural career designing churches for the new Catholic dioceses but found that the English Catholic Church tended to prefer the baroque classicism of the seventeenth-century Roman Catholic Counter-Reformation to newfangled Gothic Revivalism. To make matters worse, his usual clients were desperately short of funds, which meant that many of the commissions Pugin did secure were underfunded to a woeful extent. Added to all that, he was a perfectionist with an obsessive, unforgiving eye for detail in a world that was far less exacting. His visions were therefore often executed in a compromised or economic manner or not completed quite as envisioned. 'I have passed my life in thinking of fine things, studying fine things, designing fine things, and realizing very poor ones,' he wrote shortly before his death.[10]

The compromised nature of so many of his buildings greatly diminished the impression his architecture made at the time and still undermines his legacy. His first major church – St Mary's in Derby, started in 1838 – has a simple and almost mechanical quality to its construction, and its proposed 100-foot spire was never built. St George's in Southwark, started the following year, was also not completed as designed due to lack of funds. When the church was finally opened for worship in 1848 it met with harsh criticism, partly because of its economic structure, largely of yellow stock bricks, far from Gothic in feel, and partly because of its stunted appearance due to the failure to compete the tower or add the planned spire (wartime damage has made the church's appearance yet more denuded). More successful built examples of Pugin's Gothic theories are St Giles' in Cheadle, Staffordshire, started in 1841 for the Catholic 16th Earl of Shrewsbury (an ideal patron for Pugin), and finished in rich and high style in 1846 with much Gothic ornament, including a sensationally painted interior and polychromic floor tiles that proclaimed the pre-Puritan beauty of England's medieval Catholic ecclesiastical interiors; and St Mary's Cathedral in Newcastle upon Tyne, built between 1842 and 1844 and complete with spire. Arguably best is St Augustine's in Ramsgate, Kent, which was built from 1845, next to the home – The Grange – that Pugin had designed for himself in 1843 in functional-ist Gothic manner.

The most significant – and now best known – expressions of Pugin's Gothic are for a building he did not design and that largely relate to furniture, fabric and interior decoration rather than to archi-tectural structure. In 1834 the Palace of Westminster, incorporating the Houses of Parliament, was devastated by fire. A royal commission was established in 1835 to secure the design for a new building and an architectural competition launched, with a brief that did much to promote and legitimise the mounting interest in Gothic architecture. The new building was not to be in the long-established classical style but to be English in character, either Gothic or Elizabethan. This was partly to ensure that the new building would harmonise with the authentic Gothic and Tudor fragments that survived the fire (notably the eleventh- and fourteenth-century Westminster Hall) and also complement the early Tudor chapel of Henry VII at the east end of the nearby Westminster Abbey. The brief thrust the Gothic Revival centre stage. Ninety-seven proposals were submitted anonymously and entry number 64, showing a Tudor-style palace harmonising happily with the few surviving fragments, was chosen unanimously. The entry turned out to have been designed by the eminent classicist Charles Barry, best known in 1835 for his eclectic mix of not particularly scholarly Gothic-style parish churches and classical institutional buildings such as the Manchester Institution of Fine Arts (now the Manchester Art Gallery) of 1824, and the Italianate Travellers Club, Pall Mall, of 1830.

Having won the competition, Barry had a problem. How to deliver a convincing Tudor-Gothic-style design that would secure the commission? For that he turned to the 23-year-old Pugin (who that year had published *Gothic Furniture*), engaging him not only to produce the Gothic detail required for the Palace of Westminster interiors but also interior designs for the King Edward VI Grammar School in Birmingham. There followed a decade of unremitting toil on this and other projects. The House of Lords, with lavish and beautiful interiors created by Pugin, was opened in 1847. The monumental Clock Tower (now the Elizabeth Tower), the design of which Barry delegated to Pugin in 1843, was not finally completed until 1859.

By the 1850s, the medieval styles championed by Pugin were gaining a wider following among architects. A key figure here was George Gilbert Scott, a year Pugin's senior. He had started his architectural career working on classically inspired buildings for the architect Henry Roberts and then on simple classical workhouses with his slightly younger contemporary William Bonython Moffatt. But as a boy in the 1820s, he had developed a passion for sketching Gothic churches, and when he encountered Pugin's writings he was – as he put it in his memoir *Recollections*, published after his death in 1878 – woken from his 'slumbers' by their 'thunder'. His first significant Gothic church (St Giles', Camberwell, started in 1842) was archaeologically correct in its use of the Gothic language, materials and construction techniques. At roughly the same time he designed for a site in Oxford the equally archaeologically impressive Martyrs' Memorial (completed in 1843), based on the late thirteenth-century Eleanor Cross at Waltham Cross, Hertfordshire. Soon after these projects

The interior of the House of Lords, in the Palace of Westminster, designed by Sir Charles Barry but with details and furnishings by A. W. N. Pugin. The interior was largely completed by 1847.

the young G. E. Street joined Scott's office, where he remained until the late 1840s, seemingly engaged primarily to 'improve' the quality of the Gothic detail that the practice designed. Scott's appetite for work was voracious (he was to design or alter over 800 buildings by the time of his death in 1878) and he readily embraced the opportunities being offered for the repair of old churches. Too often, though, his repairs led to conjectural restoration and ruthless rebuilding with authenticity sacrificed. Such activities were one of the reasons why, in 1877, Shaw's former colleagues – Philip Webb and William Morris – founded the Society for the Protection of Ancient Buildings.

In parallel with Scott's early and influential Gothic Revival architecture, the art historian and polemicist John Ruskin also played a key role in promoting the style. In *The Stones of Venice*, published from 1851 to 1853, Ruskin championed the constructional potential of Gothic and its inspired use of materials. Rather than looking to northern Europe for inspiration, as Pugin had done, however, he turned to the medieval Gothic of Venice. His recommendation made some headway, and certainly his enthusiasm for Venetian 'constructional polychromy' – where colour is given to architecture not through the superficial use of paint or tinted plaster but by means of the hues of the materials of construction – struck a chord and became a significant influence on mid to late Victorian Gothic.

* * * * *

In June 1849 a meeting was held in Buckingham Palace that was to play a hugely significant role in the development of the aesthetic tastes of the nation. Ostensibly, it was primarily concerned not with art and architecture, but with industry, manufacturing, applied arts and the potential of emerging technology to change the world and create wealth, while promoting and celebrating Britain's leading role in these fields. Perhaps most significant and all-embracing was its focus on education, and the acquisition of knowledge by the British working man. Better equipped, and with his artistic taste and skills improved, those who attended the meeting believed, he would become a far more useful artisan, and in consequence be better paid and more secure. It was, in some ways, a practical and cultural response to the social and political turmoil of the 1840s and the great final rally of the Chartists in April 1848, when it was claimed by different accounts that between 20,000 and 400,000 people gathered on Kennington Common demanding political reform.[11]

Those present at Buckingham Palace that day included the energetic, progressive and astute Prince Albert – the Prince Consort – and Henry Cole, the chairman of the council of the Society for the Encouragement of Arts, Manufactures and Commerce.[12] Cole was a pugnacious and determined government official who had served as assistant keeper of the Public Record Office, and who in 1839 had become embroiled in a complex reform of the postal service that in 1840 saw the successful introduction of the uniform post-rate of one penny and the arrival of the 'penny black' stamp. In large part this success was due to the fusion of art and science: the use of the stamp was made secure by the elegance of its design and the technical sophistication of its production and printing (all things that made a convincing forgery very difficult to achieve). Although Cole did not play a major role in this particular endeavour – the dominant figure was Rowland Hill – the new stamp did epitomise his evolving interest in the integration of art with science and the manufacturing potential of the pioneering technology of the 'modern' age. These interests were combined with something else: an almost evangelical belief in the power of education to change all for the better. It was not a new idea in itself (as already observed, its origins were rooted in the Mechanics' Institute movement of the very early nineteenth century). But Cole gave it a new force and energy.

By the end of the meeting it had been resolved that a 'Great Exhibition of the Works of Industry of All Nations' should be held on Crown-owned land on the south side of Hyde Park in a purpose-built and suitably large exhibition hall, with half the space dedicated to British products, and half to products from abroad. It was to be a colossal international display of the manufacturing power and technological ingenuity of Britain's industry.[13]

The design for the exhibition hall was opened up to public

competition, and within three weeks the Great Exhibitions Building Committee had received 245 entries from Britain and Europe. All were rejected as unsuitable for a brief that demanded not only a huge structure containing over 900,000 square feet of space, but one that could be built economically and speedily, that would be temporary and that would do minimal damage to the site in Hyde Park. Driven by a growing sense of urgency, Henry Cole took matters into his own hands and turned to a man who had already established an impressive record for creating large, lightweight structures. As head gardener at Chatsworth House, Joseph Paxton had won considerable acclaim for the 'Great Stove' conservatory he had constructed there between 1836 and 1840 for the Duke of Devonshire – an ingenious and ambitious glass-sheathed structure of columns and beams of cast iron (with laminated timber for the external ribs), nearly 330 feet long and 124 feet wide, and with a vaulted central nave rising nearly 70 feet, which, at the time, was the largest glass-clad building in Britain. (Sadly it was demolished in 1920.) Paxton had then gone on, in 1849, to design the Victoria Regia House, or Lily House, also at Chatsworth, where he had managed to achieve great strength in a minimal manner by emulating the lattice-like and immensely sturdy giant leaves of the water lilies the building was designed to house. For this building he had abandoned laminated timber and fixed his glazed 'curtain walling' within semicircular arched iron frames. Elements of the design were perhaps inspired by the recently completed Palm House in Kew Gardens.[14]

Paxton's initial sketch for the Great Exhibition hall was made in early June 1850 on a piece of pink blotting paper during a board meeting of the Midland Railway, of which he was a director. The sketch was in essence a vastly enlarged version of his Victoria Regia House, utilising its ridge-and-furrow roofing system that could be glazed while also being immensely strong and quick to construct.

If Pugin represented a revival of the medieval past, Paxton stood for the possibilities of the industrial present. His embracing of cast iron, wrought iron and glass were attuned to what was now technically possible and would soon be utilised to build the stations and vast roofs of the termini of the great technological triumph of the age: the railway. At the same time, his structures possessed simple forms that were dictated almost entirely by their function, and the materials he employed meant that superfluous ornament was almost, if not entirely, absent. His plans for the Great Exhibition were not welcomed by all – in part, because their late entry breached competition rules – but Paxton, almost certainly with the encouragement of Cole, and thus no doubt of the prince, decided to bypass opposing voices and go public with his scheme, publishing his proposal in the *Illustrated London News* to almost universal acclaim.

The vast hall that followed was a triumph not just of design but of building technique. It was modular, with repetitive arch-topped prefabricated frames of cast iron that were delivered to site and assembled to form the facades, fitted with newly developed large sheets of plate glass set in minimal timber frames. Special assembly mechanisms and trolleys were designed to speed construction, so that one labourer could fix 108 panes in a day. In the end it took 2,000 men just less than eight months to build the 1,848-feet-long and 405-feet-wide 'Crystal Palace' at a cost of a relatively modest £79,800, which was well within budget. Three thousand, five hundred tons of cast iron was used, but also a considerable amount of wrought iron for the structural elements that required great tensile strength, notably the ribs forming the glazed barrel vault set above the transept that crossed the main nave-like axis of the hall. This semicircular 108-foot-high vaulted transept, with its huge terminal fanlights, does not appear on Paxton's initial sketch. It was in part a belated response to a public outcry against the removal of a number of venerable elm trees that the erection of the exhibition hall seemed certain to entail but which could be retained by being accommodated within the tall transept.

Reactions among Paxton's peers to his Crystal Palace varied. The historian and philosopher Thomas Carlyle dismissed it as no more than a big glass soap bubble. He evidently missed, in the exhibition hall's strident functionality, the expected display of cultural pedigree expressed through learned ornament. John Ruskin, predictably, felt

Inside the transept of the Crystal Palace, in Hyde Park, London, in 1851. Designed by Joseph Paxton, the palace was a temporary structure, fabricated largely of iron and glass, with the transept partly designed to accommodate the large trees that occupied the site.

much the same as Carlyle, viewing the Crystal Palace as no more than an over-grown utilitarian conservatory, a mere building, not architecture. In his opinion, a 'building', as he explained in *The Seven Lamps of Architecture*, published in May 1849, is purely functional or utilitarian. For it to achieve the poetry of 'architecture', then some 'unnecessary feature' needs to be incorporated, such as 'a cable moulding added to the outline of a bastion'. Ruskin's view was that 'architecture concerns itself only with those characters of an edifice which are above and beyond its common use'; essentially that architecture emerges through decorative additions that are 'useless' but that delight or bestow cultural pedigree.[15] So far as he was concerned, the minimalism of the exhibition building precluded any consideration of it as architecture.

Ruskin's view was not an uncommon one at the time. The notion that modern buildings constructed in a modern manner using new materials should define their own modern aesthetic was one that few, if any, contemporaries seriously entertained. Indeed, it was not until the 1890s that such a novel theory, championed by the US architect Louis Sullivan, started to take hold. In a series of manifesto-like articles Sullivan, one of the pioneers of steel-framed 'skyscrapers', argued that 'form ever follows function' in architecture as well as in engineered structures like bridges, and that buildings standing in the 'nude' – naked of history-inspired ornament – 'may convey a noble and dignified sentiment by virtue of mass and proportion' and in consequence be 'greatly to our aesthetic good'.[16]

Pugin had been engaged to create within Paxton's iron-and-glass frame a 'medieval court', in which was displayed an array of Gothic-inspired ecclesiastical sculpture, metalwork and textiles, and so to an extent his views were bound to be somewhat compromised and complex. He can hardly have approved of Paxton's use of modern materials (nowhere in Pugin's writings is there any concession to the potential offered by new and emerging building technology or to the demands made by new building types). Yet the Crystal Palace did express many of his principles of good architectural taste. Notably, structure and materials were honestly expressed rather than concealed, and 'ornament' was not 'constructed' in superficial and irrelevant manner but 'confined to the enrichment of construction'.[17] It could also be argued that, with its cruciform plan, incorporating nave, aisles, galleries and transepts, the Crystal Palace did evoke associations with ancient church architecture and that a very few cast-iron components possessed Gothic-style profiles – notably the stanchions, or vertical supports, separating the nave from the aisles – even if the consistent and coherent array of historic ornament was absent. Even so, Pugin did suggest that Paxton had best keep to building greenhouses.

The contents on display in the Crystal Palace were extraordinarily diverse. They ranged from Pugin's neo-medieval church furniture, to vibrating and well-oiled machines, as well as mass-produced and immaculately engineered weapons such as Samuel Colt's 1851 Navy revolver and Alfred Krupp's six-pound cannon. There were also sculptures of such popular Dickensian characters as Oliver Twist and Little Nell. All of these, Henry Cole hoped, would not only entertain and educate but also improve popular taste, particularly in the applied arts and in the crafts, and raise the artistic standard of British manufacturing, so making the nation more commercially successful on the world stage. He pursued this theme immediately after the exhibition closed in mid October 1851 by persuading the Treasury to provide a grant of £5,000 to start a Museum of Manufactures, of which he became director, and which was to be housed temporarily in the Crown-owned early eighteenth-century Marlborough House in St James's, Westminster.

Here he sought to further his crusade by organising an exhibition in which the rules of good taste were explained and eighty-seven objects displaying unfortunate bad taste were put on show in his 'Gallery of False Principles', with their errors described. A little tactlessly, however, this was not a Salon des Refusés, displaying objects rejected by the organisers of the Great Exhibition. Far from it. Many of the objects chosen by Cole had been displayed in the Crystal Palace. But he was fearless in his criticism, insisting that taste was an objective business governed by immutable laws. Most of these were familiar and related to proportion and geometry, or the use of colour, or involved exhortations not to take nature as too direct an inspiration or use it in an inappropriate manner, as did one hapless Great Exhibition entrant who was held up for scorn because he had designed a gas lamp to look like a convolvulus. Other of Cole's rules were derived from Pugin's strictures about the moral rightness and beauty of medieval Gothic design and construction: for example, that ornament should have a rational relationship to structure. It perhaps goes without saying that in none of his rules on taste did Cole question the use of history or tradition as inspiration for the design or ornamentation of modern artefacts or architecture. The only issue he had was the way in which history was used; for him, it was a matter of legitimate use or crass abuse.

It is often now hard for us to see where the line was drawn and what distinguishes charming and eccentric Victorian design from the banal and the tasteless. And Cole's certainties did not go unchallenged at the time. Affronted manufacturers complained bitterly. Charles Dickens took exception to what he felt was Cole's sneering at the tastes of the common man. Indeed, he went so far as to commission an article from Henry Morley for *Household Words*, published in December 1852, in which Mr Crumpet, having visited what had become known as the 'Chamber of Horrors' at Marlborough House, returns a broken man to his humble home in Brixton 'ashamed of the pattern of my own trowsers' because he has seen 'a piece of them hung up there' as an example of 'bad taste'. Cole was unapologetic. He went on to lobby for the construction of a purpose-designed building for the Museum of Manufactures on the recently acquired Brompton Estate, and when in 1857 it moved there from Somerset House (the temporary home after Marlborough House) he was retained as director. The new museum gradually expanded as it acquired more decorative and applied arts and crafts from around the world with the primary aim – true to Cole's ethos and to that of the Great Exhibition – of improving the taste and knowledge of working people involved in manufacturing. To this end the museum opened in the evenings and was fitted with gas lighting so that it could be visited after work hours, and was furnished with a cafeteria (an unprecedented concept for museums at the time). From 1899, after yet further enlargement in grandiose baroque style, it became known as the Victoria and Albert Museum.[18]

Although the Great Exhibition championed modern building techniques and manufacturing, it also inspired a backlash against them. Among those present in Hyde Park in 1851 was the seventeen-year-old William Morris, who had been taken there for the day by his family. Horrified at what he saw as the promotion of machine-age design in the pursuit of wealth, he refused to enter the exhibition. Over the following years he would become a fierce critic of technology that in his view could only reduce craftsmen to mere cogs in a vast machine of mass production which would, he argued, undermine the laws of beauty and good taste. Instead he promoted a very different world view in which traditional craft principles would assume pride of place. A return to these, he believed, would restore dignity and individuality to the craftsman, as he imagined had been the case in the Middle Ages. As for the Crystal Palace itself, it was, in Morris's view, 'wonderfully ugly'.

* * * * *

If Morris's reaction against the aesthetics of the Great Exhibition, and Pugin's and Ruskin's Gothic enthusiasms, imply that by the time Shaw came to design Cragside the way forward was clear, that was certainly not the case. For while the Gothic style continued to gain adherents, classical architecture with its many permutations – Greek, Roman, Renaissance/Italianate – still held its own for public and institutional buildings, and largely for domestic architecture, particularly for urban sites. Curiously, either style was used indiscriminately for new building types such as railway stations and termini and hotels of unprecedented large scale. As Mark Girouard observed, 'with classical Victorian country houses one always suspects either new city money or worldly owners, bringing a touch of smart London drawing rooms down to the country.'[19] In contrast the 'Old English style' was regarded as an expression of patriotic values and took two distinct architectural forms. If a client aspired to the traditional virtues of an

English country gentleman, 'he would tend to the Elizabethan' – a gentle vernacular hybrid of Gothic with some Renaissance detail and form – and if he saw himself 'as a Christian English Gentleman', he would go full Gothic.[20]

Shaw must have visited the Great Exhibition (he was, after all, living and working in London in 1851), although, as far as it's known, he failed to record his impression. Certainly, the architectural issues to which the exhibition drew attention – the rule of 'taste', the use of history in design, the role of evolving technology – cannot have failed to have made an impact on him. At that time, he, like many of his young fellow architects, was a great admirer of Pugin. Indeed, in September 1852 he, with his close friend William Eden Nesfield, made the pilgrimage to Ramsgate to view Pugin's church of St Augustine. The timing was uncanny. Pugin had died just three days before, ground down by excessive zeal and hard work which had unbalanced his reason and ultimately driven him to a nervous breakdown. His funeral was a sparsely attended affair: a few of Pugin's decorator friends, fellow Goths and church builders were there; Sir Charles Barry – recently knighted for his work at Westminster while the dead man seemed already forgotten – carried a candle in homage.[21] For Shaw and Nesfield, then just twenty and having recently entered the architectural profession, their chance attendance must have seemed a little like stumbling upon the unceremonious and hasty entombment of Christ, and the candle that Barry was carrying an architectural torch to be handed on to the next generation.[22] It seems certain that Barry, Shaw and Nesfield conversed, because shortly after, with the support of Nesfield's father, the landscape architect and Waterloo veteran William Andrews Nesfield, Barry gave the young men, during the winter of 1852–3, the chance to climb over the scaffolding still in the Palace of Westminster so they could make close-up sketches of Pugin's details. Their sketchbooks survive,[23] with the Pugin details – crestings, escutcheons, bell pulls – recorded alongside other details, some medieval Gothic, others modern.[24] These sketchbooks are a vivid reminder that for these young men history was a living thing, and while they took inspiration from the new work of Pugin, old buildings were still a vital source of information and inspiration on which to found a contemporary architecture in the Gothic style and spirit.

It must have seemed, then, that when a major new building for the Foreign Office in Whitehall was proposed in late 1858, the style adopted for it would be Gothic. Sir Charles Barry's nearby Palace of Westminster, completed just six years earlier, had already established the 'fitness' of Gothic not just for churches but for public buildings, even if by the 1850s the particular form of Gothic adopted there was thought to be something of a degenerate and repetitive one, chosen in the 1830s not out of true conviction or as an expression of antiquarian scholarship, but because it was thought to be a broadly English style that complemented that of buildings nearby. Now George Gilbert Scott, who was in line for the new Foreign Office commission, wanted to build in the earlier and purer Gothic of the thirteenth and fourteenth centuries – the 'Middle Pointed', or 'Decorated', period. In December 1858 the new project was enlarged when Scott was told he was also to design the new India Office on an adjoining site. This dramatic increase in the scale of the project created some dismay and jealousy in the upper echelons of the architectural profession. Sir Matthew Digby Wyatt, one of the main bureaucratic forces behind the success of the Great Exhibition and since 1855 surveyor to the East India Company, instantly submitted a protest to the Secretary of State for India. Wyatt argued that the design of this pair of large government offices would be too much for one architectural practice to handle. No immediate official response was forthcoming, but much must have been going on behind the scenes because in late December Scott volunteered to hand 'special direction of the interior' of the India Office commission to Wyatt, while retaining 'general command of the external design'.[25] Egos soothed, in January 1859 Scott received his letter of appointment.

Scott, aged forty-eight, the recent nominee for the Royal Institute of British Architects' royal gold medal for architecture, and at the pinnacle of his profession, must have believed that, with this generous and politic gesture to Wyatt, all the major problems with the project had been resolved. He was wrong.

On Friday, 11 February 1859, a squabble arose in Parliament when the MP William Tite asked why the first premium design for the Foreign Office by Charles Barry Jr (the eldest son of Sir Charles Barry) and his partner, Robert Richardson Banks, executed in the 'Italian style of architecture' (meaning classical), had been passed over in favour of Scott's Gothic scheme. Tite, who was himself an architect and master of the classical style, went on to observe that of the 220 competition entries, 200 had been in the 'Italian Style' and only 10 in the Gothic, an imbalance, he argued, that implied most architects appreciated that the 'Italian style would be more suitable to the wants of common life'. The MP also suggested that Scott's plans would be inconvenient and expensive. An informal debate ensued about the relative virtues of Gothic and classical architecture, during which fear was expressed that such differing views on architectural styles would result in a Foreign Office that would be Gothic and a neighbouring India Office that would be classical. The irascible Lord Palmerston, until recently prime minister and still a man of great political power and influence, had evidently been listening closely to the debate and, with a display more of sardonic humour than irritation, rose to his feet and rattled off an impromptu speech that was met with cheers and good-natured laughter. He suggested that Scott was lucky to have secured the commission, particularly since proposing a Gothic design was going back 'to the barbarism of the Dark Ages'. And, Palmerston continued, since Scott 'was a person of great talent' who had studied the Greek and Italian styles, it would be best, if he wanted to retain the commission, to put up 'a more lively and enlightened front to his buildings'.[26] It's hard not to believe that there was more than a hint of irony in this condemnation of Gothic as the tainted fruit of the barbarous Dark Ages. The criticism was, after all, being expressed by a man who at that moment was standing within the splendours of Pugin's new-minted Gothic interior of the Palace of Westminster. But if there was humour and irony in Palmerston's words, it was very much lost on Scott, who felt humiliated at such a public rebuke and horrified that it appeared to contain a threat that the commission might be taken away from him. His response was to write a hasty letter to *The Times*, published on 14 February, in which he pronounced confidently that 'any unprejudiced person would come to the conclusion that, if compared with the Post-office, the Museum, the Palace, or even the Board of Trade or Whitehall chapel, my design would carry the palm.'

These were staggeringly foolish words. They made Scott appear pompous and conceited, and invited hostility from those heavyweight contemporary classicists such as Sir Robert Smirke, who had designed the British Museum and the 'Post-office' in the City; Edward Blore, who had remodelled the east elevation of Buckingham Palace; and Sir Charles Barry, who had designed other classically inspired buildings. They also ensured criticism from those who regarded Inigo Jones's 'Whitehall chapel', or Banqueting House, as the epitome of both English classicism and architectural excellence. The reaction against Scott was predictable and extreme. He was attacked for his arrogance, his self-promotion and his unprofessional attack on his fellow architects. He almost suffered the mortification of the withdrawal of the nomination for the royal gold medal. In a panic, he immediately wrote a second letter to *The Times*, apologising for the things he had written 'in great haste and under some excitement'. His public humiliation was complete.

But Scott was not the type of man to withdraw or resign. He would hang on to the commission, no matter what it took. The 'Battle of the Styles' between those that supported the classical or the Gothic as appropriate models for modern architecture had become a public affair, and no doubt for many highly entertaining. It is easy to imagine Shaw and his fellows in Street's office, where, of course, Scott was well known, scrutinising every word published in *Hansard* and *The Times*, and wondering what on earth would happen next. Would Scott, the self-proclaimed champion of the Gothic, really turn classical to retain a valuable commission? Would he abandon his oft-declared architectural principles and sacrifice his honour?

The answer is yes. In September 1860 Scott was summoned to attend Palmerston – from June 1859 once again prime minister – at his private house in Piccadilly. The architect knew beforehand that

his Gothic scheme, which he had failed to get under way in the
months before Palmerston's return to political power, now stood no
chance. He had therefore offered an alternative: a design in a Byzan-
tine style that, it could be argued, combined some of the asymmetry
and inventive spirit of Gothic with the forms and details of classical
architecture. Palmerston was having none of it. He told Scott that he
did not want to 'disturb' his position but that he would 'have nothing
to do with Gothic' and he dismissed the Byzantine-style proposal as
'neither one thing nor t'other – a regular mongrel affair'. He insisted
yet again that Scott make a 'design in the ordinary Italian', and if he
would not, then his appointment would be cancelled.

The architect left the meeting 'thunderstruck and in sore per-
plexity' and in his *Recollections* claimed that he wondered 'whether I
must resign or swallow the bitter pill'.[27] For Scott, though, resignation
never really was an option. He desperately wanted the commission. In
any case, to resign would be to deny his family the large fees he would
earn. He therefore persuaded himself – or, rather, allowed friends to
persuade him – that a client had every right to decide the style of
the architecture they wanted for their money. In this case it was the
British nation, in the person of its prime minister, who was deciding,
and what it wanted for this most significant public building was classical, not Gothic, architecture. How could Scott possibly resist such a
wish from such a figure? So he parked his principles, obeyed his client
and got on with recasting his scheme in the Renaissance manner.

During the autumn and winter of 1860, Scott studied his old
volumes on classical design and visited Paris to imbibe the essence
of its monumental classical architecture, notably the Louvre and
the Tuileries. He seems to have generally enjoyed this but admits
in *Recollections* that, from time to time, he fell 'into fits of desperate lamentation and annoyance'.[28] This was no doubt partly because
he could not have helped but recall that the last time he had visited
Paris, in 1855, it was to explore its Gothic architecture, notably the
thirteenth-century Sainte-Chapelle that had inspired his chapel for
Exeter College, Oxford, one of Scott's best Gothic forays, which
possesses the first authentically constructed Gothic-style stone vault

built in Victorian Oxford. Ironically, Scott's exemplary Gothic essay
in Oxford was completed in 1859, just as he was being forced into
an act of treachery to the Gothic cause that from the 1840s he had
sought to lead.

By early 1861 Scott was more his old bumptious self again. He
believed that he had managed to recover some of his 'lost feelings for
the [classical] style' and in the end thought his essay in grand Renaissance classicism 'a great success'. Others agreed with him, including
one of the greatest classicists of the day, C. R. Cockerell, who after
studying the St James's Park elevation of the design wrote to Scott
in April 1861 to congratulate him 'most heartily, in the effect of your
ability and perseverance, in this glorious approachment to the new
Foreign Office'.[29]

On 8 June 1861 a debate took place in Parliament to compare and
then formally approve the designs. The result was a forgone conclusion, but the debate between Goths and classicists had been promised
by Palmerston, and niceties had to be observed. The prime minister
joined his fellow Parliamentarians at the conclusion of the debate to
congratulate Scott and declare his approved classical scheme 'very
beautiful'.[30] His imprimatur, of course, was also a vindication of the
belief he had publicly expressed that Scott had the architectural talent
to work successfully in any style.

So the first great public foray in the 'Battle of the Styles' had been
fought and lost by the Gothic fraternity, even if in ecclesiastical – and,
to a large degree, academic – architecture they reigned supreme. Now
the battleground switched from the sites where large-scale public and
institutional buildings were proposed to the realm of domestic architecture, particularly country-house design. This was still something of
an architecturally unresolved territory in the 1860s, although as early
as 1833 the garden designer John Claudius Loudon had condemned
the classical style as unsuitable for country houses because it had no
association with the English landscape.[31] A shift to the Gothic was
taking place in country-house design at the time the Foreign Office
building was being erected: between 1850 to 1854 it has been calculated that 32 per cent of new country houses were classical; by 1860

Above: The St James's Park frontage of the Foreign Office, built from 1861 to 1868 to the designs of George Gilbert Scott. The picturesquely placed tower was the suggestion of Matthew Digby Wyatt, who collaborated with Scott on the design of the adjoining India Office, where Wyatt had responsibility for the design of the interiors. Below: the Midland Grand Hotel, forming the south front of St Pancras Station, London. The hotel was completed in 1873, in splendid Gothic style, to designs by George Gilbert Scott.

to 1864 only 16 per cent were.[32] Even so, new projects offered potential prizes for the classicists as well as for the Goths, provided both sides could come up with sufficiently beguiling or novel ideas for the clients. Approaches and styles accordingly became increasingly varied as the century progressed.

The construction of the Foreign Office (and of the adjoining India Office) began in 1861 and was completed in 1868. It earned Scott the money (£35,000 in fees) and the security he craved. Despite the less than impressive way he had secured the commission, it allowed him to carry on his career with his honour largely intact. His ambition survived, too, as did his determination to demonstrate that Gothic was applicable universally. His next opportunity to champion a Gothic design for a public building came in 1865 when the Midland Railway Company launched a competition for a hotel that would form part of its terminus at St Pancras. Scott won the competition with a scheme that was clearly dependent, in spirit and scale if not in detail, on his rejected Foreign Office designs.

* * * * *

In the same year the Foreign Office was completed, Sir William Armstrong was contemplating the expansion of his building project in Jesmond Dene, just north of Newcastle, where in 1860 he had commissioned a banqueting hall from the veteran Newcastle classicist John Dobson. Armstrong used the hall, deep in the Dene, as a picturesque place in which to entertain business associates. But by the late 1860s he wanted more, and was starting to contemplate the construction of a bucolic home to which he could retreat from the noisy industrial works at Elswick, where, among other things, he was fabricating the world's most advanced ordnance. It seems that Armstrong and his wife conceived this home as an informal pile, set in apparently virgin nature and loaded with the pedigree of history and the architectural ornament of past ages. It would be an escapist evocation of an almost chivalric world that was as far removed as possible from the grim realities of Elswick and the polluted Tyne over which it presided.

Curiously, Armstrong had an indirect connection with Pugin and the Palace of Westminster, through his friend the painter John Horsley. Horsley had produced a competition entry in 1847 for one of the palace's interiors – a large canvas that showed Henry V taking the crown from his father's bedside – and when the government had ultimately declined to acquire it, Armstrong did. Horsley was an interesting, multi-talented man: the brother-in-law of the civil engineer Isambard Kingdom Brunel, with whom he collaborated on varied projects; the designer of the world's first commercially produced Christmas card (for Henry Cole in 1843); and, in 1864, a Royal Academician. When, in 1867, the Armstrongs mentioned they needed an architect to design a gallery for their Jesmond Dene banqueting hall, Horsley recommended Shaw, and in September of that year Shaw was invited north to meet Armstrong.

Why Shaw? As an independent architect he had not completed many buildings by September 1867: a few Gothic churches; from 1864 a modest Jacobean-style extension to Horsley's Georgian house, named Willesley, in Cranbrook, Kent (they had probably met through the Royal Academy); and, for Horsley's friend and a fellow member of the Royal Academy, Edward William Cooke, a house named Glen Andred in Groombridge, East Sussex, built between 1866 and 1868.[33] Glen Andred – Shaw's 'first wholly new large house'[34] – is sprawling, asymmetrical, gabled, tile-hung and with oriels, mullions and ornamental pargeting wrought in lime plaster that are very much in the Sussex domestic tradition of the sixteenth and seventeenth centuries. This relaxed, domestic style and its materials, notably tile-hanging and pargeting, was the epitome of the 'Old English style' and would in time become commonplace in English domestic architecture well into the twentieth century. In the 1860s it was novel enough to impress the likes of Horsley and Cooke.

Horsley and Cooke must have admired the fact, too, that while Shaw was something of an architectural dreamer, he was essentially a practical man. Letters between Shaw and Cooke make it clear that the architect was concerned not only with pertinent historical styles but also with such practicalities of architecture and comfortable home-making as plumbing and drainage. He also understood budgeting. In June 1866, for example, he observed to Cooke: 'I don't see why you shouldn't build the upper part of the whole house of common bricks . . . And cover them over with ornamental scalloped tiles, then you would have a Sussex house at once fire proof and cheap – and of course the walls are not half the trouble or expense and are built so much faster . . .'[35] Cooke must have been pleased with his home and his choice of architect. Horsley clearly was, too, hence his recommending Shaw to Armstrong.

Shaw's meeting with his new potential clients went well: 'they are exceedingly kind,' he wrote to his wife from Jesmond; 'I had a tremendous talk with Sir Wm about his gallery this morning and I think I am to have my own way. I dearly like my own way and not other people's!!'[36] The gallery, a modest affair, was eventually constructed, but what is more significant is that during this visit Armstrong also took Shaw further north, to Rothbury, where in 1863–4 he had built his rock-faced shooting lodge. It seems that this hilly and wooded location had become the preferred site for the Armstrongs' fantasy home, which was to be called Cragside. A few days later Shaw wrote his wife another letter, posted from Cragside: 'It will be very satisfactory working for Sir William as he knows right well what he is about.' Shaw also told her about Armstrong's 'wonderful Hydraulic machines that do all sorts of things you can imagine'.[37] He was, it must be assumed, referring to the hydraulic system Armstrong had installed to pump water uphill to the lodge and to irrigate its gardens. According to Shaw's biographer Andrew Saint, a significant event in the history of Cragside took place between the two letters Shaw sent home to his wife: 'Over the intervening weekend . . . he had sketched out the lines of the whole future fairy tale palace of Cragside while the guests were out on a shooting party.'[38]

The Cragside project got properly under way in 1870 when Shaw was asked to add a pair of reception rooms – the library and the dining room – to the north side of the existing lodge at Rothbury, with bedrooms above and plunge baths (a novelty at the time) in the basement below, fed by Armstrong's superlative hydraulic system.

This phase was completed by the end of 1872, with a second phase, involving additions to the south side of the existing house, completed by 1877.

If this makes it sound as though construction occurred in an orderly, systematic manner, that was very much not the case. Armstrong, a man of nervous creative energy, was always on the lookout for new ideas, and, consequently, was forever asking his architect to accommodate some recent technical innovation or the latest fashion in interior fittings. In 1851 his obsession had been artillery. Now it was domestic design. Shaw appears not to have been disconcerted by this constant state of flux. Provided Armstrong's dynamic new ideas didn't get in the way of his overall design, he seems to have been content with his patron's way of forging ahead.

The design of the north extension is fully dependent on historical precedent, and a powerful confirmation that, even for a technologically minded client like Armstrong and a progressive architect such as Shaw, the aesthetic model offered by the functionalist iron-and-glass structure of the Crystal Palace was entirely irrelevant for domestic design, as it would remain for fifty years or so. The pair of reception rooms, rising above a gently falling landscape, are faced with coursed and squared stone blocks of varying depth and detailed in the late fifteenth- or sixteenth-century Gothic manner, with bays furnished with large, stone-made mullioned and transomed windows topped by a battlemented parapet. On the corner the composition reads as a tower, largely because a faceted pyramid-roofed top storey suggests something of the medieval-castle style.

The theme is continued internally. The library is suitably quiet in its decoration: a congenial room for reading and reflection, and evidently a place of retreat for the Armstrongs where they could enjoy books rather than gaze at the undulating moorland. The ceiling is timber and panelled in a late Gothic manner, and there is a deep frieze, with painted leafy branches of fruits and flowers simmering with dull gold, each framed by squat, Gothic-style colonnettes. These painted panels echo the William Morris-designed glass in the upper tier of the mullioned and transomed window of the large bay, which depicts scenes from the life of St George, inspired by Dante Gabriel Rossetti cartoons. It is, in essence, both Pre-Raphaelite and patriotic in tone. The lower halves of the walls are faced with fitted bookcases, topped by a dado incorporating carving by the artist and furniture designer James Forsyth, including representations of the plants the Armstrongs favoured. The flat tops of the bookcases are used to display porcelain of Chinese inspiration or examples of the Dutch seventeenth-century-style blue-and-white tin-glazed earthenware, or majolica, that was fashionable at the time. Among these displays are large blue-and-white vases that, rather surprisingly, are capped with opaque glass spheres. These are lights: they originally housed oil-lamps but were converted to contain bulbs, which were in turn illuminated by the electricity generated by water-power that Armstrong introduced to Cragside in 1878, making it the first British house to be illuminated by electricity. By contrast the fire surround is almost abstract, with its hearth framed by three large slabs of onyx of a pale amber hue that the Armstrongs imported from Egypt in 1872.

The dining room is more strident in its architectural character, yet it's not opulent: it has the feel of a cosy 'Old English style' late medieval great hall of modest size, a place of congenial retreat and intimate dining rather than one of display. The ceiling is again panelled in timber and the walls are clad with sixteenth-century-style oak panelling with fitted shelves and court cupboard (a sideboard incorporating small cupboards and tiers of shelves for the display of plates), designed and made by Forsyth. The main focus is the fireplace, which fills much of the room's east wall. This is the epitome of late Victorian historicist work, at once scholarly and accurate in its details yet utterly fantastical in the way these details are combined. It's an inglenook – that is to say, almost a room within a room – where benches of a hybrid Gothic and Jacobean Renaissance design[39] (here lit by small windows) are placed either side of and close to the hearth and within the fireplace's all-embracing arch. The arch is rich in Gothic detail, and embraces a mighty stone lintel that was inspired by one that Shaw had sketched in the kitchen of Fountains Abbey in Yorkshire. The hearth itself, replete with a large cast-iron fire-back

The interior of the library at Cragside, designed by Norman Shaw in the early 1870s.

and burnished copper andirons (metal supports that raise logs to promote better burning and prevent them tumbling into the room), is topped by a slab of stone forming a lintel that rests on richly carved stone corbels, one of which features a cock set among foliage. The lintel itself is plain, except for a carved motto: 'East or West Hame's Best'. This quaint sentiment had been utilised a few years earlier on a fire surround at Cloverley Hall, Shropshire, a building designed in 1864 by Shaw's friend William Eden Nesfield (perhaps in association with Shaw) for the Liverpool bankers J. P. Heywood (see page 79), but largely demolished in 1927 and rebuilt. In the Middle Ages and sixteenth century, inglenooks had offered a useful way to create a snug corner in a large and draughty house. For the more affluent in the nineteenth century, they served as an expression of domestic bliss, and the carved motto encapsulates both that message and the veneration the Victorians felt for the home.

The dining room is not the only room to make an exuberant display of Gothic taste. A view of a bedroom as originally arranged at Cragside is offered in a sketch of the 'Guest Chamber' published in the *British Architect* journal of 20 May 1881, which shows a bed with a tester rich in Gothic detail, squeezed between large panelled coves that support the chamber's panelled ceiling. Tall finials, or ornaments, set on the bed's end posts feature carved owls. In consequence the bedroom and related dressing and sitting rooms, located high up at second-floor level, are now known as the 'Owl Suite'. As ever, Armstrong's love of modern convenience is on display, too. The sketches also show a staircase newel, in the form of a sitting lion, supporting a pole from which is suspended an electric light.[40]

* * * * *

Cragside continued to evolve throughout the 1870s and early 1880s, becoming ever more complex as it did so. By 1880 the house consisted of the old lodge; the large addition to its north that included the library and dining room; an extensive kitchen, scullery and pantry complex to the east (mostly built or enlarged in the early 1870s); the entrance range to the south with a top-lit 'museum room' that

A sketch by T. Raffles Davison of the bedroom in 'Owl Suite' and, left, a lion-mounted light fitting.

was soon converted into a picture gallery and that then doubled as a corridor leading to Shaw's final significant addition to the house – the grandiose drawing room, also top-lit, that was built between 1883 and 1884; and a gable-topped central tower, started around May 1872. As the historian Mark Girouard writes, Shaw 'put everything he had and perhaps more than he ought' into the design of the tower: 'panels of sunflowers and suns, twisted and moulded chimneystacks, Notre Dame gargoyles' and, as a 'crowning device ... a half-timbered [top-storey room] behind battlements'.[41] The inclusion of this half-timbering ran contrary to the ethos and aesthetics of the Arts and Crafts Movement which was highly influential at this time and championed by the likes of William Morris. The movement not only sought to promote the individual creative role of the craftsmen and craft-based vernacular Gothic architecture and thus to reverse the artistic decline that industrialisation had brought, but urged that vernacular design should be rooted in local building traditions. Shaw knew perfectly well that the half-timbering he added to the top storey had little to do with the neighbourhood. He chose it because it imbued his design with the romantic quality he craved.

The main internal spaces are linked by a long and tortuous corridor, incorporating the central spine of the old lodge and winding and rising through stairs to accommodate the uneven level of the site. It makes for an atmospheric and picturesque parade through the house from the picture gallery to the dining room, and with its twists and turns and shifts of level provides the sort of spacious and varied internal experience that was part of the emerging fashion in country-house planning. A particular 'event' on the route is the staircase to the picture gallery, with an upper portion lined, like much of the corridor, with polychromatic tiles.

* * * * *

As the partnership between the Armstrongs and Shaw evolved during the fourteen years after 1870, occasionally only just surviving collisions of personality and artistic ambition, it traced the changing pattern of domestic architectural taste and fashion in England. Some

Cragside's top-lit corridor-like 'picture gallery', dating from the mid 1870s, that eventually connected the staircase to the drawing room, which was added between 1883 and 1884.

of these fashions, indeed, were promoted and popularised by Shaw himself. All were different iterations of history-inspired designs, often coalescing in a highly romantic manner. First came the thoroughly Gothic phase, where the vernacular Gothic 'Old English style' was favoured, and where design and construction techniques rooted in local building traditions were promoted. There then followed a return to classicism – not to the symmetrical classicism of Greece or Rome but to the more informal, picturesque and individual classicism of late sixteenth-, seventeenth-, and early eighteenth-century northern Europe. The Queen Anne Revival, in which Shaw played an important role from the early 1870s, looked to Flemish and Dutch domestic architecture with its Gothic gabled forms and Renaissance trim: ornate red brickwork, white painted joinery, arched oriels and calculated asymmetry.[42] Shaw's New Zealand Chambers, in Leadenhall Street in the City of London, built in 1873 but long demolished, and Swan House, Chelsea Embankment, built in 1876, are prime and pioneering example of this emerging Queen Anne style that soon captured the public's imagination. In 1892 Swan House was described as one 'of the finest specimens of modern domestic architecture in London'.[43]

The drawing room at Cragside, completed in 1884, exemplifies the way architecture was now heading. Externally it reads as a wing, set at right angles to the south range and in part defining an entrance court. Its west-facing facade is stark, built from roughly coursed, squared stone blocks, and incorporates a tall bay of half-octagonal plan which boasts, at its top, a large mullioned and transomed window that lights the drawing room and offers delightful prospects. The angles of the bay are ornamented with boldly textured quoins, and above is a battlemented parapet. All is in the Elizabethan late Gothic style, with (apart from the quoins, perhaps) no obvious concession to classicism. Evidently Shaw was resolved to establish a visually harmonious relationship between the exterior of the drawing-room wing and the earlier entrance range with its Gothic character. Inside the drawing room, however, all is very different. The room has a Palladian double-square plan and a shallow barrel-vaulted ceiling, like a Tudor long gallery, pierced at its apex with large curving lanterns to provide generous top-lighting in a modern manner. The lower portion of the vault is embellished with Jacobean-style plasterwork, essentially classical in character.

When completed in 1884, the drawing room gave Cragside a new dimension, not least because it formed a terminal feature or point of departure in the 54-metre-long triumphal route through the house, from dining room to the new drawing room where the ritual of dinner would have started or ended. The room also contains one of Cragside's most eye-catching and startling creations: a huge inglenook fireplace, with a vast overmantel, that occupies most of the south end of the room.

Over the decades critics have struggled for words to describe this extraordinary piece of work and to define its meaning and the impression it must have made when new. For Andrew Saint, the current authority on Shaw and Cragside, it 'imbues the atmosphere with a grand sensuality', as though 'the change from Old English to Renaissance' marked 'the shifting image of Armstrong from ingenious engineer to imperial arms salesman'.[44] So arguably the reemergence of classicism from the Gothic suggests a quest for a Roman-inspired and triumphal architecture of empire – which indeed seems borne out by the rise of Edwardian baroque. The irony of course is that this triumphalist style reached its peak just as the empire started its steady decline in 1914 with the outbreak of the First World War.

The inglenook itself – seemingly in part, at least, designed by W. R. Lethaby, who in the early 1880s was Shaw's chief assistant – is a riot of Renaissance forms and details. It includes a marble-made entablature, partly supported by free-standing Roman Ionic columns and with a deep frieze occupied by pairs of putti linked by swags. Within this composition is a smaller marble fire surround and hearth, flanked by a pair of timber settles. The massive overmantel is packed with Jacobean-style strapwork, floral swags and numerous large figures of winged cherubs and heavenly maidens, carved from alabaster. Materials and workmanship are of the highest quality: the carvers were the architectural sculpting firm Farmer and Brindley, and their work is exemplary. Such is the ambition on show that it is not surprising that Shaw should have asked Armstrong, in a letter dated 13 October 1884, 'would you think me greedy if I proposed to have more than the regulation 5 per cent for the [drawing room] Chimney piece' because 'it was rather a special work & the time & trouble it took was considerable – but I shall leave myself in your hands'. Two months earlier, in August, the drawing room and its chimney piece had been 'inaugurated' by the Prince and Princess of Wales when they made Cragside their base during an official visit to Newcastle. The visit was a great success, so it is not surprising that Armstrong quickly paid Shaw a fee for the chimney piece of 10 per cent of its construction cost.[45]

The culmination of the project was the Gilnockie Tower, designed by Shaw (but based on a seventeenth-century tower house that had been a stronghold of the Armstrong clan) and probably completed in 1884. Originally it was topped by a dome serving as an observatory, but between 1885 and 1891 this was replaced by gables, as envisaged by Shaw but executed by another hand. In the same letter of 13 October 1884 to Armstrong, Shaw referred to enclosed 'tracings showing some of the alterations we proposed more especially the new tower', which Shaw thought 'might not be made a foot or two higher'.[46] This tower, combined with the earlier central tower, with its timber-framing, gables and tall chimneys, gives the entire composition the look of a Wagnerian fairy-tale confection to vie with King Ludwig II's Neuschwanstein Castle in South Bavaria, started only a few months before Shaw's additions to Cragside and built into the mid 1880s.

The completion of the Gilnockie Tower brought the curtain down on Shaw's relationship with the Armstrongs and with Cragside. A few other structures were added in the later 1880s and early 1890s, including the billiard room adjoining the drawing room, but these were not the work of Shaw.

A few letters from Shaw to Armstrong, all dating from October and November 1884, trace the final days of the long relationship between architect and client.[47] Initially all seems to have been well.

The top-lit and barrel-vaulted drawing room, completed in 1884 with Jacobean-style classical detailing. The massive inglenook fireplace and overmantel – sporting Ionic columns, paired figures of putti, cherubs, nymphs and much Jacobean-style strapwork – is a masterpiece of late Victorian eclectic and inventive classical design.

On 22 October 1884, Shaw wrote to tell Armstrong: 'I am well paid up . . . so I ought to be content & indeed I am . . . your work pays me better than most work.' He also stated how pleased he was to be able to supervise the project from London and so be 'saved all the trouble with Builders – no specifications or Contracts – no extras etc, etc'. 'So when I say I am content,' he concluded, 'I mean it. And thank you very much for all your kindness.'[48] Armstrong must have replied immediately, because three days later, on 25 October, Shaw wrote: 'I am very glad you are prepared to give me a Good Character!!! It is worth something in these queer times.'[49] Again Armstrong must have replied quickly and in a positive manner, because on 30 October Shaw wrote to thank him for his letter and to express his satisfaction that 'we do see our way and that really there are no difficulties in all sincerity.'

This letter, however, also contains a reference to a disagreement between architect and patron. 'I am sorry to say –' Shaw wrote, 'that for once – I am unable to agree with you about the upper part of the Tower, Chimney etc [of the Gilnockie Tower] . . . I think it is hardly correct to say that the back part is only seen by servants – of course it is mainly seen by servants from the court yard – but it is tremendously seen by everyone from the hillside at the back. I think the back must be a very favourite walk (I know it is mine) and therefore see the whole of the east side of the Tower etc in undiminished glory.'[50] Having the picturesque qualities of his house explained to him might well have irritated Sir William, who, like Palmerston before him, would doubtless have felt that an architect is, by the rules of his professional engagement, there to give the client what he wants. Disputes over taste and style can only go so far. At any rate, only one further letter appears to have been sent, from Shaw to Armstrong, dated 4 November 1884. Evidently, Sir William had got another architect involved by now, because Shaw, having declared at the outset that 'It should be as you wish', suggests that Sir William 'overrates' the new man 'very much' and confides that 'I return you his sketch & don't think much of it, though I hope [you will not] put this down to "professional Jealousy".' And so the collaboration between Norman Shaw and Sir William Armstrong, having run its course, quietly ended.

*****

To the contemporary outside world, Cragside, with its extraordinary combination of historical forms and avant-garde domestic technology, appeared to be, as the journal *The World* described in 1879, 'truly the palace of a modern magician'.[51] On the one hand it boasted a series of extraordinarily rich and lavish rooms, contained within an edifice that resembled a fortified medieval village set below a tall defensive tower. On the other it boasted just about every modern convenience that could be had. And this gets to the essence of the building. The magic of what Shaw created lies not just in Cragside's almost impossibly romantic form and setting but also in its function. This architectural evocation of past ages is not merely a monument to the Gothic Revival, the Arts and Crafts Movement and the late nineteenth-century return to classicism. It also incorporates labour-saving technology that was then cutting-edge – including electric lights, central heating, passenger lift and mechanised cooking spits, all operated by hydraulic power that, as the building's current owner, the National Trust, explains 'set the standard for modern living'.[52] In addition, there were water-flushed lavatories. These were far from being a novel idea in the 1870s (Sir John Harington had proposed such convenient devices as early as the 1590s, and in the mid 1770s, when S-shaped pipes and plumbing were added to chamber pots, water-flushed WCs became a realistic possibility). But it was not until the early 1860s – with the development of valves, water tanks and a ready supply of water – that such pioneers as Thomas Crapper, Thomas Twyford and Henry Doulton started to make water-flushed WCs available for the ordinary home, or at least for those equipped with drains connected to a sewage system. Armstrong was thus among the earlier homeowners to install them.

Of course, for Sir William and Margaret, labour-saving technology went only so far. As wealthy Victorians, they still required servants, of whom there appear to have been seven when the 1881 census (conducted on a day when the couple were absent) was compiled: the acting 'Head' of the house, 63-year-old butler Joseph Grey; and then two housemaids, a laundry maid, a dairy maid, a kitchen maid and a cook, Jane Elliot – all under the age of 30 and all unmarried. The eighth person in residence on that day was 36-year-old Martha Feather, who is listed as a 'visitor' and described as married to the coachman. He was absent, no doubt busy driving the Armstrongs around.[53]

By the time of the 1891 census the number of servants had apparently expanded to ten, all female apart from a 31-year-old footman, and all single apart from a 47-year-old widow, Elizabeth Jackman, who was a 'Lady's maid'. Most were born in Northumberland and a couple were from County Durham, with the exception of Elizabeth Jackman, who was from London, and the 42-year-old laundress, who came from Ireland. In addition, there were a cook, two 'under cooks', three 'house maids' and another 'Lady's Maid'. Strangely no butler is listed, nor a housekeeper, which were usually the senior staff positions.[54] All were there to look after a family that, on census day, comprised the 'Head', William Armstrong, aged 80, described as a 'Retired civil engineer' and since 1887 titled Baron Armstrong of Cragside; Margaret; two nephews (one by marriage); three nieces; and a 'visitor', a 36-year-old unmarried 'Lady's companion' from Gateshead. Theirs was indeed a very comfortable life.

For Shaw and his client, Cragside was a mutually agreed fantasy that – although extraordinary in appearance – was in tune with the spirit of its age, particularly in the way that new technology offering modern comforts was integrated with historic forms and details. Cragside makes it clear that for sophisticated taste in the late nineteenth century it was not necessary that new technology should brazenly reveal itself but rather that it should be tamed by being absorbed within tradition. This was to be a gentle evolution of taste and not a radical alteration. More revolutionary change would not come for another forty years.

As that quaint phrase chiselled into the inglenook lintel in Armstrong's refuge-like dining room suggests, the house also stands as testimony to the Victorian ideal of domesticity: 'East or West Hame's Best'. That this was, for Armstrong, a vitally important sentiment is confirmed not only by its pride of place in his inner sanctum, beside the hearth of his home, but also by the portrait he commissioned soon after Cragside was complete. The work of the Newcastle-based painter and illustrator H. H. Emmerson, himself a homely figure with, late in life, a bushy white beard, it depicts Armstrong in what must have been his favoured nook in Cragside. He is shown seated on one of the benches within the inglenook, reading a newspaper, with his dogs at his feet and with the design of the motto rearranged to make it fully legible – almost as the focal point – within the painting's frame.

For us today, there's a certain contradiction here. Armstrong was a slave to sentiment, with a liking for homely language and doggerel verse to express an idea that was little more than a cliché. Yet he was also a key figure of the new technological age – promoted by the Great Exhibition – and the projector of cutting-edge ordnance that dealt death at long distance in unprecedented manner. His house, although ambitious in scale, embodies comfortable domesticity and a romantic veneration of history. Yet its owner had made his money in a ruthless business in a ruthless era. Cragside, in fact, exemplifies a more general Victorian paradox: the promotion of home and family at a time when many homes and family were exploited and poverty-stricken. Its embrace of an imagined and cosy past at a time of rampant capitalism and commercialism – also presented so ardently by the Great Exhibition – serves to add to that sense of paradox.

Bye-law houses in Toxteth, Liverpool – a government response to the challenges that the rapid growth of Victorian towns and cities posed. The ones shown here, at the west end of Cairns Street, are slightly larger than most of the area's bye-law houses. Each has two front rooms either side of a centrally placed front door.

– 6 –

The Two-up Two-down
Toxteth Bye-law Houses
(*c*.1860–*c*.1890)

MONG THE VARIOUS EXHIBITS on show at the Crystal
Palace in 1851 was a two-storey block containing four dwellings and a well-ventilated, central open staircase and access
gallery. Designed to provide fireproof and hygienic accommodation
for the working class, it was a scaled-down version of a pioneering
'Model Houses for Families' scheme in Streatham Street, Bloomsbury, built from 1849 to 1851 on the edge of the long-notorious St
Giles slum, that Prince Albert, as the president of the Society for
Improving the Conditions of the Labouring Classes (SICLC), had
championed. After the Great Exhibition the two-storey block was
re-erected on Kennington Common, where it still stands.

The Honorary Architect of the SICLC was Henry Roberts, for
whom George Gilbert Scott had worked early in his career, and it was
Roberts who designed the Streatham Street and Great Exhibition
schemes. The society had been established in 1844 (at which point the
prince became its president) and was dedicated to providing model
dwellings for the working class. Spearheaded by the MP, committed
evangelical Christian and campaigner for social reform Lord Ashley
(better known now by his later title Lord Shaftesbury), it was a suc-
cessor to the Labourer's Friend Society, which Ashley had established
in 1830 to help allocate land to agricultural labourers for 'cottage hus-
bandry'[1] and was conceived on a more ambitious scale. Essentially, the
SICLC sought to help make available decent and affordable housing

in an era when there was no precedent, or government agency, for
the provision of what was to become known as 'public' housing for
working people. Such subsidised housing as did exist at that time was
provided in the form of almshouses by trades, professions, parishes or
private benefactors; by landowners or employers in the form of 'tied'
houses, which meant that a home went with a job; or by parishes
funding workhouse accommodation. The notion of local authorities
taking a role in the business of providing 'council' housing would start
to take root only in the 1860s, and their full involvement would not
commence until three decades later.

Even the SICLC was relatively limited in scope. The journalist Henry Mayhew, who documented 'London Street-folk' in his
London Labour and the London Poor of 1851, did no more than reflect
popular opinion when he divided the nation's 'poor' into 'those that
will work' and those that 'cannot . . . and . . . will not work'. The philanthropic housing movement concerned itself only with those who
it perceived as able and willing to work and who thus, in theory,
demonstrated that they were sober, responsible, willing to better
themselves and consequently the deserving objects of discriminat-
ing charity. And who could, of course, because of these things, be
trusted to pay rent on a regular basis.

The chronic poor and the unemployable were outside the scope
of these early philanthropists, and it would be many decades before
assistance was offered beyond that provided – frugally, grudgingly and
judgementally – by the parish-based workhouse system. Since the
Settlement and Removal Act of 1662, poor relief had been confined to
those who were natives of a parish, and to those who had established
unchallenged 'settlement' rights in a parish or who were tenants of
property worth at least £10 a year. For these eligible poor, financial
support came from a parish rate charged to local landowners and
tenants of adequate means. Parish authorities, operating through
vestries, were generally anxious to reduce the number of recipients
of aid, so the poor who could not prove their origin or rights were
ignored or rapidly removed. From 1834, smaller parishes were grouped
into 'unions', each overseen by a board of guardians, so that savings

could be made by sharing facilities. This introduced larger and yet more intimidating and impersonal workhouses. It is scarcely surprising that when the American adventurer and writer Jack London visited the East End of London in the early 1900s he described the victims of 'the prostitution of labour' as the 'miserable and despised and forgotten', 'unfit' and 'unneeded'.[2]

Organisations such as the SICLC sought to raise money on capitalist principles by offering dividends to investors, but this pragmatic approach involved difficult and often unsatisfactory compromises. In order to ensure an active programme of construction and maintenance, it was necessary to offer investors a lower rate of return than they might have obtained elsewhere (the enterprise became known as 'five per cent philanthropy'). But the very fact that there were still dividends to be paid meant tight budgets and grimly utilitarian buildings that were usually tall and densely packed, with minimal courts or open space. It also necessitated rents that were beyond the reach of all but the regularly employed 'labouring classes'.

Henry Roberts was acutely aware of the delicate balancing act that he, as architect, had to achieve. He had to provide a large number of well-ventilated, sanitary and soundly constructed dwellings that would allow for a degree of the segregation of men and women with which the prudish middle class were so obsessed. At the same time, if his buildings were to avoid looking too grimly institutional, he needed to ensure at least a minimum of visual delight. His first significant work in this field, the model dwellings in Streatham Street, Bloomsbury, achieves both objectives. It provides access to flats via open staircases and galleries in order to ensure better ventilation and security, with the galleries, to a degree, self-cleaning from rainfall. But it also achieves an almost Roman gravity and nobility through its brick-built simplicity. The ground and first floors are united to form a rusticated podium of the type associated with antique temples, while a pedimented portal leads to a courtyard within which are tiers of brick arcades. At the functional level, each of the forty-eight flats was provided with its own water closet (WC) – an extraordinary amenity at the time – and an effort was made to create shared functions, such as coal storage, to the advantage of all. Some of these ideas were continued in 1851 in Roberts's exhibit at Crystal Palace, which also made ingenious use of hollow bricks to dampen noise transmission between the small flats. Although this modest structure was conceived very much in functional terms, Roberts (and the prince) were unable to resist adding a little ornament, diluted Elizabethan in style, to give it some cultural pedigree and delight.

In the course of Queen Victoria's reign, the population of the United Kingdom rose steeply: from around 25.5 million in 1837 to 41.5 million at the time of the queen's death in 1901. As a result, while the construction of model dwellings proceeded at an increasing pace during the second half of the nineteenth century, demand invariably outstripped supply. It swiftly became apparent, therefore, that a large-scale complementary programme of privately funded building tailored to the means and needs of working people was essential. The notion wasn't in itself a new one. For generations speculative builders had, on occasion, financed the construction of modest terraced houses which, in return for limited profits, involved minimal financial outlay. Indeed, the 1774 London Building Act had specifically regulated the size and structure of modest dwellings for 'artisans' and 'mechanics'. Fourth Rate houses, as such structures were categorised, were valued at £150 or less and occupied less than 350 square feet, making them generally two windows wide, two rooms deep and two storeys high above ground. Now the pressure to provide them on a larger scale hugely increased.

In towns where demand for low-rent accommodation went hand in hand with high land values, courtyard developments of former gardens or open land became popular with developers. For example, in the burgeoning international port of Liverpool in the 1840s, such quarters housed some 86,000 people – well over a quarter of the town's population of 286,487.[3] Typically, courtyard developments took the form of narrow, blind alleys or courts squeezed on to low-value backland set behind or between larger buildings with street frontages. The alleys and courts were generally lined with short rows of two- and three-storey, poorly constructed houses facing each other.

These were invariably in multi-occupation, included minimal sanitation (usually a communal privy or two over a cesspit at the far end
of the court), and had a limited water supply that took the form of a
shared pump or standpipe in the court. Since they were built back-
to-back to save construction costs, and so lacked rear windows, they
were also invariably poorly ventilated.

Edwin Chadwick's seminal 1842 'Report on the Sanitary Condition of the Labouring Population' includes detailed observations
made by the doctor and reformer William Duncan on the grim
courtyards of the Lancashire port. There was, Duncan recorded, not
'a single court in Liverpool which communicates with the street by an
underground drain'. As a result, 'the only means afforded for carrying
off the fluid dirt' was 'a narrow, open, shallow gutter' that was 'very
generally choked up with stagnant filth'. In Duncan's opinion there
could 'be no doubt that the emanations from this pestilential surface,
in connexion with other causes, are a frequent source of fever among
the inhabitants of these undrained localities'. He then offered two
particular examples 'in corroboration' of his assertion. Of the first,
he wrote:

> In consequence of finding that not less than 63 cases of fever
> had occurred in one year in Union-court Banastre-street (con-
> taining 12 houses), I visited the court in order to discover if
> possible, their origin, and I found the whole court inundated
> with fluid filth which had oozed through the walls from two
> adjoining ash-pits or cesspools, and which had no means of
> escape in consequence of the court being below the level of
> the street, and having no drain.

Duncan ascertained that 'the court was owned by two different
landlords, one of whom had offered to construct a drain provided
the other would join him in the expense; but this offer having been
refused, the court had remained for two or three years in the state
in which I saw it.' The second example was a 'court in North-street,
consisting of only four small houses', which 'I found in a somewhat

An unknown court in central Liverpool, photographed in about 1912. It is a typical specimen of its type – built in a rudimentary manner, probably in the late 1830s or early 1840s. It is narrow, dark, gas-lit and with an open-topped central gully that might perhaps have served as a sewer.

similar condition, the air being contaminated by the emanations from two filthy ruinous privies, a large open ash-pit and a stratum of semi-fluid abomination covering the whole surface of the court.' 'Nor', he went on, 'is this the full extent of the evil; the fluid matter of the court privies sometimes oozes through into the adjoining cellars, rendering them uninhabitable by anyone whose olfactories retain the slightest sensibility.' In a cellar in 'Lace-street', Duncan noted that a 'well' into which 'stinking fluid was allowed to drain, was discovered below the bed where the family slept!'.[4]

The one example of court housing that survives in central Liverpool today is the fragmentary remains of Watkinson's Terrace and Watkinson's Building, constructed between 1836 and 1846/7, on a sliver of land behind houses and shops of the same date and numbered 35 to 39 Pembroke Place.[5] This group provides some sense of what it must have been like to live in such a development in early Victorian times. The red-brick fronts of the surviving houses, three storeys high above ground and only one window wide, were clearly designed and detailed with some care. They have elevations and windows that are pleasingly proportioned (the ground-floor windows are the deepest; those on the top floor are treated as square attics; all are topped with neatly detailed sandstone lintels), and doors that are semicircular headed, as was popular in the early nineteenth century. Nevertheless, it is only too apparent that such houses, with their almost non-existent services and communal privy, would have proved extremely difficult to inhabit with any comfort or dignity, especially when densely occupied and overwhelmed by poverty. They are agonisingly small, the rooms are cramped, there is little daylight and no prospect. Their inhabitants would have lived in perpetual gloom amid stench, stagnant air, sewage and decay.[6]

Their dark and low-ceilinged cellars, probably intended for storage and often originally with earth floors, would soon have been pressed into residential use as the city absorbed the impoverished and ill-nourished Irish migrants fleeing the potato famine of the late 1840s, 120,000 of whom arrived in the first three months alone of 1847. Duncan reckoned, conservatively, that there were upwards of

8,000 inhabited cellars in Liverpool, occupied by between 35,000 and 40,000 people. As for the condition of those cellars, he noted that a recent report by the surveyor appointed by the town council on 'court and cellar residences' had said that of the 6,571 cellars inspected, '2,988 are stated to be either wet *or* damp, and nearly one-third of the whole number are from 5 to 6 feet below the level of the street.'[7] One cellar room he came across housed sixteen people. Such dire conditions became breeding grounds for contagious disease, with cholera epidemics sweeping through Liverpool on a regular basis, notably the 1849 outbreak, which took the lives of well over 5,000 people. Not surprisingly, in Dr Duncan's view, 'Liverpool was the most unhealthy town in England.'

* * * * *

It was to a Liverpool struggling to cope with such appalling depravation, poverty, squalor and overcrowding that a twenty-year-old Welsh-born man named Richard Owens moved in 1851. He had been trained by his father as a carpenter and a joiner. He came to Liverpool to work as a clerk and then foreman for a Welsh builder named John Jones, based in Everton. Ultimately, he would be responsible for the building of hundreds of a new type of dwelling for the working families of the town: the bye-law house.

The bye-law house was a government response to the challenges, in terms of health and general well-being, that the rapid growth of Victorian towns and cities posed, and of which Liverpool afforded such an extreme example. The link between poor sanitation and disease, in particular cholera, had been made by Dr Duncan shortly after a cholera outbreak in Liverpool in 1832, which led to over 1,500 deaths; and more than twenty years before Dr John Snow, working in Soho in London in 1854, established the connection between cholera and water tainted by sewage and by the decomposition of human remains. The Chadwick Commission, to which Duncan reported, recommended a radical improvement in urban drains and sewers, the regular removal of waste from houses and streets, and the provision of readily available clean drinking water. It also proposed the creation of the post of medical officer. In 1846, accordingly, Liverpool's Health of the Town Committee secured the Liverpool Sanitary Act, which did indeed include a 'medical officer of health', along with a 'borough engineer' and an 'inspector of nuisances', all of whom were to oversee the welfare of the town's population. The first medical officer was, appropriately, Dr Duncan, whose research and campaigning had done so much to get the Act passed. He was appointed in January 1847, making Liverpool the first town (it did not become a city until 1880) in the world to appoint a medical officer of health, and in the process establishing the principle that safeguarding public health was the duty of local government. Duncan worked closely with the borough engineer, a civil engineer named John Newlands who in the late 1840s gave parts of Liverpool the world's first integrated sewage system. Further improvements came after the 1848 Public Health Act, which established a framework within which local authorities could work to achieve Chadwick's recommendations.

It was clear, though, that it wasn't just urban sanitation that needed to be improved. So did the housing provided for society's poorer members. In 1875, therefore, the Conservative government led by Benjamin Disraeli passed another Public Health Act, which, under the aegis of the Local Government Board, came into force in 1877. This provided the basis for what would become known as the bye-law house, because it required local authorities throughout the land to control the construction of privately funded low-income housing through the legal and planning mechanism of bye-laws.[8] These bye-laws were not uniform across the nation, but they did at least demand that new houses meet minimum standards of construction, ventilation, sanitation, spatial requirement and population density. All new houses had to have their own privies or 'outhouses', usually constructed as part of a rear service wing and reached via a yard. Initially privies were located over cesspits, with access for the collection of 'night soil' arranged via narrow alleys set behind or between terraces of houses. By the later nineteenth century, however, bye-laws required the provision of water-flushed lavatories connected to a sewer system (though comparable requirements were not imposed on old houses divided and converted to provide low-cost accommodation). For the first time, basic building standards were defined at a national level – and enforced – ushering in an era of reasonable quality, new-built houses for the nation's working-class population. Tens of thousands would be built by the start of the First World War. They still form around 15 per cent of the nation's housing stock. It's not surprising, therefore, that for generations of Britons the basic bye-law 'two-up two-down' house became synonymous with home.

It was within this new legislative framework that Richard Owens's business thrived. From 1855 he had worked for surveyor and estate agent Williams and Jones, which specialised in advising speculating house builders about the purchase and resale of land.[9] In the evenings he had studied architecture at the Institute of Engineering. By 1861 – when he lived at 69 Creswell Street with his wife, son, daughter, two brothers (both joiners) and a fifteen-year-old Welsh-born female servant – he was, in the words of that year's census, an 'Estate Agent and Bookkeeper'. Interestingly, his widowed neighbour's 26-year-old son, Thomas Childs, was listed in the same census as an 'Architect Surveyor'. It's tempting to think that Childs – a 'widow's son' like the biblical Hiram, reputed to be one of the master builders of Solomon's Temple – inspired Owens, a devout Christian, in his determination to change from being a tradesman and clerk to an architect and professional member of the building industry. At any rate, Owens was soon to sport a large and bushy beard that gave him the appearance of a biblical patriarch.

In 1862, or soon after, Owens set up in Liverpool as an architect, primarily serving the Welsh community and specialising in the design of chapels. One of his first, and most ambitious, was the Welsh Calvinistic Methodist chapel in Fitzclarence Street, of which he was a member and which was, when complete, one of the most costly Welsh chapels built anywhere in the world. In Wales and Welsh Liverpool, chapel and business life went hand in hand. It is unsurprising therefore that it was while supervising the construction of a chapel in Abergele in 1867 that Owens should have met the man who would become his most important business contact: David Roberts.

Roberts, another Liverpool-based Welshman, was by the 1860s a highly successful timber merchant who had invested heavily in land in the Toxteth Park area, much of it bought from the Earl of Sefton. The residential development that Roberts then put in train was closely related to the expansion and operation of Liverpool's extensive network of docks served by the Mersey, in particular the Herculaneum Dock, enlarged in 1876 and with secure casements tunnelled into its flanking sandstone cliff from 1878 for the storage of petroleum. Bye-law terraces were soon built above the cliff with some, such as those in Grafton Street, almost sitting over subterranean petroleum storage tanks. An access road leading directly from terraces to dock was constructed to accommodate the comings and goings of its local workforce, which was also served from 1893 by Liverpool's now long-gone, Chicago-style, electricity-powered Overhead Railway.

Over that period – from the 1860s into the early 1890s – Roberts developed his land as a series of estates to create nearly 4,300 new houses, with Owens as master planner, architect and building supervisor. By the time of his death in 1891, Owens had become one of the most prolific contractors in the nation's building industry, responsible for 325 acres of new building in and around Liverpool. The vast majority of these were bye-law houses of the preferred terrace form, making Owens probably responsible for planning more terrace houses in Victorian Britain than anyone else. The pair also ventured beyond utilitarian terrace houses and chapels. In central Liverpool's Dale Street, for example, with Owens as architect and Roberts as developer, the pair were responsible for Westminster Chambers, a fine Gothic-style stone-faced commercial building. It sports good-quality carving by Joseph Rogerson, including portrait busts at second-floor level and a corner entrance topped by a triangular panel, framed by snarling Welsh dragons accompanied by owls (presumably representing the wisdom of the goddess Athena), and bearing the construction date 1880.[10] The following year Owens established his own office in Westminster Chambers, where it remained, under different guises, until 1978, when it finally closed.[11]

Owens's first domestic developments with Roberts were quite

modest ones. Indeed, they continued the well-established tradition of
Liverpool's 'courts'. In the mid 1860s at Hopwood Street on the west
edge of Everton, the pair came up with a development that included
eight rows of five houses facing each other across four narrow courts
leading off Furlong Street. By the early 1870s, however, anticipating the coming of the bye-law house and rejecting the court with its
inherent problems of congestion and lack of ventilation, Owens opted
for an approach that involved straight terraces serviced by rear alleys.
Ideally these terraces were set along streets that were lined with trees
and that offered open prospects and good ventilation. And, a notable
feature, Owens rotated the axes of his grids of terraces – even when
built at a similar time on the same estate – so introducing a mildly
picturesque quality of variety into the street pattern.

The orthogonal grid pattern was by no means a novel idea. It had
become the standard strategy of planners and architects well over a
century before, as had the mixing of different scales and buildings in
varied uses within the grid. James Craig's Edinburgh New Town of
1767, which makes a major feature of minor streets in mixed use and
service alleys set between and behind the major terraces, is a good
example, as is Bloomsbury in London, as expanded from 1800 under
the control of the builders and developers James Burton and Thomas
Cubitt. Owens's first experiment with a grid of terraces rather than
courts was on the Campfield Estate, Everton, which got under way
in the late 1860s. This estate was relatively small and Owens's basic
planning strategy was, more or less, simply to continue the lines of
streets already laid out on the land adjoining the new development. It
was only when he embarked on a series of new buildings in Toxteth
(or Toxteth Park as the area was then called) that his flair as an architect really came to the fore. Indeed, what is fascinating about his work
is the degree to which he was able to apply the principles on show in
Edinburgh New Town and Bloomsbury to the mass production of
acres upon acres of humdrum bye-law housing.

In Toxteth, Roberts had four principal estates, named prosaically
but functionally, estates 1, 2, 3 and 4. Estate 3[12] – the largest – included
what have become known as the 'Welsh Streets', nineteen in all, each

named after a Welsh town or village, such as Powis, Rhiwlas, Voelas and Madryn streets – reflective of the ever-growing community of Welsh families who were moving to Liverpool in search of work.[13] It also included various streets named after Charles Dickens characters, including Pecksniff, Nickleby, Copperfield and Micawber, that were developed between, roughly, 1873 and 1875.[14] In all, 1,776 houses were eventually built on this estate,[15] which was laid out as orthogonal grids, but with the axes of the grids shifting to create a patchwork of visually distinct sets of streets. On the large Estate 4, north-west of Princes Road, Owens recorded that he built 1,900 houses, while on the much smaller estates numbered 1 and 2 he built 320 and 300 houses respectively. So 4,296 houses in all.[16]

From the early 1870s, the sheer scale of building, and the extent of land under development, meant that Owens was obliged to create a master plan for the area. And this master plan could be implemented because of Roberts's all-embracing landownership. For the historian Gareth Carr, the fact that this master plan was prepared 'by one architect for a single client' is 'significant in the context of the development of speculative housing in Liverpool, but is also potentially significant in the history of town planning in the wider national context'.[17]

Look, though, at the detailed Ordnance Survey maps produced at the turn of the twentieth century, and you can clearly see that this master plan did not involve the application of one vast overlying structure. Instead the maps show the creation of a complex urban grain, with clusters of gridiron streets, generally built at roughly the same date and under Roberts and Owens's control, orientated in a profusion of directions. There are many possible reasons for this, ranging from the artistic to the purely practical. From an aesthetic point of view the alignment of the grids of each separate development would have created long and unforgiving vistas that would have proved monotonous and unremittingly repetitive. Shifting the axis of individual clusters of gridiron developments, by contrast, creates some sense of variety and surprise as one traverses Toxteth. Certainly this approach reflects the Gothic-inspired sensibilities of the late nineteenth century, which favoured variety, and helps give each cluster of streets a sense of enclosure and individual identity that would have helped generate a feeling of community. This strategy was only possible on the larger estates – numbers 3 and 4 – and these socially subtle intentions seem to be supported by the choice of street names, with each gridded section of the larger estates often having their own very recognisable set of names, whether derived from the Old Testament, or Charles Dickens novels, or Welsh villages or towns.

So far as the various grid blocks are concerned, analysis suggests that the decision to divide the larger estates into a patchwork of orthogonal gridded streets was, at least partly, pragmatic and the consequence of the determination to squeeze the maximum amount of bye-law housing on to different parcels of land as easily and speedily as possible. A clue to this is that the orientations of grids respond to patterns of landownership, field boundaries and existing paths, rights of way and roads, often with a grid of new streets being set parallel with the nearest existing main thoroughfare. The layout of Estate 3 is a good example of this. The 1847 Ordnance Survey map of the area shows that the open land between Admiral Street to the south and North Hill Street to the north-west, on which Estate Number 3's 'Welsh Streets' were to be built, was covered with a network of small fields, gardens and building-lined yards that in fact form the basis for the alignment and location of the future streets. Similarly, the south portion of Estate 4 was covered with field boundaries that determined the orientation and location of Cairns Street and its neighbours. Theoretically, orientation towards light could have played a role in determining layout – for example, the best rooms in the best houses might face south – but there is no clear evidence of this. Such a strategy is, in any case, inevitably problematic because in two-room-deep houses an ideal orientation for a front room can mean a dismal orientation for a rear room.

Also evident, when one ponders the Ordnance Survey maps, is the way in which the numerous self-contained grids of bye-law housing were set within the broader urban structure of wide streets

Detail from the 1908 Ordnance Survey map of Toxteth showing the southern portion of David Roberts's Estate Number 3 (left) and a portion of Estate Number 4 (right) with western parts of Cairns Street and Jermyn Street. The estates are divided by Princes Road, with the orthogonal grids of groups of streets rotated to give visual variety. The 'Welsh Streets' (bottom) on Estate Number 3 run north-west to south-east. The 'Dickens' streets (top left) on Estate Number 3 run both west to east and north to south.

and parks. Late nineteenth-century Toxteth Park was a socially mixed area in which large houses – often detached and set on wider streets – were dramatically juxtaposed with the narrower and far humbler bye-law streets. Some of the wider streets mark not only the location of larger houses but also some of the non-residential buildings, including public ones and parades of shops.

Sometimes the differences in scale are subtle. For example, Kelvin Grove, marking the north-east edge of the sequence of 'Welsh Streets', is slightly wider than the streets to its south-west, and its terrace houses are larger, being three storeys high, with habitable basements and with two-storey canted, or angled, bays set in generous front enclosures, i.e. small gardens. Its ornament is also more elaborate, and includes a red terracotta eaves cornice incorporating blocks of concave-quadrant profile connected by small arches and topped by early Gothic-style 'dog-tooth' motifs – all no doubt made by the Ruabon brickworks in North Wales, which Owen favoured.

The census returns reveal that these slight differences were socially and economically of great significance and make clear why bye-law housing had, for practical reasons, to include homes of slightly differing scale and ambition. Bye-law houses were intended to accommodate not only the more ordinary, and lower-paid, working men and their families but also skilled and higher-paid workers, such as foremen, clerks and the lower ranks of civil servants and officials, such as police constables. And sometimes, as in the case of Kelvin Grove, the tenants were yet more elevated. In 1901, for example, the census reveals that number 5 was occupied by Daniel Dunglinson, the 57-year-old 'Principal Clerk H. M. Customs, Liverpool', while nearby lived Thomas Hy. Walker, a 51-year-old 'Architect & Surveyor' whose household of seven included a 21-year-old female 'General servant'.

It's not only scale that provides a clue to the status of a house within the overall social hierarchy of the area. Subtle details of design do, too. The north-west portion of Estate 3 offers a case in point. There, the individual houses in the terraces that face on to Warwick Street and in Merlin Street are, at seventeen to eighteen feet across, not only slightly wider than the 'standard' fifteen feet or less, but also boast ground-floor front rooms that are served by bay windows, of canted, here half-hexagonal, plan, each rising from a diminutive but ornately railed front 'garden', or enclosure. Geraint Street came next, with houses with canted bay windows but no front enclosures, while the houses in the other streets were given neither canted bays nor enclosures. Sadly, about 75 per cent of the Owens–Roberts terraces have been demolished since the Second World War. Fortunately, the set of early streets on the south-east portion of Estate 3 has been saved.[18]

Despite the subtle hierarchy of house types and variety of detailing, and despite the regular rotation of orthogonal grids, which, intended or not, gave some degree of picturesque irregularity, Roberts and Owens's generally repetitive bye-law housing must have made their urban quarter somewhat visually daunting. Their simple response was, when appropriate, to introduce a degree of variety by placing larger houses on the wider streets, to plant kerb-side trees, and latterly, on more important thoroughfares, to build shops with flats above to simulate a traditional high-street atmosphere.[19] But perhaps most significant in the attempt to give these estates the sense of an authentic city was, where possible, to introduce public and monumental buildings, which, apart from the particular function they were there to fulfil, acted as points of reference in the landscape as well as relieving visual monotony. These non-domestic buildings included a scattering of pubs that, given Roberts and Owens's chapel background, were tolerated by them rather than welcomed (total abstinence on these estates was not attempted and it would not have made business sense to do so). Owens made his view clear in one of his letters, where he applauded himself for building 750 houses and shops on the Campfield Estate in Everton and for ensuring that 'three Public houses only [were] allowed', none of which was permitted to open on Sundays.[20]

Most significant among the estates' non-residential buildings were the chapels and churches, notably the Welsh Presbyterian church on Princes Road (to which tree-lined Princes Avenue runs parallel) built between 1865 and 1868 with a substantial financial contribution from

Roberts. The architects were W & G Audsley, but Owens played a key role because he authorised payments for works on the building. Designed for a dominant corner site in a striking French-inspired Gothic Revival style, the church – with a pair of tall gables set at right angles and flanking an asymmetrically placed 200-foot-tall spire-topped tower – was intended to be a powerful vertical accent in a setting formed largely of domestic terraces of classical design. It could seat 1,200 people, which meant that, when it opened, it could host the largest congregation of any Welsh chapel or church in the world. Unsurprisingly, the church became known as the 'Welsh Cathedral', and not just because of its impressive scale and strident Gothic design. As the focus of the Welsh community in Liverpool, the church also played a key role in the area's working life, functioning both as a place of worship and as a labour exchange. New arrivals from Wales would go to the church seeking work; there, they would present an almost passport-like ticket given to them by their chapel in Wales that guaranteed they were of upright character. On the strength of that recommendation, they would hope to be offered employment by building contractors within the congregation.

It's important to emphasise that Roberts and Owens were not, in any significant sense, philanthropists, nor were their building activities altruistic. Both did much to support Toxteth's Welsh community. But ultimately they were businessmen. They built vast numbers of bye-law houses for the simple reason that they hoped to make a profit. And there was a profit because late nineteenth-century Toxteth and Liverpool was thriving, and the working men attracted to it had the regular jobs and the regular wages that went with them, on which the developers depended for their own income. The fact that Roberts and Owens were part of the commercial world that created these stable financial conditions was, of course, evidence of their business acumen and one of the key foundations of their success. They worked creatively within government regulations and with the city authorities to provide the type of housing required for the mutual benefit of all.

Developments tended to follow a certain pattern. First Owens would lay out the streets and determine the number of houses they could accommodate, squeezing in as many as the bye-law regulations allowed. Then Roberts leased out parcels of land to builders and building firms that ranged from plots small enough to contain no more than a pair of houses to ones large enough to accommodate entire terraces. The builders would work to Owens's designs, perhaps adding a few extra embellishments if they thought these commercially desirable, after which they would rent out the completed houses. Some houses might have been built by Roberts directly, for the benefit of rental income; others were built by building clubs formed of potential occupants; or by member-owned financial institutions, such as building societies. The object of the latter two initiatives, in particular, was to minimise land and building costs by operating in bulk.

Judging from the tone of his correspondence, Owens was an archetypal Victorian businessman: forceful and opinionated, ready to take on Liverpool's city officers over planning issues and happy to threaten miscreant debtors with the law. Sadly, his original surveys and house plans are not known to have survived. However, plans dating from 1891 for a group of eight houses in Buckland Street, which was built south of the 'Welsh Streets' and located near the Herculaneum Dock, are still extant and offer a useful insight into key aspects of the later generation of bye-law housing in Toxteth Park.[21] Signed 'Richd. Owens and Son Architect' and produced by Owens's son Hugh, who took over the family business, they reveal the standard arrangement of two main rooms per floor. On the ground floor were a front-room 'parlour' and a rear-room 'kitchen' (which no doubt also served as a dining room). On the first floor – labelled in rather grand eighteenth-century manner 'the Chamber plan' – are the bedrooms. Ground and first-floor front rooms are slightly extended and lit by shallow canted bays rising from very small front gardens.[22]

These Buckland Street houses all have water closets, reached from their rear yards. The yards themselves are serviced by a narrow alley. Curiously, next to the WCs, 'ash' stores are shown, presumably a survival from earlier times when privies were perched over cesspits and a shovelful of ash was used to bury excrement and seal

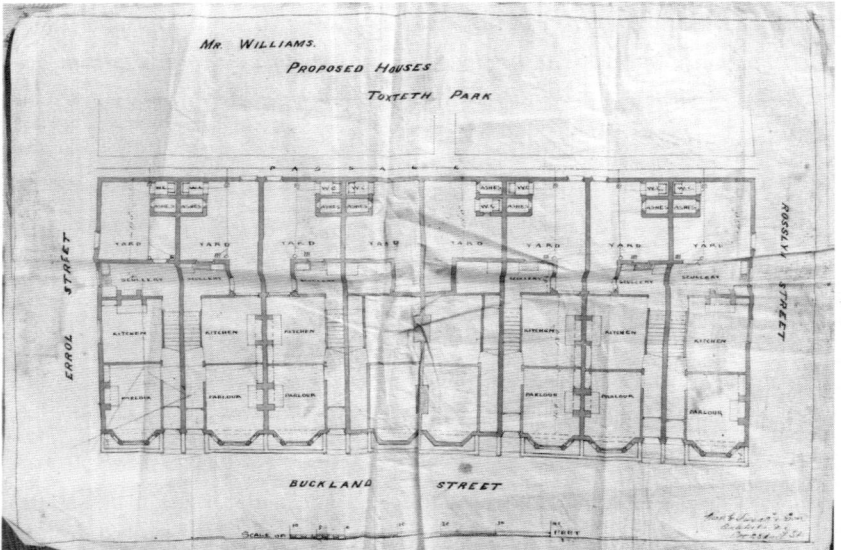

Ground-floor plan of a group of houses to be built in Buckland Street, Toxteth. The design dates from the early 1890s and is signed 'Richard Owens & Son Architects'.

in the stench. By the 1890s, such ash stores must have been used for coal. These houses also have small rear wings that at ground-floor level contain a scullery, with sink and water supply, adjoining the kitchen, and at first-floor level, in the end-of-terraces houses, the luxury of a plumbed-in bathroom adjoining a small bedroom in the wing. Where possible, houses were constructed in pairs with mirror plans, so that party walls incorporating chimney breasts that served the pairs could be built in one operation, and so achieve a slight cost saving per pair that would become significant if many houses overall were involved.

Over time, as the Toxteth houses display, amendments to the bye-laws, and additional Building Acts, laid stricter rules on would-be developers. By the 1880s walls, if made of brick, had to be at least nine inches thick. In Toxteth Park this was achieved – not through cavity wall, or double-skin, construction, which though in use in the late nineteenth century did not become common practice in Britain until the 1920s, but through the simple expedient of fully bonded, load-bearing wall construction. This was realised by laying bricks in Flemish bond, in which alternate bricks on each course are laid to present their long face (stretcher) and short face (header). When well executed, with full-depth headers, this type of construction can be very solid. Very occasionally English bond (in which courses of stretchers alternate with courses of headers) was used and even (as in the case of Elwy Street, a northward continuation of Gwydir Street) English Garden Wall bond, in which every fourth course is formed with headers. This bond was used for economy – to reduce the number of bricks required – but in this case the yellow bricks are of high quality and beautifully and precisely laid.

Well-built foundations for the walls were required, as were damp-proof courses, set at least nine inches below timber joists, the ends of which were waterproofed with bitumen. Generous floor-to-ceiling heights were also specified, as were ventilation (including under-floor ventilation) and window sizes, which meant as a rule that the area of a window had to be at least 10 per cent of the floor area of the room it served. Externally, cast-iron eaves gutters were required, and generally stone or cast-stone lintels were preferred to brick window arches, as is the case in most of the standard Toxteth bye-law houses.

* * * * *

Where they survive, the Welsh Streets of Estate 3 offer a represent-ative and fascinating insight into the scope of Roberts and Owens's Toxteth development and the nature of the houses that filled it. For a long time it was assumed that they were originally occupied almost exclusively by Welsh families that had recently settled in Toxteth Park and that they were partly built by Welsh workers.[23] Certainly, from the point of view of construction, Roberts and Owens were in the habit of importing building materials from North Wales, notably hard and fine-quality facing brick, which included red bricks used very occasionally for string course, and moulded bricks for very limited amounts of ornamental detail. It was undoubtedly the case, too, that there was not only a whole network of Welsh-speaking profession-als in Liverpool (most of who were involved in the building trade), including solicitors, estate agents, banks and even Welsh building societies, but also Welsh builders and labourers who would have sought to secure housing in precisely the sort of streets that the Welsh Streets had to offer. It's therefore not surprising to find that the 1881 census returns for Voelas Street,[24] for example, list four Welsh-born family 'Heads' in residence five or so years after its construction who were themselves involved in the building trade: David Evans, aged 39, at number 4 was a carpenter; John Jones, aged 38, at number 28 was a joiner, as was 43-year-old Thomas Roberts at number 60, while 53-year-old Owen Jones at number 56 was described as a 'Sawyer Wood' by occupation. All these lived on the south side of the street, which was possibly regarded by those who lived there as comprising slightly better houses. David Evans's house still survives, though decades of neglect and dereliction, and recent and very thorough internal repairs and rearrangement, mean that it's now virtually impossible to tell whether it was once of a fractionally superior nature or styled to reflect Evans's elevated status.

A closer study of the returns, however, reveals a slightly more complex picture. It would seem that while there was a strong Welsh presence in the Toxteth Park area in the early days of its development, by the 1880s and 1890s it was very far from being the dominant one. By 1901, indeed, the peak of the Welsh influx into Liverpool was already a generation or two in the past and most occupants of the streets, even if of Welsh origin, had been born in or around Liverpool.[25] The 1881 census, which lists the four Welsh occupants of Voelas Street involved in the building trade, also reveals that only three other heads of families could lay claim to coming from the principality, while, for the rest, there was a real mixture of occupants – and indeed of occupations. Many were of Irish and Scottish origin, and at number 22 there was 28-year-old Samuel Gittins, who had been born in New York and was a corn merchant's clerk married to a Liverpool woman. At number 23 was William Henry Phillips, a 44-year-old accountant from Halifax, 'North America'. Trades and occupations included a ship's carpenter (at number 3); a 'surveyor and draughtsman' (at number 8); a dentist (at number 11); a cabinet-maker (at number 12); a marine engineer (at number 14); a journalist, Kaufman C. Spiers (at number 29); a 'steamship Wharfinger', an operator of a commercial wharf (at number 39); a 'master mariner' (at number 58); a chemist (at number 54); Liverpool pilots (numbers 57 and 45); and 'Mariners' (numbers 13 and 27).[26]

The houses of Voelas Street are broadly uniform, consisting of two storeys furnished with single-storey canted bays and with a single first-floor window directly above. They were originally set in front enclosures with ornamental ironwork (shown in old photographs but now removed), which marks them as being slightly superior to the houses of neighbouring Rhiwlas Street to the south, whose single-storey canted bays rise directly from the pavement.[27] The tree-planting on Voelas Street also serves to set it apart a little from neighbouring streets. Where elsewhere it could be on the sparse side, here an avenue runs along the kerb, which until recently was dotted with majestic and mature trees. These were felled while repair work was being carried out and have been replaced by more widely spaced saplings.

Voelas Street. Above: the street in about 1911. Typical of the better Toxteth bye-law streets, the houses here have single-storey bays rising within small, railed enclosures. Below: a pair of houses in Voelas Street, which was completed by 1876. By 2025, the long-decaying terrace had been repaired and accommodation enlarged, rendering one door in each pair redundant. The chimney stacks have been removed, as have the front enclosures.

The Voelas Street houses are generally built in pairs with mirror plans and adjoining front doors. Above every pair of arch-topped front doors is a blank window that reveals the houses in the street to be slightly wider than a standard one-window-wide house. Each is faced with red brick laid in Flemish bond but with headers of slightly darker red brick. Further decoration is provided by a nine-brick-high lozenge within each blank window, defined by a combination of yellow and dark blue or black bricks, and by a continuous eaves cornice incorporating blocks of concave yellow brick that are set above a 'frieze' implied by a three-brick-deep band comprising a course of red bricks sets between courses of dark blue or black bricks. This frieze band aligns with the depth of the stone lintels set above the first-floor windows. Such small flourishes (and with the lozenges being special to Voelas Street) confirm its slightly elevated status. Other streets boast their own decorative touches – indeed those touches vary within streets as well as between them.[28] It is tempting to imagine that the builders and their bricklayers had an amusing time coming up with these different schemes, which would have added little to the overall cost of each house. Whether the conscious aim was to give each generally similar street a different visual character and a distinct sense of identity can now, alas, only be a matter of debate.

While brick of varied hues dominates the decorative flourishes in Voelas Street and the other Welsh Streets, cast artificial stone also plays a part (the houses of Elwy Street, for example, boast cast-stone lintels with heads of Green Men and bearded heads flanked by bunches of grapes and vine leaves – perhaps Druid bards and a nod to the area's Welsh heritage, or Bacchus, though the latter seems unlikely given that Calvinistic Methodists were the street's probable intended inhabitants).[29] Sandstone plays a part too, and is used for the lintels and supporting posts in the area's canted bays. The lintels are mostly detailed with chamfered or bevelled lower edges in the tradition of timber-frame construction, or with simple mouldings. The bays are given a little more finesse and cultural pedigree by being topped – originally at least – by gutters with the profile of a simple

classical cornice formed with concave and convex quadrant mouldings. These gutter cornices, where the originals survive, appear to be
mostly made of cast iron, which seems sensible, although some appear
to be carved of stone as part of the lintel arrangement.

The often-differing cornice levels, not to mention the rich variety
of brick decoration, suggest slightly differing building operations –
even though long facades appear to be of continuous construction
with no straight joints between houses. So it is reasonable to assume
that the individual and artistic touches were due to decisions made
by the builders of the individual portions of terraces rather than by
Owens. All are nevertheless typical products of the Owens office, and
in their plans, volumes and appointments demonstrate that he was at
the cutting edge of bye-law requirements – perhaps even to a degree
anticipating them – and apparently working to the minimum requirements that after 1875 were demanded by law when constructing speculatively built terraces houses for the labouring classes.

The internal layout of each of the houses of Voelas Street (anticipating the arrangement in the slightly later Buckland Street) involved
a small front room, a passage from the front door to the kitchen
and scullery at the back of the house, and compact bedrooms above.
Behind lay a small wing and small yard, accessed by a back door,
and in which a small free-standing privy would have been located.
The yard would have been serviced by a narrow alley – the standard
arrangement for such developments. None of the houses had a cellar
or a basement.

The basic measurements complied with the bye-laws, which required
each habitable room to have an area of at least 108 square feet of clear
space (which meant, once the square footage occupied by the staircase
and chimney breast was taken into consideration, that houses had to
have a frontage of at least 12 feet if their depth could also be 12 feet). So
far as the rear yard was concerned, however, those in Voelas Street only
just conformed with bye-law regulations, which demanded an area of
at least 150 square feet, not only to allow for the WC and storage but to
ensure ventilation and to allow daylight to enter the house. Later and
more ambitious bye-law terraces, such as those of Buckland Street, would

have compact rear wings, larger yards and even, as already mentioned, plumbed-in bathrooms.

The houses in Voelas Street were small, but they appear not to have been too densely inhabited. On the day that the 1881 census was taken, the fifty-seven houses recorded (three were listed as 'uninhabited') were occupied by 234 people, so an average of just over four people per house. Those that contained many more than the average – for example, number 2 with nine people, number 19 with ten, and number 47 with eleven – were nevertheless home to single families, with – presumably – children and unmarried adults of the same sex sharing bedrooms. Only one house, number 25, contained two separate households, but one of these consisted of just one person and the total number of occupants, on the day of the census at least, was five. Interestingly, given the generally quite humble nature of the area, seven of the households kept a 'domestic' or 'general' servant – invariably a girl or very young woman.[30]

What did the interiors of the bye-law houses of Voelas Street look like in the early 1880s? How were they decorated, furnished and serviced? The answers can only be informed speculation, because such modest, unassuming and once common homes were not fully documented, and, by being taken for granted and not much admired by contemporary chroniclers of domestic life, have fallen through the historical cracks. So reconstructing the interiors of these homes can be little more than a work of the imagination, informed by a knowledge of the tastes of the times and of the products readily available to most Toxteth Park residents.

The houses were no doubt lit by gas (after 1892 utilising newly invented incandescent 'mantles', or mesh covers fixed around a gas jet, which gave a brighter, whiter and steadier flame) but perhaps, on occasion, by candles and by lamps fuelled by rapeseed oil or by petroleum-based paraffin or kerosene, which had become cheap and readily available soon after 1850. Water was supplied to the scullery and heated on the coal-fired range in the kitchen for cooking, washing and bathing. In the houses without plumbed-in bathrooms – which were virtually all the early houses in the Welsh Streets area – a metal bath would have been placed in one of the ground-floor rooms, presumably the kitchen, and filled with water for bathing. Plumbed-in bathrooms probably only had cold water on tap and a drain, so hot water would have been supplied in the same manner, although in theory, at least, gas-powered hot-water 'geysers' had been available to householders since 1868, and since 1889 the very much safer storage-tank gas water heater. Whether these innovations were in general use in late nineteenth-century bathrooms in Toxteth's bye-law housing is currently unknown. It seems distinctly unlikely.

The now-popular perception that late Victorian working people bathed once a week at best – most likely on a Sunday – is probably correct, because it is based on not-too-distant memories. It's also hardly surprising, since heating the water and then disposing of it from baths that had not been plumbed in would have been hard work.

The kitchen would have contained a range or hob-grate on which food could easily be cooked in an open pan. Efficient ovens remained something of a luxury, were expensive to run and took time to heat up, so morsels that did not need cooking at home were popular. In river- and seaside locations such as Liverpool, all manner of shellfish were available, including whelks, winkles and mussels, and fish such as sprats, herring, sardines, pilchards and eels. Vegetables – potatoes notably, but other basics as well – would also have been available in due season. Cheaper meats that included American bacon would have been affordable for some, but in general the poor were obliged to devour a whole range of inner body parts that we would now consider inedible. Some of this dubious material was made into faggots and sausages; other offcuts found their way into stews and soups. There was 'tripe' (the lining of the stomach of cattle or sheep), 'stink' (prematurely born calves), 'broxy' (meat from an animal that had died of diseases), 'lights' (lungs of livestock) and offal generally – including the still-popular liver and kidney – along with sheep's head, cow's feet and pig's trotters, slivers of brain and slices of tongue. All cooking, when necessary, utilised coal – as did the heating of the house – which is a reminder that the bye-law streets of Toxteth must have endured a steady dark cloud of pollution.

As for interior decoration, the prevailing and standard taste of the 1880s tended towards the creation of rooms that were visually busy and ornate, thus suggesting wealth and plenty, rather than austerity and scarcity. So it is easy to imagine that parlours were piled with knick-knacks, and since a number of the houses were the homes of mariners, or of workmen connected with the docks, it is possible that many would have contained strange souvenirs gathered from ports around the world. As for art and culture, parlours were probably adorned with framed popular, and usually patriotic, prints and with furniture that aped – often in ungainly and ill-made manner – a particular historical style; Jacobean and Renaissance were particularly popular in the 1880s. Some of the more aspirational households might have possessed an upright piano, dominating one corner of the minuscule parlour, because home entertainment and music would have been an important part of life. As for books – and the wider world of art and education – these became more accessible for the residents of Toxteth when Toxteth Library opened in Windsor Street in October 1902. Designed by Liverpool Corporation architect Thomas Shelmerdine in splendid Edwardian baroque style, the library, with huge Venetian windows lighting its reading rooms, was a conscious beacon of learning and an urban ornament whose opening ceremony was attended by the Scottish-American industrialist and philanthropist Andrew Carnegie. He had supported the construction of public libraries since the 1880s, with the aim of making education more accessible, and extolled the Toxteth building as the 'ideal library'. His visit in 1902 prompted him to donate £13,000 to the city's library system.

When it came to floor coverings, by the time that Voelas Street was constructed, the painted canvas floor cloths once deployed in humbler houses would have given way to the much more durable, economic and practical floor covering linoleum, patented in 1863. Utilising linseed oil, pine resin and burlap, it offered the twin advantages of being easily cleanable with a mop and water, and being available in printed patterns or in strong single colours. It was particularly popular in those areas of the house that experienced heavy footfall:

A photograph from 1903 showing a kitchen in a house in Pretoria Avenue, Walthamstow, London. Slightly larger than the standard Toxteth bye-law houses, this London model had its kitchen located in the ground floor of a generously proportioned rear wing. Note the large and well-appointed cast-iron range, the compact dresser, ornamental birdcage, linoleum on the floor and oil lamp suspended from the ceiling. The table was probably for breakfast and informal eating, with a dining room located in the adjoining front room.

entrance passages, kitchens, sculleries and staircases. Wall covering
was a matter of taste and fashion, but it would seem that rich and
dark colours painted in cheap and stable distempers and oil paints
were favoured, with wallpaper probably being used in the ground-
floor front parlour. In most houses this would have been the best
room, almost sacrosanct, for use by the family on Sundays and on
high days and holidays.

* * * * *

Not that much had changed since 1881 in Veolas Street when the
first census of the twentieth century was taken in 1901. The average
number of people per house was virtually unchanged at 4.25.[31] A
Welsh presence was still apparent. Only three of the Welsh-born
'Heads', however, were involved with the building trade: David Evans,
a joiner/carpenter aged 59, and his Welsh wife at number 4 (their
son, aged 31, had been born in Liverpool and was not in the building
trade but was a 'shipping clerk'); John Jones, a stonemason aged 28
and his Welsh wife lived at number 28; and at number 52 was William
Roberts, a 52-year-old joiner, and his Welsh wife. There was only
one non-Welsh household involved with the building trade, a wood-
carver at number 57, and the occupations followed by the Welsh-born
heads of households who were not in the building trade were varied,
including a police constable, a printer and a warehouseman. Indeed,
the occupations and trades of the street as a whole were diverse in
the extreme and, apart from the building tradesmen, few household
heads followed similar occupations. This was a reasonably well-to-do
neighbourhood, more lower middle class than working class.

One thing that it was not was ethnically diverse. Liverpool
might have been a great port and racial melting pot, but the occupants of Voelas Street – and indeed of its slightly poorer cousin
Rhiwlas Street – were primarily English (and a large number Liverpudlian) by birth, even if, to judge by their surnames, many were
of Welsh descent. Of those born outside England the majority came
from Wales, followed closely by Scotland, Ireland, and with several
coming from the Isle of Man. Few came from more distant lands

or from countries that formed parts of the British Empire. The only exceptions were at 45 Rhiwlas Street, where the London-born foreman at a cigarette factory, Abraham Baustein, had a Russian wife; and at number 20, where the Irish furniture maker in residence had married a 'British subject' born in India. Whether she was an ethnic Indian born in an area under direct British control – in other words, an Anglo-Indian – or the child of British parents who were living in India at the time she was born is not made clear. In Voelas Street in 1901 there were none not born in the United Kingdom.

Census returns give us a snapshot view of the people of Voelas Street at various stages of its early history. They also reveal how the subtle gradations in the nature of the housing in the streets around was reflected by the character and occupations of those who took up residence there. In 1901, Voelas Street's humbler neighbour, Rhiwlas Street, contained a larger number of more menial tradesmen and a higher population density per house of just over five people. For houses with a maximum of three bedrooms this was high in the context of bye-law aspirations. Additionally, only one household – that of the Welsh blacksmith John Griffith at number 42 – appears to have been affluent enough to keep a servant, though, since she was also Griffith's cousin, it's quite possible that she lived in his house and worked elsewhere. By contrast, in Voelas Steet in 1901, three households kept servants.

Three of the small Rhiwlas Street houses contained two separate households, meaning that interior arrangements must have been awkward and cramped in the extreme. Was the ground-floor kitchen and scullery shared, or was one of the house's other rooms made into a second kitchen? This, of course, would potentially have meant a reduction in bedroom space. In number 9 there were seven people; in number 54 six people, but it was in number 55 that living arrangements must have been most problematic. One of its households was headed by Catherine Byrne, only 21, who lived with her three sisters – all single, all 'packers' in a factory, all born in Liverpool. In addition, this household contained two female 'boarders', aged six and eight, and both with the surname Williams, so presumably sisters. The other household inside number 55 consisted of a 42-year-old Irishwoman and her two sons, aged 12 and 15. It is difficult to see how nine people, of such different ages and in two separate households, could have fitted themselves into this small house. Certainly not comfortably – perhaps not even with the propriety followed by the neighbours and demanded by the age. Did all the four sisters and the two girls sleep in one room, sharing a privy in the yard with the other family? This seems to have been likely, and if so perpetuated the evils of over-dense multi-occupation that the bye-laws were meant to help eradicate.

Meanwhile, the census returns of 1891 for one of the area's slightly more aspirational streets – Cairns Street – show that each of its two-storey houses was occupied by a single family (admittedly, some took in lodgers) and that they were more likely to employ servants than those who occupied the smaller streets to the south-west. The houses at the west end of the street are particularly spacious. Originally with habitable basements and with shallow rear wings, each comprised twelve or so rooms of various sizes, with a centrally placed front door set between a canted bay serving the dining room and a square bay for the best parlour (an arrangement that became something of a convention in higher-quality bye-law housing). One of these larger houses, number 1 Cairns Street, was occupied in 1891 by a 35-year-old 'flour dealer', his three family members and a 37-year-old Welsh-born female 'domestic servant'; while number 3 was occupied by a 61-year-old man and wife living on their 'own means' and a 21-year-old female servant, also Welsh-born. The occupations listed of others in the street were sturdily 'respectable', ranging from 'bank clerk' to 'teacher' to, at number 13, 'Customs Officer'. One or two were recorded as 'living on own means', though this is perhaps a little deceptive, since in 1891 that could well mean no more than living on a meagre annuity (although in 1891 not a state pension, because these were not paid in the UK until 1909) rather than on lavish interest from invested capital. The one house that gives any indication of having been rather overcrowded was number 11, which was occupied by a 43-year-old 'Baker and Flour Merchant', his wife, nine sons and daughters (aged

17 years to 5 months) and three female domestic servants. Even for one of the larger houses in the street, this must have been a squeeze.[32]

Cairns Street, with its relatively high rents and larger houses at its west end, was clearly not primarily a place for working men but for the upper tier of skilled artisans, managers, tradesmen, superior shopkeepers, manufacturers, minor civil servants and employers. Few were involved with the sea or the docks, probably because the street was just a little too far from the Mersey. Additionally, very few of the inhabitants were Welsh-born, apart from a handful of servant girls, or had direct connections with the building world. The slightly elevated social tone of Cairns Street is reflected in the cornices of its various terraces. These display a subtle hierarchy of occupation. The larger houses at the street's west end predictably have the most ornate cornices. These are similar – but not identical – to those on the large houses in Kelvin Grove. They also are topped with 'dog-tooth' ornament, then terracotta blocks of concave-quadrant profile set over convex quadrants, which rise above a terracotta-made rope motif. The terracotta is warm red in tone, to match the colour of the house facades. Cornices on the slightly smaller houses towards the east end of the street, on its north side, have similar cornices but without the concave blocks or rope motif. The facades of these houses are also built with warm red bricks. Houses on the south side of the east portion of the street have cornices that are different yet again, mostly with terracotta blocks of concave quadrant profile topped with a band of yellow bricks and with a four-brick-high 'frieze' formed with red and yellow bricks set over a course of dark blue or black bricks. The contrast between the red brick of the facades and the yellow and blue or black brick – used also around the front doors – is most striking. This ornament is achieved in a most economic manner and here – as elsewhere in the Welsh Streets – its subtle variations relate to the varied social and economic statuses of the different classes of occupants for which the houses were intended, and is also a reminder that the generally homogeneous developments were the work of different teams of builders operating under Owens's broad control.

Meanwhile, neighbouring Jermyn Street[33] was home to the next

Top: a pair of doors, with timber-gabled surrounds, in Jermyn Street, Toxteth. Middle: detail of the ground floor of a house in Elwy Street – one of Toxteth's 'Welsh Streets'. Bottom: a richly detailed eaves cornice – made of moulded terracotta and brick – at the west end of Cairns Street. Note the intricately detailed rope moulding.

social tier up: mostly professional men or entrepreneurs, from a cotton broker and his bank-clerk son at number 21 to the 51-year-old 'Vice consul for Germany' – Edward Meyer – his wife, son, daughter and 30-year-old female 'general servant' at number 31. The one exception might seem to be the 48-year-old 'Coachman Groom', William Bridelaw, who lived at number 44 with his wife, son, daughter and two lodgers. But then coachmen and grooms were among the 'aristocrats' of the service trades: highly skilled and highly trusted.

The houses of Jermyn Street provide physical testimony to the lives and ambitions of their occupants. The standard ones are two windows wide, four storeys high, including basements and garrets, and so originally – with their two-storey rear wings – contained about nine habitable rooms, including perhaps four or five bedrooms (with servant girls probably sleeping in basement kitchens or in the sculleries). They were, in comparison with most bye-law houses, generously appointed. They also have pretty Gothic-style pointed arches above their front doors (the German vice consul's house and its neighbour, number 29, retain delicate timber porches with ornate valances), and there are eaves cornices, like those at the west end of Cairns Street but without the rope motif to be found there. The houses are faced with good yellow brick – enlivened with bands of red brick aligned with the stone lintels over the first-floor windows – have canted bays to the ground-floor front rooms, and small front gardens, originally screened from the pavement by ornate iron railings. With its elegant rows of houses and trees along both kerbs – as was usual in the superior Toxteth bye-law streets – Jermyn Street was designed to attract and please a superior class of resident.

* * * * *

By 1901 the parallel rows of trees planted along the kerbs of Voelas Street would have been starting to mature and must have formed a pleasing theatre for convivial street life and an avenue for evening promenades in the summer. They might appear a small urban detail, but, apart from their inherent attractiveness, the trees also symbolised the aspirations of the class of people who lived on that street.

The simple nineteenth-century concept for the creation of a 'model' society was based on the belief that those working people who were sensible and sober wanted nothing more than to 'improve' themselves and rise through the ranks of society. And the surest way to do this was for working people to emulate the lifestyle, habits and tastes of the upper classes: enjoying the natural world, going for convivial walks in ornamental public parks and, while doing so, engaging in respectable conversation. In such ways, and through perseverance and hard work, each citizen could, in the words of Samuel Smiles in that seminal work *Self-Help*, published in 1859, realise 'all the powers of his godlike nature'.

For the inhabitants of Voelas Street, local greenery was not confined to the rows of trees on their road. Just a short distance away were the expanses of Prince's Park, opened in 1842 and to a degree inspired in its design by the private picturesque parks of aristocratic country-house estates. It was a place where people could promenade and listen to music performed at the bandstand. Contemporary records reveal that the music played in such venues was not primarily popular airs or music-hall favourites or the offerings of local brass bands, but included works by Handel and other classical composers. Bandstands were not forlorn monuments to good intention. On the contrary, in the age just before cinema, they were regarded by the public as splendid entertainment. In the Arboretum in Lincoln, laid out between 1870 and 1872 on city-owned land, 40,000 people attended bandstand concerts in 1889 alone.[34]

Prince's Park represents something of a pioneering operation in what was to become a widespread aspect of Victorian town planning. In the early 1840s the public park – that is, a park created on publicly owned land, using public money, for the enjoyment of the public – was a new idea. It was not until 1846 that the UK's first truly public parks opened, in Manchester (Queen's Park and Philips Park) and Salford (Peel Park). The following year, Birkenhead Park opened on the other side of the Mersey from Toxteth. These were indeed public parks owned and created by the people for the people. The earlier Prince's Park is something rather different. It was an act of enlightened private patronage for public benefit, much like the pioneering Arboretum of 1840 in Derby, which was funded by the wealthy mill owner and philanthropist Joseph Strutt and laid out by the landscape genius John Claudius Loudon. Similarly, Victoria Park in east London, opened in 1845, was created by the Crown, even if its ambition – to improve the health and happiness of the local working urban population and, by doing so, make it more productive and less inclined to political turbulence – was very much that of the publicly funded parks that followed.

Prince's Park itself owes its inception to Richard Vaughan Yates – an iron merchant, philanthropist and religious Dissenter – who in 1842 bought the land from the Earl of Sefton with the intention of beautifying it as a park and opening it for public enjoyment. Its principal designer was Joseph Paxton, whose fame as the architect of the Crystal Palace (see page 172) still lay some years in the future but who had, at the time the park was being mooted, established a reputation as a gardener and designer of the Great Conservatory of 1836–41 at Chatsworth House, Derbyshire. He would go on to design the larger, much more ambitious and now far more famous Birkenhead Park. Opened in 1847, this park was in many ways the key pioneer of the publicly funded civic park, and was a primary influence on Frederick Law Olmstead when in the early 1850s he designed Central Park in New York.

Also involved in the creation of Prince's Park, if to a lesser extent, was Sir James Pennethorne. His influence was nevertheless significant. Pennethorne's career had taken off in 1826 when he became 'Principal Assistant' to John Nash, the architect to George IV, and the man responsible from 1812 for the layout of Regent's Park in London, with its periphery of speculatively built, stucco-clad classical residential terraces of uniform and palatial design, and scattering of detached villas placed within the park. Pennethorne took over elements of the scheme after Nash's death in 1835 and by the late 1840s, having by now also tucked the design of Victoria Park under his belt, was regarded as something of an expert on the aesthetics of classical architecture, urban planning and park design. His and Yates's hope was that Prince's Park would follow the model established at Regent's Park and Victoria Park, whereby the sale of house-building plots around the edge of the park would go some way to covering the costs of laying out the park itself, and rental income would pay for its maintenance. The initial aspirations for the Toxteth Park area were originally very high. It was intended to be a princely merchants' enclave.

In this respect, the park was initially something of a failure. A few large houses were built in the 1840s, notably those that survive on the corner of Sunnyside and Cavendish Gardens, which form a uniform, palatial stucco group very much in the spirit of London's Regent's Park. Some are large, detached villas, others semi-detached pairs. All are set in generous gardens. Along the serpentine frontage of Sunnyside, slightly later Italianate pairs survive, while on the eastern edge of the park, overlooking the asymmetrical lake created by Paxton, are the stucco-clad terrace of Prince's Park Mansions (built in 1843 to the designs of architect and antiquarian Wyatt Papworth) and the splendid stucco-clad and bow-fronted 1840s Windermere Terrace. However, it took until the 1860s for this elevated world of classical and Gothic palatial homes in an idyllic park setting to be fully realised.[35] To supply the requirement for domestic comfort and hygiene demanded by the large new houses and their wealthy occupants, a huge reservoir was constructed on nearby High Park Street. Built to the designs of Liverpool's water engineer Thomas Duncan, the reservoir, which opened in 1853, was capable of storing two million gallons of water to supply the residents of Toxteth with their daily needs. It has long fallen out of use but survives as a wonderland of Victorian engineering, with the robust brick vaults which form its roof supported by a forest of tall, slender but strong cast-iron columns that, glimpsed in the gloomy interior, seem to stretch into a geometrically perfect infinity.

And when the grand development was eventually completed, it was almost immediately overwhelmed by an avalanche of artistically humble bye-law terraces. What survived from its short-lived grander days was a glorious public park, an established network of large and grand houses and a series of broad and ornamental streets. These included Princes Road and Princes Avenue (at one point termed, in Parisian manner, a boulevard), which had been laid out in the late 1840s to connect the park to central Liverpool, and earlier streets created by the major landowner the Earl of Sefton as part of his late eighteenth-century development plans for his estate. He had obtained an Act of Parliament to permit building, commemorated by Parliament Street, which defines the north-west edge of Toxteth Park. These straight and wide streets, along with the park, would have made life in late nineteenth-century Toxteth profoundly different from life in the dank courts of central Liverpool.

* * * * *

Only around one-third of the houses built under Owens's supervision on Roberts's four Toxteth Park estates now survive. Hardest hit has been the small Estate 1, where all the houses have been demolished, and the large Estate 4, where around three-quarters of the houses have gone. The small Estate 2 survives pretty well intact, while Estate 3, containing the core of the Welsh Streets, retains around 50 per cent of its original houses. After years of desperate dereliction and sustained threats of demolition, what houses remain along the Welsh Streets were reprieved from imminent demolition following a public enquiry in June 2014, and most were subsequently repaired as homes. In 2015 the rejuvenation – almost reinvention – of the interiors of long-derelict houses in Cairns Street won the architecture and design collective Assemble, responsible for their resurrection, the Turner Prize. The collective had successfully demonstrated that these modest bye-law houses have a future and are capable of being transformed into desirable and characterful homes. But in spring 2025 many houses in Cairns Street as well as in neighbouring Ducie Street remain derelict, and the Presbyterian church on Princes Road – the 'Welsh Cathedral' and a building listed by the government as of special architectural and historic importance – stands as a gaunt and spectacular ruin, with one gable truncated, much of its roof gone, and its interior ravaged and laid to waste. Its fate seems emblematic of that of the Welsh community it once served and of the streets in which that community had lived.

As noted, dereliction even marks the superior housing to be found in Ducie Street, which lies parallel and immediately to the south of Jermyn Street. The terrace that once stood on its south side was demolished long ago, the site it occupied now a forlorn wasteland. The two-storey, three-window-wide houses on its north side, however, still survive. Set in generously sized front enclosures, with arch-topped stone piers flanking the paths leading to the front doors, they have central doors set between single-storey bays of differing form, and are faced with yellow brick, very finely and precisely laid in Flemish bond, which contrasts beautifully with the red brick and terracotta of their continuous eaves cornice. Yet they have been left abandoned for the best of a quarter century, and (as of spring 2025) are in an advanced state of deterioration.

The bye-law street was intended to be one of the key late Victorian strategies for self-improvement. It provided a place where a relatively genteel life could be lived in quintessential middle-class manner, and the census returns suggest that, by and large, this proved to be the case. Those who had established themselves in Voelas Street had found an admirable niche in the great city and port of Liverpool. It seems that the bye-law house had done its job. But it had not removed the nation's slums. Bye-law housing was for the lower middle class and the working-class elite. It was built as a private business enterprise to make profits, and rents were relatively high and far beyond the means of the typical urban slum dweller. A different housing strategy was required if this issue was to be addressed successfully. Its realisation led to the creation of 'public' housing: homes funded not by private speculators or philanthropists but by public authorities, notably urban or rural councils.

The Boundary Estate, one of the first large-scale, socially ambitious architectural experiments in publicly funded housing. Shown here is Marlow Buildings and Calvert Avenue seen from the mound in the centre of Arnold Circus.

The Birth of the Council Flat
The Boundary Estate, Shoreditch
(1890–1900)

P RIVATE, AND PROFIT-BASED, exercises in philanthropic
housing, such as those produced by various model-dwellings
companies, and the humble bye-law terrace house, provided
many working people with better homes than they had been used
to. But these initiatives hardly confronted, let alone solved, the core
problem of the urban slum. Clearly, a fresh approach was required.

As a small army of census enumerators collected data about
the inhabitants of Toxteth Park in 1901, others were knocking on
the doors of a brand-new experiment in working-class housing in
London's East End. This experiment did not involve the creation of
privately funded terraces, as in Liverpool, or tenements based on four
or five per cent philanthropy, such as those undertaken by the Four
Per Cent Industrial Dwellings Company or the Society for Improving the Condition of the Labouring Classes (SICLC) and other
model-dwellings companies, but of blocks of flats designed, built
and owned by a local authority – in this case the London County
Council (LCC), created just a few years earlier. The census revealed
that the new estate possessed 1,069 apartments, or 'tenements', with
an average of two or three bedrooms each, and with a planned population of 5,524 people at a density of about two people per room. This
density was reasonably high but – set in the context of the estate's
numerous amenities – offered a quality of life that was exceptional for
its late Victorian working-class occupants. Indeed, the whole notion

of the development was exceptional: this was publicly funded housing on publicly owned land, designed by a public architects' office. In essence, these were homes built by the people for the people, using in large part public revenue raised through the rates.

Neither the Boundary Street Estate in Shoreditch, on which construction started in 1893, nor the related LCC Millbank Estate in Pimlico, begun in 1897, were the nation's first publicly funded working-class housing schemes. The City of London Corporation had built tenements in 1865 along the Farringdon Road (named Corporation Buildings and designed by City architect Horace Jones, they were demolished in 1970);[1] and in 1869 Liverpool Corporation had launched an integrated municipal-housing policy when, utilising the 1864 Liverpool Sanitary Amendment Act, it built St Martin's Cottages in Ashfield Street, Vauxhall. These were blocks of four-storey tenements, with open-fronted communal staircases, that contained 124 dwellings. They were bleak and, by the time they were demolished in 1977, had been long neglected. Although they were municipal-housing pioneers, they were not epoch-making, being relatively small in scale and mean in spirit.

By contrast, when the Boundary Street and Millbank estates got under way in the early and mid 1890s, they proved to be the nation's first large-scale, socially ambitious architectural experiment in publicly funded housing. The council flat as we know it, set within an architecturally cohesive and large-scale estate, had, for good or for ill, arrived.

* * * * *

The Boundary Street Estate (soon to be called simply the Boundary Estate) involved the phased destruction of one of the largest and worst slums in London: the Old Nichol, or Friars Mount, rookery ('rookery' being a popular term at the time for particularly run-down and overcrowded districts). By the 1880s it provided homes for over 5,710 people, who were squeezed into about 730 small, old and long-neglected buildings – mostly two-storey, wide-windowed weavers' terrace houses, packed into a network of narrow streets and courts.[2]

It had also become an area notorious for its extreme poverty and decay, sense of menace and levels of crime.

When John Rocque prepared his London map of 1746, the Nichol area comprised the east–west streets of Old Nichol Street, New Nichol Street and the south side of Half Nichol Street.[3] By the time the 1872/3 Ordnance Survey map was drawn up, it had been extended to the north by a grid of streets built on the Snow Estate and had become generally more packed, with courts and cottages created on land that, behind street frontages, had once been open.[4]

Numerous accounts survive of the density of the population, the terrible physical condition of the streets, courts and houses, the paucity of the area's services and the turmoil, cacophony, stench and meanness of its fetid daily life. In *Sanitary Ramblings*, published in 1848, the physician and public health campaigner Dr Hector Gavin described the older portion of Club Row, south of what is now Bethnal Green Road and once one of the better streets bordering the Nichol area, as 'perfectly beastly', its street surface like that 'of a pig-stye [with] scattered heaps of garbage and collections of mud'. Swan Court, immediately east of Club Row, was 'abominably filthy' with 'three open privies belonging to it . . . full and most disgusting . . . dust heaps, ordure, and garbage are scattered about, as are also shallow pools of liquid foetid filth'. 'The houses convey the impression of desolation,' Gavin went on, shocked by the sense of 'great moral debasement and degradation among the occupants'. 'The medical officer at one time attended here six cases of fever, being all the occupants of one room; they all lay in one bed . . . All this disease was mainly attributable to the impure atmosphere.' The filth was the inevitable consequence of a vicious circle. The inhabitants had nowhere to dispose of their rubbish but the street itself; the garbage men refused to remove it unless paid, but the inhabitants would or could not pay; and so filth increased as, presumably, did the price of the labour for removing it. 'The inhabitants of this street,' stated Gavin, 'complained bitterly that "the people in it never died a natural death, but were murdered by the fever".'

Fifteen years after Gavin's exploration of the streets and houses of the Old Nichol, the area was again under scrutiny, this time by journalists and building and medical experts as well as by sanitary authorities. On 24 October 1863 the *Illustrated London News* published an article entitled 'Dwellings of the Poor in Bethnal Green' that catalogued the 'disgusting details' of recent cases of death from disease, dirt and neglect among the area's poor and that it was sure would shock its readers 'who have only heard of Bethnal-green as a low neighbourhood where the weavers live, somewhere in the far east of London'. It reminded them that, only twenty-five years before, the area's now 'ruinous tenements reeking with abominations' had been 'outlying, decent cottages, standing on or near plots of garden ground, where the inmates reared prize tulips and rare dahlias in their scanty leisure, and where some of the last of the old French refugees dozed away the evenings of their lives in pretty summer-houses, amidst flower-beds gay with Virginia stocks and creeping plants'. Now, however, Spitalfields' 'worst features have been exceeded by the wretched maze of streets and alleys' immediately to its north. The article described 'a population depressed almost to the last stage of human endurance'.

Thomas Archer, who was exploring the area at much the same time – and may indeed have been the *Illustrated London News*'s reporter – noted the 'ragged, dirty children, and gaunt women, from whose faces almost all traces of womanliness have faded', the appalling stench that rose from the 'blind courts' where so many lived – a mix of the stench of decaying vegetable matter, of pigs and of 'that sickly odour which belongs always to human beings living in such a state' – and the poor quality of the food available in the local shops.[5] He also touched on the sense of danger he detected in the area, where even the 'bird, dog, and pigeon-fanciers' in Sclater Street (which by then had train tracks and viaducts leading into Bishopsgate station immediately to its south) and Club Row seemed threatening,[6] and where 'regular thieves' congregated on market day: 'I have counted eleven as I stand here by the corner,' he wrote, 'and I know that I am the cause of their uneasy shifting hither and thither, and that they are watching me as closely as I am looking at them.'[7]

A note of slight caution is necessary here. That the Old Nichol was an area of often appalling deprivation is indisputable. But one gets the sense that men like Thomas Archer and newspapers such as the *Illustrated London News* and *The Builder*, which published a similarly damning report a week after the article in the *Illustrated London News* had run, had a tendency to sensationalise the worst examples and then imply that that applied to the area as a whole, in order to boost circulation of the papers they worked for. The Old Nichol was certainly overcrowded – sometimes desperately so – but while accounts in the *Illustrated London News* and *The Builder* imply that every house was bursting at the seams with people, the truth is that while some certainly were, many weren't. If the journalists are to believed, and it was indeed true that every room contained a family, then a single house could contain as many as twenty people. The 1861 census, however, yields a figure closer to ten or eleven. It's sometimes hard to separate fact from journalistic embellishment in accounts of the area.

In such accounts it's also possible to detect more than a whiff of middle-class prejudice and even fear of what was perceived as a wild and lawless domain. That there were criminals in the Old Nichol is undoubted, but there were also, as Archer himself acknowledged, 'Bandbox and lucifer-box [matchbox] makers, cane workers, clothes peg makers, shoemakers, and tailors', among many such others. Nuance, however, was not always on display in Victorian books and articles on the poor. A decade or so after Archer's account, James Greenwood included a chapter in his book *Low-life Deeps* that presents a particularly sinister portrait. He described how 'The alley-dwellers of this part [Devonshire Place, an alley off the south side of Old Nichol Street] are a terribly dirty race, and in the fastnesses of their slums seem to have deteriorated from civilisation, and gone a long way back on the road to savagery.'[8] He wrote not just of adults and children eking out a living making matchboxes, but of people collecting 'the ordure of dogs' for tanning purposes or 'hunting for cats to slaughter for the sake of their skins'. His view was that the people of the slum had been so brutalised by their dreadful ordeal that they had lost the will to fight and to lift themselves from the mire – in other words, that they were beyond help. In this context, he noted that efforts had been made to set up a public nursery in Quaker Street, immediately to the south of the Old Nichol, where 'instead of lying about in the alley gutters while their mothers were out at work or selling things in the street, [children] might be well cared for, and properly cleansed, and tended, and fed'. But, he went on, 'the response on the part of working mothers is not hearty. Whether they resent the warm bath and its changeful effects on their progeny, or whether they find it cheaper to keep their children at home, I cannot say, but at present there have never at any time been more than seven small customers in one day at this admirable home, and the number when I visited it was only five.'

In fact, the Old Nichol was a complicated quarter of extraordinary contrasts: shops and reasonably decent accommodation along its few main streets; dire, crowded, poor and filthy alleys and courts behind. Church Street (now Redchurch Street), for example, which ran east–west and roughly defined part of the south edge of the Old Nichol, had a reasonably good character. The social reformer Charles Booth's famous 'Poverty Map' (see page 57), included in his 1889 *Life and Labour of the People*, shows the buildings here as pink (or 'Fairly comfortable') along its west end, and pink and red (red signified 'Middle class') combined at the east end around the junction with Bethnal Green Road. With its shops, pubs and eating establishments, this street appeared to him reasonably well-to-do. But immediately to the north, along both sides of 'Old Nichols Street' and Turville Street, were houses that Booth coded black – his worst category – with those a little further to the north, including 'Nichols Street' (or New Nichol Street), only one shade better, at dark blue. So according to Booth, the people here were 'Very poor, casual' and in 'Chronic want', or if living in houses coloured black, 'Lowest class. Vicious, semi-criminal.'

Yet even the inhabitants of the grimmest areas, Booth recognised, had the capacity to live lives that went beyond bare survival. When he returned to the area in the late 1890s to revise his Poverty Map, he was particularly intrigued by what was going on in the area that lay on the south boundary of the Old Nichol, a 'triangle'

A street in the Old Nichol area in about 1890. This group of early nineteenth-century two-storey houses, with wide first-floor windows to light workshops or weaving lofts, probably stood in Boundary Street.

formed by Bethnal Green Road on the north, 'Fuller Street on the east [and] Sclater Street on the south'.[9] He had classed the area as purple ('Mixed. Some comfortable, others poor') on the 1889 map, and, towards Fuller Street, as dark blue with some black; and as he, his secretary and police guide wandered through it several years on, noting the 'rough class of costers, thieves, prostitutes, bird fanciers' who lived there, they also recognised that there was still vitality amid the obvious decay and 'very rough' streets. Here and there was 'a chair or cabinet factory'. Booth's secretary recorded 'several boys boxing with gloves on' and noted that 'children all looked sturdy ruffians, well fed'. Overall there was 'much life'. As far as Booth and his party could tell, the people within the triangle lived together 'as a happy family'. When 'any of them gets into trouble there is at once a whip round for money for bail or defence', his secretary wrote.[10] The inhabitants of the Old Nichol and its immediate environs had much to endure, so Booth coded the area broadly as in 1889, but they also formed a tightly knit community.

Whatever middle-class commentators might have thought of the character of those who dwelt in the Old Nichol, they had to recognise that the poor paid an extortionate price for the opportunity of living there. James Greenwood explained that women making matchboxes at home were obliged to employ the help of three or four of their children who 'by working very hard' might earn a mere 'fifteenpence a day'. Yet in one house he visited he found a 'parlour' with 'a bedstead . . . three-parts filling it' and 'a heap of ragged female attire, by way of bedclothing' that, according to the upstairs neighbour, was being rented out at three shillings and nine pence a week ('Well, you see, sir, it is let already furnished,' explained the upstairs lodger). Sarah Wise, in her magisterial analysis of the Old Nichol, argues that 'Per cubic foot, the rents of the Nichol were between four and ten times higher than those of the finest streets and squares of the West End, averaging between 2s 3d to 3s for a single room and around 7s 6d for a three room lodging.' As she points out, this startling fact meant that 'some 85% of the working-class households in London spent one-fifth or more of their income on rent', while 'half of them paid between a quarter and half of their income to their landlords'.[11] For people living at subsistence level, this was a large proportion of very small incomes.

Even at the time, speculators were generally loathed. Henry Lazarus, in his 1892 book *Landlordism*, called them 'the vampyres of the poor',[12] while the *Pall Mall Gazette* on 16 October 1883 registered shock and dismay that 'these fever dens are said to be the best paying property in London, and owners ... are drawing from 50 to 60 per cent on investments in tenement property in the slums.' As Wise points out, 'the *Gazette* had underestimated the money that could be made, and profits as large as 150 per cent per annum were not uncommon.'[13] Yet nothing concrete was done. When the highly respectable Henderson family, who owned the squalid Flower and Dean Street rookery in Spitalfields where several of Jack the Ripper's victims had lodged, found themselves in the spotlight, they simply offered parts of the estate for sale.[14] A number of houses in the Old Nichol were owned by the 3rd Duke of Buckingham and Chandos, whose family had in 1753 acquired the five-acre Nichol Estate through marriage. At that time the estate was a semi-rural oasis of weavers' cottages set on the edge of market gardens, and the family retained a sizable interest in what became slum properties even after selling a large portion, by then packed with 237 houses, in 1827. The duke's daughter, Lady Mary Morgan-Grenville, 11th Baroness Kinloss, who inherited the Shoreditch estate (which in 1836 included fifty houses) on her father's death in March 1889, concealed the fact of her ownership until 1892, when she was obliged to reveal her identity in order to collect the compensation due to her as the London County Council geared itself up to purchase the area for redevelopment as the Boundary Estate.[15] She was a dedicated churchwarden and sometime owner of the vast Stowe House in Buckinghamshire. It was subsequently discovered that numerous other houses in the Old Nichol were owned by Sir Edward Arthur Colebrooke, Lord of the Manor of Stepney. Far from being ostracised by high society for his ungallant conduct as a slum landlord, Sir Edward was raised to the peerage in 1906 and went on to be a lord-in-waiting to Edward VII, the man who in 1900, as Prince of Wales, inaugurated the new Boundary Estate.[16] Either Sir Edward's peers did not care that he was a slum landlord, or couldn't bring themselves to think about it.

* * * * *

While slum landlords continued to gather their rents, revelations about the appalling nature of the slums from which they profited continued to be made, and, by the mid 1880s, were beginning to have an impact on the government and on local authorities. In 1883, Andrew Mearns, a Congregationalist clergyman who focused on the 'abject' poor of the city, published an extraordinarily emotive pamphlet that was immediately supported and published in condensed form by the highly influential *Pall Mall Gazette*. Entitled 'The Bitter Cry of Outcast London: An Inquiry into the Condition of the Abject Poor', it described not just the physical horrors of poverty and slum life in the East End but also the moral decay that can accompany overcrowding – even suggesting that incest was a significant consequence of slum life. For Mearns, poverty, and its resultant evils, was a cancer in the heart of society and, by implication, represented a fatal threat to all. He talked on the one hand of 'moral corruption, of heart-breaking misery and absolute godlessness' and, on the other, of the fact 'that scarcely anything has been done to take into this awful slough the only influences that purify or remove it'.

Mearns evoked the horrors of slum living without referring to specific examples, but it seems highly likely that the descriptions he used to startle and rouse his God-fearing middle-class readers into action were inspired by his own descents into the Flower and Dean Street rookery and adjoining Dorset Street in central Spitalfields (described in 1901 by the *Daily Mail* as the 'worst street in London').[17] Like those who had visited these areas before him, he described the overcrowding, the filth and the grinding poverty: 'In one cellar a sanitary inspector reports finding a father, mother, three children, and four pigs! In another room a missionary found a man ill with small-pox, his wife just recovering from her eighth confinement, and the children running about half naked and covered with dirt.' He talked of those who had no choice but to 'take refuge at night in one of the common lodging houses that abound' and that were 'often the resorts of thieves and vagabonds of the lowest type'. And he highlighted the miserable circumstances of those who could not 'even scrape together the two pence required to secure them the privilege of resting in those sweltering common sleeping rooms'. These people, he said, were often forced to resort to makeshift accommodation on stairs and landings.

The emotive force of Mearns's writing inspired the founding of missions in east London, among them Toynbee Hall, which was set up by the incumbent of St Jude's church in Spitalfields, Canon Samuel Barnett and his wife, Henrietta, and which was designed to bring the affluent and the educated together with the poor and ignorant within a beautiful setting in the hope that they would form a harmonious community.[18] Combined with shocking official statistics about death rates in the Old Nichol area, where child mortality reached 252 per thousand births, as compared with 159 in Bethnal Green as a whole,[19] Mearns's work brought about significant change. Notably it encouraged the establishment in 1884 of the Royal Commission on the Housing of the Working Classes, and on the Housing of the Working Classes Act that was passed the following year and amended and strengthened in 1890. One of the key Public Health Acts of the age, it enabled county districts to obtain loans from the Treasury for housing improvements, while also granting the Local Government Board – a government supervisory board established in 1871 – the power to force indolent local authorities to close unhealthy houses and to make landlords personally liable for their tenants' physical well-being. In addition, the Act made it illegal for landlords to let out houses that fell below specified sanitary standards.

Pressure to do something about slum housing in general and the Old Nichol in particular increased. In 1887 government inspectors confirmed that there were almost 6,000 people living there, crammed into around thirty streets and courts of small, old and decaying buildings. When the area was surveyed in 1891 for clearance, it was recorded that 5,719 people lived in the Old Nichol in 730 houses, of whom 2,265 were squeezed into two-room dwellings. The high mortality rate was also noted,[20] as were the exorbitant rents the poor were forced to pay. In the late 1880s an investigative journalist named Bennet Burleigh, who worked for the *Daily Telegraph*, a philanthropist named Lady Mary Jeune, and a Shoreditch Justice of the Peace named Montagu Williams, undertook their own research into the rewards of slum landlordism, and even went so far as to reveal the names of those rich and powerful individuals who were benefiting from the misery of others. The three, along with the Bishop of Bedford, then established the Fair Rents for Healthy Homes League, which held its inaugural meeting in November 1889 at the Monarch coffee house in Bethnal Green Road, just to the south of the Old Nichol.

A further reminder of the evils such campaigners were seeking to sweep away came in the same year, when the playwright and journalist George R. Sims published his *How the Poor Live*. He provided lurid details about slum life that must, by now, have been all too familiar and which were being exposed simultaneously by Charles Booth in his *Life and Labour of the People*. Drawing on the findings of a sanitary inspector named Mr Wrack, Sims also described what death in the slums could be like. In the course of his work, Wrack regularly discovered decaying cadavers in the homes of people too deranged or immobilised by poverty even to arrange a decent burial for their dead, and Sims shared some of his grimmer findings. At 28 Church Street – probably what is now Redchurch Street on the south edge of the Old Nichol slum – Wrack had 'found in the second floor front room the dead body of a child which had died of scarlet fever on the 1st of the month'. 'The body was not coffined,' Sims went on, 'and it lay exposed on a table in one corner of the room.' Members of the dead child's family continued to occupy the room, where they 'engaged in tailors work', and, when questioned about the circumstances, explained that they were 'waiting . . . to raise the means of burying the child'.[21]

* * * * *

As Sims and Booth were cataloguing the horrors of the Old Nichol, this dismal world was finally coming to an end. In 1889 the newly

founded and democratically elected London County Council, armed
with the power to compulsorily purchase land for slum clearance,
determined to rid London of one of its worst and most infamous
slum areas and to replace it with new hygienic housing that would,
as far as was possible, accommodate those displaced by demolition.[22]
The extent to which the people who lost their homes to slum clearance could in fact be rehoused in the replacement buildings became
one of the more contentious issues of the LCC's radical and relatively
large-scale building operations. Even so, the locations chosen – the
vacant site occupied until 1890 by a large part of the huge Millbank
Penitentiary, located south of the Palace of Westminster, and the
Nichol – when both rebuilt just after 1900 provided homes for an
impressive 9,954 people. This represented a huge increase in new
working-class housing in central London.[23]

The scheme for the comprehensive demolition and rebuilding of the Old Nichol as a whole – north from the north side of
Redchurch Street to Virginia Road, and east from the east side of
Boundary Street to Mount (Swanfield) Street – was first proposed
to the relevant LCC committee on 3 November 1890. A 'clearance
order' was duly confirmed by Parliament on 3 July 1891, by which time
the calculation had been made that 5,719 people would be displaced
by the mass demolition. The order, however, required that only 5,100
be rehoused.[24] Precisely what was to happen to the other 619 people
made homeless by the redevelopment was not revealed at the time,
but it soon became clear that, regardless of the homes being created,
the vast majority of the 5,719 people who would lose their old accommodation would not be housed in the new buildings erected on the
cleared site – for the simple and brutal reason that they were too poor
and too dysfunctional to be deemed worthy of access to this fabulous
new world. The ethics, the morality, indeed the politics, of this exclusive approach worried many and it was, as we shall see, only when the
estate opened in early 1900 that the LCC fully explained its position.

The implications of a housing policy that did not tackle the core
problems of the slum were obvious to most, namely that slum dwellers
who were not rehoused would simply move on to other slums. But

in London in the early 1890s, even essentially benign local authorities did not perceive themselves as being morally responsible for the poorest of the poor: the most hopeless slum dwellers who, it was assumed, would, when demolition started, conveniently slink away. To take the most cynical interpretation, one might conclude that itinerant slum dwellers were not a constituency that local politicians felt the necessity to court.

Part of the strategy of dealing with the problem of those displaced by demolition was to organise construction work in three phases and then to filter the mass of newly homeless by insisting that all had to attempt to rehouse themselves before they could apply for, or be offered, accommodation in the new tenement blocks. As Martin Stilwell observes in his study of the Boundary Estate, 'this seems a harsh decision', but evidently the LCC 'estimated there was already sufficient accommodation in the area to take [the 2,000 people] displaced' by the first phase of demolition.[25] Predictably problems quickly arose, and in 1892 the LCC purchased land along Goldsmiths Row to build accommodation for 144 people who, owing to the demolition work, had been removed from the Old Nichol site. The Goldsmiths Row scheme, located a mile north-east of the Old Nichol, took the form of two rows of 'cottages' and was completed in 1895.[26] By then, construction of the Boundary Estate was under way. Section A, on the top north-east corner of the site, had been cleared and by 1893 Streatley Buildings, the first pair of blocks of the Boundary Estate, was complete.

* * * * *

Few seem to have been happy with the first two blocks to have been constructed, one four storeys and the other five. They were very economically built and architecturally characterless and, always unloved, would ultimately be demolished in the early 1970s. Even before they were completed, the LCC architects were having second thoughts about how best to organise and shape further development of the site. At first, while negotiations proceeded during 1892 for the acquisition of the land on which the estate was to be constructed, they thought in terms of a conventional right-angular grid of streets – much like the one that was being replaced, and not dissimilar to what was realised at the Millbank Estate. Here long, narrow tenement buildings, generally standing parallel to each other or at right angles, were placed on an irregularly spaced grid of streets organised around a rectangular open space, with only a pair of short streets set diagonally to the grid to relieve visual monotony. The advantage of following this approach on the Boundary Estate site was that the new blocks would mesh more or less seamlessly into the surrounding orthogonal networks of streets, and that two schools recently completed on the site could easily be incorporated, since they had been planned according to the old layout of the area.[27] The disadvantage was that, adopted on a large scale, the scheme threatened a certain utilitarian bleakness. At Millbank only the short streets set diagonally to the grid offered visual variety, although the neighbouring presence of the temple-like National Gallery of British Art (now Tate Britain), which opened in 1897, added more than a dash of urban drama and cultural elan. But in Shoreditch, before the LCC committed itself to a regimented grid-plan approach, a significant event took place – and one which was to produce a scheme that was far more imaginative and varied in its architecture, even if more demanding to realise.

In 1893, the year that the Streatley Buildings were completed, the Boundary Estate project was handed to the Housing of the Working Classes Branch of the LCC's Architects' Department, headed by Owen Fleming, one of the chief, and most talented, assistants to the LCC's Superintending Architect of Metropolitan Buildings, Thomas Blashill. Fleming rapidly assembled a corps of young LCC architects – notably Reginald Minton Taylor, William Hynam, C. C. Winmill and A. M. Phillips – who shared his vision for a very different form of public housing from that currently being considered. They believed that the new development should be simultaneously a place of comfort, convenience, health – and uplifting beauty. And they had the ambition, talent and experience to turn this, in some ways revolutionary, vision into a tangible reality.

If there was a general guiding principle for the LCC planners'

262 THE ENGLISH HOUSE

new ideas it was that of the qualities of 'sweetness and light', first described by the poet and essayist Matthew Arnold in his book *Culture and Anarchy* (published 1869). Arnold argued that the desire for 'sweetness', or beauty, and the application of 'light', or intelligence, had, throughout history, formed the bedrock of culture. As he put it, culture 'seeks . . . to make the best that has been thought and known in the world current everywhere; to make all men live in an atmosphere of sweetness and light'. His ideas immediately caught on with a whole generation of architects, artists and philosophers. The enthusiasm for beauty, either to behold it or to create it, became part of the Aesthetic Movement of the 1870s – the notion of 'art for art's sake' promoted by the aesthete and essayist Walter Pater and in the early 1880s personified by the poet, playwright and obsessive self-publicist Oscar Wilde. Wilde, predictably, took the notion to extremes to ensure that he would be noticed, going so far as to claim that beauty was more important than practical or moral concerns. As he put it in his 1891 essay 'The Critic as Artist', 'aesthetics are higher than ethics', with colour sense being 'more important . . . than a sense of right and wrong'. Such amoral statements as this shocked evangelical Christians, no doubt as the ever-provocative Wilde intended, and showed what was sweet for some could be bitter for others. The light of intelligence, by contrast, proved a less contentious guiding principle. It was the expression of the enlightened intellect, of the enquiring, caring and compassionate mind that would 'dissolve ugliness . . . smooth away intolerance and bigotry'.[28] The hallmarks were charity, a concern for the welfare of the poor, the promotion of health, education, free libraries and temperance.

From the mid 1870s the notion of 'sweetness and light' found architectural expression in what became known as the Queen Anne Revival (see page 196). This was a peculiar style that for a while ran in parallel with the still vigorous Gothic Revival. Indeed, it became complementary, for while the Gothic retained its dominance as the style for churches and certain public buildings, the Queen Anne quickly became the preferred approach for domestic architecture. The Queen Anne Revival was a composite style, a fusion of distinct historic prototypes rather than a revival of a particular past style, being a mix of north European vernacular Renaissance architecture of the late sixteenth to the early eighteenth centuries, particularly seventeenth-century Flemish and Dutch architecture with its love of tall, ornate and often serpentine crowning gables. From English genuine Queen Anne-era architecture, itself a product of Dutch influence, came a preference for large sash windows, inventive hand-made classical detail and a palette of red brick, off-white painted joinery, alongside a dash of Portland stone. Combined with this rich mix of Renaissance exemplars was a strong regard for the Gothic spirit, revealed most obviously through studied asymmetry (it was argued that in authentic Gothic architecture details were not disposed to create symmetry but were placed where function demanded), by the overt and honest expression of the means and materials of construction, and by the quest for a romantic silhouette, usually achieved not only by the display of looming gables but also by the striking disposition of tall chimney stacks.

The Queen Anne Revival was first used on a large scale and consistent manner in a residential area in Bedford Park, Chiswick, which got under way in 1875. The planning is picturesque and the buildings created were generally sumptuous middle-class houses, set in verdant planting. From 1877 the estate architect was the man also responsible for Cragside in Northumberland (see Chapter 5), Richard Norman Shaw.

Rather closer to home, so far as potential architectural models for the Boundary Estate were concerned, were two local schools, the Rochelle School from 1879 and the Virginia Road Primary School from 1887, constructed before the old and decayed buildings of the Old Nichol were cleared away. Both were the fruits of the Elementary Education Act of 1870, which for the first time sought to provide compulsory education in England and Wales for children aged five to ten (with those aged ten to thirteen regarded as 'half-timers' if it could be proved that their wages were crucial for the family's economic survival).[29] In terms of guiding principle, both schools represented the government's desire to alleviate the privation suffered by poor families whose children would otherwise be condemned to perpetual ignorance, and to make the working classes more capable, productive and ambitious by arming them with a better education. In architectural terms, both buildings bear the imprint of the 'sweetness and light' aesthetic, expressed here in a brick and terracotta fusion of gabled Flemish Renaissance and English Queen Anne, with distinctively large sash windows that ensure that the high-ceilinged classrooms are light and well ventilated. Designed by the chief architect of the London School Board (LSB), Edward Robert Robson, they were built to fit tight sites amid the street layout of the Old Nichol, so posing some layout challenges when the new Boundary Estate grew up around them.

The Virginia Road Primary School and the earlier and smaller Rochelle School differ from each other in many details; the Rochelle School, for example, makes more use of overtly classical details.[30] What unites them is both their resolve − very much in the spirit of the Gothic Revival − that different functions should be expressed by different and functionally appropriate forms, and their ingenuity in making the most of their small sites. At the Virginia Road Primary School, there are tiers of classrooms and assembly rooms right to eaves level, as revealed by the tall height of the second-floor windows. Stubby wings break forward towards what is now Arnold Circus, each topped by simple triangular gables, with narrow first-floor windows topped by exceptionally wide second-floor windows, all of which reflect the way different uses, requiring different forms of window, were shoe-horned together. At the Rochelle School, when an infant school was added in 1899 the playground that was lost was recreated on the top floor, and roofed out of fear that many of the area's poor children would not have coats to wear in wet or cold weather.

On the Rochelle School's short elevation to Montclare Street (formerly Turville Street), which was at least in part the entrance side, two of the three first-floor windows rise from pedestals framed by scrolls made of red brick. On each of these pedestals is a circular terracotta plaque. One bears the entwined letters 'LSB', the other the LSB's Latin motto, 'Lux Mihi Laus', meaning 'Light is My Glory'.

The Virginia Road Primary School, built in 1887 by the London School Board. It now faces onto Arnold Circus.

The light in question was the light of civilisation, the light of a fuller and richer life made possible by the education bestowed by the LSB, the light granted thanks to the enlightened action of men and woman of compassion. The schools were the ideal of 'sweetness and light' made manifest by the LSB.

A paper that Robson published in 1881 reads almost as a 'manifesto' for what Fleming and his band of LCC architects would seek to achieve at the Boundary Estate.[31] 'Architectural art', wrote Robson, 'depends intimately upon good workmanship, and upon applying rightly each material according to its nature':

> ... if we are ever to have good Art in common buildings – that is to say, if the housing of the poor is ever to be done by architects, [they] must be content to descend frequently from their lofty pedestals, and speak, think and work in simpler phrase ... be scrupulously careful about the colour and quality of brickwork, the appearance of its joints, the proper methods to be followed in carpenter's and joiner's work ... Architecture is not mere display, it is not fashion, and it is not for the rich alone.[32]

* * * * *

The new Boundary Estate scheme that Fleming and his colleagues initiated was a world away from that of the bye-law terrace house. As Susan Beattie, an authority on early public housing in London explains, the band of young architects, 'united by their idealism, committed to [William] Morris's vision of social reform', were 'compelled for economic reasons to look long and hard at the relationship between form and function in building and to abandon elaborate tricks of style'.[33] The result was a form of architecture that was both distinct and ever evolving: individual tenements located within tall blocks in communal occupation.

High-rise housing blocks were not new to London. There was, for example, the twelve-storey Queen Anne's Mansions off Victoria Street, built from 1873. But these early manifestations were designed

THE BIRTH OF THE COUNCIL FLAT

to provide luxurious Parisian-style private apartments for the well-to-do, not to provide accommodation en masse for the less well off (interestingly, though, when the owner and seemingly the designer of Queen Anne's Mansions – Henry Alers Hankey – extended part of them in the 1890s to fourteen storeys, he turned to E. R. Robson for help). In terms of high-rise working-class accommodation, the Boundary Estate, comprising numerous tall blocks with some rising to six storeys, set a new standard.

The Boundary Estate proved a pioneer in another respect, too. When in 1893 the project was handed to Fleming and the Housing of the Working Classes Branch of the LCC's Architects' Department, they decided that, rather than create a traditional orthogonal grid of streets, much in the manner of the existing street pattern, they would attempt something far more dashing, far more potentially beautiful and – as it happens – far more in tune with progressive architectural taste of the time. Out, therefore, went oblong tenement blocks set parallel to each other in a regimented manner. In came a French baroque-type *rond-point*, or circus, formed in roughly the centre of the site, with its periphery in part defined by the existing board schools. This circus, its architects decided, would be dominated by a circular garden that would take the form of a tapering mound with concentric walkways. On its flat plateau would be placed a bandstand: an emblem of civilisation and a token of the belief that the residents of this new model estate were determined to 'better themselves', and that they aspired to the tastes and habits of their social superiors whose ranks they could perhaps – through hard work, sobriety and religion – one day join.[34]

From the circus seven streets would radiate, in asymmetrical manner, to connect (two via notable cranks in axis) with the existing grid of straight streets surrounding the site. Two of these seven radial streets would spawn subsidiary streets to increase the number of potential building blocks with street frontages. Lower parts of the buildings facing the circus and portions of buildings on main streets near the circus would be faced with glazed bricks so that elevations could easily be cleaned of horse dung thrown up by passing traffic.

It was estimated that this new layout could accommodate a greater number of people than originally envisaged: 5,500 in all, in 1,069 separate tenements, or apartments. At a stroke, virtually all connection with the Old Nichol's much-tainted street network was abandoned. This was indeed to be a new world, with its attractive circus, prospect mound with promenade and bandstand acting as a potent symbol of the area's rebirth.

This adventurous, asymmetrical plan meant that the blocks forming the estate did not all have to be ruthless, barrack-like oblongs in plan. Some could have symmetrical elevations when so desired, but those fronting the circus had to have individual forms, some wedge-shaped and all with gently curving facades to the circus. The radial site plan and the pursuit of asymmetry also meant that it was possible to achieve picturesque variety, to offer delightful prospects and to place windows to catch maximum light. As the LCC later explained, 'every habitable room' in the Boundary Estate was 'provided with a 45-degree angle of light horizontally and vertically', while the buildings were 'so arranged that nearly every room commands a pleasant outlook'.[35] There were also to be plenty of trees to simulate, as with some of the near-contemporary bye-law streets in Toxteth, some of the bucolic atmosphere of Parisian boulevards.

* * * * *

When it came to the individual building's outward appearance, Fleming and his colleagues were determined to avoid the austere look of the Streatley Buildings, while also recognising the need to achieve both economy and utility. In general, the blocks were constructed in a red-brick Queen Anne Revival style. The earlier ones tend to be slightly more ornate, with bands of decoration in pale yellow or even pinkish-yellow brick, or perhaps more accurately brick-sized blocks of terracotta. Many incorporate elaborate gables. Sunbury Buildings, for example, almost certainly designed by C. C. Winmill and completed in 1896, bears a gable in the centre of each of its long elevations, each of which is seventeenth-century Dutch in style; the gable facing south incorporates concave and convex curves

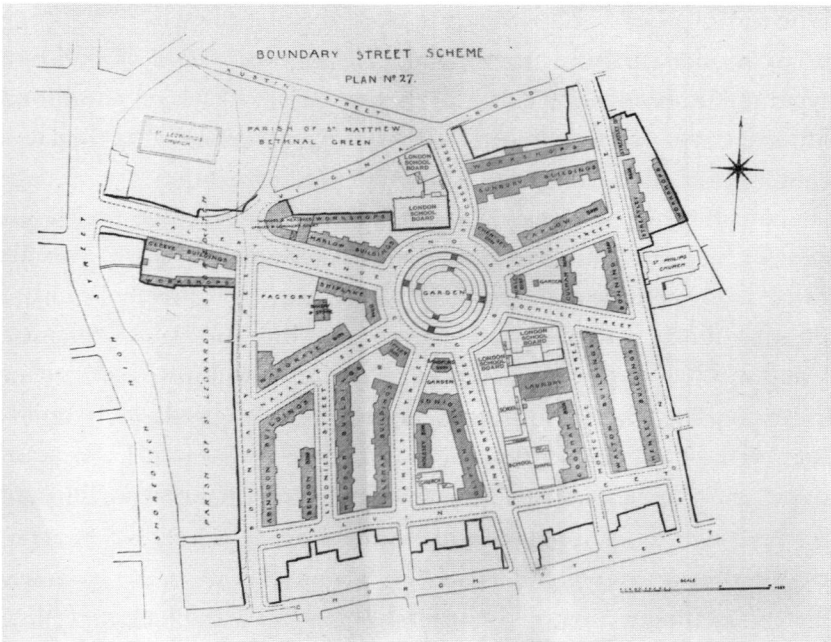

Plan of the LCC's Boundary Estate as completed in 1900. Only Streatley
Buildings and workshops, top right in the north-east corner, have been
lost. On this plan Old Nichol Street has been renamed Calvin Street (this
change of name was evidently not accepted) and Church Street is now
Redchurch Street. South of Church Street are Bethnal Green Road and
Club Row, which now extends north to Arnold Circus, replacing
Ainsworth Street.

and generous scrolls in the baroque manner, while the gable facing
north has a serrated, crow-stepped, silhouette. Winmill also probably
designed the blocks immediately to the south of Sunbury Buildings:
Taplow, Sonning and Culham buildings, all completed by 1896. [36]
Later blocks are more stripped back, while making use of powerful,
simple forms that are often sculptural and sometimes almost abstract.
One senses a band of architects at work seeking to evolve an appropriate modern architecture for the realisation of a modern building
type: public housing within tall blocks – each of which contained
different types of apartments – set within an urban plan that was
coherent yet allowed individual architectural expression.

Not all blocks were equally successful. Henley Buildings on Mount
Street (renamed Swanfield Street) and Walton Buildings on Turville
Street (renamed Montclare Street), which were designed by Rowland
Plumbe, the architect responsible for expanding and remodelling the
London Hospital in Whitechapel,[37] are disappointing, somewhat
mean-looking affairs. Plumbe was the winner of a competition organised by the LCC in 1894 to design buildings for Section E, lying on
the south-east corner of the site – a competition that presumably had
the pragmatic goal of fending off any antagonism felt by architects in
private practice to the council's newly acquired powers and its newly
fledged architects' department. Plumbe came up with blocks of yellow
brick, of a rather anaemic complexion, with red brick used only to
form ornamental bands and to face the ground floors, and no glazed
brick at ground-floor level that would have allowed for easy cleaning.
Worse still, whereas the architects of the other blocks ensured that
lavatory windows were placed deftly and thoughtfully, Plumbe elected
to situate them on the public-street elevations of his buildings, where
they make a depressing show, their narrow and shallow forms that
descend to street level stained and unsightly. Equally insensitive are
the communal stairs which spill out, open, exposed and barrack-like,
on to the yard that separates the two blocks. Evidently it did not
occur to Plumbe that the future occupants of these blocks might want
decent, and secure, front doors and entrance halls. His vision went no
further than that of the industrial dwellings companies, which had

generally made the built expression of philanthropy virtually synonymous with mean-spirited utility. Although inadvertent, this vindicated the LCC in its preference to use its own architects, who, working under the inspired control of Owen Fleming, were determined to combine the demands of function with an uplifting sense of ornamental generosity and architectural beauty.

By contrast, the buildings around Arnold Circus (under way during 1895),[38] most of which were designed by Reginald Minton Taylor,[39] and Iffley Buildings (1896–8), on the south-west quadrant, designed by Arthur Maxwell Phillips, show both architects rising superbly to the challenge. Minton Taylor's blocks (Marlow, Shiplake, Chertsey and Hurley) generally have different plan-forms depending on the nature of their sites, and vary considerably in detail, but are visually united in their use of red brick banded with yellow, pinkish yellow or biscuit colour. Little is exactly the same, while nothing is unpleasantly jarring. The buildings are also conceived in the round, with interesting rear elevations (for example, Chertsey sports a large lunette crowned with a gable and framed by plump bays) that are a far cry from the usual convention of show fronts and grim rear elevations on philanthropic buildings. All avoid the external access galleries associated with industrial dwellings.

Fleming did much to reinforce the theme of picturesque variety within general uniformity by delegating the design of Iffley House to A. M. Phillips rather than Minton Taylor. That variety, though, is relatively subtle, making it clear that Fleming wanted to ensure broad harmony regarding materials and aesthetics. So Iffley Buildings is faced with red brick, as are Minton Taylor's blocks, but with no yellow horizontal banding and, rather than the door on to Arnold Circus to be found on Minton Taylor's buildings, there is a pair of wide, Roman-style lunettes at ground-floor level that squat below a pair of full height canted bays of the type that enliven the circus elevations of Minton Taylor's Shiplake, Marlow and Chertsey buildings. The main door, a simple affair, faces the court and is flanked by a pair of short wings that break forward in a radial manner, following the radial nature of the streets flanking the site. This suggests an almost butterfly plan for the building – a fashionable form in the 1890s – and gives the block a significantly different character from Minton Taylor's similarly sized pavilions. Clearly, on the basis of this building alone, Philips' career was one of great promise, but it was interrupted by the First World War. He served in the King's Own Yorkshire Light Infantry, rose to the rank of captain and was killed at Suvla Bay, Gallipoli, on 11 November 1915, aged forty-seven.

The best of the later buildings mark a further evolution in style.[40] In the place of the playful panache of the designs of the mid 1890s there was now a reliance on form, simplicity and powerful, sculptural abstraction. As Susie Beattie puts it, Minton Taylor's earlier blocks around Arnold Circus and to the west of it are 'entertaining' but 'lack the keen originality that he and his colleagues achieved when they broke further away from [Norman] Shaw's influence and discovered the work of Philip Webb, who was a close collaborator from the mid 1850s with William Morris, pioneer of vernacular-inspired Arts and Crafts architecture and an avowed seeker after "commonplace" design'. In Beattie's opinion, Minton Taylor's finest contribution to the estate is Cookham Buildings, of 1897, 'whose elegance is dependent on proportion and an exquisite balance between sculptural and linear form'.[41] Certainly there is a greatly increased sense of simplicity and repose – almost of solemnity – with the street elevation enlivened in a sculptural manner by windows set within vertical recesses, and with brick banding – of a tonally subtle sort – used only at the upper level and within the huge, wide gable towering over the courtyard elevation. Interestingly, Hermann Muthesius, the German diplomat and scholar who celebrated English domestic architecture of the late nineteenth century in his seminal book of 1904, *Das Englische Haus*, chose this extraordinary gable composition for the single illustration that accompanied his account of the Boundary Estate.

A late Winmill contribution – Clifton Buildings of 1897 – is in Susan Beattie's opinion probably his 'most inspired' building on the estate, demonstrating the creative application of Philip Webb's simple 'architectural vocabulary' to a 'large block dwelling'.[42] The building is indeed striking: no stripes but a bold and noble simplicity, with

Boundary Estate architecture: Top left: Hurley Buildings facing onto Arnold Circus, designed by Reginald Minton Taylor and built in 1895, are a good example of the 'Stripeland' initial phase of construction. Top right: the gabled courtyard elevation of Hedsor Buildings, designed by C. C. Winmill and completed in 1899. Bottom left: the entrance of Culham Buildings, designed by Winmill and completed by 1896. Bottom right: one of the Shinto shrine-like entrance porches to Benson Buildings, designed by William Hynam.

the elevations articulated with recesses, including one placed asymmetrically towards the building's north end, set deep, topped by an arch and embracing a balcony at third-floor level. The building's top storey is pebble-dashed, or harled, and its north-facing elevation is crowned by a wide gable pediment perched above a pair of shallow, full height, canted bays. This gable is inhabited: it contains a wide window topped by an arched opening, a sort of vernacular Venetian window with, above it, a small and mysterious window that seemingly serves a yet higher floor. In the courtyard there is a most inventively detailed entry topped with a semicircular arch sporting a large-scale convex moulding that is cut across – in an eccentric manner – by the sloping slabs of a keystone and voussoirs. In Beattie's view, Winmill's 'evident delight in pure geometrical forms and in exploiting their sculptural qualities, make this the most exciting of all the blocks of dwellings on the Boundary Street Estate'.[43]

* * * * *

The boldness and novelty of the Boundary Estate plan – characterised by the introduction of the circus with its radiating but asymmetrical street pattern – and its response to the emerging desire for variety, is confirmed by the slightly later plan, drawn up by the same LCC team, for the Millbank Estate. It could hardly be more different. Here the layout is governed by strict symmetry, even to the extent that blocks each side of its central axis, defined by the short St Oswulf Street, have mirrored plans. And the central open space is rectangular, like a traditional London square, worlds away from the visual and picturesque potential offered by a circus. Why the design team made this seemingly artistically retrograde move is uncertain, though it may simply have been driven by the desire to save money. After all, constructing wedge-shaped buildings of different forms and curved frontages is neither a cheap nor a time-saving business. There is nevertheless an intriguing connection between the innovative Boundary Estate and the conventional Millbank one. The early nineteenth-century Millbank Penitentiary, which had until 1890 occupied much of the site of the Millbank Estate, had a panopticon plan that incorporated a hexagonal central court and radiating wings, each of pentagonal shape. Did this form inspire Fleming and his team when contemplating the transformation of the original orthogonal plan of the Boundary Estate? We do not know. If it did, then it does rather tend to summon up images of prisoners being under constant surveillance by their jailors, which can hardly have been the message that Fleming and the LCC wanted to convey to their future tenants, unless one takes the almost conspiratorial view that control of tenants was more important to the LCC than is acknowledged, and that a panopticon-derived plan was to remind them that they were being watched.

One of the potential problems presented by the asymmetrical approach adopted at the Boundary Estate, with its curving frontages and generally non-orthogonal plots, was, as already observed, the incorporation of the existing rectangular board schools. In fact, this problem was easily solved, not least because the designs of the tenement blocks are so varied that the schools merge with ease into the overall design. But, for those who care for such things, both schools evoke the spectre of some of the lost Nichol's most desperate streets. The Virginia Road Primary School was built to front south on to what was Collingwood Street, shown in dark blue on Booth's 1889 survey, and the Rochelle School fronted north on to Mead Street, shown in dark and light blue on Booth's survey.

As well as imbuing the estate with an artistically pleasing picturesque informality and allowing for an increase in the number of tenants accommodated, the LCC architects' new plan also led to an increase in the number of blocks, resulting in lower and less daunting storey heights, and reducing the estimated construction costs from £300,000 to £279,000.[44] The revised scheme also contained fifty-eight workshops, set in narrow yards behind a small number of the housing blocks. These workshops, built on the north portion of the estate during the first phase of construction, vary in design and size. There was a row of modest workshops behind Streatley Buildings, but those associated with Sunbury Buildings, completed in 1896, are ambitious: two storeys high with loading doors for goods, hoist jibs, or cranes, large cast-iron windows and north light roofs to maximise the amount of sunlight exposure.[45] The groups of workshops were intended for the use of the more industrious and affluent tenants, for the few successful businesses that were located within the Nichol area or that might have wanted to locate within the estate, with the workshops that were created behind Cleeve Buildings intended, apparently, for use by more modest businesses enterprises. All were there to facilitate, indeed encourage, honest and industrious toil.

There were also to be 200 sheds for the use of costermongers (those who sold goods from handcarts in the street). This was significant. As Martin Stilwell points out, 'costermongers were amongst the lowest paid of the working classes in London ... and were not normally considered to be the type of tenant to take Council's tenancies [so] to build 200 costermonger sheds indicates a reality on the part of the Council as to the expectations of the typical tenant of the new housing.'[46]

While the layout of the Boundary Estate was being resolved and the design of its architecture debated, the phased clearance of the Old Nichol slum, and the dispersal of its population, proceeded. And once the radically revised street plan had been agreed, the construction of the sewage and services system, including water and gas, was put in hand. These works were, along with paving, carried out to a high standard (costing nearly £37,000), largely to ensure that new buildings and roads would not need remedial works soon after completion. Even today, many of the streets on the estate retain their handsome York stone paving, beautifully laid and detailed, especially on radial corners around the circus. Kerbs are marked by granite slabs that subtly reinforce the geometry of the estate in which curves and straight lines merge in a delightful manner. Some streets and ramped drives retain their granite setts (especially in Boundary Street and at the west end of Calvert Avenue), but early photographs suggest that the main streets in the estate were surfaced not with setts but seemingly with some form of tarmacadam and gravel treatment (unusual for late Victorian London, even though tarmacadam had been pioneered in the 1820s). The obvious advantage of tarmacadam for residential streets is that it generates less noise than setts when passed over by vehicles with steel-rimmed wheels. An alternative was tar-clad wooden blocks, and some evidence of these has been found on the surfaces of drives leading to the courts serving blocks around the circus. Early photographs also show that the estate was lit by orna-mental street lights, with large, faceted gas-burning lanterns set atop moulded cast-iron stanchions.

* * * * *

The twenty-three different blocks that were constructed between 1893 and 1899 not only differed from one another in external detail but also varied internally in plan and in the types of apartments and services offered. Those on Arnold Circus itself tended to be the most spacious and well appointed, with, it must be assumed, the aim of attracting to this prime and leafy location the estate's higher-status tenants, who would be capable of paying the highest rents. Shiplake Build-ings, for example, offered on its second floor four-room apartments, comprising two bedrooms, a living room and a kitchen off which were a scullery and a water closet (but no bathroom).[47] Through-out, sound insulation and fire separation between apartments were provided by solid brick walls or stout wood-and-plaster partitions. By contrast, Benson Buildings, in the south part of the estate, off Old Nichol Street and parallel to Abingdon Buildings, was one of the most modestly appointed and planned blocks built on the estate, even if its architect, William Hynam, as if to compensate for the block's meanly planned interior, gave the building some most thoughtful and cultured external details (notably the porches within which are set the doors to the staircases and which, with their battered, or sloping, sides and sloping roofs, evoke distinctly oriental associations, reminiscent of Japanese Shinto shrines).[48] As for Culham Buildings, they con-tained the estate's single-room apartments, placed off long, straight corridors that terminate with pairs of two-room apartments, with communal water closets grouped around the staircase, and located off communal sculleries. All rather unpleasant. In its early years, Culham Buildings, with its array of rooms occupied by single people or couples, would have been the estate's nearest thing to a barracks or workhouse. The hierarchy of the estate was evidently complex but, presumably, tenants could, with relative ease, move up or down according to their changing circumstances.

Ultimately, according to the LCC's *The Housing Question in London*, published in 1900, the estate's 1,069 apartments accorded to one of two all-embracing plans: the 'self-contained' plan and the 'associated' plan, comprising five categories of accommodation in all.[49] Over half (601 to be precise) followed 'entirely self-contained' plans, each offering a complete dwelling within its front door, including its own water closet and generally its own separate kitchen and scullery. These apartments were usually of the larger kind, would have commanded the highest rents and were generally located in the blocks around Arnold Circus. The balance (of the 'associated' plan variety) contained a fair number (201) that, because they contained a scullery, were classed as 'self-contained' but had a WC that, while exclusive to the apartment, had to be accessed via a common corridor. Others had their sculleries and WCs located off a common landing or had to share these facilities with others.[50] Apartments varied considerably in terms of the number of rooms they contained. Over half (541) consisted of just two rooms, namely a living room and a bedroom, both heated by coal fires. Four hundred apartments included a kitchen as well. Only three apartments in the entire development could boast six rooms.[51]

It's clear from the LCC's declared ratio of two people per room that this was achievable on the Boundary Estate only if living rooms were taken into account as well;[52] and it must be admitted that while apartments on the estate offered far greater comfort and space than that afforded by the old houses in the area, they were not a significance advance on that offered for decades by superior philanthropic or industrial dwellings.[53] It has to be said, too, that the facilities were quite spartan. Those tenants who did not have kitchens would have had to cook on a range situated in the living room. Sculleries, which might include a 'copper' in which clothes could be boiled in heated water, generally contained little more than a sink, a cold-water supply for food preparation and washing plates and cooking utensils, and some storage space. Washrooms or even shared bathrooms were not included in the majority of blocks.[54] So home comforts were a little thin on the ground and, given the generally progressive and pioneering nature of the estate, this may seem surprising. Presumably even the idealists of the LCC knew that their budgets were tight and required careful handling. But the individual character possessed by the various blocks of the Boundary Estate did offer tenants the opportunity to create characterful and personal homes in which each could express their identity and pride.

What the LCC did provide, however, was a large communal laundry block and baths in Montclare Street. And it did so in considerable architectural style. Designed towards the end of 1894 by William Hynam, with construction complete by the summer of 1896, the block is a jewel of a pavilion, created in a broadly sixteenth- and seventeenth-century domestic style with fine detailing. Particularly visually striking are the elaborate cornice, the Tudor Gothic doors, the rows of boldly mullioned windows, and the tall chimney stacks vaguely reminiscent of those of Wren's Chelsea Royal Hospital. The clear object was to make a humdrum functional building into an urban ornament that – by Boundary Estate standards – was rich in historical associations. It was obviously intended to appear as something of a charming folly.

Even so, this erudite and attractive architectural display of historical sources was only skin deep. Within the building, which had an extension to the west, all was determined by function. The laundry block was, in fact, a veritable machine, with an open-plan area that contained ranks of scrubbing sinks and a rather futuristic and machine-age 'drying room', packed with hot-water pipes to heat the room, and mobile racks on rails that, loaded with wet clothes, could be run into heated drying cabinets. On top of that there were slipper baths for men and for women, and also a club room. This was clearly intended to be the heart of the new healthy, happy – and clean – community. True to the Victorian spirit of economy and efficiency, charges were kept low (for example, it cost 1½ pence per hour to use the laundry), and a small resident staff of just four (an 'engineer',

Cookham Buildings by Reginald Minton Taylor. Built in 1897, it reflects the simplicity and sculptural forms of the estate's later buildings. To its north is a corner of the estate's communal laundry block and washrooms, designed in 1894 by William Hynam. Eclectic in its rich mix of sixteenth- and seventeenth-century details and forms, the building assumes something of the character of an ornamental folly.

a stoker to keep the water hot, a 'matron' and her assistant) kept things going.[55]

As for the internal appearance of the apartments, since the LCC's *The Housing Question in London* does not include a collection of photographs of the interiors of standard apartments in occupation, much must remain conjectural. One assumes that the homes, like the estate itself, reflected and emulated middle-class standards and taste. Certainly, the *British Architect* suggests as much in May 1897, soon after the first blocks were occupied: 'The fortunate craftsmen who take up their abode here', the magazine observed, 'will, from the bay windows, command the bandstand, the hanging gardens of Virginian [*sic*] creepers and all the other delights of the workman's paradise.'[56] Evidently, as far as the *British Architect* could see, the estate possessed all the picturesque Arts and Crafts delights that one might expect to find in a middle-class housing enclave such as Bedford Park in Chiswick. Taking this as a cue, it can be assumed that living rooms would have been densely furnished, with rugs, carpets, curtains and tablecloths abounding; easy chairs would have been embellished with antimacassars to protect them from gentlemen's pomade; there would have been furniture designed in thin evocations of various past historic styles, and pot plants, including a shade-loving aspidistra or two. There would also have been an abundant display of prints on the walls, some religious and sentimental, others perhaps patriotic and, no doubt, after 1900 some celebrating Boer War 'victories' and heroes. In addition, a profusion of knick-knacks would have been strewn around. Pipes and tobacco would have been displayed as emblems of comfort and prosperity. Walls would have been painted in strong colours but also, in some cases, hung with cheap but showy wallpaper. Almost certainly some living rooms would have had the luxury of a mahogany-veneer overmantel – perhaps made by Robert Johnson of apartment 28 in Cleeve Buildings, who specialised in such things – preferably Jacobean in style, with stunted columns supporting tiny ornamental shelves and framing a sliver of mirror. Some rooms might even have been enlivened with gilded birdcages of the sort made by Thomas Porey, who in 1901 lived in apartment 30 in Cleeve Buildings.

And, of course, on many of the floors, below the rugs, would have been expanses of cheap, robust and durable linoleum.

Oddly enough there is, in fact, one photograph that shows much of this, but its history is currently uncertain. The photograph is included in Susan Beattie's book *A Revolution in London Housing*, where it is described as showing a living room in Hogarth House, on the LCC's Millbank Estate, photographed in 1906.[57] The London Archives, which holds the image, also states that it is a room in Hogarth House, although it gives a date of 1909. Yet, intriguingly, precisely the same photograph is included on page 165 of the *Municipal Journal*'s 2 March 1900 special issue on the Boundary Estate, where it is captioned in frustratingly vague terms as 'a view of one of the rooms in the Council's dwellings'.[58] Whatever the truth of the matter, the photograph shows precisely what one would expect in an aspirational Boundary Estate household. There is the dining table with its cloth covering and pot plant, an ornate gas light and a gilded birdcage hanging above it; rugs are on the floor; prints hang on the walls, including one that appears to show a religious scene. On a sideboard is displayed an elegant dining service. Ornate antimacassars are draped over the back rests of French late eighteenth-century-style dining chairs. The walls are painted a strong colour, possibly red. A large clock sits above the fireplace, flanked by ornamental items, such as plates, that look vaguely oriental. Within the fireplace is a grate that is too dainty for cooking on, suggesting that this particular apartment must have had its own kitchen, presumably the room one can glimpse reflected in a conveniently placed mirror. Whether authentic or created by the LCC, this is the image of the homes that the Boundary Estate was built to house.

Whatever virtues the estate may have embodied were, however, rather lost on the contemporary architectural press, which seemed determined to take a jaundiced view. The *British Architect* of February 1897, for example, dismissed Arnold Circus with its yellow-banded red-brick facades as 'stripeland' and sarcastically described the apartments as 'admirably lighted, artistically painted and usefully fitted with "penny-in-the-slot meters"'.[59] Presumably, pay-as-you-go gas meters

The enigmatic image of an LCC estate interior. It is catalogued as a photograph taken inside Hogarth House, on the Millbank Estate in 1906 or 1909. But the image appears in the March 1900 article on the Boundary Estate in the *Municipal Journal*, where it is captioned as 'a view of one of the rooms in the Council's dwellings'.

accepting such small sums of money were indicative of the cheapest and poorest type of accommodation and suggested that the tenants would be of the lower sort and incapable of appreciating the artistic ambitions of their new homes. The same month, no doubt to emphasise its disapproval of 'stripeland', the *British Architect* observed that Culham Buildings, perhaps started in 1894 but completed by 1896 and almost certainly an early work by Winmill, showed 'more restraint in its design' than the buildings around Arnold Circus, 'and generally we like it better'.[60] As for the laundry, this was patronised as a 'dignified little block', with an 'abominable' Tudor-style doorway.[61]

* * * * *

It was on 22 March 1898, as the estate's first tenants were moving in and the final blocks were being completed, that Charles Booth returned to the area, with his secretary and their guide and guardian, Sergeant French, from the nearby police station on Commercial Street, to update Booth's now ten-year-old colour-coded Poverty Map. It was immediately clear to them that while the estate was pristine, its immediate environs remained very rough. Those people who had occupied the Old Nichol slum were mostly too poor, too transient, too generally awkward, antisocial and criminalised by poverty, to be aided by the LCC's selective benevolence. Unable to qualify for rehousing in the new buildings, many had generally squeezed themselves into the surviving and surrounding slum streets. In Club Row market, at the west end of Sclater Street and immediately south of Bethnal Green Road and the Boundary Estate, Booth and his colleagues observed '3 and 4 storey houses, shops underneath' and noted it was the 'centre to bird fanciers, larks, thrushes, canaries, parrots, rabbits etc. in cages'. They also noticed the 'long weavers windows on top stories [*sic*]' but recorded 'no weavers now ... simply rough class'. According to Sergeant French, the population of the street was 'all thieves or receivers of stolen goods; they go "dipping" on Sunday morning, what we call larceny from the person'.[62] Booth and his secretary were of the opinion that a 'Great part of the old Boundary St. has come here'.[63]

The group walked east along Hare Street (now Cheshire Street), where Booth and his secretary noticed 'some Jews, shops underneath, the rest rough, thieves'. They then went south over 'a bridge across the Great Eastern Railway train lines' (the bridge, for pedestrians only, survives, although the world around it has been transformed). Having crossed the bridge, they found themselves among the two-storeyed former weavers' houses of Pedley Street, and from there they walked 'into Weaver Street, 2 storied houses, narrow, only fifteen feet between house and house, some Jews, others thieves. Poor.'[64] In Fleet Street (which was to the west of Pedley Street and is now itself called Pedley Street), Booth observed 'a child . . . with only one shoe, all children very dirty' and surmised that some thieves and prostitutes from the Boundary Street area had been obliged to take up residence in the ruinous houses nearby.[65]

One observation about the rough, triangular-shaped area immediately to the south of the Boundary Estate, recorded by Booth and his secretary, is particularly revealing. The party agreed that it looked like 'a remnant of Old London with ante Board School traditions and habits', with Sergeant French claiming that 'the majority of [the residents] would not know how to write their own names'. Clearly, then, despite the presence of the two quite recently erected board schools, the poorest of the poor remained beyond the reach of any formal education. Money, presumably, was the major stumbling block here, not only because education at this time was not free (the average cost in London being twopence a week) but because school attendance effectively ruled out the chance of a child undertaking some menial job that would add to the family's coffers and so help keep them out of the workhouse.

As for the Old Nichol itself, this was for the most part a vast demolition and construction site. Yet even now a small area of the old slum remained.[66] Redchurch Street was still there, with its 'thieves' and 'prostitutes' and shops where 'receivers' of stolen property were known to operate (Booth downgraded the street from pink and red to purple with a black edge). Another survivor was the Blue Anchor public house on the corner with York Row, in what is now Ebor Street. This was, according to French, 'the most noted thieves resort in London' where, 'every Sunday they congregate . . . from all parts of London'. Ebor Street itself was, Booth and his secretary noted, 'all thieves . . . black rather than the purple on the map'.[67]

This description of Redchurch Street and its environs in the late 1890s is supported by the (sometimes fantastical) memoirs of Arthur Harding, who had been born in Boundary Street in 1885 and lived in impoverished and wayward circumstances in the Old Nichol in its final desperate years.[68] He recalled the food shops of Church Street/Redchurch Street, notably a fish-and-chip shop right opposite Boundary Street where adults sent their children for 'a penny bit and haporth' (one penny's worth of fish and a halfpenny's worth of chips or fried potatoes).[69] He also recalled the Blue Anchor (even if he referred to it as the 'Jack Simmons').[70] It was, he wrote, 'the most famous pub in the east end of a Sunday morning' and the favoured resort of the 'swell mob' and the 'sporting' fraternity:

> All the top Johnnies were in there, the prize fighters, and some of the music hall artists. It had a great big bar at the front, with a little private bar round at the side. Of a Sunday morning they used to do a rare old trade. The boxers and the prize fighters and the racing people used to go in there. All the rogues and the villains – the three-card mob and all that lark.[71]

Interestingly, Harding's account also sheds some light on the operation of the board schools within the Old Nichol. He recalled that his ten-year-old sister, Mighty, was permitted, by the evidently pragmatic school inspector, to attend school just two days a week because the girl's wages helped to keep the entire family afloat. In Harding's opinion the school's staff displayed great sympathy because 'they knew what a terrible life we were living'.[72]

Evidently, what was left of the Old Nichol in 1898 was a desperate and criminalised place, the haunt of East End gangs, and its immediate environs were generally worse than they had been because they had received an exodus of Old Nichol occupants to whom the LCC could not or would not offer homes in its new tenement blocks. A strange image of the Boundary Estate in its early days is therefore conjured up. It was an island of aspiration and excellence. But it lay in an ocean of poverty which, by its construction, it had only made worse. Booth noted of Brick Lane, north of Bethnal Green Road, that 'some of old Boundary street have come here, thieves, prostitutes, bullies',[73] while Gibraltar Walk, a little to the east was, according to French, 'the beginning of a hot bed of thieves'.[74] The three men concluded that the construction of the Boundary Estate had made the streets to its east more crowded and squalid than they had been in the late 1880s 'by reason of the immigration of the worst characters from Boundary Street. Thieves, prostitutes and bullies, especially thieves.'

On 24 March 1898, Booth, his secretary and Sergeant French penetrated right into the heart of the Old Nichol area, walking east from Shoreditch High Street along Boundary Passage, the traditional entry into the Old Nichol slum from the west when, to pass the bollards – the 'posties' at the end of the passage – was to cross a boundary into a lawless land. The south side of Old Nichol Street still survived, but on his revised Poverty Map Booth shows it as demolished, while the west side of Boundary Street is shown light blue and the north side of Virginia Road dark blue, signifying the occupants were 'Poor' and 'Very poor'.[75] But he noted that new 'blocks of dwellings' had been 'built up with an elevated pyramidal garden as a common centre, on the top of which a band plays in Summer'.[76] These newly occupied blocks – not all completed – Booth colour-coded pink, denoting them as the homes of the 'Fairly comfortable' with 'Good ordinary earnings'.

While the notebook Booth and his secretary compiled does not dwell long on the fact that the construction of the new estate made things in its environs worse rather than better, at least in the short term, others felt no such constraint. Indeed, it became something of a standard observation, especially, when, after the estate was completed and the blocks fully occupied, it became known that, of the 5,500 or so people that had moved in, only eleven had been residents of the lost Old Nichol slum. It was evident to all that the blocks were not, and never had been, intended to house the very poor, the destitute and the most desperate people living in the area. These blocks were for the industrious poor. It was symbolic of the genteel middle-class aspirations imposed on the estate that there were, by decree, no public houses or even off-licences on site, even if there were plenty in the surrounding area. Some wise observers, such as Hector Gavin in his *Sanitary Ramblings* of 1848, argued, correctly, that drink and other social evils were not the cause of poverty but rather the consequences.[77] Yet demon drink remained a popular target for social reformers, which apparently included the LCC. It appeared to believe that, if nothing else, excluding pubs and off-licences from the estate was a gesture towards removing temptation. It was also a warning of the dim view it would take of drunken tenants.

The fact that virtually none of the residents of the Old Nichol were accommodated on the new estate became not only a standard observation but something of a scandal. Arthur Morrison, who had focused the public's attention on the desperate lives of the Old Nichol's impoverished inhabitants in his 1896 novel *A Child of the Jago* (his name for the Old Nichol), pointed out that this failure to rehouse its population meant the evils of the old slum lived on: 'The Jago, as mere bricks and mortar,' he wrote, 'is gone ... the Jago in flesh and blood still lives, and is crowding into neighbourhoods already densely over-populated.'[78] In 1899 George Haw, the author of *No Room to Live: The Plaint of Overcrowded London*, made a similar point but in more specific terms. He complained that philanthropic or municipal authorities 'never entirely re-house the people displaced from cleared sites' and that the newly homeless were therefore compelled to 'overcrowd into the already overcrowded smaller properties that lie around'. As far as Haw could see, 'Chief among the offenders is the London County Council, as its high rents hold the poorer classes at bay.' Haw had discovered, from the Chief Sanitary Inspector of Bethnal Green, that 'the Boundary Street scheme turned over 3,000 people into the other overcrowded quarters of his district, very few of whom returned to the new block dwellings.'[79] The Californian novelist and journalist Jack London formed a very similar impression of the new estate in late 1902. In his somewhat slapdash *The People of the Abyss* he observed that 'while the buildings housed more people than before' (typically London was wrong about this) and were 'much healthier', this was because they were 'inhabited by the better-class workmen and artisans'. As London put it, echoing Morrison, Haw and Booth, 'The slum people had simply drifted on to crowd other slums or to form new slums.'[80]

It was self-evident to most that slum clearance projects that did not involve rehousing the slum's occupants meant that the core problems of urban poverty and deprivation were not solved. They had simply been moved from one place to another. In 1851 Charles Dickens had made precisely this point in *Household Words* when pondering the new thoroughfares that were being cut through London by the Metropolitan Board of Works. Intended largely to improve communications, they had the secondary ambition of clearing away the slums; indeed, routes were usually manipulated to cut through the poorest areas. But, as Dickens complained, those who engineer 'our . . . new streets' do so 'never heeding, never asking, where the wretches whom we clear out, crowd'.[81]

Even so, despite the criticism from such informed observers as Morrison and Haw, the LCC's Boundary Estate was, when completed, regarded as a model to be emulated. It also received the royal imprimatur of the Prince of Wales. On 3 March 1900, he and the Princess of Wales travelled to the East End where they were met at the junction of Calvert Avenue and Boundary Street by Lord Welby, chairman of the LCC, and by D. D. Waterlow, vice chairman of the LCC's Housing of the Working Classes Committee. The royal carriages then took a tour of the estate, eventually arriving at a pavilion erected between Hedsor Buildings and Laleham Buildings. Various speeches were delivered, including one by the prince in which he declared that 'there is no question at the present time of greater importance than the housing of the working classes', a subject in which, the prince reminded the audience, he had 'long taken a deep interest'. He professed himself to be 'greatly pleased with the design of the buildings' and concluded by wishing 'the LCC all success in the great and good work in which they are engaged – the erection of good and wholesome dwellings such as those around us'.[82]

After formally opening the estate, the prince and his entourage was taken to 'inspect a specimen tenement in the new buildings'.[83] The 'specimen' was in fact Benson Buildings, immediately to the west of Hedsor Buildings. This was one of the more recently completed blocks and so probably still empty, which would obviously have been convenient. But Benson Buildings also contained some of the most humble homes on the estate. If this choice of 'show house' was closely considered by the LCC, then it has to be concluded that council officials did not want the prince to form the opinion that they were being profligate in their use of public funds and housing the working classes in too princely a fashion.

The *Municipal Journal*'s special issue of 2 March 1900, which is headed 'Municipal Housing in London . . . from Slums to Model Dwelling', commemorates the Prince and Princess of Wales's inauguration of the 'LCC Dwellings in Bethnal Green' and forcefully proclaims the virtues of the Boundary Estate, contrasting the qualities of the 'hard-working, self-respecting community' who have taken the place of the 'self-contained colony of criminal and semi-criminal people' who had lived in the 'old evil haunts'. 'It represents something more than good homely dwellings in place of unhealthy hovels,' the journal argued. 'It represents a moral as well as a sanitary change. Healthy homes in place of unhealthy ones generally do bring moral changes in their train' that 'in this instance . . . will make for good throughout the whole of the two populous districts of Shoreditch and Bethnal Green.' The journal acknowledged that provision had not been made for most of those ousted from the slums, and that it was quite possible that they might have gone on to 'create another "Nichol" in some other quarter', but argued that, if so, 'it cannot . . . be as bad as the old place . . . nor . . . as big', since 'many of the former tenants have been scattered over several districts'. '[T]he most that such clearance schemes can do,' it concluded, 'is to sweep away foul rookeries and put healthy homes in their place. The healthy dwellings in themselves are the best guarantee against a criminal population.'[84]

To support its somewhat strident and uncompromising journalistic position, indeed to inform and sustain it, the journal published a long article written by R. M. Beachcroft, the chairman of the LCC Housing Committee. He was a little more apologetic, admitting that the 'great problem' facing his committee was of 'housing those displaced, who ought', he acknowledged, to have had 'accommodation found for them on site'.[85] When the issue was first considered back in 1890, he wrote, the LCC calculated 'that probably half of the whole number displaced would not be seriously inconvenienced by having to leave the neighbourhood altogether' – suggesting that around 2,700 of the Nichol's population were little better than vagrants and so could simply be moved on elsewhere. But, he also claimed, a 'primary' desire of his committee in 1890 had been 'to avoid wholesale clearances and to provide accommodation beforehand for those displaced'. Back then it had been hoped that the management of the displaced population would be achieved by the phased demolition of the old buildings, whereby 'vacant accommodation in the neighbourhood would provide for those whose removal was primarily called for (some 2,000) and that the new buildings would accommodate the rest.'[86] Ten years later, Beachcroft had to concede that this had not, in fact, happened, and that virtually none of the displaced residents of the Old Nichol had been rehoused in the new buildings. Instead, he confirmed that, 'according to the sanitary inspector of Bethnal Green, the inhabitants displaced simply crowded into the previously overcrowded houses in the neighbourhood, and it is to be feared, as the scheme developed, this was so.'

Beachcroft told the story of a blind man named Conolly whom he had interviewed in 1890. Conolly had made matchboxes and rented two rooms in the Old Nichol for which he paid five shillings and three pence in rent a week. One room he occupied with his family and the other he sublet to another family for two shillings and three pence per week. In all, eleven people had lived in the two rooms. 'Poor Conolly', wrote Beachcroft, 'could not be expected to pay 6/- for two rooms (and our regulations would probably require him to take three at 8s 6d) without permission to sublet one of them.' Conolly, priced out of the new LCC paradise, was simply regarded as beyond help.

Ultimately Beachcroft felt that the advantages of the Boundary

Estate outweighed the losses its construction entailed. 'The truth is', he argued, 'that the new dwellings are of so superior a character that they have naturally attracted a better class'; that 'no one who looks at these buildings will wonder that the old tenants have not returned to them'; and that 'The lesson to be deduced is, that if clearances on a similar scale are to be affected, all idea must be dismissed of rehousing the people dispossessed, and we must rest content with the assurance of the political economist that the provision of a high standard of house accommodation produces a general shift and serves to raise the standard all round.'[87]

In his final reflections one nevertheless senses some little, if late, uncertainty about the morality of it all. While clearly proud of the new estate, he acknowledged that, when it came to the fate of the dispossessed of the Old Nichol, 'personally I am not content with this as a solution.' 'I hold', he suggested, 'that the bounden duty of the Council is to see that such of the persons displaced, as must of necessity reside in the immediate neighbourhood, should have provided for them proper dwellings, into which they may move before being displaced.'[88]

This was, in a way, another first for the Boundary Estate. The morally compromised way in which it had replaced the existing denizens of the Old Nichol slum, awkward and impoverished as they were, with a new population launched the conviction among local authorities that the rights and aspirations of established communities had to be properly regarded in mass demolition schemes, certainly those undertaken by councils. There was now a more widespread belief that strenuous efforts should be made to protect a community and, as far as possible, to rehouse it on site, particularly when it was thought to possess economic or social potential. This conviction was not, of course, always acted upon, especially when the rebuilding project was largely commercial or industrial rather than residential, but it did become a guiding principle and promised a change in the LCC's housing policy.

* * * * *

As for the inhabitants of what Beachcroft described as the new 'model village', we get a very good sense of their overall composition and nature by looking at those who settled into Cleeve Buildings on Calvert Avenue, designed by R. Minton Taylor and occupied from July 1896. Minton Taylor was, as we have seen, one of the LCC team's more able architects and responsible for most of the buildings on the prime sites around Arnold Circus. Indeed, Cleeve Buildings has, in its architectural details, much in common with Minton Taylor's Shiplake and Marlow buildings stretching along Calvert Avenue and looking on to the circus. Like them it has large shops on most of its ground floor – in fact eight in number – and crowning gables embellished with broad, closely set bands of brick, darker in hue than the red brick walling. But unlike Shiplake and Marlow, each strikingly asymmetrical and L-shaped on their distinctive sites, Cleeve Buildings presents a strictly symmetrical elevation to Calvert Avenue.[89] The end gables are of Minton Taylor's simple, abstract, flat-side type and are each one storey high, with small round windows lighting the roof space. The gable in the centre is more ornate – incorporating stone scrolls, urns (now lost) and a minuscule crowning pediment – and is two storeys high, making the building in its centre six storeys high.[90] Behind the building, and related to it, are sixteen single-storey workshops. They remain in use, much as originally intended.

In terms of the accommodation offered, Cleeve Buildings hovered between the extremes of the more generous apartments around Arnold Circus and the more utilitarian ones of Culham Buildings. It was given an 'associated' plan, but of a reasonably generous sort: sculleries were shared, but each apartment had its own private WC (although located off a common corridor). The size of the accommodation varied from two to four rooms, with two or three being the most common. No apartment boasted a kitchen, or even an externally located one nominated for their use. All rooms were, as elsewhere, heated by coal fires and lit by gas. Sculleries, accessed off corridors, were each shared between four apartments. They were grouped with the private WCs, presumably for the ease of water supply and drainage. As Stilwell observes, although the apartments were not 'advanced' in terms of layout, they were nevertheless 'spacious and considered a cut-above the normal quality of

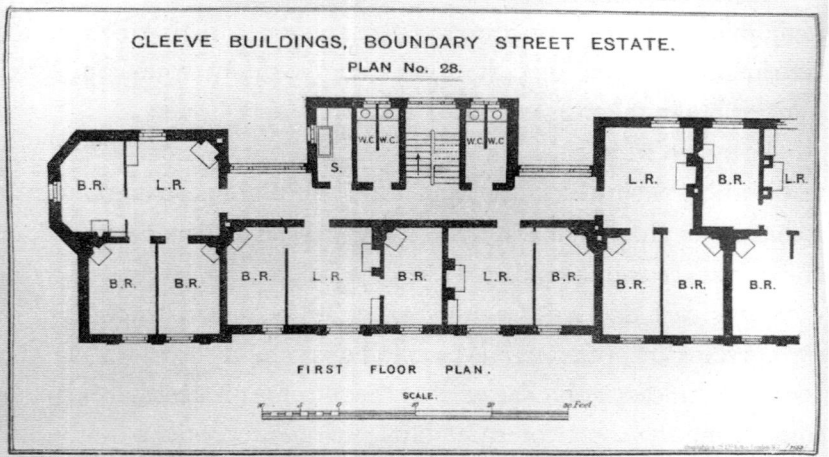

Above: Cleeve Buildings on Calvert Avenue, before bomb damage during the Second World War. The architect was Reginald Minton Taylor and the building was occupied from July 1896. Below: An early upper-level plan published by the LCC, showing the mix of four-, three- and two-room apartments. L.R. indicates living room, B.R. bedroom and S. scullery. Each of the four apartments in this group has its own W.C., but reached via the communal corridor/landing.

the time'. Stilwell also suggests that 'unusually, baths were provided on each floor'.[91]

The 1901 census returns for Cleeve Buildings (or House as it, and many of the Buildings, have been re-christened) list thirty-two apartments. On the day the census was conducted, 142 people were in residence. In addition, there were three 'visitors' in two separate apartments. So there were on average nearly four and a half people per apartment, or, since the building contained 103 rooms,[92] an average of around 1.4 people per room (or around two if only bedrooms are included), so just within the limits of what the LCC deemed acceptable, but problematic for families that included a large number of older children or adults. Number 16 offers a case in point. Here the McCarthy family lived: Dennis McCarthy, a 41-year-old 'G.P.O. Linesman' (a General Post Office worker who maintained the telephone lines), his wife, and their eight children, five girls and three boys, aged from 17 years to 10 months.

LCC rules banned subletting, so all the apartments in Cleeve Buildings were theoretically in single-family occupation. The census returns suggest, however, that the rules may on occasion have been bent or broken. Number 32, for example, was occupied by the four-person Leach family (Alfred W. Leach, aged thirty-six, who was listed as 'Head' of the household, and his three children, aged from seven to eighteen) and Sarah Day, Alfred's widowed mother-in-law. But on the day the census was taken a Florence Jacobs and her four-year-old daughter were also staying there. Florence Jacobs may possibly have been the 'visitor' she claimed to be, but it has to be said that it all seems a little suspicious. Certainly, if seven, perhaps eight, people lived in this four-room apartment it must have felt dreadfully overcrowded.

The trades followed by the occupants of Cleeve Buildings were almost invariably more skilled than those pursued by the denizens of the lost Old Nichol slum, who, according to census returns, generally eked out a living making matchboxes or working as costermongers, street hawkers, labourers or porters (leaving aside those who, in common opinion, were little better than street loafers and petty criminals). In 1901 there were a roofer, a 'fancy box maker', two butchers, a pastry cook/bread maker, several cigar makers (very much a local industry in the later nineteenth century), a bootmaker; a foreman cap maker and two postmen. At a slightly more elevated level of employment at apartment number 5 was 53-year-old James Ward, an 'Engineer's assistant', his wife and their 26-year-old son, who was a 'Musical Director'; at number 14 was Arthur Eve, a 69-year-old 'Author Journalist', his wife and niece; at number 23 was 32-year-old Joseph Harnorsky, a cabinetmaker, and his wife and brother – all Russian-born; and at number 24 was George Seaward, a 36-year-old police inspector, with his wife and daughter. The more exotic occupations, some catering for the luxurious interests of late Victorian Londoners, included the maker of overmantels, Robert C. Johnson, at number 28, and the 'bird cage gilder', Thomas Porey, at number 30. All were just the sort of industrious people who, imbued with the spirit of sweetness and light that inspired the design of the Boundary Estate, were well able to start the process of upward mobility the planners of the estate hoped for its occupants.

* * * * *

The early years of the Boundary Estate never remained entirely free from controversy. First came the concerns that so few of the previous inhabitants of the Old Nichol had been offered housing in the new development. Then, in 1903, Samuel Forde Ridley, the MP for Bethnal Green South-West, opened up a new line of attack. In an inflammatory statement in the House of Commons on 18 February of that year he claimed that: 'The model dwellings which the County Council has put up on the Boundary Street area were now full of aliens who lived in the most undesirable conditions.' By aliens, he meant Jewish immigrants from eastern Europe.

Ridley was something of a maverick and a distinctly oddball MP for Bethnal Green. A Conservative and Unionist, born on the Isle of Wight, who worked for the family firm that made the linoleum that must have lined the floors of so many of the Boundary Estate apartments, he was an opportunist and a populist, and his resolutely pro-British, anti-Boer rhetoric had played well with the patriotic voters in

Bethnal Green during the election campaign of 1900 that followed the outbreak of the Boer War. Ripley's anti-alien stance must also have played well with elements of the local community, and he managed to wrest the seat away from the incumbent Liberal – and very progressive – MP Edward Pickersgill, though Ripley was swept away in the Liberal landslide victory of 1906, which saw the seat returned to Pickersgill, and was subsequently dropped by the local Conservative association.

Ridley's description of the Boundary Estate was clearly part of a political agenda, but was he in fact correct in his assertion that it had become an enclave of foreign Jews? *The Times*, which reported his statement, clearly smelt a rat. On 16 March 1903, less than a month after Ridley's Commons intervention, it published the fruits of its own, rather hasty investigation, which relied, in a distinctly unscientific manner, on the surnames recorded in the LCC annual census of the estate in December 1902 to determine what nationality the inhabitants of each of its various apartments might be. Its conclusion was that 'out of a total of 1,044 tenements on the Boundary Street estate, 283, or 27 per cent, are occupied by persons who would appear by their names to be foreigners' – hardly evidence that eastern European Jews were taking over the estate. It also investigated Ridley's claim that tenants were living 'in the most undesirable conditions' and, again, concluded that he was exaggerating: 'Out of these 283 tenements only one was occupied by such number of persons as to transgress the Council's regulations as to overcrowding,' it reported. The 1901 census returns for Cleeve Buildings confirm *The Times*'s scepticism, with little or no evidence of overcrowding and – if one uses surnames as a crude guide – there is no suggestion that Jewish residents predominated. In fact, just over 15 per cent of the occupants of Cleeve Buildings could be described as (possibly) foreign (and not necessarily Jewish), if the family's origin is defined by the place of birth of its 'head', and under 15 per cent if the place of birth of all family members is considered.[93] Among them, in number 10, was Solomon Klebensky, a 34-year-old bootmaker, and his wife, Adilade, both of whom had been born in Russia, and their four children, named Jacob, Abey, Sarah and Amie, all of whom had been born in Whitechapel or

Stamford Hill. The oldest, Jacob, was aged fifteen, which suggests his parents had arrived in London during the early 1880s, just when the pogroms in Russia were getting under way. At number 23 was Joseph Harnorsky, his wife, Rebecca, and a 15-year-old brother, Hyman, all of whom had been born in Russia.[94] Over three-quarters of their neighbours were British-born.

Ridley's provocative observations were unsavory, but they were, in fact, no more than a reflection of the deep-rooted fear of the 'alien'. Even Charles Booth, in the section on 'Poverty' in the 1902 edition of his *Life and Labour of the People in London*, revealed a strain of unsettling prejudice, presumably provoked by the perception of an all-engulfing wave of immigrants. 'Just outside the old City walls', reflected Booth, 'have always lived the Jews, and here they are now in thousands . . . seeking their livelihoods under conditions which seem to suit them on the middle ground between civilisation and barbarism.'[95] Moreover, Booth had, in relation to this perception, specific observations about the Boundary Estate. Like many contemporary observers, Booth argued that, because 'the various expenses incurred in effecting the clearance had been enormous', rents were too high and 'the regulations to be observed under the new conditions demanded more orderliness of behaviour than suited the old residents.' As a result, not only had the displaced residents of the 'demolished dwellings . . . overrun the neighbouring poor streets' but the 'different class' they had made way for were 'largely Jews'.[96]

Why, one wonders, did Charles Booth not analyse the 1901 census returns when editing the 1902 edition of his monumental work of London poverty? Presumably he could not get access to them. If he had, he would have seen that it was incorrect to state that the occupants of the new Boundary Estate buildings were 'largely Jews'. In fact, the estate was principally occupied by precisely the 'respectable' English working people for whom it had been intended.

The popular perception, however, proved hard to shift, and in time led to parliamentary action. The Aliens Act of 1905, while presented as a means of preventing criminals and paupers entering the country, was clearly framed to control Jewish immigration from central and eastern Europe. A few years later, in 1914, it was strengthened by the Aliens Restriction Act, which introduced controls, and systems of registration and deportation. Immigration had become a political issue.

* * * * *

The Boundary Estate still flourishes. The blocks have long been listed, and protected, as buildings of special architectural or historic interest. It is a conservation area, the planting is mature, lush and well maintained, with many tall and handsome plane trees, and physical damage through the decades has been slight, apart from the wartime destruction of one corner of Cleeve Buildings. The estate is much loved and much visited, especially by foreign architects and planners. It is, after all, a pioneering exploration of, and monument to, the potential of 'council' or social housing and estate planning and, despite its seemingly quaint Queen Anne Revival and Arts and Crafts manner, is a bold, even revolutionary, experiment in socially progressive, relatively 'high-rise' architecture and in the creation of a sense of community. More than ever the estate, with its ornate beauty and gabled buildings rising amid mature planting, looks like a fantastical fairy-tale 'model village', albeit formed with five-storey buildings, embedded in Shoreditch. But, perhaps more important than the estate's abiding architectural beauty is the fact that it still does what it was built to do: it provides housing – about 50 per cent for local authority tenants, with the rest managed by housing associations or owner-occupied. The LCC was abolished in 1965, so the authority now largely, but not entirely, in control is Tower Hamlets Council, with a small part of the estate controlled by Hackney Council. One of the board schools, the Virginia Road Primary School, still functions as a state school. The Rochelle School long ago ceased to be an educational establishment. For a while, parts of it were used by artists and for a restaurant. Now it contains office space and apartments, but with the restaurant still in operation.

As a living and still largely council-owned housing enclave, the Boundary Estate has to exist in the real world, and at times endure it. Despite being in a conservation area and with its external fabric at least reasonably well maintained, both of which factors make the blocks attractive for private investors, there is very little evidence of gentrification. There have clearly been long-term issues over running costs, which mean that a lot of external joinery needs a lick of paint and the courts between blocks, which originally contained large informal gardens and areas for drying clothes and for children to play, are now generally bleak places with expanses of easy-to-maintain tarmac, usually dotted with large wheelie bins. The comparable courts within the Millbank Estate are far more congenial, with concrete brick paving and profusions of potted plants. This presumably reflects the economic differences between the east London councils and Westminster City Council, which now owns the Millbank Estate and runs it through a tenant management organisation whose board is elected from the resident population (half of whom own their apartments on private leaseholds).

The Boundary Estate's community is mixed, with families of Bangladeshi origin now forming a significant proportion in many blocks. The purpose-built shops on Calvert Avenue generally still function as shops, some most exquisite, such as a high-quality children's clothes and toyshop and a pair serving as a superior delicatessen and café. There is also a 'community' launderette which functions as the self-appointed community centre, a place not just for washing clothes but also for gathering and posting information, exchanging concerns and as a mobilisation point for action. It seems to work, and certainly residents do band together to clean the gardens, to frown upon unsympathetic development proposals (these now mostly seem to involve turning workshops – many of which have been sold off by the local authority – into exclusive high-rent commercial spaces), and to fight antisocial behaviour. There has also recently been vigorous debate over local authority proposals to restrict traffic on the estate and to extend its planting, which superficially seems a sound idea but could compromise the estate's surviving original landscape design, funnel through-traffic along limited routes and result in damage to early paving schemes.

Internally the blocks have changed significantly following successive waves of modernisation and service upgrades with, in a few cases, additional accommodation having been inserted within commodious roof spaces. Overall, apartments have been extended in size and their population density reduced. Now around 2,000 people live on the estate.

One of the largest and more obvious physical changes has been the fitting of locks to the main doors to the individual blocks, in part a response to the fact that, some years ago, Arnold Circus and nearby St Leonard's churchyard became minor battlegrounds in a turf war between rival drug gangs. It was nasty for a while, but the community weathered, and finally saw off, the threat. There is also a heavy sprinkling of satellite dishes (technically not permitted on the facades of listed buildings), which suggests that many tenants do not particularly appreciate that they are living in historic buildings of national significance or, if they do, are unwilling to accept that this puts some limitations upon their habits of occupation. But, being philosophical, this is a price worth paying for the estate to remain primarily a place where people live and make their homes, to their individual tastes, rather than being a museum quarter. And at least there are no uPVC windows.

Presiding over all, perched as if on a primeval mound, is the bandstand. It became run-down and was disfigured with lewd graffiti during the turf-war years, but recently has been restored. Music is not generally performed within it, but then perhaps it never was. Indeed, the bandstand, although planned from the start and mentioned in 1897 in the *British Architect* article, is a late arrival in its present majestic form. Photographs taken in 1907 show its site delineated, and perhaps used by a band, but it was not until 1910 that the existing bandstand was definitely in place. Now, as in the past, the bandstand is much more a symbol of intent than a practical structure. Once it represented aspiration to middle-class gentility. Now it is, perhaps, a romantic evocation of a lost, late Victorian ideal world – the Shoreditch working man's paradise – that was realised for some but that, for the desperately poor of the area, remained forever out of reach.

New Ways, Northampton, shortly after its completion in 1926.
Top: the entrance front. Bottom: the garden elevation.

– 8 –

The First 'Modern' House
New Ways, Northampton
(1925–6)

THE AMENITIES OFFERED TO the tenants of the Boundary Estate in 1900 were typical of much housing in Britain at the start of the twentieth century. There were water closets (though often located in the corridors), gas for lighting, and fireplaces in which to burn coal for heating and cooking, as well as running water that was probably unheated (although, as previously noted, gas-fired 'geysers' were available in England from 1868 and storage-tank gas water heaters from 1889). Over the next few decades, however, significant changes were made to improve the comfort and ease of everyday domestic life. By the 1930s, internal toilets (as WCs were now more commonly called) and bathrooms were becoming common, and coal fires were being replaced by gas-burning heaters. Electricity, virtually unknown in most houses in the early part of the century, was on its way to becoming commonplace. In 1919 only 6 per cent of housing was connected to the National Grid. By 1939 just over 60 per cent was. Some features of the home that today we take for granted – central heating, for example – were known but not widely deployed. Radiators pumped full of steam or, latterly, of scaldingly hot water had been around since the mid nineteenth century, but would not be common in more modest homes until the 1970s and 1980s. Fridges became available to a very limited and wealthy few from the 1920s, but as late as 1948 were to be found in only around 2 per cent of homes. The fact remains, though, that the average house of the

1920s and 1930s was far better appointed and easier to run than its Victorian predecessor.

The arrival of the modern caused a degree of nostalgic backlash in certain quarters. The retreat from the coal- or log-burning open fire, for example, provoked a fear that the loss of flames and an open hearth as the natural gathering place in the home could lead to the loosening of sociable ties, even to the breakdown of family life. In 1945, in an article that he penned for the *Evening Standard* entitled 'The Case for the Open Fire', George Orwell argued that since open fires heated only one part of a room they had the power to encourage family members and friends to group together. He painted a rose-tinted picture of the role of the open fire: 'To one side of the fire-place sits Dad, reading the evening paper. To the other side sits Mum, doing her knitting. On the hearth rug sit the children, playing snakes and ladders. Up against the fender, roasting himself, lies the dog. It is a comely pattern . . . and the survival of the family as an institution may be more dependent on it than we realise.' In this article Orwell also had a dig at members of the artistic avant-garde, particularly joyless functionalists: the 'small but noisy minority' that 'want to do away with the old-fashioned coal fire' were, he suggested, also 'the people who admire gaspipe chairs and glass-topped tables' and 'argue that the coal fire is wasteful, dirty and inefficient' and that 'fogs in our cities are made thicker by the smoking of thousands of chimneys'. Orwell admitted that this 'is perfectly true, and yet comparatively unimportant if one thinks in terms of "living" and not merely of saving trouble'.[1]

Given the views of the likes of Orwell it is perhaps scarcely surprising that, despite the gradual embracing of emerging technology in the home, architectural taste remained cautious and traditional. The Boundary Estate managed to be both pioneering and, in terms of appearance, rooted in the past. A few years later, Hampstead Garden Suburb, conceived in 1906 as a radical attempt to provide decent housing for a wide mix of people in a garden-city-like context (see page 363), took an entirely historicist approach to planning and look. The most eminent of its architects, Sir Edwin Lutyens, was content to design houses and churches in a classical idiom inspired by Wren and the Renaissance and, for the most part, in traditional brick. The distinction Lutyens's architecture possesses, and it is considerable, comes primarily from his idiosyncratic and skilful use of traditional forms and building techniques.

That history haunted early twentieth-century British domestic design is made clear by a book, *Small Houses: £500–£2500*, published in 1937, that was inspired by the house-building boom that started, as the book's editor writes, in 1923 to 1924 and only began 'to fall off in 1936'.[2] Of the sixty relatively small, economically built and generally free-standing new-built houses illustrated, just over forty are designed in a more or less historical style. All of these have pitched roofs; a few are fully-fledged neo-Georgian. The remaining houses are in various permutations of what might be termed a more 'modern' style, with flat roofs, large areas of glazing and minimal history-inspired ornament. Even then, their internal arrangement is traditional, and virtually all of them retain chimney stacks and open fires, at least in their main rooms. The book's editor is accepting, if faintly disapproving, of this architecturally unadventurous tendency, mostly because 'the parody of famous historical styles', as he puts it, and their inevitable ornament have a tendency to lead to a significant increase in building costs for no practical gain. In the editor's view, 'the simpler the better seems a loose way of defining good architecture today.'[3] The modern was nevertheless, as *Small Houses* demonstrated, making gradual, cautious inroads, and the aesthetics it promoted slowly won some support among the more progressively minded.

A significant and intriguing figure within this more adventurous cohort is the early twentieth-century architectural patron Wenman Joseph Bassett-Lowke. Born in 1877, he was the son of a Northampton boilermaker and the founder in 1898 of a highly successful mail-order firm that specialised in the sale of construction sets (including those that it designed and produced), his focus being on model trains, boats and ships. He was a committed lecturer on the magic lantern (a simple type of image projector) and an enthusiastic author of books on model railways – all in all, something of an evangelising showman for a miniature world of modern transport. And he was also fascinated by contemporary design.

Such was his interest, indeed, that in the course of barely a decade he commissioned two architects of world renown to work on two very different houses for him in his native Northampton. First, from 1916, the Glaswegian architect Charles Rennie Mackintosh slightly extended and extensively remodelled the newly acquired Bassett-Lowke family home at 78 Derngate. Then, in 1926, the German-born and Berlin-based Peter Behrens designed Bassett-Lowke a completely new house in leafy Wellingborough Road, on the outskirts of Northampton city centre,[4] a house that would be described by *Ideal Home* magazine in January 1927 as Britain's 'first modern house', and one that would be subsequently acclaimed by the influential architectural pundit J. M. Richards as the 'first modern building in England'.[5] By 'modern' Richards meant that the house was a pioneering example in Britain of what became known as the 'modern movement', or 'modernism'. This was a form of architecture, with its origins in the very early twentieth century, that was based not directly on historic precedent, sentiment or regional tradition but on seemingly objective rationalism, functionalism and technological opportunism that was international in its identity and in which ornament, certainly that based on established architectural styles, was ruthlessly eschewed. Appropriately enough, the house was given the name 'New Ways'.

* * * * *

At the time Bassett-Lowke commissioned Mackintosh to work on 78 Derngate, the architect was living in semi-retirement in Chelsea, west London. His career had not, in its latter stages at least, been an easy one, and in recent years had been in decline. He had started to make his name in the late 1890s as an avant-garde designer with international aspirations, who focused initially on the creation of self-consciously exquisite interiors, often carefully integrated with the design of furniture. His chief influence was the Vienna Secession movement that had been established in 1897 by avant-garde

Austrian architects and artists who resigned in protest from the long-established, tradition-orientated Association of Austrian Artists, and instead embraced the innovative ideas of art nouveau. Another major influence on Mackintosh was oriental, specifically Japanese, art and design, which had been a key source of inspiration for Western artists since the 1870s. The consequence of this fusion of influences was that Mackintosh mastered the production of very pleasing designs that included delicate, almost abstract, detailing and studied asymmetry. His architecture was in a similar vein, with all coalescing to create a style, forged in union with his talented artist wife Margaret Macdonald, that captivated many in the first years of the twentieth century.

During the early part of his career, Mackintosh's reputation grew rapidly. In July 1897 his work was published in the highly influential London-based *Studio* magazine; in November 1898 it featured in an article in the German *Dekorative Kunst* ('Decorative Art') magazine, owned by the highly influential Alexander Koch, and in 1899 it was included by the Arts and Crafts Exhibition Society in its London exhibition. In 1900 Mackintosh was invited to participate in the Vienna Secession exhibition, with his work being again promoted by Koch. This appears to have launched Mackintosh in Germany, where he was supported by the highly placed Germany architect, architectural pundit and diplomat Hermann Muthesius, who wrote a glowing article on Mackintosh for the March 1902 edition of *Dekorative Kunst* and subsequently included him in his epoch-defining three-volume celebratory report on British domestic architecture and progressive 'garden city' town planning, *Das Englische Haus*, published in 1904.

But despite his soaring international profile, Mackintosh's professional life in Glasgow ran a less successful course. In 1896–7 he had designed the Glasgow School of Art, which, large in scale and inventive, was in many ways Britain's most compelling essay in a native idiom of Secessionist or art nouveau architecture. The project was undertaken with the eminent architectural practice of Honeyman and Keppie, with whom in 1901 Mackintosh bought a partnership. This was, in theory, a sound business move that should have provided a steady income. But the relationship between the partners gradually came under strain. Doubtless the growing gap in reputation between Mackintosh and his once-close friend John Keppie, accentuated in 1909 by the completion of Mackintosh's design masterpiece, the library in the Glasgow art school, played a part in this. Nor can it have helped that Mackintosh's high reputation was not matched by the value of the work he brought to the practice, which in fact was considerably less than that generated by Keppie, and that this had an impact on the division of the firm's profits and the allocation of commissions. His unpredictability and unreliability did Mackintosh no favours either. He had a tendency to deliver schemes late and unresolved, and his relationship with clients was, as a result, often tense. Not surprisingly, perhaps, he was manoeuvred out of the practice in 1913.

Mackintosh seems not to have been upset by this parting of ways, his view being that obligations to the business had trespassed upon his creative time and compromised his artistic independence. But the practice he set up on his own soon demonstrated the value of the Honeyman and Keppie connections he had once been able to draw on. Little business came his way and his health, not good since 1911, collapsed, almost certainly undermined by an excess of alcohol. In July 1914 his wife removed him from Glasgow and, when aged only forty-six, into semi-retirement, during which, it was hoped, his anxieties would recede and his health improve.

At Walberswick, in East Anglia, where the couple rented a studio, Mackintosh worked on his landscape and seascape watercolours and on the ultimately fruitless task of planning urban blocks for towns in India being designed by his architect friend Patrick Geddes. While this peculiar combination of escapist activities was being set in motion, Mackintosh was dragged into the brutal and hostile contemporary world. Since August 1914, Britain and its empire had been at war with the German and Austro-Hungarian empires and, strange as it might seem, Walberswick stood on one of the front lines. The coastline of East Anglia had long been regarded by the authorities and by amateur military pundits as a likely invasion location for German forces, sailing at speed and in secret across the North Sea from the German Frisian Islands. As early as 1903, Erskine Childers had suggested such a possible course of action in his whistle-blowing novel *The Riddle of the Sands*, which warned of the bellicose expansionist ambitions of the increasingly militarist German Empire, and highlighted the defensive weakness of England's east coast.

By early 1915 the war had taken an unpredicted and alarming turn, with siege-like trench warfare leading to military stalemates in Belgium and France. To British strategists fearful of German military prowess, this made an outflanking invasion of East Anglia a distinct possibility. The construction of steel-reinforced concrete gun emplacements and 'pillboxes' got under way, and in the process accelerated the development of the building technology that was to characterise early post-war architectural modernism. In parallel to the rapid construction of static defences, coastal communities were scoured for possible spies or German sympathisers. Mackintosh was denounced as potentially pro-German, perhaps because the British security authorities were mistrustful of the professional connections he had forged with designers and architects in Germany and Austria and of the sympathetic reception his work had received in what were by 1915 enemy nations, but more probably because he cut a suspicious figure in cape and slouch hat striding over the headlands at dusk with a sketchbook and lantern.

In May 1915 his German and Austrian papers were seized and read. They were returned after six weeks and no further action was taken, but suspicion lingered, and Mackintosh and his wife were ordered to leave the East Anglia coastal area. Under something of an anti-patriotic cloud in a nation in which military hysteria was mounting, the couple moved to a studio in the sophisticated and tolerant artistic community of Glebe Place in Chelsea. Here they produced watercolours and distinctive textile designs and entered the circle of the dancer and highly successful choreographer and dance teacher Margaret Morris. She had been a long-time companion and artistic collaborator of the author John Galsworthy and in 1915 founded the Margaret Morris Club in Chelsea. This soon became the meeting place of the artistic avant-garde in a London increasingly preoccupied with the bloody business of an unfathomable war of attrition that, aided by the technology offered by industry, seemed set to plumb the depths of suffering. Members of the club included Augustus John, Jacob Epstein, Katherine Mansfield, Ezra Pound, Siegfried Sassoon, Wyndham Lewis and Mackintosh. It was within this context that the ailing architect/artist, beset by health and financial problems, was approached by Bassett-Lowke.

Precisely why Bassett-Lowke should have chosen Mackintosh to enlarge and decorate his modest 1820s Northampton terrace home remains unclear. Presumably he knew of the designer's previous high reputation. Certainly he was impressed by him when they met, even if he could not later quite recall precisely when and how they had done so. Bassett-Lowke thought that an introduction had probably been made by a mutual friend 'in connection with the Glasgow School of Art', presumably Francis Newberry, Mackintosh's client for, and director of, the Glasgow art school. Whatever the precise circumstances of that first meeting, it would seem that Bassett-Lowke must have mentioned that he had recently submitted plans (drawn up by a Northampton-based architect named Alexander Ellis Anderson) to the town's authorities for a flat-roofed bay to the front of the Derngate house and a two-storey rear extension.[6] He must also have invited Mackintosh's comments, because on 31 July 1916, in Bassett-Lowke's first surviving letter to Mackintosh, he thanked the architect for 'the drawings' he had sent and confirmed that he had that day taken possession of the newly acquired house in Derngate.[7]

Mackintosh never visited Northampton to view the site or to supervise the works for which he now took responsibility. It's possible that he believed, initially at least, that he could work remotely and simply recycle a number of earlier designs. Certainly, the wall panels and related fittings he had designed in 1911 for the Cloister Room and the Chinese Room in the Ingram Street Tea Rooms in Glasgow seem to have been a key inspiration for Derngate, since the stylised, brightly coloured geometric references to the leaves of a weeping willow tree that are present in the tea-room designs make a reappearance here. But his designs for the Derngate Street project, as finally executed, demonstrate that he swiftly went beyond any thoughts of settling for a lazy exercise in self-plagiarism. Rather, it would seem that he increasingly came to view the commission as an opportunity to make one final statement. If he failed to visit the site, this was not because he was indifferent to the project but because he believed he knew precisely what he wanted to achieve. He realised that his work, which had once beguiled a sympathetic public and profession, was regarded as old-fashioned in 1916, even passé. The Derngate house was his chance to demonstrate that he had evolved, that he had developed a Chelsea style, that he still had his finger on the pulse, even that he was ahead of taste. It would show that Mackintosh could still create magical and innovative interiors.

And it can be argued that this is precisely what he succeeded in doing with Bassett-Lowke's house. Each room possesses a different visual and decorative character. The interior wall surfaces are made almost frantic by Mackintosh's determination to express himself, and since he was permitted to conceive a total scheme, the design of some furniture and fittings is his, too. It may be that the geometric abstraction and stylisation apparent here was intended to evoke the industrialised processes of production on which Bassett-Lowke's business was partly based – certainly the fire surround, with a frame that is tiered in section and that breaks back and forth with mechanised precision in the hall/lounge, is a striking specimen of the geometric style. What is undoubtedly the case is that the bold colours and geometric patterns of the Cloister Room (initially a men's smoking room) in the Ingram Street Tea Rooms foreshadow, in uncanny manner, the art deco movement that in 1911 was still in its earliest infancy, but that in time (the mid 1920s) would become a distinct style in its own right through its focus on geometric, streamlined and jazzy decoration, strong colours and love of such motifs as ziggurat forms and concentric 'sunburst' circles.[8] Among such a riot of detail at the Derngate house, there was evidently little room left for Bassett-Lowke to put his own mark on things before the interior was completed by March 1917. For such an ebullient man, this could have proved a problem.

A slight complicating factor in all this is that Mackintosh's

The hall/lounge of 78 Derngate, Northampton, designed in 1916 by
Charles Rennie Mackintosh for Wenman Bassett-Lowke. The interior was
significantly altered over the years: the original design drawing suggested
that the joinery was to be painted dark grey, but in fact it was executed in
matt black, offset with brightly coloured abstract stencilled patterns, and
then in the 1920s changed to 'French Grey'. In 2003 the room was carefully
repaired and returned to its original appearance.

complete absence from site meant that Alexander Ellis Anderson, who appears to have initiated the works, was responsible for the execution of Mackintosh's designs. This raises the question: how much of the Derngate design is his and how much belongs to Mackintosh? It's a question that is surprisingly difficult to answer, and particularly intriguing, because the relationship between Mackintosh and Anderson was an involved and complex one. Although based in Northampton by 1916, Anderson had been born in Dundee and his elder brother William James Anderson had been an academic, and an authority on Greek, Roman and Renaissance architecture, who from 1894 had been the director of the Architectural Department at the Glasgow School of Art and Mackintosh's close colleague. William also practised as an architect, specialising in the design of economic, fireproof, functional structures, often proto-modernist in character with large windows. All went well until 1898, when one of William's buildings in Dundee suffered a partial collapse during construction. Five workmen died in the tragedy. In 1900 a sixth victim was claimed when the stricken and inconsolable William took his own life. This grim event cast a shadow over the lives of many, and it is hard to imagine it did not, for good or for ill, influence the working relationship of Mackintosh and William's brother Alexander Anderson at Derngate, or some of the details designed, individually or in unison, for the house. One example can be seen in the rear extension to the original 1820s house, which is white-rendered in a simple manner and contains wide first- and second-floor windows fitted with large panes of glass. The window lighting what appears to be the second floor, when viewed from garden level, is recessed within a balcony that serves the main bedroom. This surprising design has fuelled the myth that, towards the end of his career as an architect, Mackintosh became something of not only an art deco but also a modernist pioneer, as if picking up the spirit of the coming age. But it is evident that his rear addition is a collaborative affair, the initial idea for its functionalist design being Anderson's, with Mackintosh extending it by a storey and adding the recessed balcony. This collaborative work can be seen as a subtle and personal memorial to the functional architecture of a long-lamented brother and colleague whose promising career had been cut short in such appalling circumstances and who by 1916 was all but forgotten.

Memorialisation and mourning more generally must have stalked Northampton in 1916. Many local men would have volunteered for, or from March 1916 been conscripted into, the Northamptonshire Regiment. It had sent two battalions to the Western Front by late 1914, a third to Suvla Bay in August 1915 as part of the ill-fated Gallipoli campaign, and four of its battalions (just over 4,000 men) took part in the murderous Somme offensive from 1 July 1916. By the end of this battle in mid November, British and imperial forces had suffered appallingly high casualties, a significant number of whom would have been Northamptonshire men, including many 'Pals' of the New Territorial armies, who from early 1915 had been recruited on the basis that men who joined together, and who knew each other in civilian life, would serve together. What this meant on the appalling killing fields of the Somme is that whole communities died at the swivel of a single German machine gun. So when in early 1917 Mr and Mrs Bassett-Lowke moved into their vibrant new home, financed in large part by the sale of German-made or German-inspired model railways, the streets of Northampton must have been sad and bleak indeed, with many of the bereaved having no grave at which to mourn their loved ones whose bodies had been atomised by explosives or buried anonymously in graves marked only with the epitaph, selected by Rudyard Kipling, grieving for his own soldier son killed in 1915, 'Known unto God'.

It's tempting to think that some of Mackintosh's work in the house reflects this sombre national mood. In the hall/lounge, for example, the brightly coloured glass and triangular stencil pattern sit in stylish openings in walls that are painted a solemn black and overlaid with machine-like grids of panels. The colour and repetitive grid can be seen as an expression of the modern industrial age and factory production in general or, more specifically, as symbolising the military technology that was overwhelming the beauty of nature and snuffing out the dreams of the living. In around 1920, a softer and brighter 'French Grey', and a new stencil design, were substituted for the original darker colour, presumably at the request of Bassett-Lowke, who, one assumes, found the first scheme a trifle oppressive. In recent restoration works it is the first scheme that has, to a large degree, been recreated.

Of course, it's possible that the sombreness of some of the design reflected Mackintosh's gloomy contemplation of his declining career and his mortality. Number 78 Derngate proved to be his last significant piece of architecture. He subsequently, in 1919, undertook a small project for Bassett-Lowke's brother-in-law – a dining room in number 5 The Drive, Northampton – and that was it. Work dried up, as did funds, and in 1923 Mackintosh and his wife, Margaret, moved to Port-Vendres on the Mediterranean coast of France because the food and drink were good, living was cheap and the landscape and seascape beautiful and an inspiration for their lives as watercolourists. But neither really prospered and in 1927 they returned to London for medical reasons. The couple lived for a while in Willow Road, Hampstead, where Mackintosh succumbed to cancer in December 1928. Margaret, who had been suffering from ill health since 1921, died in Chelsea in 1933.

*****

By 1925 Bassett-Lowke, now forty-eight and at the peak of his business success, had tired of life in 78 Derngate. It is not known why. Perhaps he had indeed found Mackintosh's intense scheme of decoration too intimidating or perhaps too dated, or perhaps he simply wanted a larger home, built from scratch, to reflect his increased wealth, status and evolving tastes. Evidently by the early 1920s he had moved away from lingering art nouveau combined with a twist of what was to become art deco and towards more mainline modernism. The models he was making and marketing display the same shift of interest. As well as model railway buildings, such as stations, of traditional late Victorian design, he was also starting to produce modernist structures that remain, within the context of model railways, quite startling and certainly novel. Now in the spring

of 1925 he started to look around for an architect able to realise the
type of progressive home he had in mind: functional, comfortable and almost futuristic in its realisation of the potential of new
technology – in short, modern in its operation and in its appearance.
Such an architect, he rapidly discovered, did not exist in Britain. He
therefore turned to a German one.

Given the business he was in, this was not a particularly surprising decision. During the interwar period, Germany was the
centre for top-quality model-making, particularly of trains and
train-set paraphernalia, and Bassett-Lowke forged significant professional relationships with several German manufacturers that for
a while enabled his company to corner the growing British market.
He produced, or commissioned for sale in Britain, models of the
highest quality, mostly at the relatively large 'o' gauge,[9] and in the
process established a high reputation (his models are now much
coveted and highly valuable collectors' items). Bassett-Lowke's
main German connection was a toy-manufacturing company called
Gebrüder Bing ('Brothers Bing'), founded in 1863 in Nuremberg,
that specialised in immaculately made clockwork and live-steam-
powered model locomotives, and that by the early twentieth century
was the largest toy manufacturer in the world. Gebrüder Bing
established a benchmark in excellence, having introduced 'o gauge'
model train sets in 1895, and the canny Bassett-Lowke commissioned the company to design and make model trains inspired by
British prototypes for the British market. His exploration of such
high-quality, craft-based companies, combined with his leaning to
'progressive' politics (he served on the executive committee of the
socialist Fabian Society from 1922 until 1924), led him to become
familiar with the evolving culture in Germany of design in the
service of society that expressed egalitarian ideals. This led to connections with the Deutscher Werkbund – an association of artists,
architects, designers and industrialists, launched in Munich in 1907,
that promoted design that would improve the quality of life in a
broad spectrum of society[10] – and to membership of its British functionalist equivalent, the Design and Industries Association, which

was founded in 1915 and which championed utility and took as its motto 'Fitness for Purpose'.

It was through his business associations with Germany, and his admiration for German culture, crafts and industry, that Bassett-Lowke came into contact with the architecture of Professor Peter Behrens. Later he was to recall that when he first decided to build a new house he 'could not find any ... architect with modern ideas in England'. Then, 'when looking through a German publication called *Werkbund Jahrbuch* of 1913', he encountered some work by Behrens which he thought was 'very simple, straightforward, and modern in its atmosphere'.[11] Bassett-Lowke obtained Behren's address through the German Consulate, contact was made, and a meeting was then held in 1925 in Paris between Bassett-Lowke, his builder Charles Green, and Behrens. It must be assumed that Bassett-Lowke and Green took a lot of information with them to Paris, including a draft plan of Bassett-Lowke's 'ideal home' and a requirement that some of the Derngate details be duplicated or removed and incorporated in the proposed new house,[12] because Behrens, like Mackintosh before him, was never to visit the site nor in any way to supervise the work. It was, and remains, an unusual and potentially high-risk form of architectural practice. At the very least it demands that much information is gathered and relayed from the site by the client or his advisors, who must also be obliged to make many decisions that are usually the prime preserve of the architect.

The then 58-year-old Peter Behrens had trained and practised in the Arts and Crafts tradition, but from the early years of the twentieth century became attracted to what would ultimately grow into, and be termed, 'modernism'. One early strand of this movement was a search for artistic unity in which all elements, including graphics and decoration, were integrated to create a 'total work of art' (*Gesamtkuntswerk*). This started to characterise German and Austrian architecture from the late nineteenth century and became a key part of the expressionist movement, which was a dominant avant-garde and proto-modernist artistic force in central and northern Europe until the First World War.

In architecture, expressionism tended to promote the creation of powerful, often elemental, forms calculated to engage the emotions of observers.

Another important aspect of early modernism was the belief that, when a building is designed, the poetry of architecture should lie primarily in the honest and overt expression of the materials and means of construction, with the forms chosen derived directly from function and utility. These were, of course, among the basic tenets of the early nineteenth-century archaeologically inspired phase of the Gothic Revival, as defined in Britain by A. W. N. Pugin (see page 163), but in the early twentieth century this approach led to the abandonment of ornamental evocations of past historic styles that had marked European architecture for centuries. Finally, there was a growing desire to make the most of the potential of new technology and building materials.

In Behrens's case these strands first came together in 1909 in Berlin when he completed the vast Turbine Hall for AEG (Allgemeine Elektricitäts-Gesellschaft, or General Electric Company), a leading generator of the modern power source of the age. Designed to present an extremely abstracted exterior of stripped-classical style, it utilises new technology to achieve a large open-span hall, 25.5 metres wide and 123 metres long, formed with a steel frame that incorporates a wall of huge windows, with glass set in slender steel frames supported in part by steel stanchions that rise on massive hinge joints. This wall of glass lights the hall in a fantastically dramatic manner, allowing machines and work areas to be illuminated with almost startling clarity. This was a building for machines that was itself designed and executed with the ruthless precision and practical perfection of one, and it established Behrens's status as one of the godfathers of modernism. The building made clear that new technology could achieve functional and aesthetic wonders, while historic precedent, when confronted with the demands and structural potential of the coming world, was of only limited relevance. The building's vaguely classical appearance and some of its external detailing, such as the steel-reinforced concrete piers that appear to be rusticated because they are divided into bands by steel straps, may make it appear as a temple of power, and as such reveal Behrens's expressionist tendency to imbue his architecture with emotive associations. But this evocation of temple architecture is probably little more than the coincidental consequence of the application of the principles of utilitarianism. The fact that the building can be perceived in different ways is a hallmark of expressionist architecture and evidence of the building's intriguing complexity. Arguably, the central point being made is that history is irrelevant as a prime source of architectural inspiration for functional buildings of the modern age.

Such was Behrens's achievement with this building and so high his reputation that by 1912 three of Europe's leading young architects, all eventually to become giants in the modern movement in architecture, or the International Style, had gravitated to his office. Here, it must be assumed, they first encountered many of the ideas they were to later exploit with stunning success. Walter Gropius, who worked on the Turbine Hall, became the director in 1919 of the inspirational Bauhaus School and in 1925 at Dessau designed its functionalist and largely glass-walled and minimalist main studio building. Ludwig Mies van der Rohe, who worked in Behrens's office from 1908 to 1912, went on to dominate steel and glass architecture in the USA in the years immediately after the Second World War. The Swiss-born, French-based Le Corbusier, who worked in Behrens's office for four months from late 1910, pioneered 'pure-form' white architecture from the early 1920s, and then béton brut (steel-reinforced concrete, its surface patterned by the texture of the timber moulds into which it was poured) as a very precise expression of the conviction that materials and means of construction become a building's primary architectural ornament. Le Corbusier also dreamed of high-rise garden cities of towers flooded with light, and in which uses were zoned and functions segregated to create open and healthy living spaces and places. This was in opposition to what he perceived as the dark and congested canyon-like streets of traditional cities in which people and traffic fought for dominance and where communities lived and worked cheek-by-jowl, often in

The AEG Turbine Hall in Berlin, built in 1909 to the designs of Peter Behrens. A pioneering modernist structure, functionalist in spirit and utilising new building technology, the hall is nevertheless also Expressionistic in its powerful elemental forms. The fact that it can be seen as a 'temple of power' suggests a link to the classical tradition, too.

atmospheres polluted by industry and traffic. Le Corbusier became
the key artistic and visionary force within the early phase of the
modern movement, instilling it with an almost spiritual – certainly
crusading – quality.

* * * * *

Shortly after Behrens's Turbine Hall was completed, work was under
way on one of the earliest houses that can be termed modernist: the
Steiner House in Vienna of 1910. Its architect, Adolf Loos, would
become one of the most influential, if idiosyncratic, modernists of the
early twentieth century, and the house itself sheds fascinating light
on some of the principles that Behrens would come to apply at New
Ways some fifteen years later.

Loos, the son of a stonemason, had received a broad if unfocused
education that leaned towards engineering and architecture. In 1893,
at the age of twenty-three, he went to the United States to visit the
World's Columbian Exposition in Chicago, a world's fair held to celebrate the 400th anniversary of Christopher Columbus's arrival in
the New World. The experience had a galvanising effect, prompting
him to stay for three years in order to absorb the bubbling architectural energy of the powerful new nation. He admired the pioneering
achievements of the Chicago School, with its early high-rise structures utilising wrought iron, steel, terracotta, glass and brick, and fell
under the spell of the proto-modernist writing of architect Louis
Sullivan. Particularly important for Loos was Sullivan's 1892 essay
in the *Engineering Magazine*, entitled 'Ornament in Architecture',
which promoted a doctrine that was to become a cornerstone of the
aesthetics of modernism. Sullivan observed that it was 'self-evident
that a building, quite devoid of ornament, may convey a noble and
dignified sentiment by virtue of mass and proportion', and argued
that 'it could be greatly for our aesthetic good if we should refrain
entirely from the use of ornament' and produce buildings that are
'comely in the nude'. Sullivan was not against all ornament, though:
it depended on its source and how it related to the primary structure of the building. He finessed his bold declaration by asserting

that although 'excellent and beautiful buildings may be designed that shall bear no ornament whatever', ornament that was 'harmonically conceived' and 'well considered' could be beautiful, especially when it was 'part of the surface or substance that receives it' rather than looking 'stuck on'. As for the character of the ornament used, Sullivan rejected direct reference to historic styles and, in the manner of art nouveau, recommended that architects 'turn to . . . the heartening and melodious voice [of] nature' and 'learn the accent of its rhythmic cadence'.[13] In 1896 Sullivan, with Dankmar Adler, gave most dramatic and persuasive expression to these ideas with the high-rise Guaranty Building in Buffalo, New York.

Loos was one of the first to bring Sullivan's ideas to Europe, and from 1896, based in Vienna, started his personal revolution in architectural taste by penning a series of startling essays that challenged convention and attacked what he perceived as meaningless decoration. His initial target was the aestheticism and architecture of the Vienna Secession. This he dismissed out of hand, criticising its indulgence and extravagant use of what he saw as superficial, irrelevant and unnecessary ornament. In 1913 he published an essay, conceived in 1908 and delivered as a lecture in 1910, entitled 'Ornament and Crime', which crystalised the nature of his complaint against the florid excesses of Secessionists and against all self-consciously artful architects and clients who craved 'meaningless' adornment. The opening passage of the essay was calculated to offend the Secessionists and is vivid in its imagery and direct (and patronising) in its analogies:

> The Papuan tattoos his skin, his boat, his rudder, his oars. He is no criminal. The modern man who tattoos himself is a criminal or a degenerate. There are prisons in which 80% of the prisoners are tattooed . . . It is possible to estimate a country's culture by the amount of scrawling on lavatory walls. In children this is natural, but what is natural for a Papuan, or a child is degenerate for modern man . . . cultural evolution is equivalent to the removal of ornament from articles in daily use.

An industrialist's escape: Cragside in Northumberland, commissioned by William Armstrong and his wife Margaret and designed in large part by Richard Norman Shaw. The south-west corner shown here is made up of a mixture of different structures, with Shaw's work dating from the early to late 1870s.

Housing the urban working class: some of the larger and higher-quality bye-law houses erected in the late 1870s in Jermyn Street, Toxteth, Liverpool. The photo-graph (c. 1910) shows the street's pleasant avenue of trees and small front areas or enclosures defined by ornamental iron work.

Early council housing: the Boundary Estate in Shoreditch, London. Hedsor Buildings, shown here – designed by C. C. Winmill and completed in 1899 – is typical of the more abstract and sculptural design that characterises the final phase of the estate.

Augustus Welby Northmore Pugin, a pioneering proponent from the late 1830s of the archaeologically correct Gothic Revival style. The portrait shows him in 1840 at the age of twenty-eight, probably wearing a smock suitable for working in his studio. His attire is somewhat sombre in comparison to the strong palette he used in his interiors, which include the lustrous parliamentary chambers in the Palace of Westminster.

A Victorian patron: William Armstrong, later Baron Armstrong of Cragside, possibly at the time of his marriage to Margaret Ramshaw in 1835.

One of the nineteenth century's most prolific and successful architects: George Gilbert Scott. This portrait was painted just a year before his death in 1878.

A fin-de-siècle architect: Charles Rennie Mackintosh. His artistic attire and determined expression in this mid 1890s photograph proclaim his innovative architectural direction and drive to succeed.

A modern pioneer: Peter Behrens, shown at his desk in his flat in Berlin in about 1913. Here he seems more businessman than innovative architect.

Behren's sketch of late 1925 or 1926 for the lounge in New Ways.

The patron of England's 'first modern house': Wenman Joseph Bassett-Lowke, shown here in the mid 1920s at around the time he commissioned Peter Behrens to design New Ways in Northampton.

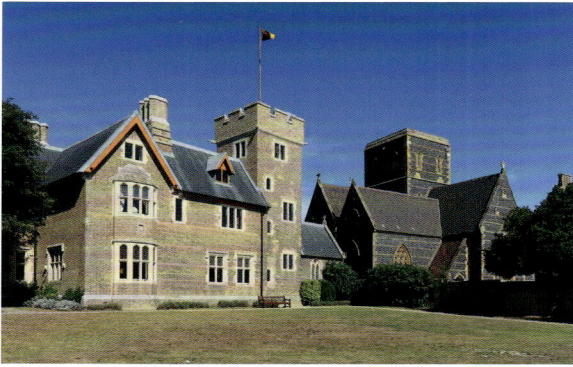

The Gothic Revival: The Grange (left) and St Augustine's Church, Ramsgate, Kent, both designed by Pugin in the 1840s and intended to serve as a manifesto for his ideal of creating a modern architecture based on the Gothic tradition.

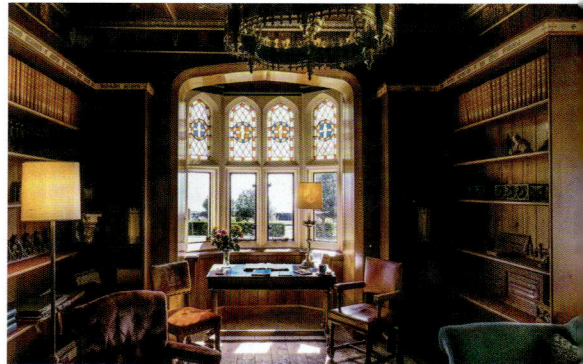

The library in The Grange, Pugin's family home. The design reveals Pugin's vision for how Gothic Revival taste would define the modern domestic interior.

Multiple influences: a mix of late Gothic, classicism, and the vernacular architecture of the Arts and Crafts Movement defines Marshcourt, Hampshire, built between 1901 and 1904 to the design of Sir Edwin Lutyens.

Detail of the great hall in Marshcourt. The interior illustrates Lutyens's imaginative mix of historic styles, most of them classical with details including fluted pilasters and late seventeenth-century-style baroque plasterwork.

A mid nineteenth-century bedroom. The washstand, jug and hip-bath suggest a well-appointed bed-sitting room, evidently created within a roofspace, suitable for a young governess who was neither the social equal of the family nor classed as a servant.

The bathroom in 28 Ashley Place, Westminster, in 1893, complete with modern innovations which include a linoleum-covered floor and a bath and canopy with a row of external controls with which to operate the shower.

The kitchen in Cragside shown in 2013. Although much cooking was evidently still done on coal-fuelled cast-iron ranges in the more traditional style, this represented the height of kitchen technology at the time: a utilitarian and hygienic space, with easy-to-clean white-tiled walls and electric lighting.

The staircase at ground-floor level, and part of the front room, at Sambourne House, 18 Stafford Terrace, Kensington, London, built in the early 1870s. Decorated and furnished from 1875 by illustrator Edward Linley Sambourne, the interior survives much as it was when Linley Sambourne died in 1910.

Middle-class tastes: the interior of Sambourne House, typical of late nineteenth-century domestic design. Inspired by the Aesthetic Movement, which celebrated the power of 'art for art's sake', the house is packed with seductive ornament including William Morris wallpaper, polychromatic floor tiles, stained glass showing sunflowers, and blue and white Chinese porcelains.

Wallpaper with cockatoos and pomegranates, printed using wooden blocks, designed in 1899 by a leading member of the Arts and Crafts Movement, the artist and book illustrator Walter Crane.

The birth of the modern? The entrance hall of New Ways, Northampton, designed by Peter Behrens and built in 1926. The architectural style of the hall, indeed of the house, remains debated – modernist, expressionist, moderne or pioneering Art Deco.

Art Deco: Florin Court, Charterhouse Square, London, built as a block of luxury flats in 1936 to the design of Guy Morgan. Its streamlined sinuous walls, quadrant corners and bands of glazing are typical of the Art Deco style.

1–3 Willow Road, Hampstead, built from 1937 to 1939 to designs by Erno Goldfin-ger. The central house served as the architect's own home.

The first-floor interior of Goldfinger's house on Willow Road. The pair of rooms, with their split floor level, are flexible in their use, and have large windows overlooking the garden.

Post-war design: a house in Parkside, Wimbledon, London, designed by Su and Richard Rogers in 1967 for Richard Rogers' parents. A pioneer of British High Tech architecture and following Mies van der Rohe's Farnsworth House, it boasts a minimal steel frame, front elevation of glass, and flexible open-plan living.

A portion of the 'Byker Wall' social housing estate, Newcastle-upon-Tyne, started in 1968 to the design of Ralph Erskine. The tall elevation is enlivened by the use of panels of differently coloured brick in an attempt to evoke a sense of joy among inhabitants.

Minimal, open-plan and transparent: Michael Hopkins inside the house he and his wife Patty designed for themselves in 1976 in Hampstead, London.

In the same year – 1910 – he gave physical form to his theories through his work on the Steiner House.

As one would expect from Loos' writings, the Steiner House is rationally conceived, making it an early example of the Rationalist persuasion within modernism. To the street it presents a single-storey front elevation topped by a curving metal-clad roof incorporating a single, centrally placed dormer that lights the studio of the artist Lilly Steiner, who commissioned the house. The bold simplicity of the rendered, white-painted and unadorned exterior, and the functional and asymmetrical disposition of the windows, anticipated the 'white box' architecture of Le Corbusier and the International Style by almost a decade. The garden elevation is three storeys, due to the fall in the level of the land, and gives the house a more monumental and geometric quality. From the rear and side it also becomes clear that the curving roof over the front elevation is no more than a quadrant in form. Internally the house reflects Loos's penchant for built-in furniture. As he explained: 'The walls of a building belong to the architect. There he rules at will. And as with walls so with furniture that is not moveable.' Loos believed that, through the use of built-in furniture, he had the right to create the interior and so ensure the full realisation of his architectural vision. The overall impression the house gives is of functionalism, a machine-age aesthetic and the retreat from historically based ornament.

If that suggests that Loos eschewed all decorative details, though, that is not the case. As with his mentor Sullivan, his target was not so much ornament *in toto* as the type used, and its relation to structure and its purpose. Where Loos found ornament unsound, he simply condemned it as 'degenerate' or 'illegitimate' but, as his work reveals, ornamentation was never entirely abandoned. A Vienna house he designed a few years later, the Rufer House of 1922, overtly demonstrates this. Exemplifying Loos's theory of *Raumplan* ('spatial plan' of volumes) – the complex organisation of internal spaces[14] – its facades have asymmetrically placed windows whose locations are dictated by functional internal demands. In order to permit the creation of open-plan and flexible interiors, Loos had come to rely on external load-bearing masonry walls, supplementing these with columns, or pilotis, when necessary. In the Rufer House, he went one step further, incorporating a multistorey column within the centre of the house that not only plays a structural role but also contains the plumbing. Yet, at the same time, on one elevation he installed three panels that are copies of slabs from the Parthenon frieze. One has to assume that these decorative elements possessed for Loos – and his client, the music scholar Josef Rufer – a cultural value and intrinsic beauty that transcended debates about degenerate or illegitimate embellishment.

Within four years of the completion of the Steiner House, Le Corbusier started to promote his own structural and spatial principles. Like Loos, he favoured an open floor plan and modular structure, opting for floor slabs made of steel-reinforced concrete (a relatively new material at the time that possessed the tensile strength required) supported by reinforced concrete columns in his Dom-Ino House theoretical studies of 1914–15. Such an approach, which largely relieved external walls of structural responsibility, also allowed for flexibility of room arrangement and generous ranges of windows to let light and air flood inside. By 1923, in his manifesto entitled *Vers une Architecture* (titled *Towards a New Architecture* in its 1927 English edition),[15] he had coined the memorable description of a house 'as a machine for living in', and by 1926 had distilled his thinking into five guiding principles, or 'points', for the 'New Architecture'. The points were essentially intended to inform the design of new homes, although they were also, to a degree, meant to be universally applicable to all building types. The first point specified the use of pilotis to support the floor slabs, and thus facilitate the second point, the free or open plan, achieved by the pilotis, which removed the need for load-bearing internal and external walls and allowed the plan to be as flexible and adaptable as possible. Point three was the 'free facade', the natural expression of piloti construction and the free plan, which meant that external walls (since they were largely non-structural) could be almost fully glazed. Point four, utilising the potential of the free facade, promoted the notion of the long, horizontal sliding window. The final point was a roof garden or terrace that, in theory, restored the amenity of open space lost when the house was constructed.

Related ideas soon emerged within Le Corbusier's design repertoire, notably the 'promenade architecturale' through the house, from the entrance hall, via the staircase to the roof terrace. The promenade was intended, rather in the spirit of late seventeenth-century baroque planning, to act as an axis through the building that would fully display the spatial novelty of the new home. Closely related to the artistic purpose of the promenade was the almost sculptural treatment of the roof terrace, where structures and ramps were given pure geometric forms, in a spirit pioneered by Russian constructivist architects (members of a wider art movement that sought to express the modern and egalitarian principles of the 1917 Bolshevik Revolution).[16] Many of these points had been tested and refined in Le Corbusier and Pierre Jeanneret's Villa La Roche in Paris. Built from 1923 to 1924, the villa is L-shaped in plan, and incorporates a home and a gallery for the avant-garde art owned by its client, a Swiss banker named Raoul La Roche. The elevations are plain and white and feature horizontal bands of windows. There is a free plan pierced by a sculptural ramp-like staircase forming part of a promenade architecturale, and floor slabs are supported on pilotis. The villa's forms have an overtly cubist quality that no doubt echoed the art in La Roche's collection.

One other domestic building is worth mentioning in the context of New Ways: the Schröder House in Utrecht. Conceived to be like no other house before it, and, when completed, arguably not only the most innovative house in the world but also the most visually radical, it was commissioned in 1924 from the architect Gerrit Rietveld by a client, Truss Schröder-Schräder, who initially wanted a house without walls. What she in fact got is a house of planes, one of the ultimate expressions of architecture emulating an artistic movement, and rendering the imagery of two-dimensional painting as a large-scale three-dimensional inhabited and essentially functional object. The artistic movement was De Stijl (meaning 'The Style'), or neoplasticism, which had emerged in the Netherlands in 1917. The movement explored and presented an art of pure abstraction that would be applicable universally. It sought this through reducing all elements to essential forms and colours that, it argued, were embodied in the primal geometry of squares, rectangles, vertical and horizontal planes or lines, and by the primary colours (including black and white). This theory is expressed most clearly in the paintings executed by Mondrian from the second decade of the twentieth century until his death in 1944.

In various writings Mondrian defined the aims of the movement. As early as 1914 he wrote to the art critic and collector H. P. Bremmer to argue that 'it is possible that, through horizontal and vertical lines constructed with awareness, but not with calculation, led by high intuition, and brought to harmony and rhythm, these basic forms of beauty . . . can become a work of art, as strong as it is true.'[17] In 1917, in an essay in the journal *De Stijl* entitled 'Neo-Plasticism in Pictorial Art', Mondrian further explained the new movement. The 'plastic idea' would, he suggested, 'ignore the particulars of appearance, that is to say, natural form and colour' and instead 'find its expression in the abstraction of form and colour . . . in the straight line and the clearly defined primary colour'.[18] It was these theories that Mondrian expressed through his paintings, and that Rietveld sought to express through his architecture.

The process of evolving the almost abstract notion of a house liberated from associations with traditional domestic architecture was predictably difficult. In plan the Schröder House is unconventional for the time but now hardly exceptional, with a first floor conceived as a flexible space manipulated by sliding and rotating partitions, perhaps in part influenced by traditional Japanese minimalist domestic architecture, still in vogue in the West in the 1920s. The exterior is artistically far more radical. It seems the client and architect agreed upon the basic idea that the elevations of a De Stijl house should be pretty much a three-dimensional representation of a Mondrian De Stijl painting. The elevations are composed of a collage of planes that overlap and glide over each other and that frame, embrace or act as supports for the horizontal lines of projecting balconies. Vertical lines are provided by slender posts that help support balconies and projections of the building's flat roof, which provide additional horizontal

Modern houses. Above: the interior of the Steiner House, Vienna, designed in 1910 by Adolf Loos. Despite Loos' radical attitude towards history-based decoration, the interior is, in many ways, traditional in atmosphere, with the honestly expressed structure of is floors evoking associations with medieval timber-frame construction. Below: the Schröder House, Utrecht, the Netherlands, designed in 1924 by Gerrit Rietveld – conceived as a three-dimensional inhabited abstract painting and like no house built before.

lines. The horizontal and vertical lines, created by the posts and the edges of balconies, are painted in strong primary colours, notably red and yellow, while the planes are painted in neutral white and grey. The client had expressed a desire to break down the division between the house's interior and exterior, and this is reflected in the decision to continue lines, horizontal planes and colours without regard to location. Indeed, when the windows are open it is hard to tell where the facade of the house stops and the interior begins. Essentially the conventional mass of the building gives way to seemingly floating planes, interpenetrating volumes and lines of vibrant colour. It was completed just a year before work got under way on Bassett-Lowke's new Northampton house.

These house designs by Loos, Le Corbusier and Rietveld have some primary points in common – for example, in the latter two cases ensuring that the internal space is both flexible and adaptable. All, of course, eschew the application of traditional, history-derived ornament; and all are, in their own ways, structurally rational and artistically consistent. They also reveal the avant-garde architectural context within which Behrens, in collaboration with Bassett-Lowke, designed New Ways. That Behrens would have known these houses well, and would have been familiar with the theories of their architects when designing New Ways, is evident from the fact that in 1926 his former assistant Mies van der Rohe invited Behrens to contribute a set of cubic apartment blocks to the Weissenhof Estate, part of a 1927 exhibition entitled 'Die Wohnung' (The Dwelling) in Stuttgart, organised by the Deutscher *Werkbund.* The houses on display here, including works by Le Corbusier (the Citrohan House), Mies van der Rohe and Walter Gropius, took twenty-one weeks to construct, which suggests that, since work started on site in early 1927, they must have been designed in the course of 1926, at roughly the time when Behrens was working on New Ways.

* * * * *

In November 1926, New Ways was the subject of an article in the *Architectural Review* (the *AR*),[19] a magazine that promoted international architecture and design, old and new, to a largely professional and informed readership. When featuring British architecture, the *AR* tended to favour that built on tradition and historical precedent and thus intrinsically and distinctly British in character and native to the soil. But the anonymous author of the article, who went by the byline 'Silhouette', was clearly intrigued by this Northampton manifestation of modernism in Britain, even if one senses a certain reservation about its clearly foreign, 'cosmopolitan', even alien, appearance and reliance on such tokens of modernity as steel reinforced concrete and flat roofs. '"New Ways"', the article declared, 'is . . . startling in that here the latest continental model . . . is revealed on English soil in a suburban landscape.' '[T]the significance of this phenomenon can hardly be ignored', it went on, adding that '"New Ways" is symbolical of a new phase of thought . . . Whether the final verdict condemns or acquits . . . there is . . . as with all pioneer work . . . much that appeals and likewise much that will arouse criticism and possibly condemnation.' Two months later, *Ideal Home* magazine ran its article that proclaimed New Ways as unequivocally Britain's 'first modern house'.[20]

That this is how Bassett-Lowke hoped his new home would be perceived is clear from a short silent film he made about the house very soon after its completion. Introduced by the smiling, indeed seemingly self-satisfied, visage of Bassett-Lowke himself, it opens with a view of the garden gate opening by way of welcoming the viewer to the house, which a card describes as 'The Super-Modern Home of Mr. W. J. Bassett-Lowke, at Northampton – a fore-runner of the house of the future'. Subsequent cards fully express the modernist ethos that Bassett-Lowke had evidently embraced and that he assumed his new home reflected: 'straight lines and direct treatment of the interior strike an ultra-modern note . . . the long triangular front window, which traps the light . . . the two wide-windowed storeys that tell their own story about the value of light and air . . .'

It's scarcely surprising that New Ways should have struck a distinctly modern note in the England of the mid 1920s. The front facade with its flat roof (itself a novelty in 1920s British housing) does indeed display the 'straight lines' of simple and honest modern-ist design, with pure white walls that, in sunlight, give the building a sculptural quality. There are, however, several idiosyncrasies and, indeed, a significant amount of decoration. The major idiosyncrasy is the entire absence on the front facade of first-floor windows. This is an unusual design decision for the front of a villa-like house and one that imbues it with a somewhat industrial quality, or, alterna-tively, that gives it the appearance of the minimalist North African vernacular architecture that so impressed some early modernists. Was this Behrens's intention? And, if so, why? Then there's the ornament, which takes the peculiar form of stunted concrete posts along the edge of the flat roof. It's possible that these had a practical purpose. Certainly, they help visually to break up what would otherwise be a somewhat unforgiving silhouette. Alan Windsor, author of *Peter Behrens: Architect and Designer*, offers the intriguing possibility that the posts might be an essay in empathy – Behrens's attempt 'to evoke the style of Mackintosh', or even that of Josef Hoffman, who was one of the founder architects of the Vienna Secession.[21]

And then there is the 'triangular front window' that rises full height in the centre of the elevation, above the front door, and in jaunty manner bears the date '1926'. This elongated triangular-plan fully glazed bay certainly lets light into the house, and so has an admirable and practical purpose. But it is also somewhat incongru-ous on a domestic building, looking like a detail one might expect to find on an interwar factory or office block, on which comparable windows illuminate staircases and entrance lobbies.

As for the internal layout, this reveals no serious attempt on Behrens's part to develop or express a modernist sense of space. Le Corbusier's earlier Dom-Ino House, with its extensively glazed eleva-tions and open plan, it certainly is not, nor does it possess the spatial panache of the Turbine Hall. Indeed, it is traditional in form. Double doors link the entrance hall and dining room and align the entrance door with the glazed door to the garden loggia beyond the dining room to create a vista and route through the house that is firmly in the baroque tradition. The large rectangular lounge adjoined by a study follows the 4:3 proportion favoured during the Renaissance. The disposition of rooms is much as one would expect to find in almost any house of this period – or, for that matter, of houses built a century or so before.

The consequence of Behrens's overall approach is that, while New Ways is obviously in the modernist manner, connoisseurs find it difficult to categorise, and there is, as a result, an ongoing debate about its nature and the origin of its architecture. For Historic England it is a building of architectural and historic interest that is 'in the German Expressionist Style'. For the Twentieth Century Society,[22] it is 'sometimes billed as Art Deco' but could 'more properly be defined as Modern Movement or Expressionist', and, the society suggests, it also shows 'the influence of the Vienna Secession'. Certainly, the art deco label some have applied seems a little premature for an English building of the mid 1920s. In any case the term is, it has to be said, a slightly problematic one, in that, while it was derived from the Exposition Internationale des Arts Décoratifs et Industriels Modernes that was held in Paris from April to October 1925, it was not actually coined until the 1960s.[23] And to make things more complex there is a moral dimension. What we now generally accept as art deco can be seen as a distortion of the all-embracing social and artistic crusade of modernism into mere fashion – indeed into a highly commercialised superficial style in which form no longer reflected function nor the materials employed. Art deco – showy and decorative – embodied a certain theatrical amorality. But, however distinctive we now regard it as being, at the time it would have been covered by the very broad term 'moderne'.

And it's that broad term 'moderne' that probably describes Bassett-Lowke's ambition for his new house most accurately. His preoccupation was with the modern in general, rather than with any particular movement within it. If he was attracted to aspects of nascent art deco, it was to the streamlining aesthetic that it incorporated and that became so significant in the design of another of his passions – up-to-the-minute types of transport. The supreme architectural exemplar of this aesthetic is the Chrysler art deco skyscraper in Manhattan, designed by William Van Alen in 1928 for the eponymous automobile company. Here forms and motifs are curved and streamlined, like the company's cars. All is characterised by a go-ahead approach to architecture and to life. As Van Alen proclaimed, before he designed the Chrysler, 'No old stuff for me, no bestial copyings of arches and colyums and cornishes! [*sic*] Me, I'm new! – avanti!'[24] This could have been Bassett-Lowke speaking in the early 1920s when at least part of his obsession with modern transport was a belief that revolutionary new trains, ships and planes were emblematic of the exciting new age and that, as Le Corbusier argued, the application of cutting-edge technology could improve the world. It's significant in this respect that the *Architectural Review* noted that New Ways 'was evolved by Mr Bassett-Lowke with certain definite intentions'.

Some of these 'definite intentions' involved the layout of the house in general and the function of individual rooms in particular. Bassett-Lowke clearly wanted a traditional central entrance and staircase hall, with the dining room set on an axis with the front door, and with the lounge and study on one side and the service areas on the other. This layout, which the *Architectural Review* unequivocally states was 'evolved by Mr Bassett-Lowke', was applauded by its correspondent as 'extremely efficient and praiseworthy . . . with an entire absence of waste space'.[25] Other requirements in Bassett-Lowke's brief included: 'a spacious communal room, large enough for dancing [the lounge], a dining-room reduced to a purely meal-taking apartment, and a study, or spare room, available if required as a nursery . . . bedrooms . . . adjacent to dressing-bathrooms . . . and a spacious hall with modern conveniences'. Below the service rooms there would be a basement, containing a wine cellar, a pantry, a store and what the *Architectural Review* describes as a 'wash-house'. In the *AR*'s view, all these various 'specifications' set the architect 'a task of considerable magnitude'.[26]

If that makes it sound as though Behrens simply acquiesced to his client's demands, the truth is probably rather more nuanced. Houses that he designed before the First World War – for example, Villa Cuno at Eppenhausen, dating from 1910 – are often also conventional in plan, indeed in many ways similar to New Ways. Of course,

Cuno was designed when Behrens was still something of a classicist (indeed, Cuno is furnished with a full-height portico of semicircular plan dressed with piers, within which rises the staircase) and before the explosion of modernist ideas that followed the war. It is possible that Bassett-Lowke had seen the Cuno plan and made it the basis of his draft design, rather than seeking to establish what European architects of the mid 1920s might have regarded as more cutting edge. Behrens, after all, was a generation older than Mies van der Rohe and Le Corbusier, and had trained in the Gothic-inspired Arts and Crafts tradition. It's also possible that the design of New Ways was a response on the part of Behrens and Bassett-Lowke to the established suburban context for which the house was intended, where a traditional approach might have appeared more seemly and sensitive, although it should be noted that the artistically radical Schröder House was built on a similarly somewhat cramped and conventional suburban site. What is more certain is that Behrens surrendered to his client the responsibility for designing and fitting out a number of the interiors. The *Architectural Review* is helpful here in assigning overall responsibility for different aspects of the house: 'the design for the lounge, dining-room and exteriors ... belong to Professor Dr Behrens,' Silhouette wrote, 'but the study is a reproduction of the hall in the earlier house designed for Mr Bassett-Lowke by C. R. Mackintosh, of London [and] the bedrooms, bathrooms and kitchen, the heating and other details are largely the original work of Mr Bassett-Lowke.'

Whatever debates might have been had about the overall appearance of the house, it is certainly the case that Bassett-Lowke was, as Silhouette put it, 'determined to incorporate into one building every modern aid to comfort and efficiency'.[27] There were to be 'two fully-equipped bathrooms ... electric power in every room' and 'central heating in most rooms'. In the basement would be housed 'heating boilers for the domestic and radiator supplies'. There would be 'ducts beneath floors, giving easy access to the water pipes, electric cables and so forth'. The lounge would contain 'sunk storage space ... for logs and fuel ... reached by a trap door in the floor'. Even the private

Villa Cuno, Eppenhausen, Hagen, Germany, designed by Peter Behrens in 1910. It is stripped-back classical in feel, with its central full-height concave bay with minimalist piers that read as a portico.

room for the maids, and the first-floor bedroom for the live-in maid, was 'equipped with hot and cold running water' – a luxury that was taken by the *Architectural Review* as evidence of Bassett-Lowke's progressive architectural and social attitudes. It's worth noting, though, that while the main bedroom, overlooking the garden and furnished with an open fireplace and a traditional bed alcove, had a large en-suite bathroom, the smaller 'maid's bedroom' that lay on the other side of the bathroom lacked its own bathroom or even a lavatory. Presumably the maid was expected to use the small ground-floor WC adjoining the maids' sitting room (a room described by the *Architectural Review* as 'a cheerful apartment')[28] and bathe in the basement 'washhouse', unless she was expected to use a tub in her bedroom. Some might argue that the fact that Bassett-Lowke employed maids does little to suggest a commitment to the egalitarian principles he supposedly espoused as a Fabian socialist and indicates that his approach to society was not as modern as his approach to architecture.

* * * * *

New Ways still stands, and, although long detached from the Bassett-Lowkes, is still in single family occupation. The extent to which Bassett-Lowke preserved or enhanced the 1925–6 scheme of internal decoration and furnishing in subsequent years is unknown, but the major external and internal features, including the windows, hall floor, lounge fireplace and windows, radiator cover and staircase, survive unaltered. Overall, indeed, the house still exudes the simplicity of design, and emphasis on maximum daylight and health-giving fresh air, that were the basic aspirations for all who sought to design socially responsible modernist domestic architecture. It is also charmingly idiosyncratic.

The entrance, set in the smooth, white facade, is itself a striking composition. A pair of flush doors, each with a small window fitted with coloured glass in an abstract manner, are flanked by shallow casement windows of horizontal form, all sheltering beneath a wide and deep reinforced concrete hood. This is apparently supported in its centre by five narrow concrete beams that project from the elevation and read rather like large-scale dentils of the type found in ornamented classical cornices. This composition is, to put it mildly, eccentric, with probable connections to Adolf Loos and German expressionism. On each side of the elevation of the centre block of the house are two shallow wings, set well back and also with windowless front facades. The wing to the right (west) of the main house contains the study and lounge and to the left the service and staff accommodation.

The front door opens via a small vestibule into the entrance and staircase hall. This is essentially a circulation space of traditional type and with a muted scheme of decoration that is in striking contrast to the strident and richly embellished hall at 78 Derngate. The implication in the *Architectural Review* is that the hall was the work of Behrens, not Bassett-Lowke, and the detail it most admired is the floor. It declares that the floor, with encaustic tiles (made using inlays of different coloured clay) in white, grey and black, is 'extraordinarily subtle', and specifically states that it was Behrens's design. It is in fact conceived as a large abstract painting, formed of square and oblong grey and black tiles set against a background formed by a grid of square and oblong white tiles – somewhat like a monochrome Mondrian but with a nod to function with thresholds generally marked with black tiles.

The door from the hall leading into the entrance vestibule is recessed within a frame flanked by lower recesses surrounding smaller doors which lead to a cloakroom and a WC. The flat lintels, stepped in relation to each other, create a slight ziggurat form that was to become a favoured art deco motif. There are, in addition, doors to the study, lounge, dining room and to the service wing. Those here, and 'throughout the house' noted the *Architectural Review*, have flush surfaces made of plywood 'veneered or enamelled and furnished with continental lever handles'. Such streamlined doors, perceived as rational and easy to keep clean, replaced traditional framed and panelled doors, with their numerous dust ledges, and became one of the earliest emblems of the modern and hygienic home. New Ways must be one of the first British examples to contain this soon-to-be-ubiquitous detail. The treads of the staircase rise between one of the walls of the hall and, in lieu of a handrail, a broad but squat wall of stepped profile, with each step of the wall reading as a shelf. The hall also contained a 'piscina . . . and a small fountain' – delightful details usually associated with Renaissance palazzi.

The study, relatively small and decorated by Bassett-Lowke in homage to the hall/lounge of the abandoned 78 Derngate, included Mackintosh-designed fittings that were either transferred or reproduced. The *Architectural Review* describes the walls as painted 'primrose yellow' and decorated with a stenciled 'motif in flat colours' of red, blue, grey and yellow. Mackintosh, who was by then living in France, appears not to have been consulted about the creation of this new, Mackintosh-style, interior. Additional information about the study is offered by the article on New Ways in the *Ideal Homes* magazine of January 1927. It includes a photograph of the study, taken by Bassett-Lowke, which shows the radiator cover, or a very exact version of it, designed by Mackintosh for the hall/lounge at Derngate. This cover survives in New Ways. It has small panes of coloured glass, with arched tops, set in lead cames, or strips. Bassett-Lowke's photograph confirms that the study also contained a ceiling light that was moved from 78 Derngate and adapted, as well as a cloak cupboard, smokers' cabinet and a domino clock that were all of Mackintosh design. The design of the wall stencilling, based on examples in Derngate, can also be clearly seen.

The lounge was the main room of the house, and Behrens, or his office, prepared a perspective suggesting a scheme of decoration. The view offered by the perspective is from the study towards the four large panes of glass forming the window looking on to the garden.[29] The main features depicted are the broad fireplace, framed by abstract pilasters, and the layered and geometric treatment of the walls and ceiling, which possess something of the character of a large abstract painting. This ceiling, like the hall floor composed of a pattern of squares and oblongs, particularly impressed the *Architectural Review*, which describes it as 'delightful . . . with varying levels [that] form a severe pattern, on which the changing light casts romantic shadows by day and night'. This is a most perceptive observation that suggests Behrens wanted to capture some of the theatrical and dynamic quality of traditional baroque design, but using a new, abstract architectural vocabulary.

The Behrens scheme possesses more of the showy character of a cinema lobby than of a family lounge, and perhaps it was for this reason that it was not strictly followed by Bassett-Lowke. Nevertheless, he did want this room to be used in a convivial manner, hence his specifying that it must be large enough for dancing. The imposing fireplace, a traditional emblem of hospitality and festivity – which, the *Architectural Review* suggests, anticipating George Orwell, was added 'on account of its sentimental value and human appeal' – is shown in a drawing produced by Behrens and was executed much as designed. It is a massive, blocky and geometric affair that, once again, expresses the style that was soon to be known as art deco. Square piers, with block capitals and bases and rusticated blocks in the centres of their stubby shafts, support a slab-like mantelshelf. All is very elemental, indeed expressionist. This composition frames an opening that is clad with square white tiles and, again, composed upon the theme of the square and the oblong, with these shapes defined by darker coloured tile strips. The opening for the grate is a perfect square, and topped by five vertical coloured strips of tile that imply a keystone. The classical language of architecture hovers over all, as it did with Behrens's temple-like AEG Turbine Hall in Berlin.

On each side of the fireplace are windows fitted with coloured glass arranged to form large abstract asymmetrical compositions – secular modernist stained-glass windows – each being a precise mirror version of the window it adjoins. The *Architectural Review* was fascinated by these windows, which admit 'light by day and [are] artificially illuminated by night'. The glass, it noted, 'is a Berlin production of a metallic pigment, which yields similar colour effects by transmitted light as by reflected light, and, withal, a delightful warmth and richness'. The colourful carpet in the lounge was provided by 'Primavera of Paris, while some of the ornaments hail from other parts of Europe'. It was this in particular that caused the *Architectural Review*

The lounge at New Ways as presented in the *Architectural Review* of November 1926. With its large armchairs it evokes a sense of comfort; the colourful carpet 'provided by Primavera in Paris' adds a fashionable, avant-garde note.

to conclude that New Ways was, 'indeed, a most cosmopolitan house'. The Atelier Primavera, established in 1912 in the Parisian Au Printemps department store, specialised in the sale of modern interior design and from the mid 1920s showcased art deco. Buying from Primavera meant that Bassett-Lowke was dealing with a key maker and purveyor of Continental avant-garde taste.

The dining room is far simpler, its main features being a large ceiling light formed by panes of opaque glass of differing sizes and mellow colours, and timber 'pilasters' placed on facing walls that support a rail that runs around the room at the height of the window lintels. The pilasters, displaying exotic timber grain, have 'capitals', each formed by pairs of block-like abstracted classical Doric triglyphs.

The original flavour of some of the other rooms can still be experienced thanks to the photographs by Bassett-Lowke that illustrate the 1927 *Ideal Homes* article. The kitchen, seemingly his own creation, was a utilitarian space, designed and fitted out to be functional rather than a pleasure to inhabit. It was evidently conceived as a machine-like and hygienic room in which staff simply prepared, cooked and served food. The walls were clad with white tiles; the floor was also tiled; a gas cooker was placed in one corner; and a long sink, with draining board on each side, stretched along most of one wall. In the centre of the room was a table brought from 78 Derngate.

The house's first floor was largely given over to bedrooms that are far simpler in detail than many of the rooms below, although the ceiling above the staircase continues the square motifs used on the hall floor and lounge ceiling and fireplace (it was presumably designed by Behrens). Here squares – reminiscent of classical coffering but most with a U-shaped addition along one outer edge – form a band around a deep oblong recess in which is set a diminutive plaster barrel vault. Once again, the inspiration is classical. The staircase landing is fitted with large cupboards, with art deco-style ziggurat or stepped plans. On the garden front, above the dining room loggia, is an enclosed first-floor verandah reached via a room termed the 'Den' which, with an open fireplace, was presumably intended as a retreat for the master of the house.

Bassett-Lowke clearly loved his house, since he remained there until his death in October 1953. At Christmas 1940, he dispatched a jolly card showing a dazzling montage of details of the house and its garden, including an image of him taking tea with his wife. Bassett-Lowke had used similar cards in the 1930s, but Christmas 1940 – by which time the British army had been pushed out of France; Coventry had, just a month before, been blitzed (the flames were visible from Northampton); the City of London was being bombed; and an implacable and powerful foe seemed about to invade – was surely a strange moment to circulate such a playful architectural concoction. Perhaps this was no more than a display of buoyant spirits in the face of adversity, of uncurbable optimism and faith in the future, but with hindsight it seems a little odd. The sentiment printed on the card, 'with the season's greetings from Mr & Mrs Bassett-Lowke, New Ways, Northampton', was in 1940 joined by another message, not found on earlier versions of the card. It was evidently intended both to strike a patriotic note and to celebrate Bassett-Lowke's architectural adventures in home-making. The motto reads: 'The foundations of the empire are in the homes of the people', and the source of this uplifting quote, elevating house construction into a patriotic undertaking, is given as King George V, who had died nearly four years earlier.

* * * * *

Although secreted within a suburban street in the provincial town of Northampton, Britain's first 'modern house' became almost instantly well known among those interested in such things, thanks to nationally significant and popular publications like *Ideal Home*, and to its promotion by the extrovert and well-connected Bassett-Lowke. No doubt the celebrity friends he invited to visit would have told their own similarly influential friends about the novel features of the house they had encountered. Bassett-Lowke seems to have cared deeply about the opinions of such people. He invited his fellow Fabian George Bernard Shaw to stay in 78 Derngate, and must have been disappointed when, on asking his guest how he had slept in one of

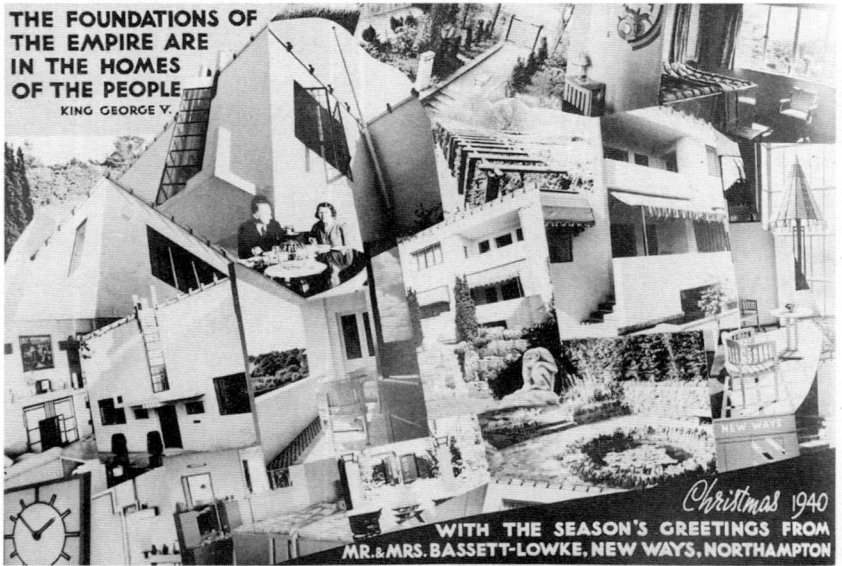

THE FOUNDATIONS OF
THE EMPIRE ARE
IN THE HOMES
OF THE PEOPLE
KING GEORGE V.

Christmas 1940

WITH THE SEASON'S GREETINGS FROM
MR. & MRS. BASSETT-LOWKE, NEW WAYS, NORTHAMPTON

The Bassett-Lowkes' Christmas card for 1940, featuring a collage of images of New Ways. The accompanying quote, which is credited to the late King George V, expresses a sentiment that certainly aligns with the king's known commitment to tradition and belief in the importance of family values, but since there is no record of George V ever having used the phrase, it seems to be a Bassett-Lowke concoction.

the robustly decorated bedrooms, received the answer that, like most people, Shaw had slept with his eyes shut. It was, quite possibly, unappreciative comments like this, probably made in 1922, that persuaded Bassett-Lowke to forsake the strident Mackintosh interior.[30]

Not all who encountered New Ways thought it worthy of emulation. The *Architectural Review*, for example, marginalised its significance, arguing that it was 'the product of many brains', and that while it was 'intended not only to be but to look a modern house' and had 'character', its 'somewhat bizarre exterior [was] conditioned not so much by the demands of internal efficiency as by the fact that its owner desired an exercise in modernity'. In the *AR*'s view, the house was not the spearhead of a new architectural movement but a one-off exercise in 'most cosmopolitan' taste and style that was, in reality, little more than an individual and somewhat eccentric architectural folly of suspiciously foreign origin. In short, it was just one more playful and passing excess in Britain's rich history of architectural oddities.

Nevertheless, in 1929 New Ways won a place in Alphonse Barrez's *Maison d'habitations*: a seductive and exclusive photographic compilation, published in Paris, of modernist houses recently built in Europe and the United States.[31] And it proved not only to be a trailblazer but to have immediate progeny. In 1927 the Scottish architect Thomas S. Tait was commissioned by the Essex industrialist Francis Henry Crittall to design progressive housing for his workers in the village of Silver End, incorporating the firm's metal casement windows that were to become synonymous with British interwar modernism. The houses, two storeys high and with flat roofs and white rendered facades, were evidently inspired by New Ways; one even has a windowless first-floor front elevation and a tall, narrow central window of triangular plan perched above the front door. Frederick R. McManus, an architect and assistant to Tait, later confirmed that New Ways 'acted as the catalyst for the Silver End houses'.[32] And the 1937 book *Small Houses* includes Starlock House in Rye, Sussex, designed in 1929 by Frank Scarlett, which possesses a garden front that is startlingly similar to that of Bassett-Lowke's house.[33]

It seems that Behrens's contribution to British modernism became almost instantly iconic.

The Silver End houses also serve as an important reminder that, while Behrens might have designed New Ways for a wealthy client, the modernist movement more generally had a social as well as an aesthetic aim. Le Corbusier's Citrohan House of 1920, for example, was envisioned as an affordable, functional home that was to be realised through industrial processes of mass production, yet could also be seen to possess abstract aesthetic appeal. The house was first shown in built form in July 1927 on the Weissenhof Estate in Stuttgart, as part of the showcase organised by the Deutscher Werkbund. The showcase demonstrated how industrial design in Germany, having embraced many of the ideals of William Morris and the English Arts and Crafts Movement, had moved these into the realm of mechanised mass production with the aim of making well-designed artefacts that were relatively cheap and so available to all. In Le Corbusier's ambitious and all-embracing vision, the Citrohan House was to be as practical and machine-like in its efficiency as a modern car – an association made explicit by the house's name, which was inspired by the Citroën automobile. The car, with aeroplanes and mighty streamlined steam engines, were Le Corbusier's design ideals.

Le Corbusier would soon draw attention away from older and more formal architects like Berhens, and his uncompromising modernism and use of structurally revolutionary techniques would make New Ways look timid, and in some senses – particularly with its unadventurous plan – almost reactionary. It's not surprising therefore that the English house that should have secured the tag of being 'the first truly convincing essay of the International Style in England' is not the house in Northampton, but the far more pioneering High & Over at Amersham in Buckinghamshire.[34] Started in 1929 to the designs of New Zealander Amyas Connell for Bernard Ashmole, the head of classical sculpture at the British Museum, this has a reinforced concrete frame, abstract elevations with large areas of horizontal glazing, and an open-plan and a striking Y-shaped form – all calculated to let light flood inside and to offer stunning views over the surrounding country.

But if High & Over captured the high ground of early interwar British modernism, it is reasonable to suggest that New Ways – more solid in appearance, with its comfortable and familiar plan and with its modernism being little more than a question of surface decoration and details – provided the workable model for Britain's house builders of advanced taste. Thus, New Ways launched the construction of thousands of bypass moderne houses[35] calculated to appeal to buyers who saw themselves as artistically progressive and forward-thinking or, as Van Alen put it: 'avanti!'

Afterword

NEW WAYS WAS COMPLETED a hundred years ago, but many of the design principles it embodies, or which were pioneered in contemporary houses by architects such as Le Corbusier, have continued to define mainstream and avant-garde domestic architecture right up to the present day. An adaptable open-plan design with split-level floors; generous areas of glazing made possible by a structural frame wrought of reinforced concrete or steel; an avoidance of history-based ornament and forms; and a focus instead on simplicity and practicality. All these precepts express the modernist conviction that, ideally, form should follow function and that the means and materials of construction should be both openly revealed and openly celebrated. They also embody the belief that, rather than looking to the past for inspiration, each age should have its own distinct architecture, reflecting changing patterns of life and taking full advantage of the potential offered by evolving technology.

Within less than a decade of New Ways' completion, England's first modernist high-rise block of flats arose. Highpoint I in north London was designed in 1933 by the Russian-born architect Berthold Lubetkin as a sleek and functionalist eight-storey apartment building. Lubetkin, working closely with engineer Ove Arup, made much use of steel-reinforced concrete. Load-bearing column-like pilotis ensured that the split-level, white-painted ground-floor entrance hall, with its wall of glass, was as open as possible. And the building's cruciform plan and generous glazing allowed light to flood inside. The architect and his client – the industrialist Sigmund Gestetner – had been inspired by avant-garde Soviet housing models arranged on the 'collective' principle, where facilities and services were shared by the residential community. So at Highpoint I there were a laundry and canteen on the ground floor, and gardens that all could enjoy.

The original ambition was that the block would contain exemplary 'workers' housing' for Gestetner's employees, but this changed as the building was being designed. By the time it was completed, Highpoint I had become a speculative venture, its high-quality flats sold to those who could afford them. Interestingly, when Lubetkin came to start work on Highpoint II on an adjoining site a year after Highpoint I was completed in 1935, he opted for a modernism with a slightly different aesthetic character and included a large porch that was supported in part by a pair of reproductions of the caryatids (a caryatid being a column in the form of a tunic-clad woman) that adorn the fifth-century BC Erechtheion that stands on the Acropolis in Athens. This may seem a surprising choice for a modernist, but then the veneration of the ancient world – for its elemental forms, precision of thought, and logical systems of harmonically related proportions – is a binding thread through the work of early modernists (notably in the work of Le Corbusier). A particular reference for Lubetkin might have been the casts of the sculptural panels from the Parthenon that Adolf Loos used to embellish the otherwise simple facade of the Rufer House in Vienna of 1922 (see page 323).

While Highpoint I 's construction process was rationally conceived, things did not quite work out as intended. The external walls, which are constructed from concrete poured into moulds and reinforced with steel bars, may give the exterior an extraordinary monolithic appearance and, potentially at least, a strong load-bearing capacity. But in his desire for elegance, Lubetkin made the thickness of the concrete cover of the steel too minimal, with the eventual result that even hairline cracks allowed water to penetrate. The steel reinforcing then rusted and expanded, making the cracks larger and water penetration more serious. This initiated a cycle of decay that ultimately necessitated a high level of maintenance and much concrete repair and replacement.

Such problems, perhaps inevitable with pioneering and experimental construction techniques, were to become something of a

Highpoint I, Highgate, London, on the left, built 1933 to 1935 and, to the right, Highpoint II, built from 1936 to 1938. Both were designed by Berthold Lubetkin. The view is from the extensive garden that's in communal use by the occupants of the two buildings.

recurring theme with numerous modernist buildings. The rationally conceived flat roofs beloved by many modernists often leaked. Concrete made using High Alumina Cement, which was intended to harden quickly, turned out to be prone to rapid decay. The 1970s Southgate Estate in Runcorn New Town, Cheshire, is a case in point. Designed by James Stirling, its 1,500 'residential units' were constructed largely out of pre-cast concrete panels, with repetitive housing blocks connected by a network of raised walkways. By 1990, this reinvention of the concept of urban living along Rationalist lines had become irredeemably uninhabitable, and all the units were demolished to make way for housing of a more traditional design.

In mid 1934, a year before Highpoint I reached completion, another pioneering modernist housing block came to maturity that, again, sought not only to transform the appearance of the modern home and the way people lived, but to create an ideal urban community. The Lawn Road Flats in Hampstead, designed by Wells Coates for the progressive-minded clients and plywood furniture entrepreneurs Molly and Jack Pritchard, is a four-storey reinforced concrete block with a roof-top penthouse offering ultra-modern and minimalist accommodation, with open-plan flats reached via generous external access galleries inspired by Soviet constructivist architecture (see page 325) and designed in a highly sculptural manner. Like Lubetkin, Coates assumed his flats would function as a Soviet-style 'collective', with a communal laundry, a bed-making service, a centrally placed dumb waiter to circulate food, and a restaurant. And, again like Lubetkin, Coates applied rational first principles to design, though whereas at Highpoint I, Lubetkin reconsidered the forms of bathrooms, lavatories and lavatory-paper holders, at Lawn Road Coates adopted a functionalist approach to furniture design, using the Pritchards' connections to create furnishings made of plywood (something of a wonder material at the time). Initially, at least, the apartment block (often referred to as the Isokon building after the development and design company founded by the Pritchards and Coates) became a centre of intellectual and artistic life in north London. Agatha Christie moved in, as did modernist émigré

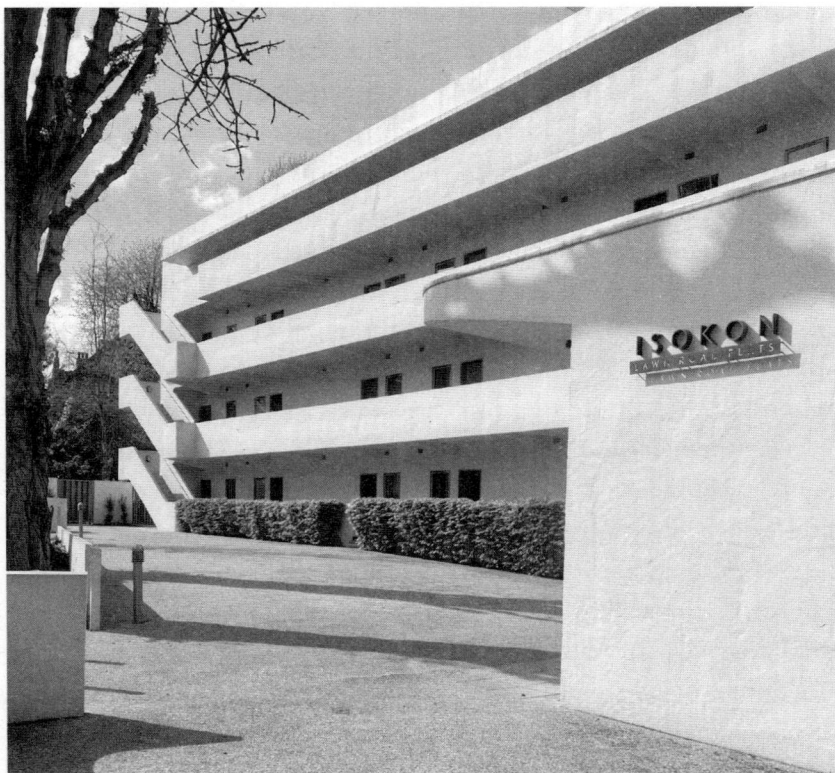

The Lawn Road Flats, also known as the Isokon Building, in Lawn Road, Hampstead, London. The reinforced concrete-built structure, with sculptural access galleries and staircase and minimal detailing, was designed and developed between 1929 and 1934 by architect Wells Coates and entrepreneurs Molly and Jack Pritchard.

architects Walter Gropius and Marcel Breuer, who designed the restaurant at which Henry Moore, Barbara Hepworth and Ben Nicholson were regulars.

Highpoint I and Lawn Road were exercises in the creation of
the utopian modern home, but they were also ultimately private-
enterprise projects intended for the well-heeled. A similar utopian
spirit and aesthetic did, however, also inform some public housing
of the period. The art deco bull-ring of St Andrew's Gardens, Liverpool, for example, which dates from 1935, was initially intended
for council tenants. It is brick-faced and five storeys high, with an
inner garden court framed by sculptural tiers of access galleries that
is reached through a large, semicircular arched opening. The windows
are small and repetitive, suggesting uniform and utilitarian interiors. This was political architecture designed by Lancelot Keay and
John Hughes in solidarity with near-contemporary workers' housing
schemes in Berlin (the Britz Horseshoe Estate by Bruno Taut and
Martin Wagner) and in Vienna (the Karl-Marx Hof by Karl Ehn).

A more nuanced and far more site-specific application of modernist domestic principles was pursued by Hungarian-born architect
Erno Goldfinger, who in 1939 completed the construction of three
houses, organised as a uniform three-storey group (four-storey from
garden level), on Willow Road in Hampstead. One was to serve as
Goldfinger's own home, so this was a very personal affair and for him,
at least, clearly a great success because he continued to live in the
house until his death in 1987. The project did not have a particularly
auspicious start. Construction involved the destruction of a group of
late Georgian houses, which drew protests from local residents. Goldfinger ultimately had his way and was able to deploy the language of
modernist design in his new building, while also seeking to mitigate
criticism by matching the scale of the lost buildings and by echoing
some of the essential character of the area's Georgian architecture.
So his building is faced with brick and the use of proportion, in the
relationship between windows and between wall and windows, is in
a sense traditional. But the podium-like ground floor includes a row
of Corbusian pilotis, the first-floor *piano nobile* favoured in Georgian

houses (see page 96) is achieved by a continuous range of large windows, and the second-floor windows are square in the Georgian tradition. The street frontage is a subtle and sophisticated fusion of the new and the old. But the garden front, liberated from the need to harmonise with history, has more generous glazing, with large horizontal window arranged in a way that is far from Georgian. Internally the houses have first-floor open plans – achieved by running rooms together by opening large double doors – and split-level floors, introduced to define differing functions within the same space.

After the Second World War, house building focused on the replacement in cities and towns of the estimated 4 million homes lost to or seriously damaged by bombing. This set in motion a programme for the construction of large-scale housing estates, often high-density and often at least relatively or partially high-rise. In terms of overall approach and spirit, these were a continuation of a tradition of which the Boundary Estate in Shoreditch (see Chapter 7) offers an early example. They were funded by local or national authorities on public land. They were often designed by public architectural offices. They were built quickly and economically. And they were inspired by the ambition to provide better homes – healthier and far more comfortable – than the urban quarters and dark dwellings that had been swept away during the war. The reality, of course, turned out in many cases to be very different from the vision.

If there were English precedents for these high-rise blocks – including not just the Boundary Estate but the various philanthropic tenements that were constructed from the late 1840s onwards – perhaps the most important ancestor, in terms of architectural influence, was a Russian one: the Narkomfin building in Moscow, designed in constructivist manner by Moisei Ginzburg and completed in 1932. In its inclusion of collective amenities – including a roof garden, penthouse and solarium – it proved a model for Highpoint I and the Lawn Road Flats. In its adoption of a plan that contains tiers of flats of different types (some two-storey maisonettes) that are reached via a wide access gallery, complete with a row of pilotis, and form an internal street, it pointed the way to the design of post-war housing blocks. Le Corbusier made reference to a set of Narkomfin plans when in 1947 he designed the twelve-storey slab-like *Unité d'Habitation* in Marseilles, which was completed in 1952 and which, in his view, made a major contribution to the realisation of his long-held ideal for '*La City Radieuse*' – the Radiant City – of the future. Le Corbusier's scheme in turn had a profound influence on English post-war domestic architecture.

Built of steel-reinforced poured concrete, with board marks from the timber shuttering forming a surface pattern, the external appearance of the *Unité* is a rational expression of its materials and means of construction. Indeed, this béton-brut aesthetic of rough-cast concrete, which anticipates the look of much British brutalist architecture from the 1950s to the 1970s, is its prime ornament. The *Unité* contains 337 apartments of twenty-three different layouts, and an internal street that includes shops, a hotel and a restaurant. The ground floor is treated like a cloister, with ranges of downward-tapering slab-like concrete pilotis supporting the building above, while the rooftop is dedicated, Narkomfin-style, to communal use, with a running track and pool and ventilation towers in the form of huge abstract sculptures. The development as a whole embodies Le Corbusier's ambition to create a housing scheme capable of evolving into a self-contained community.

Among the earliest of the English high-rise housing blocks to be influenced by the *Unité* was the Golden Lane Estate, built on a site on the north-west edge of the City of London that had been heavily bombed during the Second World War. Built from 1952 to designs by Chamberlin, Powell and Bon – architects in private practice who won the commission through competition – it incorporates a mix of housing blocks set in split-level gardens and courts with some buildings in communal use. But the main block – of slab form, rising sixteen storeys and with a partly open ground floor – evidently owes much to Le Corbusier's Marseilles project. Even more directly inspired by the *Unité* is the Highcliffe portion of the Alton West Estate in Roehampton, west London. Designed by the London County Council Architects' Department and completed in 1959, it

Unité d'Habitation, Marseilles, France, completed in 1952 to the design of Le Corbusier. Containing a wide variety of domestic accommodation as well as an internal street with shops, *Unité* provided a model for much post-war public housing. Above: exterior. Below: the interior of a flat inside the building.

includes five tall slab blocks that incorporate ground-floor pilotis to allow them almost to float over the lush landscape (a Corbusian ideal), and two-storey maisonettes as at the *Unité* and also at the Narkomfin. Meanwhile, as the Roehampton project was in its final stages, construction was under way on the Park Hill Estate in Sheffield, planned (in 1953) by the city architect J. L. Womersley, and designed by Jack Lynn and Ivor Smith. Comprising articulated rows of béton-brut slab block, linked by snaking access decks, each incorporating a mix of apartment types and wide, street-like galleries, it was, when the first tenants finally moved in, in 1961, the largest *Unité*-inspired public housing scheme in England. As often turned out to be the case with such large-scale, visually repetitive and radical housing schemes designed to replace Victorian slum housing or bomb sites, the Park Hill Estate proved unpopular with tenants, and the blocks became run-down to the point where they ended up in much the same condition as the slums they replaced. It was a similar story at Keeling House in Bethnal Green in east London. Designed in 1954 as social housing (or 'collective housing', as it was described at the time) by Denys Lasdun, it consists of four 16-storey towers clustered – in radial fashion – around a central service core incorporating lifts and staircase. Each tower contains mostly two-storey maisonettes reached by short access galleries, simulating in Lasdun's view the 'two-up two down' plans of the area's traditional Victorian houses. His hope was that the galleries would function as streets in the sky, where neighbours could gather in a convivial manner. Unfortunately, his optimism was misplaced. The block became unloved and uncared for, and by 1992 Tower Hamlets Council had declared that it could not afford to maintain or renovate it. Demolition was considered.

The subsequent history of the Park Hill Estate and Keeling House developments suggests that poor housing management and lack of maintenance were arguably far more significant factors in such developments' fall from grace than faulty conception or inappropriate design. Park Hill had been listed in 1998 as being of historical and architectural significance, so ultimately, instead of being demolished, the estate was in part privatised and turned into aspirational flats. Keeling House had been listed in 1993, and so rather than press for demolition Tower Hamlets Council finally agreed in 1999 to sell it to a private developer who undertook repairs, took on a concierge and added gates to improve security, and constructed eight penthouses in what had been the roof-top service area. Keeling House is now a success story, even if it no longer fulfils the social purpose for which it was built.

The Barbican Estate, designed by the Golden Lane team of Chamberlin, Powell and Bon, and built from 1957 on a vast City bomb site, enshrines many of the characteristics – and the issues – of the post-war modern home placed within a visionary city setting. The variety of homes offered by the Barbican is extensive – there are 2,000 flats but also maisonettes and small houses, some of studio form with barrel-vaulted roofs over double-height volumes with galleries, mostly placed in medium- and low-rise blocks and terraces. The flats tend to be in the three 44-storey towers, whose tiers of balconies give them dramatic serrated edges when viewed in silhouette. The high residential density that these towers achieve allows much of the site to be given over to gardens, lakes and waterways, so the built fabric, which ranges from brutalist bush-hammered cast concrete to brick, is set within a relatively small but attractive landscape, where housing blocks soar over water on tall pilotis and ground levels are split as if in a gigantic interior. Some blocks are effectively megastructures, perhaps reminiscent of ancient ziggurats, while others coalesce to form a gigantic residential circus, free of traffic and often of people that – with its louvre-screened tiers of balconies – is a distinctly surreal piece of introspective urban theatre. Functions are rich and varied, with an arts centre, library, shops, bars and restaurants that make the Barbican – for its residents – a self-contained community of the type envisioned on a much smaller scale within the *Unité*.

Attitudes to the Barbican have changed radically over the decades. In its early days it was not infrequently described as the ugliest building in London. Now it is more generally appreciated, not least because its owner, the City Corporation, generally maintains the buildings and gardens well, security is good, and the people who live

Above: The Park Hill Estate in Sheffield, a large public-housing scheme inspired in part by Le Corbusier's *Unité,* and constructed between 1957 and 1961. The estate fell into disrepair and is shown before recent remodelling. Below: a central portion of the Barbican Estate, City of London, showing apartments raised on tall pilotis and spanning a small lake. The estate, which contains over 2,000 apartments, was built from 1957, with its arts centre not completed until 1982.

in the estate want to live there. In many ways the Barbican vindicates the Corbusian urban vision: it offers homes set apart from traffic and set among open space and gardens within a lively community.

The notion of housing blocks as urban megastructures has led to other manifestations of the modern home. The Brunswick Centre in Bloomsbury (begun in 1967 to designs by Patrick Hodgkinson) and the Alexandra Road Estate in Camden (begun in 1972 to designs by Neave Brown of Camden Council's Architects' Department) both employ reinforced concrete to create structures with a stepped section and a staggered profile of ziggurat form. Both incorporate parallel and almost identical terraces facing each other across a central court and both use the step-section form stretching across much of their sites to achieve high-density accommodation, without having to resort to building dauntingly high edifices and so risk the sense of visual oppression that they can entail. The configuration also allows for each home to have a balcony, fully glazed external elevations and striking prospects. The Brunswick Centre, after a shaky first few years, now contains a mix of social and private housing and a shop-filled central court raised on a plateau-like podium that is bustling with life.[1] The Alexandra Road Estate contains public housing, divided between flats and maisonettes. It benefits from the fact that its designers were obliged to take account of the findings of the 1961 Parker Morris Committee, which determined that the spatial and amenity stand- ards of social housing had to improve to reflect a general rise in the nation's standard of living. Enshrined in law in 1963, these precepts may not always have led to the creation of homely flats, but, as the Alexandra Road Estate demonstrates, they did at least ensure that the space on offer to tenants became a little more generous. It's now a listed building, as is the Brunswick Centre. Once regarded as radical and challenging experiments in housing, the two projects are now firmly part of the capital's stock of built heritage.

Forming a strong contrast with these two step-section reinforced- concrete megastructure estates is the 'Byker Wall' in Newcastle upon Tyne, begun in 1968. Generally eight to ten storeys high, and planned as a continuous, slightly undulating series of 620 public housing maisonettes, it was originally conceived as a sound barrier against a motorway that was never constructed. The architect, Ralph Erskine, made much use of colour and a mix of material – including timber and brick – in an attempt to evoke a sense of joy. He also pioneered what in the 1970s would become a fashion for 'community' architecture by living on site and entering into lengthy consultations with potential residents. The scheme, which was finally completed in the early 1980s, was not only much discussed at the time but also greatly admired.

In parallel with inner-city explorations of the potential of novel design and construction on modern homes was the New Town Movement, which sought to ease the nation's housing problems through the founding of new settlements on open country or by sub-stantially expanding existing ones, and which was created through a series of Acts of Parliament from 1946. By the 1960s and 1970s the scale of its operations – overseen by development corporations – had increased markedly. Simultaneously, the character of its archi-tecture had changed. Innovation, combined with a high quality of design, became ever more valued as planners increasingly recognised that such qualities were essential if the new communities being formed were to acquire their own identity and sense of distinction. Milton Keynes, which was developed over the course of the 1970s and 1980s, is a case in point: a demonstration project of avant-garde housing curated by its development corporation and realised by a wide spectrum of young architects. By 2002 there were twenty-one new towns in England, providing some 500,000 homes for over 2 million people.

When it comes to the building materials that 'define' modernism, concrete is perhaps the first one that comes to mind, whether the béton brut associated with brutalism or the many and varied types on display today. But glass has also played a central role.

Ludwig Mies van der Rohe (see page 319) arguably pointed the way with the 'curtain wall' glass facades he designed for the Seagram office tower in New York (completed in 1958). He also created the epitome of the 'transparent house' with his single-storey, flat-roofed Farnsworth House, in Plano, Illinois (built between 1945 and 1951), where a minimal steel frame holds and supports walls that are wholly glazed. This approach clearly has a functional aspect to it since it makes maximum use of daylight and offers open prospects. It also possesses dramatic potential because, by night, the house, luminous like a lantern, puts virtually all life on display, unless purposely concealed, almost as though the occupants are existing in a self-conscious work of art. Such transparency, of course, can also be something of a trial, not least because the interior of a glass-box-like house always runs the risk of being excessively cold in the winter and overly hot in the summer. In the case of Farnsworth House, the client, Edith Farnsworth, clearly felt that ultimately the disadvantages outweighed the advantages because, while she initially collaborated very closely with van der Rohe, by the end she had tired of her toy to the point where the architect had to sue her to get his final fees paid.

Despite the practical limitations of such seemingly functional architecture, the idea of the transparent house – the minimal and rational ultimate solution to home-making – has continued to haunt the imagination of architects. So, for example, Richard and Su Rogers' single-storey house at Parkside in Wimbledon – designed in 1967 for Richard Rogers' parents – has a minimal steel frame, a front elevation entirely of glass and an open-plan interior with areas for different functions defined by screens (some fitted with mirrors) and by furniture. There is a separate, similar, pavilion for additional uses, including a pottery studio. This house is also an early manifestation of High Tech architecture, within which Rogers was a key figure, partly because of its utilisation of prefabricated components, including neoprene rubber gaskets which help to seal junctions, and cushion and absorb vibrations within the glazing panels.

Almost a decade later, in 1976, architects Patty and Michael Hopkins created their own, highly transparent, family home and office in Downshire Hill, Hampstead, using prefabricated steel components to form a two-storey frame (one storey set below street level), with diagonal steel bracing and the sections of the frame filled with glass. Inside all is open plan, with few permanent interior partitions, and functions flowing freely, indeed overlapping, in the main spaces,

The Farnsworth House, Plano, Illinois, USA, built between 1945 and 1951 to the design of Mies van der Rohe. It is a masterpiece of late modern minimalism, but the satisfying if simplistic logic of its architecture – slender steels for structure and glass for walls – while producing a light-filled building, made for a home that was difficult to occupy with ease, comfort, convenience and necessary privacy.

rather as in a fifteenth-century great hall. Even highly modernist buildings, it would seem, can evoke older models.

* * * * *

While modernist principles have maintained a strong grip on domestic design over the past hundred years or so, the alternative and parallel strand in English house design – the pursuit of tradition and historic precedent – continues to have a rich story to tell. The Arts and Crafts Movement of the later Victorian age, with its focus on vernacular architecture – that is, using local building material and historical forms and details, and taking inspiration from nature – remained a strong influence well into the twentieth century. It served as partial inspiration, for example, for the Garden City Movement, initially promoted from 1898 by Ebenezer Howard, which envisioned the creation of new but traditionally designed housing set amid rich planting for all classes of society who would, it was hoped, form flourishing and self-sustaining communities. To a degree this movement was, in its planning at least, a model for England's post-war new towns.

Letchworth Garden City in Hertfordshire, started in 1903, and Hampstead Garden Suburb in north London, dating from 1906, both based on master plans by Barry Parker and Raymond Unwin, contain new houses of traditional form, with much display of history-inspired detail and decoration. In Hampstead Garden Suburb, the architect Sir Edwin Lutyens confirmed the dominance of history by designing houses around the Central Square as erudite essays in the brick-built, late-seventeenth-century, Wren-revival style. In architectural terms, the two garden cities are a world away from large-scale modernist housing schemes. In social terms, on the other hand, they unfortunately have a shared problem, in that – broadly, at least – both have failed to realise the ambition that drove their creation. Modernist housing projects have all too often failed to appeal to those for whom they were intended. Garden cities, which were initially intended to bring different social classes together in happy harmony, have rarely succeeded in so doing. In both cases, brave experiments in creating balanced communities have struggled to withstand the tests imposed by the hard economic realities of market forces, with less wealthy potential occupants tending to be priced out.

The ornamental aspect of the tradition-based architecture that helped shape the look of the early garden cities, and so much other domestic architecture of the period, remained an important and evolving element of new housing throughout the middle decades of the twentieth century. For a time in the 1930s more historically based themes tended to give way to the abstract motifs – radial curves, streamlining and ziggurat forms – of art deco. During the Second World War the architectural practice of Tayler & Green came up with an approach for the modest council houses it undertook for a rural district council in south Norfolk that creatively fused more 'modern' abstract ornamental brick detailing with such elements of traditional design as low-pitched roofs, colour-washed brickwork and, on occasion, carved bargeboards fixed to the gables of houses. The 600 council houses the practice built in the area between 1943 and 1973 may not be much known or noticed today, but in a way that is their triumph. Tayler & Green's houses are so sympathetic to their setting, so self-effacing, that they become, in a sense, an invisible part of the landscape. If they run the risk of being taken for granted by many, they nevertheless remain sources of quiet pleasure for the discerning.

The traditional strand of domestic architecture that Tayler & Green represent is arguably more overtly expressed in the work of Raymond Erith, who from the late 1930s into the early 1970s kept the flame of the classical orders very much alive. One of his first projects, from the late 1930s, was to rebuild the Great House in Dedham, Essex, after a calamitous fire. Here he worked in a simple classical style reminiscent of the early nineteenth-century Regency period, but the result is far more than an essay in the neo-Georgian. Even his extensive repairs and alterations from 1958 to numbers 10, 11 and 12 Downing Street (number 12 being an almost complete rebuild) manage to be a combination of respectful erudition and impressive invention. His successfully realized ambition was to show that historical forms and traditions remain alive and continue to be capable of evolving to meet the demands of a new age.

This ambition was (and continues to be) further pursued and given tangible expression in the last great tradition-inspired, large-scale house-building project of the twentieth century: Poundbury, outside Dorchester in Dorset, commissioned in 1988 by the then Prince of Wales for land owned by his Duchy of Cornwall estate and based on a master plan produced by the polemical urbanist Léon Krier. The scheme, which got under way in 1993, was conceived as a standard commercial house-building exercise, but its primary significance was as a demonstration project, intended to show that it is possible to create new-build communities that possess the qualities so admired in historic towns and cities: architecture on a human scale; a stimulating complexity of street plan that creates a sense of intimacy; a variety of design and of detail within a broad aesthetic harmony, but favouring classicism; and a sense of visual beauty and delight. In effect, Poundbury was to be a self-contained small town, ideally in which people both lived and worked, with a rich mix of different types of housing (including some for low-income residents) and of buildings serving different purposes, many arranged around informal public spaces.

Construction has been a continuous process, with houses financed as speculations by private house builders. A key object from the start was to imbue the scheme as a whole with the character of a traditional community, built over a period of time as different enterprises. Achieving a convincing sense of variety – of building materials and details – was therefore deemed essential, and this was attempted by engaging a large number of architects, all of whom were given a degree of leeway as they drew up detailed plans but who also had to adhere to the Krier master plan and to a broad design brief that involved creating buildings inspired by historical models and rooted for the most part in the vernacular classical idiom.

In its early days Poundbury proved divisive, quickly becoming the lightning rod in a wider debate between modernists and traditionalists, and between those providing mass public housing where tight

A diverse group of houses, mostly constructed from the mid 1990s
by various house builders and architects, that forms one edge of the
Great Field in Poundbury, Dorset. Sheep graze on the field, as they did
for centuries when this was farmland, and the new houses, mostly
vernacular classical in manner, are inspired by local historical examples,
with the aim being to give this large development – ultimately for
6,000 people – a distinct regional character.

budgets are often a deciding factor and commercial builders of houses for private occupation working in a less financially constrained way. It pitched, as it were, those who admire the style of a Maister House against those who, like Bassett-Lowke and Behrens at New Ways, favour architecture that is more overtly forward-looking. But after more than thirty years, the debate has died down, the optimum mix of uses seems to have been resolved, a distinct community has been formed, and the houses are much desired. The vision behind Poundbury's creation has been tested by unforgiving commercial forces and, within its own economic terms, found to work. It confirms that, for many, houses of traditional design, set in familiar streets, crescents or squares, remains an ideal. In 2024 Poundbury housed 4,600 people and when completed in 2028 it will provide homes for 6,000.[2]

The arguments over Poundbury are, of course, nothing new — conflicting views of architectural style and approach stretch back to the mid Victorian 'Battle of the Styles' between the Gothic and classical traditions (see page 184), and earlier. And those arguments — about urban planning, about the best ways to provide housing for all and about the design of individual houses — will continue. Home-making is both a complex business and a fascinating, never-ending story.

Glossary

apse: a niche or recess, often curved in plan, set in a wall.

architrave: the bottom part of a classical **entablature**. Also the name of mouldings (derived from entablature mouldings) framing a door or window.

balusters: an ornamental post, usual formed of diminutive columns and urns, supporting the handrail of a staircase or 'balustraded' wall.

barrel vault: a ceiling or roof of semi-cylindrical form.

béton brut: concrete poured into timber moulds and over steel reinforcing, with the texture of the moulds, or formwork, forming a surface decoration when the concrete has dried. From French, meaning 'raw concrete', béton brut became a popular modernist building technique in the mid twentieth century and in Britain became known as brutalism.

bolection: a decorative serpentine moulding, composed of semicircular and quadrant, convex and concave profiles, framing panels that project beyond the surrounding wall surfaces.

cabinet: a small room, also termed a **closet**, where informal meetings could take place.

capital: the top of a column or **pilaster** in classical architecture.

caryatid: a supporting column sculpted in the form of a draped female figure, Grecian in origin.

chamfer: a flat surface made by cutting off the edge or corner of a block of wood or other material.

closet: a small, private room used for prayer or study, intimate meetings or prayer, also termed a **cabinet**. Occasional the location for a close-stool or privy.

coffering: a decorative sunken panel in a ceiling, dome, **soffit** or vault.

collar-beam: in roof carpentry, a horizontal timber set halfway along the length of a rafter to give extra solidity to the roof truss, or structure, and prevent it from spreading.

colonnade: a row of columns, supporting a flat **entablature** or arches.

colonnette: a small column.

corbel: a bracket of stone, wood, brick or other building material, projecting from the face of a wall and generally used to support a **tie-beam** or arch.

cornice: the top member of a classical **entablature**. Often used in isolation to ornament the top of an external elevation, usually at the junction with the roof, or the top of an internal wall at the junction with the ceiling.

Corinthian: the most ornate of the three main **orders** of classical Greek architecture, characterised by a slender fluted column with an ornate bell-shaped **capital** decorated with acanthus leaves.

crown post: in roof carpentry, a post – sometimes ornamented – rising from a **collar-beam** or from a **tie-beam**, and supporting a collar plate that in, turn, helps support the ridge of the roof. Once sometimes called a king post, but this usage has now been abandoned.

crow-stepped: a step-like design along the raking sides of a roof gable. Visually striking, it also provides a convenient way to terminate courses in a brick-built structure.

cyma: a classical moulding of sinuous concave and convex quadrant profiles. A cyma recta has the concave quadrant at the top, and the arrangement is reversed for the cyma reverse. The cyma mouldings of a cornice were originally placed at the eaves of a pitched roof and contrived to throw rainwater off the walls below.

Doric: the simplest of the three main **orders** of classical Greek architecture. Grecian Doric is characterised by massive columns with shallow flutes and plain, saucer-shaped **capitals** and no base. Roman Doric is slightly more ornate, including columns of more slender girth and with bases.

dentil: a detail, reminiscent of teeth, in a classical **cornice**.

egg-and-dart mouldings: also known as egg-and-tongue mouldings, these are set within an **entablature**, particularly **cornices**, and composed of bulbous, egg-like forms separated by dart, or tongue-like, motifs.

enfilade: a set of rooms arranged in a linear manner in which doors are aligned to offer a vista when opened, an arrangement typical of seventeenth- and eighteenth-century baroque architecture.

entablature: the upper horizontal element of a classical building, often actually or visually supported by **pilasters** or columns. All entablatures comprised three elements: the **architrave** at the bottom, then the frieze, then the **cornice**. Although largely symbolic and ornamental by the Roman period, the entablature – like many elements of the **orders** – was functional in its origin.

fielded: a panel with bevelled edges, so that its surface appears raised above the surfaces of the frame within which it sits.

finial: an ornament on the top of a building. In classical architecture typically placed above the **entablature**, parapet wall or balustrade. Often in the form of an urn or pineapple.

flute: a concave vertical recess in the shaft of a column.

gable pediment: a pediment that is the expression of a pitched roof, or a diminutive pediment set at the apex of a gable.

gargoyle: a sculpture – usually serving as a waterspout – carved in the form of a grotesque face or creature and projecting from the building, especially in a Gothic building.

impost block: a projecting masonry block, resting on a column set above a **pilaster** or embedded in a wall, on which rests the lowest **voussoir** of an arch.

Ionic: the type of Greek column characterised by scroll-like decorations. See the **orders**.

keystone: a wedged-shape block at the crown of an arch – curved or slightly cambered – to consolidate its structure.

lantern (roof): a generously glazed and relatively lightweight structure – usually made of timber or iron and typically with a pitched roof and vertical sides, used to light interiors.

lintel: a horizontal support – of any suitable material – across the opening of a door or window.

loggia: a room or porch with at least one side open and usually defined by a **colonnade, piers** or an arcade of Gothic or classical design.

lunette: an opening or recess of crescent, semicircular or half-elliptical form containing a window or sculptural ornament. Open or glazed variants of lunettes are also known as Diocletian or thermal windows because of their use in Roman bathhouses.

mullion: a vertical division – of timber or masonry – in a window opening to which hinged casements of frames, containing panes of glass, are fixed.

muntin: in timber wall panelling, a narrow upright that helps to frame a panel or wide plank and is fixed to upper and lower horizontal rails. Similar to a **stile** but not part of a structural system because muntins do not usually extend between, nor are fixed to, floor and ceiling joists. In doors, a vertical upright between panels. In the US it refers to glazing bars.

nave: the main, central and usually highest space in a building of basilica form, usually flanked by aisles and separated from them by screens of columns, **piers** or shafts.

newel: a vertical post, often in the form of a small column, placed at the bottom or top of a flight of stairs and at the point where the flights change direction, that supports a balustrade or handrail and that gives the staircase structural stability.

the orders: by the Roman period there were five 'orders' of classical architecture, ranging from the simple Tuscan through the progressively elongated and ornate **Doric, Ionic** and **Corinthian** to the Composite order. The Doric, Ionic and Corinthian are of Grecian origin; the Tuscan and Composite, Roman. Each order possessed its own sets of proportions, ornaments and attributes but all included plinths, columns, **capitals** and **entablatures** of varied proportions, profiles and ornamentation.

oriel: a projecting structure – rising from the ground but more usually cantilevered or supported by **corbels** – containing windows and contrived to form a notable architectural feature.

ovolo: a moulding in classical architecture of convex quadrant, or quarter circle, form.

pediment: a triangular or curved form set above an **entablature** – often supported by columns or **pilasters** – marking the main entrance to, or forming the central feature of, a classical building. The form is derived from the functional expression of the triangular end of a pitched roof. As well as being triangular, semicircular, segmental or – in baroque architecture – formed of sinuous concave and convex forms, pediments can be open or broken, with parts of their horizontal lower entablature or their **keystone** removed for visually dramatic effect. In addition, the area defined by the pediment – the tympanum – can be filled with allegorical and ornamental sculpture.

piano nobile: the main floor of a building, usually a house. Derived from Renaissance practice when, typically, the first floor was treated as the *piano nobile* and had the greatest floor-to-ceiling height, the richest interior decoration and the most ornamental exterior decoration, especially to its windows, which would be the highest in the elevation.

pier: a vertical structural support; if free-standing, typically square or rectangular in plan. Also refers to the continuous vertical masonry structure separating openings such as windows. In classical architectural composition, piers, topped with simplified **capitals**, can be used to terminate **colonnades** of frame **porticoes**.

pilaster: a flat equivalent to a column, usually furnished in classical architecture with a **capital** in one of the **orders**. Structurally, a buttress, strengthening the wall to which it is attached and helping to carry a load imposed on that wall. In this role comparable to the function fulfilled by types of **piers**.

piloti: a column, often made of steel-reinforced concrete, used without ornamentation in twentieth-century modernist architecture.

portico: a sheltered entrance or porch leading to a building or a covered way. In classical architecture often formed by the projection of a **pediment** or **entablature** supported on columns.

proscenium arch: a frame – usually arched – that surrounds a stage in a theatre, separating performers from the audience and presenting the play or opera as if it were an animated painting, taking place in a world removed from daily life.

putti: statues or paintings of naked male children; when with wings they are more commonly called cherubs, which, although angelic in appearance, can have the attributes – as well as the appearance – of Cupid.

quoins: rectangular stone or brick blocks used at the corners of walls to offer structural support – or at least to suggest strength – and to ornament a composition and give emphasis to selected features.

rustication: the decorative treatment of a stone or brick wall to suggest strength of construction, much favoured in Roman architecture for buildings where solidity and endurance were to be expressed. Rustication is achieved by emphasising individual blocks of stone – or panels of brickwork – by cutting back the edges of real or implied joints. The cutting back can be achieved in varied ways – notably by bevelling edges or by creating narrow channels between blocks.

sill course: a horizonal masonry band projecting from an elevation, at the level of, and combing with, window sills. Generally used to visually divide an elevation into separate portions to achieve proportions. See also **string course**.

soffit: the visible underside of an arch, beam, **architrave** or any horizontally laid element such as a stair tread.

solar: in medieval and Tudor domestic architecture, a private family room adjoining a great hall.

spigot: a tap, or in the US a faucet, for controlling the flow of liquid, especially in external or utilitarian locations. Also, in the UK, a timber stopper for a vent in a barrel.

stanchion: a vertical support, usually of very simple form and of cast iron, supporting a roof or superstructure generally.

stile: in timber panelling, a vertical upright within which panels are framed and which plays a structural role by extending between floor and ceiling joists by being fixed to top and bottom rails. See also **muntin**.

string course: a horizontal, projecting band running along an elevation and used as decoration, to mark floor levels or – more usually – to divide surface areas into admired proportions. See also **sill course**.

stucco: a render of varied materials – traditionally lime or from the late eighteenth century 'Roman cement' – applied to a brick surface, then painted in oil, lime-washed or frescoed to suggest stone.

tabernacle frame: a frame, often around a painting fixed within an overmantel above a fireplace, formed by a bold **architrave**, frequently with its corners articulated or 'lugged', topped by a frieze and **cornice** or **pediment**. On occasion, side architraves are replaced by columns or **pilasters**. Derived from Renaissance altarpieces and like a miniature temple front or tabernacle.

tie-beam: in a timber roof, the main horizontal beam connecting the ends of rafters to form a structurally strong truss of triangular form.

torus moulding: in classical architecture, a convex moulding of semicircular form.

tracery: a pattern of interlacing ribs, especially as used in Gothic windows.

transept: projections from, and set at right angles to, the **nave** and aisles of a Christian church of basilica plan. The transepts are placed towards the altar end of the church so that, in plan, the church has the form of the Christian Latin cross.

transom: a bar made of stone, timber and on occasion moulded brick and used from the Middle Ages into the mid seventeenth century to form the horizontal component in mullioned and transomed casement windows.

triglyphs: in the **Doric** order, the three vertical and abutting elements in a frieze, derived from the timber origins of classical temple architecture, with triglyphs representing the ends of three planks joined to form a beam. In classical architecture triglyphs are usually flanked by square metopes, or spaces, and generally ornamented.

truss: a rigid structural framework – rectangular or arched – usually formed of timbers or metal to bridge a space, with each end resting on supports at regular intervals. Also the triangular form created in timber roof construction, with the outer edges formed by rafters and a **tie-beam**.

volume: the amount of space occupied by a three-dimensional object or region of space.

voussoir: a wedge-shaped element, typically a stone used in building an arch or vault.

Notes

INTRODUCTION

1. Steep Hill connected the Roman upper city (Lindum) – started as a fortress in about AD 60 by the 9th Hispanian Legion – with the lower city (Lindum Colonia), built from AD 90, when the legionary settlement expanded. Remains of the Roman south gate of the upper city survive in 44 Steep Hill.

2. There is another contender for this coveted title: Saltford Manor House, near Bath, in Somerset, which is widely regarded as the nation's oldest continuously occupied house. It could date from *c*.1150, which on stylistic grounds is credible but precise documentary evidence is lacking.

3. English Heritage supports this claim.

4. This storm was weathered, but in 1255, when a Christian boy known as 'Little Hugh' was found dead in Lincoln, the Jewish community was accused of ritual murder and, with no evidence, eighteen Lincoln Jews were summarily executed at the Tower of London. 'Little Hugh' rapidly assumed the status of Christian martyr, with a shrine in the cathedral to which pilgrims flocked, bringing offerings, and thus apparently confirming the guilt of the Lincoln Jews. There was an uneasy peace until 1290, when all Jews were expelled from Lincoln along with the rest of England, by order of Edward I.

5. The Vicar's Close is regarded as the oldest continuously inhabited, coherently planned and uniform street to survive in Europe. Commissioned by the Bishop of Wells Cathedral, which it closely adjoins, to house his community of choral vicars, it was almost certainly designed and executed by masons working on the cathedral, where the choir and retrochoir were under construction during the 1340s. The Close is therefore architecturally exceptional and packs a great visual punch. Most strikingly, each of its small houses is utterly subservient to the realisation of a monumental conception, dominated by uniformity, repetition and relative simplicity. The layout of the terraces tapers slightly as it moves away from the cathedral to create a false perspective – a most sophisticated concept – so that, when entering the Close from the cathedral, it appears to look surprisingly long.

The houses are constructed from coursed mudstone rubble, presumable sourced locally, with stones roughly squared, and with larger, more regular quoins marking corners. In the history of English housing the Close, due to the exceptional conditions of its design and construction – being evidently a cathedral project for cathedral 'staff' – is far from typical. But in its designer's desire for uniformity, mini-monumentality and relative simplicity, it is tempting to see the Close as a harbinger of a national architectural spirit, and as an urban model that was to find ultimate expression in house design of the seventeenth, eighteenth and early nineteenth centuries, in such cities as Bath and London.

6. The house, which dates from the very early fifteenth century but appears to have been significantly altered after fifty years or so, originally stood in Chiddingstone in Kent. It has now been re-erected in the Weald & Downland Living Museum in West Sussex.

7. Beckley Park, Oxfordshire, brick-built in 1540, is a good example.

8. See Nottingham County Council Historic Environment Record, https:// her.nottinghamshire.gov.uk/Monument/MNT17644/, and Eric Mercer, *English Vernacular Houses* (London: HMSO, 1975). Urban, and late, examples of the lobby-entry plan survive in Nelson Street, King's Lynn, where numbers 22 to 28 date from the early seventeenth century. See Nikolaus Pevsner and Bill Wilson, *The Buildings of England, Norfolk 2: North-west and South* (London: Penguin, 1999), p. 493.

9. Nikolaus Pevsner, *The Buildings of England, Essex* (London: Penguin, 1954), pp. 183–4.

10. From south to north, in roughly linear fashion, Nelson Street, St Margaret's Place, Queen Street and King Street to Tuesday Market Place.

11. A good example is the early seventeenth-century 29 Queen Street, King's Lynn, which has an L-shaped plan form incorporating a hall and solar range behind the main house, and originally a long range of warehouses running parallel with the hall and solar range. The variation, or combination, of uses for these rear ranges – residential and warehouse/industrial – was typical of sixteenth- and early seventeenth-century urban buildings. See Pevsner and Wilson, *The Buildings of England, Norfolk 2: North-west and South*, pp. 464 and 485.

12. See Alec Clifton-Taylor, *The Pattern of English Building* (London: B. T. Batsford, 1965), pp. 22–6, for a brilliant introduction to the nation's traditional building materials.

13. Arguably the Inigo Jones-designed Queen's House in Greenwich, conceived in 1616, has a double-pile plan, but in this case its pair of double-pile ranges were originally separated by a public road and linked by a

room serving as a bridge. So perhaps an exceptional and not generally applicable example of the type. Architectural historians have not infrequently claimed that the design reached maturity with Coleshill House, Berkshire, built around 1650 to the designs of the gentleman-architect Roger Pratt, but tragically destroyed by fire in 1952.

14. *Oxford English Dictionary*. Initially used in reference to fortifications.

15. At Hengrave Hall in Suffolk, dating from 1525 to 1538 (although much altered in the late eighteenth and late nineteenth centuries), a passage runs around three sides of the central court (with the volume of the great hall providing the connecting link), ensuring that the main chambers are not used as semi-public thoroughfares. Similarly, functional passageways are to be found in Hardwick Hall in Derbyshire. But architecturally conceived corridors, as opposed to humble passages, remained something of a novelty in the very early eighteenth century: as late as 1716, architect Sir John Vanbrugh had to explain to his client for Blenheim Palace in Oxfordshire, the Duchess of Marlborough, what a corridor was. As Vanbrugh, who had proposed architecturally glorious, as well as most convenient, 'vaulted corridors' for the palace, wrote in a letter to the duchess, 'The word Corridore Madam is foreign, and signifys in plain English, no more than a Passage'; see *Complete Works of Sir John Vanbrugh*, vol. 4, *Letters*, ed. Geoffrey Webb (London: Nonesuch Press, 1928), p. 71.

16. Examples of corridors being added for convenience to existing houses are those at Wilton House, Wiltshire, where in 1811 a Gothic-styled corridor was fitted within the courtyard of this sixteenth- and seventeenth-century house, and Felbrigg Hall, Norfolk, where a late seventeenth-century wing of interconnecting rooms had a corridor added in 1751.

17. Indeed, Book III of Serlio's *Tutte l'Opere d'Architettura*, published in 1537, includes drawings of a square-plan house with four square-plan corner towers and, as at Hardwick, columnar screens along two sides. See *Sebastiano Serlio on Architecture*, vol. 1, ed. Vaughan Hart and Peter Hicks (New Haven, CT: Yale University Press, 1996), pp. 242–3.

18. As Mark Girouard points out with regard to the passion for devices: 'This characteristic of the Elizabethans can be traced … in their architecture', which contains 'a great number of ingenious geometrical plans', including Hardwick Hall, where Girouard suggests the plan is formed by a pair of Greek crosses, each 'imposed' upon by a square. This reading is possible if the three square-plan towers attached to each of the outer edges of the two large squares are interpreted as the arms of Greek crosses, with the missing arms subsumed into the volume of the central hall. See

Girouard's *Robert Smythson and the Elizabethan Country House* (London: Yale University Press, 1983), pp. 21–5.

19. According to Ronald Brunskill, the eminent historian of England's vernacular architecture, the mid sixteenth century marks the point when people became more likely to employ a building professional to design their homes, with, as he puts it, 'large houses from the end of the 17C onwards [tending] to be designed by architects in the prevailing style'. See Brunskill's *Vernacular Architecture: An Illustrated Handbook* (London: Faber & Faber, 2000), pp. 25–9.

20. Both are 'prodigy houses' (large, ostentatious houses), but the extent of Smythson's involvement has not been fully established, although he seems to have worked largely as a mason at Longleat and as an architect at Wollaton.

21. As Mark Girouard points out, 'there is no evidence, in the accounts or in his drawings, for connecting' Smythson with any detailed designs at Hardwick, and the surviving 'building accounts have no payment for a design'. See Girouard, *Robert Smythson and the Elizabethan Country House*, pp. 146–8.

22. Sadly Oldcotes, completed in 1599, was long ago demolished.

23. By 1590 the countess had 'a lifetime's experience of building' and 'clearly set out to create the perfect house'. Girouard, *Robert Smythson and the Elizabethan Country House*, p. 145.

I. ARCHITECTS AND PATRONS

Pallant House, Chichester (1712)

1. The house was built in the mid 1680s by a speculating builder named John Steele under a lease issued by Richard Frith and William Pym, who held the head lease from the Crown and from 1696 from William Bentinck, the Earl of Portland. Built as two houses that were united to become one residence in 1696, the building survives and is now numbered 10, although there is little early fabric within apart from a very robustly detailed, rather old-fashioned-looking, timber staircase. Cutter had been in possession of the house from 1703, at which time he was described as 'then Captain of His Majesty's ship of war the Newcastle'; see *Survey of London*, vol. 33, *The Parish of St Anne, Soho*, ed. F. H. W. Sheppard (London: Athlone Press, 1966), pp. 63–4.

2. Sibylla Jane Flower, Roy Strong and David Coke, *Pallant House: Its History, Architecture and Owners* (Chichester: Pallant House Gallery, 1993), p. 30.

3. According to Alexander Hay's 1804 history of Chichester, the house was built 'around the year 1712'; see Alexander Hay, *The History of Chichester, Interspersed with Various Notes and Observations* (Chichester, 1804), p. 190.

4. At that time occupied by a malt house.

5. The City Minute Books for 1685 to 1737, p. 250, West Sussex Record Office, County Hall, Chichester.

6. National Archives Kew, C11/2334/11/ Sheet 4 of 5. With thanks to Alan Baxter Associates and Vicky Simon for the transcription of this document and with whom in 2020 I worked preparing a report on Pallant House.

7. Elizabeth, Lady Wilbraham, born in 1632, has been proclaimed as England's first female architect, although this is purely speculation based on circumstantial evidence since there are no signed drawings or documents connecting her directly to any projects. She did own architectural books that she evidently studied closely, including Palladio's *I quattro libri dell'architettura* of 1570, and it is possible that she did design her own home – Weston Park, Staffordshire – built in 1671, but the house is also associated with another architect, William Taylor. Other notable women in the field include Lady Anne Clifford, who in the mid seventeenth century appears to have been actively involved in the maintenance and improvement of the Clifford family's extensive estates in Cumbria, on occasion, acting as architect. Queen Mary II also had a great interest in the arts, crafts and architecture, and over thirty years after her death in 1694, the architect Nicholas Hawksmoor spoke of the queen's 'great passion for building' and admitted that she was the 'real foundress' of the Royal Naval College at Greenwich, and that its architectural glory was the result of 'her Majesty's fix't intention for Magnificence' (Hawksmoor's *Remarks on the Founding of the Hospital* (1728), quoted in Kerry Downs, *English Baroque Architecture* (London: Zwemmer, 1966), p. 51) Sarah Churchill, the Duchess of Marlborough and the key client for Blenheim Palace, Oxfordshire, designed in 1705 by Sir John Vanbrugh, was a highly opinionated and acerbic architectural patron, apt to be impatient and aggressive and suspicious of all professional pretentions and most careful and astute when it came money. The first female member of the Royal Institute of Architects, Ethel Charles, was admitted in 1898, but she failed to gain significant recognition, or commissions, in the male-dominated world of architecture and building, and it was not until the late 1920s that a female architect secured a major commission, when Elizabeth Scott won the competition to design the Shakespeare Memorial Theatre in Stratford-upon-Avon.

8. Dan Cruickshank, 'The Eighteenth Century and the Rebuilding of St Bartholomew's Hospital, in *St. Bartholomew's Hospital: 900 Years*, ed. Ann Robey (London: Barts Heritage, 2023), p.77.

9. Information given to the author by the architectural historian Richard Hewlings.

10. There were surveyors to the great cathedrals, to the King's Works, and so on.

11. Eight gave depositions to 'His Majesty's High Court of Chancery' on 14 October 1717, then sitting 'at the house of William Castle bearing the sign of the Black Horse' in Chichester, where they were examined or 'interrogated' to establish the veracity of their depositions. The commission was issued to, and the examinations conducted by, John Woodyer, 'clerke'; William Tutte, 'gent'; William Woodyer Esq.; and Mr John Peckham, 'gent.', presumably a relative of Henry's. See National Archives Kew, C11/2334/11/ Sheet 4 of 5.

12. The London prototype for the 'Modell' that the Peckhams could have seen and admired – and that Pallant House in some respect emulates – could have been one of a number of high-status homes lately completed in 1712. There was Buckingham House, at the west end of St James's Park, which was brick-built between 1703 and 1710 to the designs of William Winde and was three storeys high over a basement. Located nearby was Marlborough House, completed in 1711 and designed by Sir Christopher Wren and his son for the Duke and Duchess of Marlborough. It was originally only two storeys high and to judge by its current but much altered condition probably possessed ground- and first-floor windows of equal height – as was to be the case with Pallant House. And there was of course Inigo Jones's seminal Queen's House at Greenwich – built from 1616 to 1635 as a royal home and in the early eighteenth century famed for the authority of its Renaissance-inspired design and a place of architectural pilgrimage. The Peckhams must have viewed it, and being two storeys high above a basement, seven windows wide and with its main north elevation raised on a terrace, the Queen's House is in a sense a model for Pallant House.

13. When the staircase was constructed the use of mahogany for architectural elements such as doors and staircases was still a decade away, with one of the earliest examples being the interior of Houghton Hall, Norfolk, fitted out for Sir Robert Walpole in the early 1720s and designed by Colen Campbell and Thomas Ripley, perhaps with James Gibbs.

14. See, for example, Rainham Hall, Essex, built in 1729.

15. John Aubrey, *Natural Historie of Wiltshire* (1691; Wiltshire Topographical Society, 1845).

16. The room, incidentally, also contains a well, which may predate the construction of Pallant House.

17. Most of the other builders who worked on Pallant House concurred with this figure. However, James Burley, a 35-year-old Chichester joiner, who also acknowledged the important role of Mrs Peckham in the design and decision making during the construction of Pallant House, suggested that it cost 'five & twenty hundred pounds'.

18. Isaac Ware, *A Complete Body of Architecture* (1756; London, 1768), p. 347.

19. In the evidence he gave, John Page listed some other works on the house that he had executed directly on Mrs Peckham's orders, notably the replacement of a small window on the rear elevation with a larger window, the fabrication of 'ffolding doors from the Backbuilding into the dwelling house', the 'laying of the fflowers [floors] in the Outhouse', the 'setting out plates for Chimneys & setting up the furnace' and the construction of a 'deale partition in the Cellar of the dwelling house to make a Larder'.

20. The inventory of August 1759 for the composer George Frideric Handel's early eighteenth-century London house on Brook Street includes the following items in its kitchen: 'Large Rainge with Cheeks . . . a Crain and Pott Hooks . . . a Fender (&) Shovel Tongs & Poker & Bellows . . . 3 flat Irons . . . a Jack compleat with Lead Weight . . . 2 standing Spitt Racks and three Spitts . . . a Gridiron and two Trivetts . . . 8 Brass Candlesticks . . . 2 Coffee Pots . . . a Drudger and 2 Pepper Boxes . . . a Copper grater . . . a Warming Pann . . . a Copper Drinking Pott . . . a Fish Kettle Compleat . . . 2 Stue pans and Covers . . . 2 Frying Panns . . . 5 Saucepans and 3 Covers . . . a Copper water Candlestick . . . 12 Pewter Dishes and 24 Plates . . . a tea Kittle . . . a Coffee Mill . . . 2 Wainst (oak) tables . . . 5 Old Chairs . . . a plate rack . . . a chopping Board . . . a Spice Drawer . . . a Box wth 12 Knives and 12 Forks . . . 4 Glass Salts and Mustard Glass . . . 2 Coal Boxes . . . a Meat Screen & a Cleaver'. In Handel's house, the 'Back Kitchen' and the 'Area' and 'Vault' beneath the pavement contained items that were probably located in the scullery wing of Pallant House. These included: 'a Stove . . . a Copper Fixed & iron work [a copper tub heated by a fire in which fabric could be boiled and cleaned] . . . 2 Forms and 5 Washing tubbs . . . A Cloaths horse & horse to Dust cloaths on . . . a Large Lead Cistern & Brass Cock & beer Stylion.'

21. A pamphlet entitled 'Pallant House Chichester', seemingly published in 1996 and with the author uncredited, calls the room Mrs Peckham's 'Parlour Chamber'.

22. The 'Pallant House Chichester' pamphlet, which calls the smaller of the first-floor front rooms (that to the north-west) a 'study/sitting room', does

not offer evidence to support this use. However, it does persist, without explaining why, that the room was 'clearly not designed as a bedroom'.

23. For the term 'pig', see, for example, C. M. Westmacott, *Mammon in London, or, The Spy of the Day* (London, 1823): 'You'll see wives and their sisters pigging together with the same man . . . and lighting each other to the same bed'. i, p. 314); And *An Open Elite? England 1540–1880*, ed. Lawrence Stone and Jeanne C. Fawtier Stone (Oxford: Clarendon Press, 1984).

24. This room has, according to the 'Pallant House Chichester' pamphlet and to the 1905 survey of the house, been much altered, with areas of panelling removed, obscured and replaced. Rather dramatically, the 1993 publication *Pallant House: Its Architecture, History and Owners* states unequivocally that this 'bedroom was originally plastered and decorated with wallpaper' and that the 'present panelling dates from 1780' (p. 14). No evidence is offered for this rather startling statement, and no explanation why, in 1780, when timber panelling was out of fashion, this room would have been panelled in the style of *c.*1712.

25. Now, with panelling removed and details that date from the late eighteenth or early nineteenth century.

26. It is worth noting that the 1905 survey of the house suggests there was no door connecting the anteroom and the first-floor chamber to its south. But the existing panelling and related joinery around this door, which is now open, suggests very convincingly that it is original and was merely sealed when the 1905 survey was undertaken.

27. Perhaps more in the way of baroque planning was attempted originally, but the early nineteenth-century remodelling of the south pair of ground-floor rooms – arguably the house's main reception rooms – makes the original intention here impossible to discern. However, there appears to have been a wide opening (now filled) between the corresponding rooms above, where there is evidence that part of the brick wall between these rooms is earlier than the construction of Pallant House. There could have been a similar arrangement in the ground-floor pair of south rooms, but the resolve to incorporate elements from an earlier structure on the site might, to a degree, have inhibited baroque spatial gymnastics.

28. The cornice in the hall is most peculiar. It is placed on a fascia board framed by staff beads (a standard hall detail; see, for example, the hall of the Minister's House, Christ Church, Spitalfields. London designed in *c.*1726–1730 by Nicholas Hawksmoor's office) and comprises a deep cyma recta topped by a smaller cyma reversa. All pretty standard for 1712, but between the two is a fillet embellished with a series of small spheres. This is most unusual and reminiscent of the sort of abstracted

and idiosyncratic classical language devised by Sir John Soane from the very late eighteenth century. Presumably this cornice is, in its current form, the consequence of a late eighteenth- or early nineteenth-century alteration. If not (and details on the adjoining staircase suggest the detail might date from *c.*1712), then its designer was, in 1712, a most interesting man indeed who had studied some very exotic references.

29. No doubt this room correctly is, as termed in the 1996 pamphlet, the 'dining room'. The buffet arch to the south does not now contain a door, or a serving hatch as shown on the 1905 survey. It is possible that there was originally a door or serving hatch, and if there was a door it was probably a jib door, so, when closed, would have been flush with the wall within the buffet arch and not easy to see from within the dining room.

30. The panels framed by the bolection mouldings are flat, not raised and fielded as on the first-floor screen and anteroom.

31. On the top of the roof was a terrace or walk – a fashionable feature in the late seventeenth century (indeed, the houses on the east side of Soho Square, well known to Mrs Peckham, possessed such an agreeable attribute). The roof-walk, with its balustraded edge, is shown in the image of Pallant House included in Samuel and Nathaniel Buck's 1738 *Prospect* of Chichester. This view also shows a staircase tower much as the existing one, although the balustrade has gone. From this rooftop terrace Mr Peckham could have enjoyed a fine view of Chichester's harbour, where his merchandise would have been delivered.

32. *Letters to His Son by the Earl of Chesterfield on the Fine Art of Becoming a Man of the World and a Gentleman* (1748).

33. The one significant alteration to its layout was undertaken in the early to mid nineteenth century when, as mentioned earlier, the ground-floor rooms on the house's south side were radically redecorated.

2. A HOME FOR IMMIGRANTS

19 Princelet Street, Spitalfields (1718)

1. See *Survey of London*, vol. 27, *Spitalfields and Mile End New Town* (London: Athlone Press, 1957), pp. 187–9.

2. The Wood-Michell estate was bounded to the north by the existing thoroughfares of Brown's Lane (now Hanbury Street) and to the east by Brick Lane and a small freehold estate developed by the brewer Joseph Truman. The Wood-Michell estate stretched south to encompass the south side of what became Church Street (now Fournier Street), and to the west to

Red Lion Street, which in the mid nineteenth century was widened and lengthened to become Commercial Street.

3. Worrall lived in a detached house adjoining his building yard set between Princelet Street and Fournier Street. Smith and Tayler lived in palatial houses – in a sense, show houses – of 1725 on Fournier Street, now numbered 4/6 and 14 respectively. Worrall's house, built in 1722, is numbered 18 Princelet Street.

4. Similar examples of the top-floor arrangement suggested by 19 Princelet Street survive in Spitalfields. For example, in 6 Wilkes Street, built as a speculation on the same estate by Samuel Worrall and only a few years later in date than 19 Princelet Street, there is a small top-floor room, located at one end of the one-room-deep house, that is provided with a large mullioned window with leaded lights. This is positioned in the rear slope of the roof and allows morning light to flood into the room. The front slope is lit by dormers. In 1724, the year this Wilkes Street house was completed, Worrall assigned the lease to a glover, who perhaps used the top, well-lit room for work purposes (*Survey of London*, vol. 27, p. 185). The adjoining number 2 Princelet Street, also built by Worrall in 1723/4, was occupied from 1728 by Anna Maria Garthwaite, a key figure in the Spitalfields silk industry, who no doubt used the top floor of her house as a studio.

5. The beams are each 11½ inches wide and 8 inches deep and are separated from each other at the centre of the house by about six feet. Joists run between beams and from the beams to the front and rear walls. The six-feet area in the centre of the house is, with its short-length joists, particularly stable and it is upon this strong footing that the timber partitions separating front and rear rooms are placed. The solidity of the floors suggest that Worrall wanted to ensure that the partitions between back and front remained non-structural and so could be as slight as possible and pierced by door openings. From the beams in the rear rooms larger joists, or stringers, roughly 2½ inches wide, run to the rear wall. These, with the beams, define the volume within which the staircase rises.

6. The most obvious external clue is the pier separating the front facades of numbers 19 and 21. It is only a brick and a half wide – so around thirteen inches. There is simply not space for a party wall, as simple external and internal observation makes clear.

7. A similar scheme was found on plank-and-muntin panelling on the ground floor and staircase compartment of 17 Elder Street, of 1727.

8. *Survey of London*, vol. 27, p.188. Samuel C. Melnick, in *A Giant Among Giants: A History of Rabbi Shmuel Kalman Melnick and the Princelet Street*

Synagogue (Edinburgh: Pentland Press, 1994), p. 36, asserts that the 'nee-dleworker' was in fact John Nevill, who in 1722 bought the freeholds of 19 Princelet Street and the abutting 30 Hanbury Street (also built by Worrall) for £270. Unfortunately Melnick offers no evidence to support this claim.

9. *The Victoria History of the County of Middlesex*, vol. 2, *General*, ed. William Page (London: Constable, 1911), pp. 132–7.

10. Overall, between about 1670, when the level of persecution started to rise significantly, and 1710 it has been estimated that around 50,000 to 80,000 Huguenots fled France, more than half of them coming to England. Some current estimates suggest that more than 50,000 settled in the British Isles (information from Tessa Murdoch, chair in 2023 of the Huguenot Society). Of these, more settled in London than in all other British locations combined. Of the capital's population of around 575,000 in 1700, Huguenots may well have formed at least 5 per cent; see Robin Gwynn, 'The Number of Huguenot Immigrants in the Late 17th Century', *Journal of Historical Geography*, vol. 9, no. 4 (1983), 384–98.

11. Other Huguenot refugees were attracted to the area near the French church in the Savoy, off the Strand, and so contributed to Soho's rapid and large-scale expansion and development in the 1680s and 1690s, when it became the focus of the Huguenot precious metals industry.

12. In 1675 Joseph Trevers in his *Essay to the Restoring of Our Decayed Trade* estimated that there was then, 'in and about the City of London', 'an hundred thousand people small and great' who 'depend upon' the silk trade, (pp. 36–7), but this is almost certainly a great exaggeration. There was evidently confusion among contemporary observers, who were not sure how to calculate the number of tradesmen in London. In 1705 Daniel Defoe estimated that in 1679, just before the arrival of Huguenots in significant numbers, there were 50,000 silk-ribbon weavers in London, and even this number is probably an exaggeration. Puzzlingly, in 1722, when writing his *Journal of the Plague Year*, Defoe took Trevers' number and claimed that in 1665 there were a 'hundred thousand riband-weavers' in London, 'the chiefest number of whom lived ... about Spitalfields'. Other estimates suggest that, more realistically, by 1661 there were around 40,000 silk weavers in London.

13. Trevers, *An Essay to the Restoring of Our Decayed Trade*, pp. 36–7; M. Dorothy George, *London Life in the Eighteenth Century* (Harmond-sworth: Penguin, 1978), p.178; Norman G. Brett-James, *The Growth of Stuart London* (London: George Allen & Unwin, 1935), p. 490.

14. Robin Gwynn, an acknowledged authority on the Huguenots in England, suggests that this indicates 'a genuine generosity of heart' on the king's part, and goes on to say: 'In 1666, even as he was declaring war on France, Charles chose to welcome French Protestants into his country. And when the *dragonnades* began in 1681, he acted with speed and decisiveness in offering the Huguenots both a home and significant privileges, so that those who came to British shores were well treated for the four years before his death in 1685'; see Robin Gwynn, *Huguenot Heritage: The History and Contribution of Huguenots in Britain* (Brighton: Sussex Academic Press, 2001), p. 166. The king also, perhaps, perceived that the arrival of the Huguenots offered economic benefits that outweighed possible political disadvantages and domestic difficulties.

15. Funded by a national tax on coal, these new places of worship would, it was hoped, serve as visually dominant religious statements in newly developed areas of the city or ones with large Dissenting populations.

16. As Catherine Swindlehurst points out, 'France and the French silk industry were both the nemesis and the spur towards development of the English silk weaving trade in the late 17th century. For many London weavers, the French trade was something to be both revered and copied, as well as to be scorned and protected against'; see "An Unruly and Presumptuous Rabble": The Reaction of the Spitalfields Weaving Community to the Settlement of the Huguenots, 1660-90', in *From Strangers to Citizens: The Integration of Immigrant Communities in Britain, Ireland and Colonial America, 1550-1750*, ed. Randolph Vigne and Charles Littleton (Brighton: Sussex Academic Press, 2001), p. 368. Despite the perceived cruelty and intolerance of its Catholic king, France was also, paradoxically, admired for its economic success and as a centre of taste and fashion. So the establishment of French tradesmen, enterprise and taste in England promised the potential of successful competition with France in the production of luxury goods. The long-established Weavers' Company, which took the view that the arrival of the French represented, on balance, an opportunity for creative cooperation and self-improvement rather than a commercial threat, won a royal charter in October 1685 that gave it authority 'over all persons practicing the art of weaving within the Cities of London and Westminster, the Borough of Southwark, and all other places within twenty miles distant'; see Alfred Plummer, *The London Weavers' Company, 1600-1970* (1972; Oxford: Routledge, 2006), p. 461. In *From Strangers to Citizens*, p. 370, Swindlehurst observes of the Weavers' Company: 'as the 17th century progressed [it] became less able to deal effectively with the weavers' concerns; especially as the Huguenots tended

to settle in areas like Spitalfields, which were beyond the legal jurisdiction of the Weavers' Company.' She is referring to the situation in 1683 and presumably it was to resolve this that the 1685 charter was granted. This, potentially, gave the company the power to reconcile Huguenot and English weavers, within Spitalfields and adjoining areas, to their mutual benefit.

17. Daniel Defoe, *A Brief State of the Question Between the Printed and Painted Callicoes and the Woollen and Silk Manufacture, as Far as It Relates to the Wearing and Using of Printed and Painted Callicoes in Great Britain* (London, 1719), p. 5.

18. John Strype, *Survey of the Cities of London and Westminster* (London, 1720), vol. 2, Book Four, p. 48, includes a map of 'Spittle Fields and Places Adjacent'.

19. La Patente Huguenot chapel was founded in Crispin Street in 1688; the congregation moved to Paternoster Row by 1707, had moved to a different building in Crispin Street by 1716, and then from 1740 until 1786 had relocated to a building in Hanbury Street (formerly Brown's Lane) that had been built in about 1719.

20. *Publications of the Huguenot Society of London*, vol. 11 (1898), p. iii; *The Victoria History of the County of Middlesex*, vol. 2, *General*, pp. 132–7; *Survey of London*, vol. 27, p. 143.

21. See Anne J. Kershen, *Strangers, Aliens and Asians: Huguenots, Jews and Bangladeshis in Spitalfields, 1660–2000* (London: Routledge, 2005), p. 171; and M. Weber, *The Protestant Work Ethic and the Spirit of Capitalism* (London: Unwin, 1938).

22. The Ogier genealogy, from Pierre and Jeanne to William born in 1812, is published as figure 8.4 on p. 127 in *The Spitalfields Project*, vol. 2, *The Anthropology, The Middling Sort*, by Theya Molleson and Margaret Cox with A. H. Waldron and D. K. Whitaker (York: Council for British Archaeology, 1993).

23. It was essential for him to become a freeman of the City of London and thus eligible to practise his trade within the City and deal with City-based businesses. See *Extracts from the Court Book of the Weavers' Company of London, 1610–1730*, ed. William Chapman Waller (Huguenot Society of London, 1931), vol. 32, p. 77.

24. 'The Spitalfields Manufacturers and the Young Pretender', *Proceedings of the Huguenot Society of London*, vol. 2 (1887–8), pp. 453–6; *London Gazette*, 5 October 1745.

25. In 1743 and 1750 the house is recorded as being in Ogier's occupation (Land Tax returns for the Parish of Christ Church, Middlesex, London

Archives, CLC/525/MS06008/001-2 [736/8]); Dan Cruickshank, *Spital-fields: The History of a Nation in a Handful of Streets* (London: Random House, 2016), p. 342; *Survey of London*, vol. 27, p. 188).

26. John Ogier married Louise Françoise Maillard in 1719 and died in 1777; see *The Spitalfields Project*, vol. 2, fig. 8.4, p. 127.

27. Natalie Rothstein, 'Huguenot Master Weavers: Exemplary Englishmen 1700–c.1750', in *From Strangers to Citizens*, p. 167.

28. National Archives, PROB.11/649 sig. 5.

29. At the time of the 1743 Land Tax returns for Christ Church, Middlesex (London Archives, CLC/525/ /MS06008/001-2 [736/8]; see also *Survey of London*, vol. 27, p. 188). The assessors, of whom one was Samuel Worrall, who himself lived in a house in the large yard between Fournier (Church) Street and Princelet (Princes) Street, noted eleven neighbours for Peter Abraham on the north side of Princelet Street. They were clearly well-to-do: annual tax valuations of their houses range mostly from £9 to £14, with one as high £20, suggesting that in some cases named occupants might well have been in possession of two houses. Ogier himself was assessed to be liable for the average tax of £14. The returns also make it clear that he was, in addition, the occupant of a house in Hanbury Street. It was probably the one backing on to his Princelet Street house. The 1719 conveyance of 19 Princelet Street to Worrall included 30 Hanbury Street, which Worrall had also built. Presumably the joint ownership of these houses continued into Ogier's time (*Survey of London*, vol. 27, p. 188). Most of the names listed in the returns are French, as one might expect given the period and the location. So, for example, what is now 1 Prince-let Street – on the corner with Wilkes Street – was occupied by John 'Bellynew'. Other residents included Sam Delors, John Baptiste Bowe, Daniel Pilon and Rene Turguan.

30. Dan Cruickshank and Neil Burton, *Life in the Georgian City* (Harmond-sworth: Viking, 1990), pp. 180–9.

31. Paint analysis thanks to James Howett.

32. Larger gardens are one of the distinctive features of the houses on the north side of Princelet Street and the houses on Fournier Street.

33. Jonathan Swift, 'A Panegyric on the Reverend Dean Swift' (1729–30).

34. Probably he died in 19 Princelet Street, but it is not currently known where he and his wife, Esther, are buried. Huguenot temples generally did not possess burial grounds or vaults; Huguenot families were happy to make use of the facilities offered by their Protestant parish churches. Consequently, members of the family were either interred in the vault within Christ Church or, more probably, in its churchyard – including

their daughter Mary (1734–8) and another daughter, Esther (1723–1803), who specifically asked in her will to be buried at Christ Church 'in the best ground'. Parts of the vault were 'public', where bodies were placed at the discretion of the sexton. But other parts were 'private' and used by the rich of the parish, who were happy to pay a rent to secure an exclusive resting place for family members until the trumpet sounded at the end of days. When the vaults were emptied in 1984–6, no traces of Peter Abraham or his wife, Esther, were discovered. It seems most likely that they found their final resting place somewhere in the churchyard, where they almost certainly remain in graves that have long been unmarked following removal of headstones and altar tombs from the 1850s.

35. *The Spitalfields Project*, vol. 2, pp. 98 and 127, figure 8.4 showing the genealogy of the Ogier family.

36. Her bones resided for some time in the Natural History Museum, under the catalogue number 2309.

37. *Survey of London*, vol. 27, p. 188.

38. *Household Words*, 5 April 1851.

39. National Archives, HO 107/1542, district 12.

40. Interestingly, one of the historians of 19 Princelet Street, Samuel Melnick, comes up with an additional set of names of occupants. His suggestion is that from sometime after 1826 until 1847 the house was occupied by Alfred Lavey, a professor of music, from 1851 until 1857 by a wholesaler of pickle and sauce named Lewis Abrahams, and then, in turn until 1864, by Mary Ellen Hawkins, who ran an industrial school in the house, and by Isaiah Woodcock, a carver and gilder, and finally until 1869 by an engineer named George Flint; see Melnick, *A Giant Among Giants*, p. 37. These occupants could have been missed by composers of census returns or were in occupation during the decades between census compilations.

41. The building was occupied by the Loyal United Friends Friendly Society, and the founding group was led by Jacob Davidson, a bootmaker, who lived and worked in what was then numbered 15–16 Princes Street and included Coleman Angel and Harris Levy. A. Heiser was employed as secretary. The story of the synagogue is told in great detail by Samuel C. Melnick in his lecture 'The Princelet Street Synagogue in Victorian Times', delivered in 1988 to the East London History Society. A faintly typed transcript resides in the Tower Hamlets Local History Library and Archives in Bancroft Road, London, E1, filed under 'W/PRI/8/12'; see p. 4. The story is also told, at greater length, by Melnick in *A Giant Among Giants*.

42. Melnick transcript, p. 2.

43. Melnick transcript. The extended text in Melnick's *A Giant Among Giants* tells the story of Rabbi Shmuel Kalman Melnick, who was involved with number 19 from 1896 until 1920 (see pp. 8 and 22). Melnick's writings are crucial to the reconstruction of the nineteenth-century history of 19 Princelet Street because he appears to have had access to original documents that are now missing, although not many are specified in detail. In his 1988 lecture, Melnick refers to his sources, including 'a number of account books' in the Museum of London and 'two minute books elsewhere'. A librarian has added a handwritten note to the lecture transcript confirming that in the late 1980s the minute books were 'in private hands, whereabouts not known'. They have now been located. In 2014 the daughter of Bernard Reback and granddaughter of Myer Reback – both of whom had served as shammas (beadle) to the synagogue – donated the two books, covering the period from 2 June 1874 to 16 June 1907, to the Jewish Museum in London. They are catalogued 2014.7.1 and 2014. 7.2.

44. Melnick transcript, p. 2 The physical evidence generally supports this chronology and account of the formation of the synagogue, so it would appear to be accurate, although no documentary evidence is offered. The robustly built retaining walls in the basement, which resist the lateral thrust of the earth from the adjoining gardens, were constructed with pale red and dark yellow bricks that look as if they date from the late 1860s, although many may be salvage and thus far older.

45. Melnick transcript, p. 2. All this information is delivered without documentation and was presumably largely extracted from obscure 'newspapers reports and advertisements' in which, Melnick admits, he was obliged to place 'great reliance'. Cross-checks and observation support Melnick's account. There was indeed a local architect named John Hudson, who was responsible a few years later (1878) for rebuilding the Wycliffe Chapel Charity School in Whitechapel (*Survey of London*, vols. 54 and 55, *Whitechapel*, ed. Peter Guillery (London: Yale University Press, 2022). vol. 55, p. 567.

46. The 1870 date makes the synagogue, according to Melnick, 'the first purpose-built of the so-called minor synagogues in London'. It is also, he points out, 'the third oldest synagogue building still surviving in London' (Melnick transcript, p. 2). The consecration service was conducted by the Rev. Aeron Barnett and Rabbi Bernard Spiers and from the start the synagogue employed a paid reader, initially the Rev. Barnett. The synagogue's 'Society for Chanting Psalms & Visiting the Sick' (Chevra Tehillim u'mishmorim) was the first such society to be founded in England. Isaac Kaliski was secretary of this society and a similar society

in Old Castle Street (see Tower Hamlets Local History Library and Archives, TH/8262/139.1-2). The term 'minor' is a reference to the Federation of Minor Synagogues, founded in 1887. Its specific aim was to focus on assisting poor synagogues in east London. By contrast, the United Synagogue founded in 1870 by Act of Parliament acted for all Orthodox synagogues, with its founder, Nathan Marcus Adler, bearing the title of Chief Rabbi of the British Empire; he was succeeded on his death in 1890 by his son Hermann Adler, who was a prominent figure in the story of 19 Princelet Street.

47. Melnick transcript, p. 5.
48. Melnick transcript, p. 5.
49. Melnick transcript, p. 7.
50. Melnick, *A Giant Among Giants*, pp. 73–4.
51. Tower Hamlets Local History Library and Archives, W/PRI/3/2.
52. As for the business of finance and funds, the pamphlet announced that the 'proposed alteration' would cost 'about £500', which was presumably in addition to the £200 already borrowed from the Friendly Society. The Federation of Synagogues helped with a loan of £100 in the form of a mortgage repayable at £10 per annum, and since the synagogue's 'Committee find themselves unable to carry out the necessary improvements unaided', donations were invited.
53. The pamphlet recording the reopening is among the records relating to 19 Princelet Street in the Tower Hamlets Local History Library and Archives.
54. Solomon became architect to United Synagogues, and in 1908, as Honorary Architect of the Federation of Synagogues, he converted the Wycliffe Chapel, consecrated as the Philpot Street Great Synagogue, to form a new home for the Shalom veEmeth ('Peace and Truth') congregation. Additional works for the federation include the design in 1921 of the Congregation of Jacob Synagogue on Commercial Street, Whitechapel, and in 1923 the East London Central Synagogue on Nelson Street, Whitechapel. By the time these synagogues were built, Solomon was working with his architect son, named Digby Lewis Solomon in honour of his father's old master, and together they created synagogues for Orthodox congregations that are classical in design, with the neo-Georgian Nelson Street synagogue possessing a particularly richly detailed interior. Both these synagogues still function – despite the almost complete exodus since the late 1960s of their congregations. Lewis Solomon died in 1926. See *Survey of London*, vol. 27, pp. 188–9; *Jewish Chronicle*, 18 September 1908; 29 June 1923;

1 January 1943; with additional information from Sharman Kadish, *Jewish Heritage in Britain and Ireland* (London: Yale University Press, 2011); 2nd edn (London: Historic England, 2015); and records at Tower Hamlets Local History Library and Archives, W/PRI; Melnick, *A Giant Among Giants*, p. 131.

55. Rachel Lichtenstein, draft publication 'Strategic Vision for a Jewish Quarter in East London', written in 2019 and read in private correspondence, pp. 7–8.

56. Melnick transcript, p. 7. This event surely led to the improved access to the synagogue erected in 1892.

57. LSE, B351, pp. 124–5.

58. Census return RG12/273, district 4.

59. The building still exists, but since the early 1980s has functioned as a mosque serving the Bangladeshi community.

60. Pamphlet in possession of the Spitalfields Historic Buildings Trust and Tower Hamlets Local History Library and Archives.

61. Melnick, *A Giant Among Giants*, p.109.

62. See Rachel Lichtenstein and Iain Sinclair, *Rodinsky's Room* (London: Granta Books, 1999).

63. Melnick, *A Giant Among Giants,* p. 109.

64. Despite being long abandoned and partly ruinous, the building had to be safeguarded because it was listed by the government as being of architectural and historic interest and stood at the heart of the Spitalfields prime conservation area that from the late 1970s had become the focus for numerous groups campaigning to save the buildings and life of the area. The Federation of Synagogues took responsibility for what was clearly a liability, hence the sale to the Spitalfields Historic Buildings Trust, which had been founded only in 1977 but, operating as a revolving fund favouring direct action, had already by 1980 acquired, successfully repaired and sold several important early eighteenth-century houses in Spitalfields to form new private homes; see *A Giant Among Giants,* p. 109.

65. The author is a founding member of the Spitalfields Trust and one of its first trustees to enter the building in 1980, so much here is personal memory.

66. The many books that remained were boxed up and removed, initially in collaboration with the Museum of London, and after remaining safe but virtually untouched in storage for over forty years, the opening of the boxes, by archivists from Tower Hamlets Local History Library and Rachel Lichtenstein, utilising charitable funds, commenced just before Christmas 2024, and their secrets were slowly revealed. What is striking,

as Lichtenstein points out, is the international nature of this small synagogue – with books coming from many different countries – making it clear that the congregation was, in its way, at the heart of an almost boundless world of Jewish faith, drawing for inspiration from Ashkenazi Jewish communities across central and Eastern Europe. Over 500 books have now been moved to the library.

67. Information given to the author by Heisar's descendant David Lewis.

68. Copy of pamphlet 'Rules and List of Officers for 1893 – 5653' with the Spitalfields Historic Buildings Trust and Tower Hamlets Local History Library and Archives.

69. Information given to the author partly by Baruch Baigel, descendant of Rabbi Schwartz.

70. The Machzike Hadath and the synagogue in 19 Princelet Street were evidently affiliated – an ancient photograph of Rabbi Werner, Rabbi of Machzike Hadath until his death in 1912, still adorns a wall in 19 Princelet Street. There was a strong network of connections linking 19 Princelet Street with most, if not all, of the Ashkenazi synagogues in the streets of Spitalfields, notably with those in Booth Street and Wilkes Street. Rabbi Kook and Rabbi Schwartz had probably met soon after Kook's arrival in London's East End, and they appear to have been close. This seems to be confirmed by their surviving letters. In one, hand-written in Hebrew and dated 7 August 1919 on paper headed 9 Princelet Street, Kook commends Schwartz's attributes and scholarship. It is essentially a reference, perhaps for a post in the synagogue at 19 Princelet Street. The letter reads, in part: 'I have been well acquainted with my honorable friend, the great, God-fearing teacher and rabbi, Rabbi Chaim Aharon Schwartz . . . since living here. And I have had numerous pleasant encounters with him discussing various areas of Jewish law in the Torah and teachings, including relating to fables and the fear of God, and I found him to be full of expertise in practical Jewish law, as one of the prominent and highly respected rabbis in Israel. He is an expert in the Torah text, with the ordination of the greatest scholars of the generation [and] I, too, add my humble priestly blessing for the aforementioned dear rabbi and scholar, may he continue to succeed . . .' (information given to the author by Rabbi Schwartz's descendant Baruch Baigel).

71. Genesis 12:1; 12:7; 15:18–21; Deuteronomy 7:6.

72. Melnick, *A Giant Among Giants*, p. 100.

73. His funeral in Jerusalem is said to have been attended by 20,000 mourners.

74. Information given to the author by Baruch Baigel.

75. Originally this would have been served by a spigot connected to a large lead cistern, no doubt with an ornamental front and located near the sink (sadly no trace remains).

76. For example, cast-iron columns of barley-twist form survive in the 1850s auditorium of Wilton's Music Hall located nearby, off Cable Street.

77. Melnick, *A Giant Among Giants*, p. 38.

78. His book contains a useful cross-section diagram of the building.

79. This door leading to the front room is slightly smaller than the other door and must be a later insertion. Certainly a top rail is absent, and the panel above the door is in fact a painted pane of glass. Its purpose is confirmed by the floor of the front room, beyond the door. It retains evidence of a now-removed partition forming a narrow corridor leading from the smaller door to one of the windows. Missing floorboards in front of the window reveal the corridor once led to a lavatory that must have damaged the boards in which it was placed. This speculation is confirmed by a lead and iron soil pipe that survives below, partly secreted in a recess next to the front door. This arrangement must date from the later nineteenth century when the house was divided and in multiple occupation and mixed use.

80. Mezuzah, the Hebrew for 'doorpost', relates to an ancient Jewish religious ritual that praises God and aims to protect the home and its inhabitants from evil and from danger. In part it is connected with Passover, also known as Pesach, when Moses, relaying God's instructions, told Jewish families in Egypt to mark their homes with lamb's blood so that the 'Angel of Death', directed by God, would pass over their homes when punishing the Egyptians – the Jews' oppressors – with the last of the ten plagues. The aim of the plagues was to force the Egyptians to release the Jews from bondage, and the final 'plague' was the most fearful: the killing of all first-born children. The first prayer on the mezuzah scroll is from the Book of Deuteronomy, 6:4–9: 'Hear, O Israel: The Lord our God is one Lord: And thou shalt love the Lord thy God with all thine heart, and with all thy soul, and with all thy might. And these words which I command thee this day, shall be in thine heart . . . And thou shalt bind them for a sign upon thine hand . . . And though shalt write them upon the posts of thy house, and on thy gates.' The second prayer is from 11:13–21 and promises abundance and fruitfulness to the faithful and obedient and dire punishment to those who 'turn aside, and serve other gods'. The Scripture instructs that this command is to be written 'upon the door posts of thine house'.

81. Well over 30 per cent of the city – around 60,000 people – were Jewish, with the Jewish population nationwide being around 240,000.

82. Soon after acquisition the Spitalfields Trust leased the building to another trust to transform it into a 'heritage centre' and place of meeting for the diverse communities of Spitalfields. This trust became moribund, and in early 2024 the Spitalfields Trust regained possession. The plan now – in 2025 – is to complete repairs, to restore nothing that has been lost, and to open the building to the public not as a museum but as a place of reflection that will chart the histories and experiences of the diverse immigrants that have – from the late seventeenth century – made Spitalfields their home. The Bengali community – which settled in Spitalfields in large numbers before and after December 1971 when the new nation of Bangladeshi arose to replace the state of East Pakistan – has no direct or major historical associations with 19 Princelet Street. Yet the Bangladeshi community plays a vital role in the story the building seeks to tell, because it does much to form the context within which number 19 exists, and is the latest of the significant and culturally rich waves of immigrants that have done much to give Spitalfields its very distinct and diverse character.

3. A HOUSE BUILT BY CONNOISSEURS

Maister House, Hull (1743–c.1760)

1. The Minster is also one of the first British buildings since Roman times to use a substantial amount of brick in its construction.

2. A small portion of Crowle House at 41 High Street, dated 1664, also still survives. Losses include 196 High Street (the battered remains of the once richly decorated mid eighteenth-century Travis House) and 200 to 203 High Street (in the portion of the street known as Dock Office Row), with numbers 200 to 203 forming a three-storey and stately terrace, with fine exterior brick detailing and the remains of high-quality panelled interiors. These houses probably dated from the 1730s. Ivan and Elizabeth Hall suggest c.1756–7 but this is almost certainly too late; see their *Georgian Hull* (York: William Sessions, 1978), p. 68. Numbers 200 to 203 High Street sported a number of early eighteenth-century details, including keystones to windows and timber eaves cornices, which it is difficult to dismiss as mere expressions of a provincial lag behind high fashion. Undoubtedly these details remained in use in mid eighteenth-century Hull, forming part of its well-established vernacular classical tradition; but in Hull in the 1740s and 1750s a number of houses were

designed that were at the cutting edge of fashion and metropolitan in their aspirations – Maister House being the major surviving example. Of this characterful High Street group, the seven-window-wide number 202 alone survives, but only as a facade over a largely new interior. There is an additional, comparable, surviving group: numbers 23 to 24 High Street, dated 1751 and abutting Wilberforce House. These have keystone embellished windows like 200 to 203 and form a united six-window-wide composition, with front doors grouped below a wide and eruditely composed Ionic pediment.

3. The exact construction date for Blaydes House is a matter of debate. The Halls suggest *c.*1760 in their *Georgian Hull*, p. 60, but elements could date from *c.*1735 with many probably dating from *c.*1740. It is of solid if slightly provincial Palladian design, with its ground-floor corner quoins being a Palladio motif popularised by William Kent. The designer for the 1760s work was probably Joseph Page, also involved with Maister House. Joseph Pease was one of the wealthiest of Hull's merchants in the first half of the eighteenth century, the town's first banker and a pioneering industrialist, and his mansion stood at 18 High Street. But it was demolished soon after the Second World War, largely unrecorded. A similar relationship between house and riverside warehouse was found behind 23 and 24 High Street and the adjoining Wilberforce House, where warehouses and wharfs rose next to the riverbank.

4. Hull University Archives, Hull History Centre, GB 50 U DP/82.

5. The Maisters' trading partners included several women: Sarah Virtue, Mary Hurst and Jane Stephenson.

6. Gordon Jackson, *Hull in the Eighteenth Century: A Study in Economic and Social History* (Oxford University Press for University of Hull Publications, 1972), pp. 110, 113, 148–9; the Maisters owned Partington Manor until 1829 as part of their Winestead Old Hall estate.

7. Jennifer C. Rowley, *The House of Maister* (North Humberside: Hedon and District Local History Society, 1982), p. 6; M. Edward Ingram, *The Maisters of Kingston upon Hull 1560–1840* (Todmorden, Lancs.: privately printed, 1983), pp. 32, 36–8.

8. Information regarding Lord Burlington's extensive Hull connections thanks to David Neave. And see David Neave, 'Musgrove, Lord Burlington and the Building of Maister House, Hull', *Georgian East Yorkshire: Journal of the Georgian Society for East Yorkshire*, vol. 3 (2025), pp. 4–13.

9. Dan Cruickshank, 'An English Reason', *Architectural Review* (April 1983), 49–58.

10. Howard Colvin, *A Biographical Dictionary of British Architects, 1600–1840*, 2nd edn (London: John Murray, 1978), p. 128.

11. Wisdom of Solomon, 11:20, included among Protestant Apocrypha. The historian Rudolf Wittkower explains the importance of this passage in sixteenth-century architectural thinking.

12. Rudolf Wittkower, *Palladio and English Palladianism* (London: Thames and Hudson, 1983), p. 197.

13. Leon Battista Alberti: *On the Art of Building in Ten Books*, trans. Joseph Rykwert with Neil Leach and Robert Tavernor (Cambridge, MA: MIT Books, 1988), Book IX, Chapter 5, p. 305.

14. Alberti, *On the Art of Building*, p. 303.

15. Bruce Boucher, *Andrea Palladio: The Architect in His Time* (New York: Abbeville Press, 1984, p. 239.

16. Only the gateway and piers survive to commemorate the creative union of these men.

17. Robert Morris, *Essay in Defence of Ancient Architecture* (London, 1728), pp. 68–9.

18. Robert Morris, *Lectures on Architecture, Consisting of Rules Founded upon Harmonick and Arithmetical Proportions in Building* (1734), Preface and Lecture V, p. 74.

19. A local architect named Ralph Tunnicliffe had initially been engaged in the very early 1730s by Malton, but following consultation with Burlington in *c.*1734 and Tunnicliffe's death in 1736, Burlington's London-based protégé Henry Flitcroft was brought in to finalise the design and oversee construction. The Tunnicliffe–Flitcroft design takes the form of a pedimented and porticoed cubic centre flanked by lower wings that are in turn flanked by yet lower wings that terminate with towers of double-cube volume topped with tall lanterns. The design of the elevation is broadly inspired by Colen Campbell's third theoretical design for Wanstead House, published in 1725 in volume three of *Vitruvius Britannicus*. Thomas Watson-Wentworth, who had inherited the house and land in 1723, served as a Whig MP until 1728, when he was raised to the peerage as Baron Malton. In 1734 he became the Earl of Malton and in 1746 the Marquess of Rockingham.

20. Ingram, *The Maisters of Kingston upon Hull*, p. 41.

21. Information given to the author by David Neave; and see Neave, *Georgian East Yorkshire*, p. 9; and Chatsworth MSS, Venison accounts 1733–93, Devonshire Collection Archives, Chatsworth.

22. Information given to the author by David Neave.

23. Significantly, the subscribers to Gibbs's book included George Crowle, while Cuthbert Constable of Burton Constable Hall, just outside Hull, subscribed to Kent's *Inigo Jones*.

24. All Nathaniel Maister's letters to Henry are in a folder catalogued 'U DAS/26/2' in the Hull History Centre. Joseph Page was born in Barton-upon-Humber in 1716, apprenticed in Hull in 1733 as a bricklayer, by 1740 was a freeman and by 1743 had become an expert stuccadore, which is not surprising given that in the East Riding of Yorkshire bricklaying and plastering were synonymous trades (Ingram, *The Maisters of Kingston upon Hull*, pp. 44–5). He has long been credited as the architect of Maister House, but as David Neave, the authority on the architecture of Hull and the East Rising and currently working on a monograph on Hull's High Street, says: 'There is no evidence that Page designed Maister House. I am sure that he was just responsible for the plasterwork . . . I suspect the carcass of the house could have been the work of the builder Samuel Spencer, with Burlington and perhaps William Kent involved with the interior' (in conversation with the author). It is also worth pointing out that Rupert Alec-Smith, in his excellent *National Trust Guide to Maister House* (undated but probably 1968), does not attribute the design of the house to Page, while Ingram states categorically that Page has been 'incorrectly described as the designer' of Maister House (*The Maisters of Kingston upon Hull*, p. 132). See Neave, *Georgian East Yorkshire*, pp. 4–13. It seems more certain that Page was the designer of Blaydes House.

25. Samuel Spencer had been apprenticed in February 1711 to Samuel Barton and in 1719 admitted a Freeman of Hull, which dates the completion of his apprenticeship. Spencer was, it would appear, the master builder in charge of the construction of Maister House (Ingram, *The Maisters of Kingston upon Hull*, pp. 42–3).

26. Information given to the author by Richard Hewlings.

27. See Register of Persons Bound Apprentice to Freemen, 1720, Hull History Centre, C/BRG/7/39); Ingram suggested in 1983 that Thomas Musgrave, admitted to the Freedom of Hull in 1694 upon completion of his apprenticeship, was perhaps a 'superior craftsman' who acted as 'a kind of overseer' for the construction of Maister House (*The Maisters of Kingston upon Hull*, p. 43).

28. The suggestion that it was Henry Musgrave who was involved in Maister House has been made by David Neave in his as-yet-unpublished book on the architecture of Hull's High Street. When he died in 1718, William Constable left his 'natural son' £2,000 in his will (information thanks to David Neave and Neave, *Georgian East Yorkshire*, pp. 5–8; East Riding Archives (ERALS), DDCC/134/4, 135/60). Dunbar's nephew, Cuthbert Constable, had subscribed to Kent's *Inigo Jones* and inherited Burton Constable. David Neave confirms that it was Cuthbert Constable who

supplied the £1,500 surety required in 1728 to secure Musgrave the lucra-
tive post of 'Collector of Customs' at Hull, and that 'Musgrave was in the
Yorkshire circle of Lord Burlington', who in letters to his wife records
Musgrave being present at the Burlington's Londesborough Hall in
October and November 1739; see Neave, *Georgian East Yorkshire*, pp. 8–
10; and letters from Lord Burlington to Lady Burlington, Devonshire
Collection Archives, Chatsworth, CS1/127.22.

29. In the folder catalogued 'U DAS/26/2' in the Hull History Centre. The
house for Andrew Perrott was built at 22 High Street by 1745 and 'demised'
(the right to occupy transferred by lease or will) to Henry Musgrave in
his position of Collector of Customs; see Neave, *Georgian East Yorkshire*,
p. 12, and ERALS Deeds Registry, S/24. The house was demolished in
the late 1940s after suffering war damage.

30. Dan Cruickshank, *The Secret History of Georgian London: How the Wages
of Sin Shaped the Capital* (London: Cornerstone, 2009), p. 210.

31. Ingram, *The Maisters of Kingston upon Hull*, p. 41.

32. See the folder catalogued 'U DAS/26/2' in the Hull History Centre.

33. Ingram, *The Maisters of Kingston upon Hull*, p. 41.

34. Originally it would appear to have been conceived as a free-standing
house, certainly on one side. This is evident because its basement was lit
by a window in its now-obscured north elevation, while a narrow passage
along its south side, leading to a door to the cellar or basement and to
rear vaults, still separates the house from the adjoining building. But if
virtually free-standing, the house had only one show-front: that facing
the High Street. So it was designed in the manner of a terrace house.

35. See the Halls, *Georgian Hull*, p. 52.

36. Morris, *Lectures*, p. 43.

37. Morris also suggested that 'the Ionick Order is the most proper where
Nature . . . requireth Art to assist and embellish her, and the Liveliness
of the Ionick Order can deck and garnish the Glebe [with] its Parts . . .
analogous to Nature' (*Lectures*, p. 43). By 'Glebe' he meant land that
generates an income for its owner, again appropriate for this particular
building on the High Street.

38. The layout echoes not only Burlington's now long-demolished Round
Copping in Buckinghamshire and his Chiswick House but also, more
significantly, Renaissance and Palladian villas, such as the Villa Rotunda.
The house at Round Copping was free-standing, but had windows only
on its front and rear elevations, and the first plate in Robert Morris's
Rural Architecture of 1750 is for 'a little plain Building' in the form of
a thirty-foot cube, with windows on two sides and with ground- and

first-floor windows of double-square proportion linked by sill courses, and second-floor windows of square proportion – all, of course, much like Maister House.

39. Although the underside of the beam shows a swirl of tendrils, seemingly acanthus and of a type found in Palladio's work – for example, in plate XLVIII of the Fourth Book of his *I quattro libri* – so more Burlingtonian.

40. Palladio illustrates a Greek-key pattern in plate VIII of the Fourth Book of his *I quattro libri*.

41. The Victoria County History suggests a French influence in the way in which the staircase handrail rises in an unbroken line, defining a square open well with quadrant corners (*The Victoria History of the County of York East Riding*, vol. I, *The City of Kingston-Upon-Hull*, ed. K. S. Allison (London: Oxford University Press, 1969), 'Secular Buildings', pp. 443–59). Ivan and Elisabeth Hall even suggest a particular source, J. F. Blondell's *Maisons de Plaisance* of 1737–8 (see *Georgian Hull*, p. 53).

42. Benjamin Yates, who continued Robert Bakewell's business after his death in 1752, produced an almost identical design in 1766 for St Helen's House, King Street, Derby. Information thanks to Richard Hewlings.

43. The construction of 22 Arlington started in 1740, with its carcass completed and roofed by November 1741 and with the interior ready for painting and occupation by May 1743. See Nicholas Thompson, '22 Arlington Street in the 18th Century', in *A House in Town: 22 Arlington Street, Its Owners and Builders*, ed. Peter Campbell (London: B. T. Batsford, 1984); and 'Building Accounts' from 1740 to 1754 in the British Architectural Library of the Royal Institute of British Architects, p. 108.

44. This landing now has a segmental apse set behind a pair of Ionic columns, which is a conjectural restoration dating from the 1980s and undertaken to reverse earlier damage inflicted on this important space (Campbell (ed.), *A House in Town*, p. 183). The main staircase stops at this first-floor landing with a secondary staircase, in its own adjoining compartment, giving access to the floor above. The upward view from that landing was calculated to impress, even if its exact original character remains debated. Now the view is through a square opening in the second-floor gallery that offers a glimpse of a Roman-style coffered barrel vault of the type promoted by Palladio and admired and emulated by Burlington and Kent. Within, the vault beams are decorated with large-scale Greek-key patterns – so a possible connection with, or inspiration for, the Maister House staircase. So far as the upper part of the staircase is concerned, Nicholas Thompson points out that 'no mention is made' in the Building Accounts 'of a gallery at second floor level' and argues that the existing

gallery is 'a copy of one existing before the 2nd World War, and which might have been a later insertion' (Campbell (ed.), *A House in Town*, p. 109). Intriguingly, a 1950s photograph of the underside of the second-floor gallery shows that each square space between supporting brackets was filled by a large plaster-made rose much like those below the gallery in Maister House. In its current form, created in the 1980s, the gallery no longer has these roses.

45. Horace Walpole, *Anecdotes of Painting in England*, vol. 4 (London, 1787), p. 234. In his early nineteenth-century Royal Academy lectures, the architect Sir John Soane described the staircase at 44 Berkeley Square as 'a splendid specimen of what may be done even on a small scale, by a man of genius', noting in particular that Kent had 'availed himself ... of the twisted steps so much praised by Palladio' (*Lectures in Architecture by Sir John Soane*, ed. Arthur T. Bolton (London: The Sir John Soane's Museum, 1929), p. 136).

46. The colonnade, by being extended by one bay on either side and with these bays topped by circular niches with antique-style busts to suggest an attic, is transformed into a type of triumphal arch, far more elaborate than that below.

47. One significant difference between the designs is the treatment of the lofty volume above the staircase. At Maister House it is capped with a glazed octagonal lantern, but in the London houses Kent indulged in the Palladio-inspired antiquarianism that so delighted him and Burlington. The ceiling above the staircase in Arlington Street is formed with a coffered barrel vault, but that in Berkeley Square is far more ambitious. It also has a barrel vault with octagonal coffering, but which is flanked by coffered apsidal or half-spherical vaults that Palladio illustrated in his *I quattro libri*, taken from Roman examples. But Kent manipulated the model for practical ends. The coffering in the apse opposite the screen is fully glazed so that, to a significant degree, the staircase and its landings are top-lit. This was a bold and imaginative manipulation of sources that included, for example, the Basilica of Maxentius that Palladio reconstructed and illustrates in the Fourth Book of his *I quattro libri*. Kent also seems to have been inspired by the niches completed with Giovanni da Udine in Giulio Romano's domed saloon and arcaded loggia (an open-sided gallery) of the early sixteenth-century Villa Madama in Rome.

48. She probably met him first through the Burlingtons, with whom Kent lived for thirty years in London, or through the royal household, for whom Kent had undertaken several projects and where she served during the 1730s and 1740s, becoming 'Lady of the Bedchamber' to George II's

daughter Princess Amelia. Kent's royal projects dated from this period, including a picturesque hermitage and grotto for Amelia's mother, Queen Caroline, built in Richmond Park in 1730 and that incorporated four busts of 'thinkers admired by the Queen', among them John Locke (George Vertue, *Notebooks Relating to Artists and Collections in England*) 6 vols (Oxford University Press for Walpole Society, 1929–50), vol. I, p. 121; vol. III, pp. 51, 66; vol. XXVII; index to vols I–V, 1947).

49. Quoted in Juliet Learmouth, 'The London Town House of Lady Isabella Finch', *Georgian Group Journal,* vol. 25 (2017), pp. 73–94; letter dated 1 September 1742 from Lady Isabella to Lord Malton, Sheffield Archives, WWM/M8/51.

50. Learmouth, 'The London Town House of Lady Isabella Finch', p. 82; letters from Lady Isabella Finch to Lady Burlington, 28 August 1744, Devonshire Collection Archives, Chatsworth, CS1/219/17.

51. Building accounts from September 1742 that are preserved in Sir John Soane's Museum make it clear that she received all tradesmen's invoices personally 'From the Hands of Wm Kent Esqr', scrutinised them, perhaps discussed them and if all was well paid them (Sir John Soane's Museum, 'Building Accounts', 39 B).

52. Learmouth, 'The London Town House of Lady Isabella Finch', p. 82; Lady Isabella Finch to Lord Rockingham (formerly Malton), 31 December 1748, Sheffield Archive Office, Wentworth Woodhouse Muniments, WWM/M8/88.

53. Learmouth, 'The London Town House of Lady Isabella Finch', p. 90. Intriguingly, there is one other connection between the staircases in London and that at Maister House. All three feature floral garlands and seashell motifs, and those in 44 Berkeley Square and Maister House include niches, one of which on the Berkeley Square staircase probably contained a bust of Locke – similar to that in Queen Caroline's Hermitage – that Kent had presented to his client.

54. Paint analysis has failed to reveal what the original colour scheme would have been, but the choice of colours that suggest entrance spaces are somewhat like exterior spaces is appropriate. Such schemes can be found in canal-side Renaissance palazzi in Venice (with which Burlington and Kent would have been familiar), where domestic life and commerce often met and mixed at ground level, as in Maister House.

55. This decoration is probably of carved pine, but might be of plaster. Pulvinated friezes incorporating carved or moulded oak or laurel leaves, or scales, are illustrated on plate 55 of Kent's *Designs of Inigo Jones* (1727). Such door surrounds were deployed by Burlington in his York Assembly Rooms,

of 1730–35, where he used laurel leaves, which were no doubt Roman in inspiration, to echo the Roman basilica and bath that were his models. So this detail is perhaps yet more evidence of the extent of Burlington's – and arguably Kent's – involvement in the creation of the Maister House interior.

56. Almost all the panelling appears relatively modern, as do the non-functional window shutters and fire surround. At one point this room had a nineteenth-century bow window added to its facade and when this was removed external brickwork was recreated, as it seems was much internal joinery.

57. See Halls, *Georgian Hull*, p. 52. A local connection might have come through Henry Sheemakers, who worked with William Kent and Cheere in the early 1730s and whose brother Peter Scheemakers, who also worked with Kent, made the splendid equestrian statue of Willian III that remains in the Hull Market Place. Gilded like a statue in Venice or Rome, it rides high on a stone pedestal on which is proclaimed, through neatly carved letters, that 'THIS STATUE was Erected in the Year MDCCXXXIV To the Memory of KING WILLIAM The Third OUR GREAT DELIV-ERER.' So a potent reminder of Hull's Protestant allegiance in the early eighteenth century when William, dead for over thirty years in 1734, was still celebrated for delivering the nation from the threat of resurgent Roman Catholicism and autocratic and malign kingship.

58. Ingram, *The Maisters of Kingston upon Hull*, pp. 44–5.

59. Plate XXV in the Second Book of *I quattro libri* and in plate VIII of the Fourth Book.

60. Halls, *Georgian Hull*, p. 53. The underside of the beam partly support-ing the first-floor landing is also embellished with a bold and large-scale Greek-key pattern, above which is a view of the second-floor landing, which takes the form of four walkways around a square open-well offering a prospect of the crowning lantern roof. The underside of the second-floor landing is a showcase of Palladian Kentian detail. The landing is supported by shallow serpentine brackets – as, for example, in Chiswick House – that define square areas. The brackets and the squares are framed by the lower mouldings of an Ionic cornice, with the upper mouldings of the cornice running around the edges of the gallery. It is very logical and illustrated several times by Palladio in his *I quattro libri*.

61. Halls, *Georgian Hull*, p. 53.

62. See, for example, the notes on the house by the Georgian Society of East Yorkshire: gsey.org.uk/maister-house-hull/.

63. By 1969 the Victoria County History records that after he 'completed his apprenticeship in 1740' Page 'was designing the new Maister House, at no.

160 High Street' (*The Victoria History of the County of York, East Riding*, vol. I, p. 445), and in 1979 Ivan and Elisabeth Hall asserted in their authoritative *Georgian Hull* that 'Henry Maister rebuilt his house to the designs of Joseph Page' (p. 52). These claims are now countered by new research and interpretation (see note 24) and appear confirmed by a letter Henry Maister the younger wrote in 1750 to John Grimston, in which he referred to Page as 'the Man who was employed to do the Stuco in my house' (Ingram, *The Maisters of Kingston upon Hull*, p. 44). If Page had been the architect, surely Maister would not have described him as a mere stuccodore.

64. Blaydes House might in part date from as early as the 1730s, but its front facade and external details probably date from around 1760, as English Heritage and the Halls suggest (Halls, *Georgian Hull*, p. 60).

65. This central King Street building is a powerful late Palladian composition with a first-floor Venetian window set above the arch that is, in turn, topped by a square second floor window and an eaves pediment. A first-floor Venetian window also embellishes the rear elevation and offers a charming view of the modestly built and gradually curving frontage of the houses in Prince Street.

66. Ingram, *The Maisters of Kingston upon Hull*, p. 37.

67. Ivan and Elisabeth Hall suggest *c.*1760 (*Georgian Hull*, p. 20).

68. The front portion of the first floor, overlooking the High Street (originally two separate rooms) comprised one that was almost square in plan and the other with a plan almost 3:2 in proportion. The upper portions of the walls are plain plaster, presumably intended originally to be painted, wallpapered or even hung with fabric. The lower portions of the walls have flush dado panelling topped by a cornice-like dado rail to read as a classical pedestal. This would probably have been painted a light stone colour, with doors (which are each formed with six fielded panels) and the skirting's kick boards painted a mahogany colour. All this would have been typical of advanced taste in the 1750s and early 1760s.

69. As is suggested by *The Victoria History of the County of York East Riding*, vol. I, pp. 443–59. The fireplace design rewards close attention. The functional focus of the lower fire-surround is, of course, the hearth, which is framed by yellow sienna marble slips. These in turn are framed by a carved, eared architrave, the sides of which are supported visually by shallow serpentine scrolls, also largely of marble. The architrave itself supports a bulbous enriched frieze capped with a dentil cornice. The frieze incorporates a central tablet replete with a floral swag. All this is still, essentially, in the late Palladian taste, although more delicate than the designs of Burlington and Kent. Similarly, the overmantel above the

cornice of the fire-surround takes the form of a 'tabernacle frame' of the type favoured by Burlington and Kent and found in Kent's *Inigo Jones*. This is an architectural treatment, sometimes incorporating pilasters and entablature or, as here, eared architraves enriched with egg-and-dart mouldings. But this affair is also delicate in its details and is topped by a curvaceous swan-neck pediment that, in its ornament, strikes a note that is too baroque for Burlington. Entwined around the architrave, in an exceptionally playful rococo manner, is a vine complete with bunches of grapes. This detail is more likely made from carved timber not plaster.

70. Ingram, *The Maisters of Kingston upon Hull*, pp. 45–6.

71. Ingram, *The Maisters of Kingston upon Hull*, p. 45.

72. Little evidence is now visible because this level was ruthlessly altered in the years soon after the Second World War, with even the lower flight of the stone staircase removed.

73. The walls of the cabinet are clad with raised and fielded panelling topped with a Doric-profile timber-made box cornice that appears of prodigious size because it is placed upon a deep fascia board. This board reads like a frieze that rises from a convex and concave composite moulding. All in all, the composition looks impressively massive for such a relatively small room – particularly so if it was painted to make it stand out.

74. Topped by a tabernacle frame with lugged corners within which are set rosettes.

75. Letter from Lord Burlington to Lady Burlington, Devonshire Collection Archives, Chatsworth, CS1/127.22,27; Neave, *Georgian East Yorkshire*, p. 9. The game was popularised by the publication in 1742 of Edmond Hoyle's *Short Treatise on the Game of Whist*.

76. Letter of 7 November 1744 from Nathanial to Henry Maister.

4. A PIECE OF URBAN THEATRE

Heywood's House and Bank, Liverpool (1798–1800)

1. John Booker, *Temples of Mammon: The Architecture of Banking* (Edinburgh University Press, 1991), p. 26. The Liverpool volume of the *Pevsner Architectural Guides* echoes the point, stressing that this is an 'exceptionally early purpose-built bank', combining 'office and living accommodation in the traditional way' although here 'the house is an appendage to the business part rather than the other way around'; see Joseph Sharples, *Pevsner Architectural Guides: Liverpool* (New Haven, CT: Yale University Press, 2004), p. 135.

2. Barclays Group Archives, Records of Arthur Heywood, Sons & Co, Liverpool, bankers, 1725–1928, NatWest Group.

3. Daughter of Samuel Ogden of Mossley Hill.

4. They were initially based in Lord Street and Castle Street but by 1775 were trading from Hanover Street. However, William Moss's *Liverpool Guide: Including a Sketch of the Environs* of 1796 (published by Crane and Jones, London) records 'Messrs. Arthur Heywood, Sons and Co.' being located in Castle Street. It also records that banks in Liverpool were 'open from nine till three, every day except Friday, when they are shut at one' (p. 104).

5. 'The total of slave trading voyages with direct Heywood ownership totals 133. This involved the transportation of an estimated 42,000 people, 6,000 of whom died before reaching the Americas': 'The Heywoods' by Nancy Adams, *Rylands Blog*, University of Manchester, https: //rylands-collections.com/2023/09/18/the-heywoods/; see also 'Manchester's Slave Trade Dynasty: The Heywoods and the University', *Guest Blog*, Global Threads Project (Manchester, 20 September 2023), https://wordpress.com/post/globalthreadsmcr.org/4437. For background, see the collection of papers in *Liverpool and Transatlantic Slavery*, ed. David Richardson, Suzanne Schwartz and Anthony Tibbles (Liverpool University Press, 2007). See also revealinghistories.org.uk, run by eight museums in Greater Manchester.

6. Kenneth Morgan, 'James Rogers and the Bristol Slave Trade', *Historical Research*, vol. 76, no. 192 (May 2003), pp. 189–219; Kenneth Morgan, in *Liverpool and Transatlantic Slavery*, ed. Richardson et al., p. 15; Kenneth Morgan, in *Slavery, Atlantic Trade and the British Economy, 1660–1800* (Cambridge University Press, 2000), states that Liverpool had by 1800 'become the most important slave trading port in the world' and 'between 1699 and 1807 . . . dispatched 5,199 slaving vessels out of a total of 12,103 clearances from Brtish ports' (p. 88); David Richardson, 'The British Empire and the Atlantic Slave Trade, 1660–1807', in *The Oxford History of the British Empire*, vol. 2, *The 18th Century*, ed. P. J. Marshall (Oxford University Press, 1998), pp. 441–2; David Richardson, 'The Bristol Slave Traders: A Collective Portrait', pamphlet (Bristol Historical Association, 1985).

7. As the Archives Centre in Liverpool's Maritime Museum explains: 'In the 1790s Liverpool controlled 80% of the British slave trade and over 40% of the European slave trade . . . Virtually all the leading inhabitants of the town, including the Mayors, Town Councillors and MPs, invested in the slave trade and profited from it. The prosperity and growth of the

town was closely connected with its involvement with slavery' ('Liverpool and the Transatlantic Slave Trade', Information Sheet 3).

8. Daniel Defoe visited Liverpool in 1680, 1690 and again in about 1716, and in the early 1720s enthused in his *Tour Through the Whole Island of Great Britain* (1724–7) that 'Liverpoole is one of the wonders of Britain . . . what it may grow to in time, I know not.'

9. According to the *Pevsner Architectural Guides: Liverpool*, this was the 'first commercial enclosed wet dock in the world' (p. 7). However, this claim is open to debate because the ten-acre Howland Great Wet Dock in south London had been constructed between 1696 and 1699 by John Wells, although, it should be pointed out, it was not an 'enclosed' commercial dock like that in Liverpool because it lacked walls, warehouses or other commercial facilities. What is certain, though, is that Liverpool's Wet Dock – later known as the 'Old Dock' – must when new have made a strong impression. It is assumed that the construction of both docks was supervised by the civil engineer Thomas Steers, who moved to Liverpool in 1710. According to Howard Colvin, Steers, who lived in Liverpool until his death in 1750, 'played a leading part in the affairs and development of the town' (Colvin's *A Biographical Dictionary of English Architects, 1600–1840*, 2nd edn (London: John Murray, 1978), p. 778). The Old Dock was regarded as cramped and awkward by 1826, when it was filled in.

10. According to Howard Colvin, the dock 'laid the foundation of the town's greatness as a seaport' (Colvin, *A Biographical Dictionary of English Architects*, p. 778).

11. Between 1750 and 1775 it has been estimated that over a hundred slaving voyages to Africa set sail from Lancaster (see Historic England's notes on the Maritime Museum, 26 St George's Quay, Lancashire; list entry number 1289088). This connection is hardly surprising since Lancaster's extraordinary prosperity in the eighteenth century was based on slaving. With its quay on the River Lune offering direct access to the sea, Lancaster grew into the fourth-largest slave port in England after Liverpool, Bristol and London. Many prominent local families were involved, some of whom built and operated slave ships while others invested by fitting out ships with trade cargoes.

12. As Kenneth Morgan points out, 'in terms of market share, this made him the twelfth leading British slave trader and the second largest Bristol slave merchant in the decade after 1785'; see Kenneth Morgan, 'James Rogers and the Bristol Slave Trade', *Historical Research*, vol. 76, no. 192 (May 2003), pp. 189–216. See also Richardson, 'Bristol Slave Traders: A

Collective Portrait', p. 30; David Richardson (ed.), *Bristol, Africa and the Eighteenth-Century Slave Trade to America*, vol. 4, *The Final Years, 1770–1807* (Gloucester: Alan Sutton publishing for the Bristol Record Society, 1996): D. Eltis, S. D. Behrendt, D. Richardson and H. S. Klein, *The Trans-Atlantic Slave Trade: A Database on CD-ROM* (Cambridge University Press, 1999).

13. Sharples, *Pevsner Architectural Guides: Liverpool*, p. 135.

14. The church was demolished in 1897.

15. The pedimented central range, with its two tiers of arcaded windows, is perhaps inspired by Palladio's mid sixteenth-century Basilica in Vicenza, and by Wren's Trinity College Library in Cambridge of 1676–84. The architectural language of brick with stone corner quoins and architectural trim had been well established by Wren as a smart but economic structural and decorative system, for example with the Royal Observatory of Greenwich of 1674 and St James's Church, Piccadilly, of 1684. Indeed, brick with quoins was the favoured language for institutional buildings and almshouses by the early eighteenth century, so the Blue Coat School was following a conventional pattern. Another Wren-derived detail is the heads of cherubs adorning the keystones around the court – probably intended as an evocation of the Temple of Solomon in Jerusalem, described in the Old Testament. A further clue to this inspiration is provided by an early eighteenth-century print of the Blue Coat School that shows the court paved with black and white stone slabs set in a chequerboard pattern. Such a pavement was said to have been used in the temple.

16. Sharples, *Pevsner Architectural Guides: Liverpool*, p. 43.

17. It is possible the Woods were involved in the square's design, but there seems to be no stylistic evidence to support this attribution and Wood the Elder died in early 1754.

18. The number of Liverpool merchants involved in the trade is suggested by studies made by Cambridge economic geographer Professor Robert. J. Bennett: *Local Business Voice: The History of Chambers of Commerce in Britain, Ireland and Revolutionary America, 1769–2011* (Oxford University Press, 2011) and *The Voice of Liverpool Business: The First Chamber of Commerce and the Atlantic Economy, 1774–c.1796* (Liverpool Chamber of Commerce, 2010). Bennett analysed the Liverpool Chamber of Commerce between 1774 and 1795 and lists eighty-eight merchants of whom thirty-two were – to a greater or lesser extent – involved in slaving, usually operating in partnerships.

19. Parr took a lease on the land in 1797 and the complex he soon constructed was described in the late nineteenth century as 'one of the best extant

examples of the establishment of a first-class Liverpool merchant of the period' (J. A. Picton, *Memorials of Liverpool: Historical and Topographical*, 2 vols. (London: Longman, 1875), vol. 2, p. 278).

20. Moss, *The Liverpool Guide*, p. 99.
21. Moss, *The Liverpool Guide*, p.100.
22. Moss, *The Liverpool Guide*, p. 100.
23. *The Journal of Rev. William Bagshaw Stevens*, ed. Georgina Galbraith (Oxford: Clarendon Press, 1965), p. 436. Jane Longmore, in *Liverpool and Transatlantic Slavery*, ed. Richardson et al., asks to what extent were Liverpool houses built in the last quarter of the eighteenth century 'cemented . . . by the blood . . . of Negroes'. Coordinating known Liverpool slave traders with speculating builders, she discovered that 'substantial merchants, including many slave traders, leased . . . large blocks of land [from Liverpool Corporation,] often retaining the holding until the demand for housing triggered development'. Arthur and Benjamin Heywood probably used 'some of their profits from the slave trade to build their matching houses in Hanover Street from 1759', because 'at this stage they were in the midst of a sequence of eight slave voyages, lasting from 1753 to 1764' (pp. 232–6).
24. Genesis 9:24–7.
25. *Leviticus* 25:39–46. Additional sanction appeared to be supplied in the New Testament, where the Apostle Paul – anxious not to be perceived to be inciting rebellion among Rome's slave population – argued in his epistle to the Ephesians: 'Servants, be obedient to them that are your masters according to the flesh, with fear and trembling, in singleness of your heart, as unto Christ', adding that 'whatever good thing any man doeth, the same shall he receive of the Lord, whether he be bond or free' (in the biblical texts, as in Rome, the terms 'servant', 'bonds-man' and 'slave' were essentially synonymous). Paul believed that masters should forebear from threatening their slaves, since God would be judging them for their actions (Ephesians 6:5–9; and also *Colossians* 4:1) but, as he reiterated elsewhere, it was essential that 'servants . . . be obedient unto their own masters, and . . . please them well in all things; not answering again, not purloining, but shewing all good fidelity, that they may adorn the doctrine of God our Saviour in all things' (Titus 2:9-10).
26. James Boswell, *The Life of Samuel Johnson*, 5 vols. (London: J. Richardson, 1821), vol. 4, p. 44.
27. Somerset had been born in Africa, carried to the American colonies as a slave and purchased in Boston, Massachusetts, by a Scottish-born American customs officer and merchant named Charles Stewart. In 1769 Stewart brought Somerset to England, where he continued in servitude.

But in 1771 Somerset absconded, was quickly seized by Stewart and confined in a ship that was bound for Jamaica, where Somerset was to be sold to a plantation. However, things took an unexpected turn for Stewart. Three godparents appeared – evidently Somerset had been baptised while in England – who obtained a writ of habeas corpus, resulting in Somerset appearing before the Court of King's Bench, which was to decide if his imprisonment and transportation were lawful. The case, eventually heard in February 1772, was of great public interest, although the arguments aired during the hearing did not turn on profound moral issues but on legal detail and interpretations.

28. See copy of the advertisement in Liverpool's International Slavery Museum, located within the Merseyside Maritime Museum, Royal Albert Docks.

29. A. H. Arkle, 'Transactions: The Early Coffee Houses of Liverpool' ('Read 21st November 1912'), p. 6, hslc.org.uk/wp-content/uploads/2017/06/64-2-Arkle.pdf.

30. Iain Whyte, *Scotland and the Abolition of Black Slavey: 1756–1838* (Edinburgh University Press, 2006), p. 187.

31. In Samuel Johnson's opinion, 'The laws of Jamaica afford a Negro no redress. His colour is considered as a sufficient testimony against him.' In his view, he concluded, it was 'to be lamented that moral right should ever give way' to the temptation of the financial gain offered by the brutal exploitation of the free labour afforded by slavery, and he expressed himself 'certain that the justice of the court will declare him free'. Boswell recorded his response to Johnson's 'opinion', and if taken as a barometer of popular opinion it is as interesting as it is bizarre. He protested against Johnson's 'general doctrine with respect to the Slave Trade' because, asserted Boswell, it was based on 'prejudice, and imperfect information'. This was due, in Boswell's opinion, to Johnson listening too closely to those locked in a 'wild and dangerous attempt . . . to abolish so very important and necessary a branch of commercial interest' rather than to 'the vast body of Planters, Merchants, and others, whose immense properties are involved in that trade' (Boswell, *Life of Johnson*, vol. 4 (1821), pp. 41–5).

32. By the time the ship finally reached Jamaica on 22 December, 142 Africans had been killed or had died as a direct result of slavers' murderous actions. Collingwood himself died three days after the ship's arrival.

33. Barclays Group Archives, 'Arthur Heyood and Sons, Liverpool', https://home.barclays/archive-barclays/founding-banks/arthur-heywood-and-sons-liverpool/.

34. Colvin, *A Biographical Dictionary of British Architects 1600–1840*, p. 316.

35. Although constructed from *c.*1798 to 1800, Heywood's house and bank was 'possibly' built to a design of 1789 by John Foster Sr; see *Pevsner Architectural Guides: Liverpool*, p. 135.

36. John Foster Jr was born in about 1786, joined the family office in around 1805 and turned out to be an architect of genius. He had been articled in London to the architect Jeffry Wyatt (who later changed his surname to Wyatville and worked for George IV at Windsor Castle), had designs accepted for display in the Royal Academy of Arts annually from 1805 to 1807, in 1809 travelled to Greece with architect C. R. Cockerell and in 1810 was instrumental in the epic exploration and documentation of the fifth century BC Temple of Apollo Epicurius at Bassae (see page 157). In 1816 Foster returned to Liverpool, rejoined his father's office and in 1824 succeeded to the post of surveyor to the corporation. He steadily refined his austere, erudite and exquisite neoclassical manner. The loss of the Liverpool Custom House building was – and remains – a cultural tragedy for Liverpool and for the nation.

37. The Lower Castle Street elevation that abuts the main building is two storeys high and one window wide at ground level, where an arch-topped window echoes those on the ground floor of the main building, with its arch springing from impost blocks aligned with those in the neighbouring rusticated elevation. At the first floor there is a tripartite window, with narrow windows flanking a slightly wider central window. Evidently this lit a staircase. The sliver of facade to the south is also one window wide, but three storeys high, with a ground-floor arched window and a square second-floor window, as on the main building.

38. Even the staircases at Heywood's house and bank are not original. One is an early twentieth-century creation, curiously with banded rods, or fasces, serving as balusters. The other, which starts at first-floor level, might be in its original location but is now a late seventeenth-century-style 'Wren revival' affair – dating probably from the 1890s – with an open well, barley-twist balusters, square-plan newels and cherubs in its plaster frieze.

39. This interpretation is supported even if only in a circumstantial manner by some of the small amount of early internal decoration that survives at first-floor level. For example, windows tend to be framed by panelled pilasters topped with minimal Doric capitals that each incorporate fluting and three round rosettes. These capitals might date from the early twentieth century, but stylistically they could well be of 1800, and they relate visually to the pilasters that frame the stone front-door surround on to

Brunswick Street, on which the capitals each have three round discs. If original, these internal pilasters are appropriate for a room of conventional height, and would no doubt have supported now lost or concealed entablatures that marked a ceiling height set below the second-floor level.

40. In a letter from Nevis, sent in 1764, Pinney recorded a view of the slave trade that was perhaps typical at the time, indeed to a degree echoes the opinions of James Boswell, and helps explain why many seemingly thoughtful individuals did not protest against the trade's obvious evils. Pinney was, he wrote, 'shock'd at the first appearance of human flesh exposed to sale' but concluded that 'surely God ordain'd 'em for ye use & benefit of us: otherwise his Divine Will would have been made manifest by some particular sign or token.' See Madge Dresser, *Slavery Obscured: The Social History of the Slave Trade in Bristol* (Bristol: Redcliffe Press, 2007), p. 58.

41. Colvin, *Biographical Dictionary of British Architects 1600–1840*, p. 627.

42. This was in large part due to the Naval Stores Act of 1721, which removed all duties from timber imported into Britain from British colonies. One of the immediate beneficiaries of the Act was Sir Robert Walpole, the first Lord of the Treasury and de facto prime minister who from 1721 started to benefit personally from the repeal of the duty when he used large amounts of mahogany to beautify the interiors of his new house, Houghton Hall in Norfolk.

43. Adam Bowett, 'The 1721 Naval Stores Act and the Commercial Introduction of Mahogany', *Furniture History*, vol. 30 (1994), pp. 42–56.

44. James Peacock, under the pseudonym of Jose MacPacke, *Nutshells: Being Ichnographic Distributions for Small Villas* (1785). Peacocke worked as assistant clerk of the works to the City of London under George Dance the younger. See Dan Cruickshank and Neil Burton, *Life in the Georgian City* (Harmondsworth: Viking, 1990), p. 187.

45. Moss, *The Liverpool Guide*, p. 78.

46. *Lloyd's List*, no. 3031, 14 September 1798. Marine List, 'The *Parr*, Christian (master), from Africa to the West Indies, blown up on the coast of Africa. 29 of the crew and about 200 Negroes saved.'

47. See Historic England's listed building description for 57 Parr Street.

48. James Walvin, *Questioning Slavery* (London: Routledge, 2006), p. 158. It's worth noting that up to £20 million was paid by the government in compensation when slavery was outlawed in the British Empire, but the money went not to liberated slaves but to former slave owners for the loss of their property. The father of William Ewart Gladstone, the Liverpool-based MP and future prime minster, was one of those to

benefit. A tobacco and cotton merchant, who had amassed a vast fortune, largely through investing in numerous West Indian slave estates, he was awarded £107,769 to compensate him for the financial loss he suffered by being obliged to free the 2,508 slaves he owned. See Historic England's listed building description for 62 Rodney Street, Liverpool, where it is stated that the Gladstone family was awarded over £90,000 in compensation.

5. A QUESTION OF STYLE

Cragside, Northumberland (1869–95)

1. Howard Colvin, *Biographical Dictionary of British Architects: 1600–1840*, 2nd edn (London: John Murray, 1978), p. 17. An idiosyncratic but most entertaining history of the architectural profession in Britain is offered by Andrew Saint in *The Image of the Architect* (London: Yale University Press, 1985). In Chapter 3, 'The Architect as Professional: Britain in the Nineteenth Century', Saint refers to Charles Dickens's novel *Martin Chuzzlewit*, in which the unctuous, self-promotional and greedy Seth Pecksniff – 'architect and land surveyor' – makes an appearance and, in the process, observes Saint, 'offers not a few clues to the true "state of the profession" in Dickens's day, at a time (1844) when Britain alone could boast a substantial, organised body of architects' (p. 51).

2. Samuel Smiles, *Self-Help* (London: John Murray, 1859).

3. David Watkin, *The Life and Work of C. R. Cockerell* (London: Zwemmer, 1974), p. 65.

4. Andrew Saint, *Richard Norman Shaw* (London: Yale University Press, 2010), p. 25.

5. *The Times*, 12 October 1843; Friedrich Engels, *The Condition of the Working Class in England* (Oxford University Press, 1993), p. 45.

6. A. W. N. Pugin, *The True Principles of Pointed or Christian Architecture* (London, 1853), p. 1.

7. Pugin, *The True Principles of Pointed or Christian Architecture*, p. 2.

8. Pugin, *The True Principles of Pointed or Christian Architecture*, pp. 2–3.

9. Pugin, *The True Principles of Pointed or Christian Architecture*, p. 3.

10. Phoebe Stanton, *Pugin* (New York: Viking, 1972), p. 189; Saint, *Richard Norman Shaw*, p. 13.

11. Chartist leaders claimed 400,000 people had gathered, while *The Times*, downplaying the event, estimated the number at 20,000. It is now thought that 15,000 to 25,000 attended.

12. The society had been founded in 1754 to promote the creative fusion of art, science and industry to improve manufacture. Since 1843 the Prince Consort had been its president and in 1847 – as a sign of his support for its endeavours – secured the society the reward of a royal charter, but it was not until 1908 that it obtained the right to use 'Royal' in its name, becoming the Royal Society of Arts (RSA).

13. The direct inspiration was the Exposition des produites de l'industrie française, which had opened in Paris in June 1849 to showcase French technology. The Great Exhibition was initially opened to season ticket holders – in other words, the relatively wealthy. But from 26 May 1851 the entrance fee was set at one shilling per day, from Monday to Thursday, to make its wonders accessible to poorer Londoners, although even a shilling was quite a large sum considering that a bed in a common lodging house at the time was four pence a night and a loaf of bread one penny.

14. The Palm House in Kew Gardens was built between 1844 and 1848 to the design of Decimus Burton (who also worked on the 'Great Stove') and iron master Richard Turner. This structure represented the world's first large-scale architectural use of wrought iron, here used for curved ribs, combined with cast iron for internal columns.

15. John Ruskin, *The Seven Lamps of Architecture*, Chapter 1, 'The Lamp of Sacrifice', Aphorism 4 (Orpington, Kent: George Allen, 1889), pp. 8–9.

16. See *Engineering Magazine* (August 1892) and *Lippincott's Magazine* (March 1896).

17. Pugin, *The True Principles of Pointed or Christian Architecture*, pp. 3–9.

18. The Great Exhibition had been a colossal success, certainly within the terms it had set itself; and having achieved a surplus of £186,000 in receipt the commissioners were granted a supplementary charter to extend its existence in perpetuity, allowing it to disburse the profits in pursuit of some of the key aims of the exhibition. Primarily this involved the purchase of the mostly open land to the south of the exhibition site – as far as Brompton Road – to form an estate on which Prince Albert's dream of an educational and inspirational museum and academic quarter could be gradually realised. Brompton was renamed South Kensington (probably Cole's idea) to create a connection with the majesty of nearby Kensington Palace, tracts of land were let to speculative builders to create profitable upscale housing, and a series of institutions and museums eventually constructed – including Imperial College, the Science Museum and the Natural History Museum – so that the area became something of a self-contained town, especially after the Metropolitan Railway's underground station and related parades of shops opened in 1868. By then this

new London quarter had become known informally as 'Albertopolis', in honour of the 43-year-old prince, who had died most unexpectedly in December 1861.

19. Mark Girouard, *The Victorian Country House* (London: Yale University Press, 1979), p.53.
20. Girouard, *The Victorian Country House*, p. 53.
21. Saint, *Richard Norman Shaw*, p. 13; Richard Phené Spiers, *RIBAJ*, vol. 2 (1895), p. 607.
22. Saint, *Richard Norman* Shaw, p. 13.
23. Nesfield's sketchbooks are in the RIBA; Shaw's are in the RA.
24. Saint, *Richard Norman Shaw*, p. 17.
25. See https://gilbertscott.org/buildings/the-gothic-foreign-office; https://gilbertscott.org/buildings/the-building-of-the-foreign-and-india-offices; https://gilbertscott.org/buildings/the-classical-foreign-office. See also George Gilbert Scott, *Personal and Professional Recollections* (London: Sampson Low, Marston & Co, 1879).
26. https://gilbertscott.org/buildings/the-gothic-foreign-office; *Hansard*, Friday, 11 February 1859, vol. 152, cc. 760–73); *Spectator*, 12 February 1859, p.10.
27. Scott, *Personal and Professional Recollections*, pp. 197–8.
28. Scott, *Personal and Professional Recollections*, p. 199.
29. https://gilbertscott.org/buildings/the-classical-foreign-office.
30. https://gilbertscott.org/buildings/the-classical-foreign-office.
31. J. C. Loudon, *An Encyclopedia of Cottage, Farm and Villa Architecture and Furniture* (London: Longman, 1833).
32. Girouard, *The Victorian Country House*, p. 52.
33. Saint, *Richard Norman Shaw*, pp. 44–5; John Calcott Horsley, *Recollections of a Royal Academician*, ed. Mrs Edmund Helps (London: John Murray, 1903), pp. 338–42.
34. Saint, *Richard Norman* Shaw, p. 50.
35. Saint, *Richard Norman Shaw*, p. 51.
36. Saint, *Richard Norman Shaw*, p. 80.
37. Saint, *Richard Norman* Shaw, p. 80.
38. Saint, *Richard Norman Shaw*, p. 80; Reginald Blomfield, *Richard Norman Shaw RA* (London: B. T. Batsford, 1940), p. 20.
39. They were designed by Forsyth.
40. The sketch is by T. Raffles Davison.
41. Girouard, *The Victorian Country House*, pp. 308 and 312.
42. The Queen Anne Revival was in part a response to the argument expressed by the primary theorist of the Gothic Revival, Charles Eastlake, who in *Hints on Household Taste in Furniture, Upholstery and Other Details*

(1868), regretted the absence of picturesque sensibility in contemporary urban architecture (Saint, *Richard Norman Shaw*, p. 152).

43. A. McGarel-Hogg and W. Hargreaves Raffles, 'Rambles in London Streets', *British Architect*, vol. 6, 12 December 1892, p. 38.
44. Saint, *Richard Norman Shaw*, p. 85.
45. Saint, *Richard Norman Shaw*, p. 85; Tyne & Wear Archives, letters from Shaw to Armstrong on 13 October 1884, DA/A/1/32/1, and on 22 October 1884, DA/A/1/32/3. Information thanks to Andrew Saint.
46. Tyne & Wear Archives, DF/A/1/32/1.
47. Letters now in the Tyne & Wear Archives.
48. Tyne & Wear Archives, letter from Shaw to Armstrong, 22 October 1884, DF/A/1/31/3.
49. Tyne & Wear Archives, DF/A/1/32/4.
50. Tyne & Wear Archives, DF/A/1/32/5.
51. Quoted in Girouard, *The Victorian Country House*, p. 307.
52. Cragside has largely escaped twentieth-century alterations and additions, and so still exists in much the form in which it was originally conceived.
53. 1881 census, RG11/5137. Information from Andrew Saint.
54. 1891 census, RG12/4272. Information from Andrew Saint.

6. THE TWO-UP TWO-DOWN

Toxteth Bye-law Houses (*c.*1860–*c.*1890)

1. This was prompted by the Swing Riots of 1830 – a Luddite-like reaction by agricultural labourers fearful for their livelihoods as mechanisation was introduced – and which culminated with the allotment movement.
2. Jack London, *The People of the Abyss* (London and New York: Macmillan and Isbister, 1903), Chapter 24, 'A Vision of the Night'; Dan Cruickshank, *Spitalfields: The History of a Nation in a Handful of Streets* (London: Random House, 2016), p. 561.
3. This total includes inner suburbs; see *The Victoria History of the County of Lancaster*, vol. 4, ed. William Farrer and J. Brownbill (London, 1911), pp. 37–8. Figures vary slightly, however: the 1841 census suggests the population was 293,963. According to the National Museums Liverpool, in the mid nineteenth century as much as 40 per cent of the population of Liverpool lived in desperate conditions, generally in courts that often contained back-to-back houses and a large proportion of dank subterranean accommodation.

4. Edwin Chadwick, 'Report on the Sanitary Condition of the Labouring Population', prepared for Her Majesty's Principal Secretary of State for the Home Department, from the Poor Law Commissioners (1842), pp. 8–19; see also William H. Duncan's paper entitled 'On the Physical Causes of the High Rate of Mortality in Liverpool', 'read before the Literary and Philosophical Society, in February and March 1843' (Liverpool: Joshua Walmsley, 1843): copies in the Wellcome Collection, London.

5. They are absent from M. A. Gage's Liverpool map of 1836 but appear on the first edition of the Ordnance Survey map, dating from 1847. Back-to-back houses, significantly larger in scale, survive in Duke's Terrace off Duke Street. They were built in 1843 and were once set in a court but now, handsome and well repaired, they preside over a garden.

6. As a lone survivor these buildings are now conserved by the National Museums Liverpool, but in spring 2025 the court buildings remain derelict and abandoned.

7. 'Report on the Sanitary Condition of the Labouring Population', Section II, 'Arrangements External to the Residences by which the Sanitary Condition of the Labouring Population is Affected', pp. 18–19.

8. This Act was part of Disraeli's promised 'social reform', aimed at elevating the circumstances of working people, and was accompanied in 1875 by the Artisans' and Labourers' Dwellings Improvement Act (or the Cross Act, named after the home secretary Richard Cross), which gave local councils the power to purchase slum areas for clearance without the owner's consent and then, rather than redeveloping the areas themselves, to sell them to commercial house builders. A key requirement was that homes had to be 'through-houses' and not back-to-backs.

9. See Gareth Carr's PhD thesis 'The Speculative Development of Workers Housing in Victorian Liverpool: An Analysis of the Work of Richard Owens, Architect and Surveyor, 1863–91', vols. 1 and 2, submitted to the University of Liverpool in 2014, and his evidence given in 2014 on behalf of Save Britain's Heritage in the public inquiry into a proposal to compulsorily purchase and largely demolish what survived of the bye-law housing in the Toxteth Welsh Streets (copy made available to the author by Save Britain's Heritage, with additional information and insight offered most generously by Dr Carr in conversation with the author). See also Gareth Carr, 'Richard Owens of Liverpool, Architect and Surveyor, 1831–91', *Liverpool History Society Journal*, vol. 17 (2018); and 'Richard Owens and the Welsh House-builders of Mid-Victorian Liverpool', *Liverpool History Society Journal*, vol. 20 (2021). Dr Carr now teaches at Wrexham University.

10. Joseph Sharples, *Pevsner Architectural Guides: Liverpool* (New Haven, CT: Yale University Press, 2004), p. 144 (where it is misnamed Westminster Buildings).

11. Its archive was deposited with the Merseyside Record Office, subsequently absorbed into the Liverpool Record Office and now in Liverpool Central Library (information from Gareth Carr and included in his 2014 proof of evidence, 2.8).

12. Copy Letter Book 7, covering correspondence from October 1871 to November 1873, records that works were starting on Estate 3, with Gwendeline, Enid and Geraint streets being mentioned. See Gareth Carr's report for Save Britain's Heritage. The Letter Books are held in the Liverpool Record Office of Liverpool City Council, based in Liverpool Central Library.

13. The sites of these Welsh Streets were bounded on the north-west by the north-east/south-west-aligned North Hill Street, on the south-east by South Street, on the south-west by Admiral Street and on the north-east by Princes Road. This represented about half of Estate 3, which extended to the north-west.

14. See Copy Letter Book 8, covering correspondence from November 1873 to February 1875. The southern portion of the grid of Dickens streets was at more or less right angles to that of the Geraint Street block and aligned roughly with Windsor Street. Hierarchy was not apparent in these Dickens streets, in which all the houses were of the simplest sort: flat fronted with facades rising directly from the pavement and with no front enclosures. The south portion of the Dickens streets has been destroyed.

15. Copy Letter Book 10 (correspondence from September 1876 to October 1878), p. 257.

16. Copy Letter Book 10, p. 257. The dates of the construction of the streets on Roberts's four principal estates (those numbered 1 to 4) have been established by Dr Carr. He has explored Owens's office ledgers deposited in the Liverpool Record Office and, using the Letter Books containing copies of Owens's outgoing correspondence, has pieced together a chronology (see Copy Letter Books 1 to 15, (part) LRO 720 WDL/1/1-15, 1864–1891). Copy Letter Book 1 relates to Owens's earliest projects and dates from July 1864. Copy Letter Book 7 (correspondence from October 1871 to November 1873) marks the start on Estate 3. Copy Letter Book 8 (correspondence from November 1873 to February 1875), includes streets named after Charles Dickens characters. Copy Letter Book 9 (correspondence from March 1875 to August 1876), mentions a start being made on the set of streets with biblical names and Welsh names, including

Gwydir Street and Madryn Street. Copy Letter Book 10 (correspondence from September 1876 to October 1878) records more building taking place on Estate 3 and on Estate 2.

17. Gareth Carr, 2014 proof of evidence, 4.3. p. 7.

18. Information thanks to Dr Carr. In his 2014 evidence opposing the demolition of these streets, Gareth Carr argues that Owens's planning of the streets on Estate 3 was subtle and sophisticated. It demonstrated Owens's 'recognition of the differing environments which lay' around the site 'and the skill with which the simple bay-window and resultant streetscape might be utilised in accommodating the gradual transition from one urban context to another' (Carr, 4.16, pp. 10–11). Madelaine Street, east of the Geraint Street block and also mentioned in Letter Book Number 8, was more ambitious: its houses were of the best sort, with canted bays rising from small front enclosures. Only the east side of Madelaine Street survives.

19. Notably along Granby Street in Estate 4. The Granby Street area is generally a little later in origin than the Voelas Street area of Estate 3. Estate 4 was perhaps under way in the mid 1870s. Granby Street is mentioned in Copy Letter Book 9, covering correspondence from March 1875 to August 1876.

20. Copy Letter Book 10, p. 256.

21. The plans and section are now in the Liverpool Central Library.

22. Presumably to save on the cost of construction, no basement or cellar is shown.

23. Referenced by Gareth Carr in his 2014 proof of evidence; see James Allanson Picton, *Memorials of Liverpool: Historical and Topographical*, vol. 2 (London: Longman, Green, 1875), p. 353. Thomas Roberts, in 'The Welsh Influence on the Building Industry in Victorian Liverpool', asserts that 'The urban development of Victorian Liverpool was different [in comparison with other Victorian towns] and unique in the sense that it was undertaken in the main by Welsh migrants and their families'; see *Building the Industrial City*, ed. M. Doughty (Leicester University Press, 1986), p. 106.

24. Voelas Street and Rhiwlas Street, mostly built from 1875 and 1876, stand parallel to each other, with the terrace on the north side of Rhiwlas Street being separated by a narrow service alley from the terrace on the south side of Voelas Street. Of the 114 households in this pair of 'Welsh Streets' in 1881, only eleven had Welsh-born 'heads', and of these eleven only eight were involved with the building trade. The terraces generally survive in Rhiwlas Street (of its sixty houses, six at the east end of the north side have been lost), and in Voelas Street a little over half of its sixty houses have been demolished.

25. Although it is clearly unsafe to make a judgement about the ethnic identity of the majority of the residents of these streets on surname alone, Gareth Carr's analysis of documents has come up with results that seem to support the census readings. Based on the 'predominance of Welsh names' in Owens's administrative record during the period of construction of the estates in Toxteth Park, Carr observes that during the late 1860s 'typically' Welsh names increased and became more common than 'typically non-Welsh names' and remained significantly more common until the early 1880s. After this they plummeted below 'typically non-Welsh names', so that by 1890 non-Welsh names were far more common. Quite often only the husband was Welsh-born, as in the case of William Jones, a 34-year-old 'Commercial Clerk' for a steamship company, who lived in 2 Voelas Street, and John Herbert, a 34-year-old 'Mariner' in number 24. In both cases their wives were Liverpool-born.

26. The 1881 census captures life in Voelas and Rhiwlas streets just a few years after their houses had been completed. Many of the residents listed must have been the streets' original occupants. The dilution of the presence of Welsh-born builders in these Welsh Streets from the 1880s – suggested by the census returns for Voelas and Rhiwlas streets – can be explored by looking very briefly at two streets immediately to the south, Madryn Street and Kinmel Street. These streets were slightly more modest than Voelas Street and Rhiwlas Street – their houses are without bays – and it's tempting to speculate that, in the early 1880s, Welsh-born builders and their families tended to congregate in these less expensive streets. However, the 1881 census for Madryn Street reveals that, of its sixty houses, only two were occupied by Welsh-born members of the building trade – number 2 with John Griffith, a joiner, and number 20 with James Page, a blacksmith. Kinmel Street was more Welsh, with twelve houses occupied by Welsh-born 'heads', who in eight or nine instances were building tradesmen, including bricklayers at numbers 5 and 46; joiners at numbers 8, 42 and 56; a carpenter at number 13; and a carter at number 15.

27. The streets to the south, including Powis Street and Gwydir Street, are simpler still, with neither bays nor front enclosures.

28. The variation of detail is almost dazzling. In Wynnstay Street, immediately to the north of Voelas Street, the houses are faced with red brick and have single-storey bays and cornices as in Voelas Street. But although the lozenges are absent from the first-floor blank windows, the arched door surrounds are more strongly emphasised by being framed with pale yellow and black bricks. In Rhiwlas Street, cornices on the north side, where the houses are faced with reddish-brown bricks, are simpler,

with yellow-brick concave quadrant blocks but no bands of coloured bricks. However, on the south side of the street some houses have bands of yellow and black brick beneath their cornices and – a most peculiar detail – horizontal bands of yellow bricks framed with black bricks cut across their brown-brick facades at the centre point of their first-floor windows. Can the ultimate influence for this be the bands that often emblazoned medieval architecture of Italy, and John Ruskin's promotion during the 1850s of 'structural polychromy' in his *Stones of Venice*? There are also houses with window and door openings framed with yellow stretchers. In Powis Street, where the red-brick houses are flat-fronted, there are cornices formed by bands of black brick set below yellow-brick blocks, and groups of doors framed by yellow stretchers that alternate with dark grey headers and with arched tops formed with yellow bricks incorporating keystones formed of grey bricks. In Madryn Street and Kinmel Street the cornices of the red-brick houses are formed with standard bricks set diagonally to create a herringbone pattern – a cheap option – and some have no brick bands below the herringbone cornices while others have bands of black or of yellow bricks. Also in Kinmel Street yellow bricks are used as voussoirs on many of the door arches. In Gwydir Street, arguably the most modest of the surviving Welsh Streets, yellow bricks project at eaves level to imply a dentil cornice with, below, alternating red stretchers and black headers forming a frieze. In addition, and more idiosyncratic, black-brick bands cut into the centres of first-floor and ground-floor windows and travel around the perimeter of the door arches. Above ground-floor windows the lintels have a rough stone texture set within flat margins, as in the masonry of ancient Rome.

29. Cast stone was also used for the rough-textured lintels in Gwydir Street and Madryn Street.

30. The profile of the sixty houses on Rhiwlas Street is similar to that in Voelas Street, but with even fewer Welsh-born 'heads' of households (for more on which, see below). The population of the street on the day of the 1881 census was 246 but, as with Voelas Street, three houses were uninhabited, so that the average number of people per house was 4.3, just a little more than in Voelas Street. The houses were essentially the same size as those on Voelas Street, but with their design, notably the absence of front railed gardens, suggesting a subtly lower status. But the occupations of the street's inhabitants hardly confirm this. There were a few more humble residents – such as labourers and porters – but also those who were skilled tradesmen, superior artisans and aspiring professionals; for example, a watchmaker, a master mariner, a 'steam ship

engineer', a 'captain' in the 'merchant service' and a 'civil engineer'. One house – number 55 – seems to have been a 'common lodging house' and two of the street's small houses contained two separate households, which would have made them crowded. But on the other hand, six households kept servants; indeed, that at number 48, occupied by the 48-year-old civil engineer Albert Nelson Barnes, had two servants. So evidently the street was socially mixed but, once again, what was strikingly absent was a large Welsh-born population. There were only five Welsh-born 'heads' of households in the street, but most of these operated in the building trades. For example, at number 4 was David Evans, a 31-year-old 'Joiner & Builder'; at number 20 lived 39-year-old William Williams – also a joiner. At number 32 was William Hughes, a 'plasterer'; and his lodger, John Hugh and also Welsh-born, was a joiner. Finally at number 44 was Hugh Williams, a 'Railway Porter', his Welsh wife and a Welsh lodger named John Beedle, who was also a joiner, and at number 59 was 57-year-old Alfred Lewis, a 'warehouseman'.

31. With all sixty of the Voelas Street houses occupied in 1901, and accommodating 255 people at the time of the census, there was a density on average of 4.25 people per house.

32. Apart from the Cairns Street houses all being in single occupation and with no inhabited cellars or basements, the street is also notable for its generally low density of 4.25 people per house. This, of course, is in striking contrast to the court housing of central Liverpool.

33. It is not until Copy Letter Book 11, covering correspondence from October 1878 to November 1881, that the construction of twelve houses in Jermyn Street is mentioned.

34. See notes on the Arboretum compiled and published by the City of Lincoln Council.

35. For example, the Gothic Revival house of 1862–4 on Devonshire Road (with additions by Alfred Waterhouse) for the dock engineer George Fosbery Lyster (see Sharples, *Pevsner Architectural Guides: Liverpool*, pp. 276–80).

7. THE BIRTH OF THE COUNCIL FLAT

The Boundary Estate, Shoreditch (1890–1900)

1. J. N. Tarn, *Five Per Cent Philanthropy: An Account of Housing in Urban Areas between 1840 and 1914* (Cambridge University Press, 1972), pp. 42, 61.

2. See Sarah Wise, *The Blackest Streets: The Life and Death of a Victorian Slum* (London: Bodley Head, 2008), pp. 3–12.

3. The five-acre Nichol Estate had been acquired in the late 1650s by a Gray's Inn lawyer named John Nichol.

4. The Snow Estate stood to the east of the Nichol and stretched north from a narrow frontage on Redchurch Street. The estate was owned from the early eighteenth century by the Turville family, who had inherited the land in the 1680s from Elizabeth Snow.

5. He writes, for example: 'Cow-heels, bullocks'-hearts, kidneys, and livers, thin and poor-looking tripe, and sheep's-heads are amongst the uncooked portion of the stock; while the cooked viands are often represented by piles and chains of bruised, and often damaged-looking, saveloys, black-puddings, and a sort of greasy cake of baked sausage-meat, known as "faggots", sold for a penny or three farthings, and made of the harslet and other internal portions of the pig'; see Thomas Archer, *The Pauper, the Thief and the Convict* (London: Groombridge & Sons, 1865), pp. 21–2.

6. Archer, *The Pauper, the Thief and the Convict*, pp. 21–2.

7. Archer, *The Pauper, the Thief and the Convict*, pp. 26–7.

8. James Greenwood, *Low-life Deeps: An Account of the Strange Fish to be Found There* (London: Chatto & Windus, 1876).

9. Booth notebooks in London School of Economics (LSE), Booth/B/351, pp. 168–9.

10. LSE, Booth/B/351, pp. 170–71.

11. Wise, *The Blackest Streets*, p. 10.

12. Henry Lazarus, *Landlordism* (London: General Publishing Company, 1892), p. 6.

13. Wise, *The Blackest Streets*, p. 11.

14. At the time of the Ripper murders in 1888, the Hendersons were the 'epitome of respectability', as historian Jerry White points out. In 1888 Kenneth Henderson was 'an army officer', Henry Henderson was 'an active member of the Conservative Club, St James's St', and other family members were 'in the church'; see White's *Rothschild Buildings* (London: Routledge and Kegan Paul, 1980), p. 27.

15. 'Bethnal Green: Estates', in *A History of the County of Middlesex*, vol. 11, *Stepney, Bethnal Green*, ed. T. F. T Baker, (London, 1998), *British History Online*, pp. 155–168.

16. Wise, *The Blackest Streets*, pp. 51–2.

17. See Fiona Rule, *The Worst Street in London* (Hersham, Surrey: Ian Allan Publishing, 2008).

18. Toynbee Hall was the first of what would become a significant number of east London 'University Settlements', where volunteer students from

Oxford and Cambridge undertook a wide range of 'good works', as explained in 1902 by Howard Angus Kennedy: 'The wise men came from the East; and now, thank heaven! A few of these are going back there – back to the . . . East-End of London . . . that densely-peopled wilderness . . . Settling in little colonies, to live helpful and simple lives among the poor, not as missionaries . . . but as neighbours, brothers, and fellow citizens'; see Kennedy's 'London Social Settlements', in *Living London*, ed. George R. Sims (London: Cassell, 1902). In 1893 the Barnetts expanded their educational activities with the opening, in collaboration with the enlightened benefactor Passmore Edwards, of a large public library in Whitechapel High Street. In 1901 came the Whitechapel Art Gallery, designed by Charles Harrison Townsend, and intended to fulfil the biblical aphorism that 'man shall not live by bread alone' (Matthew 4:4). While 'bread' feeds the body, man also needs art – beauty – to feed the soul and, as Canon Barnett put it, to counter the 'paralysing and degrading sights of our streets'; see J. A. R. Pimlott, *Toynbee Hall* (London: J. M. Dent, 1935), p. 168, and Asa Briggs and Anne McCartney, *Toynbee Hall* (London: Routledge & Kegan Paul, 1984), p. 57. Jack London took a contrary view. Visiting 'an exhibition of Japanese art, got up for the poor of Whitechapel with the idea of elevating them', he wrote: If 'the poor folk are . . . taught to know and yearn after the Beautiful and True and Good, the foul facts of their existence and the social law that dooms one in three to a public-charity death . . . will be only so much of an added curse to them'; see London's *The People of the Abyss* (London and New York: Macmillan and Isbister, 1903), Chapter 26, p. 309.

19. Martin Stilwell, 'Housing the Workers: Early London County Council Housing 1889–1914, Part 3 – The Schemes in Detail, 11 – Boundary Street Estate, Bethnal Green' (August 2015), p. 3, https://stilwellhistory.uk/wp-content/uploads/2024/05/early_lcc_housing_part_3_11-boundary_street.pdf.

20. The mortality rate in the late nineteenth-century Nichol area was 40 people per thousand, as compared to 22.8 in Bethnal Green generally; see 'Bethnal Green: Building and Social Conditions from 1876-1914', in *A History of the County of Middlesex*, vol. 11, *Stepney, Bethnal Green*, pp. 126–32; Stilwell, 'Housing the Workers', p. 3.

21. George R. Sims, *How the Poor Live, and Horrible London* (Chatto & Windus, 1889), pp. 61–3.

22. Action was sweeping and it was rapid, largely because the Housing of the Working Classes Act of 1890 – supplementing the similarly named Act

of 1885 – for the first time gave local authorities like the LCC the legal power to compulsorily purchase land for slum clearance and to construct working-class tenement homes and estates. The Artisans' and Labourers' Dwellings Improvement Act 1875 had given councils the power to compulsorily purchase and clear slums, but not the power to build new housing on their site. This had to be done as a private initiative by house builders (see page 419). This meant that until the advent of the powerful LCC, councils could clear slums but did not have the mechanism to build houses directly, which was a formula for inaction.

23. Stilwell, 'Housing the Workers', p. 3.
24. Stilwell, 'Housing the Workers', p. 4.
25. Stilwell, 'Housing the Workers', p. 4.
26. Photographs of the LCC cottages in Goldsmiths Row are in the London Picture Archive under the record numbers 260035 and 259626. The Goldsmiths Row scheme is described in 'Bethnal Green: Building and Social Conditions from 1876–1914', in *A History of the County of Middlesex*, vol. 11, *Stepney, Bethnal Green*.
27. During this initial planning phase, it also emerged that estimates about the number of homes that could be created were too optimistic and the target number of people that could be accommodated in the scheme was lowered to 4,700.
28. Mark Girouard, *Sweetness and Light: The 'Queen Anne' Movement, 1860–1900* (Oxford University Press, 1977).
29. Wise, *The Blackest* Streets, pp. 161–2.
30. There are pilaster strips topped with strangely elongated Doric triglyphs and a dainty Doric cornice, above which rises an attic storey with square windows that are in striking contrast with the larger classroom and hall windows on the storeys below.
31. As described by Susan Beattie, *A Revolution in London Housing: The LCC Housing Architects and Their Work, 1893–1914* (London: GLC and Architectural Press, 198), pp. 23, 31.
32. E. R. Robson, 'Art as Applied to Town Schools', *Art Journal* (1881), pp. 137–40, quoted in Beattie, *A Revolution in London Housing*, pp. 23, 31.
33. Beattie, *A Revolution in London Housing*, p. 17.
34. The *rond-point* ingeniously served as a convenient dumping ground for demolition rubble from the site. Perhaps an inspiration for the mount is the fact that the west boundary of the estate was defined by Mount Street and the area had long been known as Friars Mount.
35. C. J. Stewart, *The Housing Question in London* (London: LCC, 1900), pp. 209.

36. Winmill initialled and approved the design drawings for these buildings –
    see Susan Beattie, *A Revolution in London Housing*, pp. 33–4. The gables
    on these three buildings are generally simpler than those on Sunbury
    Buildings, but make it clear that in the early 1890s Winmill loved a
    Dutch baroque gable and, given the opportunity, liked to demonstrate
    his powers of invention. The gables on Sunning and Culham are a happy
    mix of raking sides and concave curves topped by semicircles of brick-
    work. All are fairly abstract, merely evoking the sense of history. But the
    gables on Taplow Buildings are different, with the one in the centre of the
    south side almost as historically accurate as those in Sunbury Buildings,
    incorporating large-scale carved stone baroque scrolls and a crowning
    semicircular pediment. Winmill was not just inventive with his gables
    but also with his walling. For Sonning and Culham, he deviated from
    the general convention for the early phase LCC-designed buildings on
    the estate and used yellow brick for the walls and red brick for banding
    at upper levels, with the bands getting thinner as they get nearer to the
    ground. On the adjoining Hurley Buildings, by contrast, bands of red and
    pinkish-yellow brick are of equal depth. Winmill was also responsible,
    along with Reginald Minton Taylor, for most of the blocks in Section
    B, on the northern portion of the site and around part of Arnold Circus,
    which were named after wholesome town and villages west of London
    close to the Thames (west to east: Cleeve, Shiplake, Marlow, Hurley and
    Sandford). All the blocks around the circus, with the exception of Iffley
    Buildings, were completed by 1896.

37. *The Buildings of England, London 5: East*, ed. Charles O'Brien, Bridget
    Cherry and Nikolaus Pevsner (London: Yale University Press, 2005), p. 588.

38. The centre portion of the estate, with Arnold Circus at its heart, was –
    with the areas to the north, west and east – the first part of the estate to
    be built. It also – as one might expect – contains the most architecturally
    ambitious buildings. This was not just because the circus is the estate's
    showpiece but also because the sites, with their curved frontages and
    somewhat wedge-shaped plots, offered opportunities for architectural
    adventure and flights of fancy.

39. Like most of the LCC architects who worked on the estate, Minton
    Taylor remains something of a misty character. But what little is known
    is revealing. In the 1880s he had made a special study of brick architecture
    in the Netherlands and in 1911, when he applied for licentiate member-
    ship of the Royal Institute of British Architects, his supporters included
    W. R. Lethaby – one of the powerhouses of British late nineteenth-
    century architecture who, arguably more than anyone else, led the creative

leap from Gothic- and vernacular-inspired Arts and Crafts design to a modern architecture, inspired by history but characterised by a rational simplicity of form. Minton Taylor was also responsible for Cleeve Buildings on Calvert Avenue.

40. The construction of the blocks on the south portion of the estate were generally a year or so behind those to the north, with, for example, Abingdon Buildings, at the south end on Boundary Street, being built between 1896 and 1899 to the designs of A. M. Phillips and, immediately to its north, Wargrave Buildings, completed in 1897, probably to the designs of William Hynam, who initialled the design drawings. Also completed in 1897 and early 1898 were Molesey Buildings and Clifton Buildings, both by C. C. Winmill, and Cookham Buildings by R. Minton Taylor. Laleham Buildings, by Winmill, and Benson Buildings, by William Hynam, were completed by the end of 1898 or in 1899, as was Hedsor Buildings, running north off Old Nichol Street (which was at one time to be renamed Calvin Street). It was designed by Winmill, and the completion of these blocks finalised the construction of the estate.

41. Beattie, *A Revolution in London Housing*, p. 32.

42. The evolution of Winmill's contributions is immediately evident in his attitude to gables. Those on Hedsor Building, completed to Winmill's designs in 1899, are strange, partly because what can be taken to be the building's main elevation faces the courtyard rather than the street. The hierarchy here is a little difficult to decipher but, probably significantly, the windows generally face the street, and the building's major gables face the courtyard. They are of matching design and curious affairs, quite unlike Winmill's earlier, meticulously detailed seventeenth-century baroque-style gables. Those on Hedsor Buildings, as on the adjoining Laleham Buildings, also of 1899 – are wide, rough-cast, straight-sided and elemental, or basic, and all embrace simple, classical five-bay arcades. On both buildings the portions of their elevations crowned by the gables break forward slightly and are flanked, in a most memorable manner, by tall, rectangular-plan or half-cylindrical and very sculptural towers, one of which on each building is topped in a most idiosyncratic and surprising manner by a white-painted gable pediment. The capping of a cylindrical form with a triangular form gives these courtyard elevations great visual distinction. As Susan Beattie explains most perceptively, there was no doubt a sound – almost symbolic – reason for the careful detailing of the block's less public elevations. The fact that the 'inventive' and 'fastidious' attention to detail 'embraces not only their principal facades but rear and side elevations' can be seen as an act of 'deliberate defiance of the

rule of uniformity that had been imposed upon the poor' by the utilitarian housing blocks usually constructed by the 'charitable trusts' (Beattie, *A Revolution in London Housing*, p. 23).

43. Beattie, *A Revolution in London Housing*, p. 41. There is another contender for the most interesting example of late Winmill design. Molesey Buildings on Camlet Street, completed in 1898, is another extraordinary essay in the simplified and inventive final phase of the estate. There are no stripes and, on the street elevation, tall towers of polygonal plan-form house sculleries and frame a two-storey inhabited gable pediment of a most simple shape. There is nothing curvaceous or baroque here, just straight raking sides. Below the pediment are two tiers of balconies serving as an outdoor space for the apartments they adjoin. Molesey Buildings had an 'associated' plan, with mostly three-room apartments, some incorporating sculleries and most with WCs accessed via common corridors.

44. Stilwell, 'Housing the Workers', pp. 4 and 5.

45. The workshops behind Marlow Buildings (of a similar date) are also two storeys high and with joists, but slightly smaller windows. On the other hand, the workshops behind Cleeve Buildings, also of 1896, are single storey and structurally simple.

46. Stilwell, 'Housing the Workers', p. 5.

47. See Shipley Buildings upper-floor plan in the London Archives, ref: LCC/AR/HS/03/176-256. The *Municipal Journal*, 2 March 1900, p. 190 (Bishopsgate Institute library reference: London Collection Pamphlets Number Q20/2 Class D3.4).

48. Benson Buildings was completed at the same time as Abingdon Buildings – sometime soon before 1900 – with this pair probably being the last housing blocks completed on the estate. Plans of Benson Buildings indicate that at a typical upper level it contained sets of three two-room apartments and one three-room apartment. The two-room apartments comprised a bedroom and a living room, both heated in the traditional manner by coal fires, with that in the living room also used for cooking. Some apartments included a small scullery off the living room while others had a scullery located off the common corridor. On typical upper levels all the apartments had their own water closets, but some were accessed via the corridor. (See upper-floor plan of Benson Buildings in the London Archives, ref: LCC/AR/HS/03/176-256.)

49. Stewart, *The Housing Question in London*, p. 209.

50. Ninety apartments had 'private W.C. and private scullery' located off the common landing; 142 had private WCs set 'outside' their front doors but with sculleries 'in common with others'; 35 apartments used the WC

and scullery 'in common with others'. The number of different types of apartments – 601, 201, 90, 142 and 35 – add up to the total of 1,069 apartments on the estate.

51. There were 103 four-room apartments (i.e. with an extra bedroom). Fifteen apartments had just one room. Seven had five rooms.

52. The 1,069 apartments contained 2,762 rooms (excluding sculleries and WCs) so at two people per room – which was the LCC's declared ratio – these rooms were to house 5,524 people.

53. See for example the Streatham Street 'Model Houses for Families' in London's Bloomsbury of 1849 by Henry Roberts, p. 205.

54. Martin Stilwell claims that Cleeve Buildings had one bathroom per floor ('Housing the Workers', p. 8), as did Hedsor Buildings. Extensive interior alterations made in recent years mean that it is now physically difficult to confirm the presence of these original bathrooms.

55. It is interesting to consider the laundry block alongside the other non-residential building constructed on the estate to the design of the LCC's architects. At the west end of Calvert Avenue is a most curious and highly asymmetrical structure that, at casual glance, you might think was intended to serve as a community hall for the estate. Built in 1898, it in fact served as the LCC's Weights and Measures Office, with a coroner's court occupying what looks, externally, to be a pleasant hall intended for convivial gatherings. As with the laundry building, the architectural sources are eclectic. There are Tudor Renaissance mullioned windows along with seventeenth-century-inspired details including a handsome arch – that presumably led to the court – which incorporates a large keystone emblazed with the interlinked letters 'LCC'. This was the estate's only public building, but it does not seek to express its exceptional role. Instead, it gently merges with the estate's domestic architecture while only in a subtle manner signalling that it is in some way different.

56. *British Architect*, 14 May 1897, vol. 47, pp. 343–4.

57. Beattie, *A Revolution in London Housing*, p. 60.

58. The working drawings for Hogarth House are dated December 1897, so its rooms could have been furnished by late 1899, when presumably the photograph would have been taken. But why would the journal show a room from the Millbank Estate in an article about the Boundary Estate? A simple mistake? Perhaps.

59. *British Architect*, 12 February 1897, vol. 47, p. 110, quoted in Beattie, *A Revolution in London Housing*, p. 32.

60. *British Architect*, 26 February 1897, vol. 47, p. 146, quoted in Beattie, *A Revolution in London Housing*, p. 35.

61. *British Architect*, 12 March 1897, vol. 42, p. 180, quoted in Beattie, *A Revolution in London Housing*, pp. 31–2.
62. LSE, Booth/B/351, pp. 158–9.
63. LSE, Booth/B/351 pp. 170–71.
64. LSE, Booth/B/351. pp. 160–61.
65. LSE, Booth/B/351, pp. 158–75.
66. Notably mostly Church Street, which had been the west end of Bethnal Green Road and is now Redchurch Street, along with much of the south side of Old Nichol Street, which effectively formed the south edge of the Boundary Estate. At one point these streets seemed to have been due for demolition (indeed they are shown as demolished on the 1896 edition of the OS map) but were spared.
67. LSE, Booth/B/351, pp.174–5.
68. Raphael Samuel (ed.), *East End Underworld: Chapters in the Life of Arthur Harding* (London: Routledge & Kegan Paul, 1981).
69. *East End Underworld*, pp. 5–6; Samuel refers to 'Directories' that list James Julier at the fried fish shop at number 19 from 1890 to 1896.
70. The 1891 *Post Office Directory* and census returns record that the landlord of the Blue Anchor was Thomas George Symonds. The *Directory* records Symonds was still there as late as 1915. The Blue Anchor appears to have been in fact located at 2 Chance Street on the corner with Redchurch Street. On the south side of Redchurch Street, between Chance Street and Ebor Street, is the long-established 'Owl & Pussycat' public house, which occupies what is probably an early eighteenth-century building refaced in opulent manner in the mid nineteenth century. How this related to the Blue Anchor is not clear, but it seems they were neighbours.
71. *East End Underworld*, p. 17.
72. Quoted in Sarah Wise, *The Blackest Streets*, p. 114.
73. LSE, Booth/B/351, pp. 182–3.
74. LSE, Booth/B/351, pp. 184–5.
75. LSE, Booth/B/352, pp.178–9.
76. LSE, Booth/B/351, pp. 180–81, 182, 183.
77. Dan Cruickshank, *Spitalfields: The History of a Nation in a Handful of Streets* (London: Random House, 2016), p. 426.
78. Morrison's preface to the third edition of *A Child of the Jago* (Chicago: Academy Victorian Editions, 1995), p. xiv.
79. George Haw, *No Room to Live* (London: W. Gardner, Darton & Co., 1900), p. 49.
80. London, *The People of the Abyss*, Chapter 6. Sarah Wise, in *The Blackest Streets*, offers a breakdown of the fate of the dispossessed population of

the Old Nichol. Quoting an LCC record of 1895, she reveals that of the 1,035 people the LCC documented 56 per cent moved within a quarter mile, 30 per cent between a quarter and a half mile, 9 per cent between a half mile and one mile, with only 5 per cent moving more than a mile away (pp. 265–6). Charles Booth was seemingly correct when he observed that the former denizens of the Old Nichol had largely swelled nearby slum areas.

81. *Household Words*, 14 June 1851, p. 167.
82. *Municipal Journal*, 9 March 1900, pp. 193–4; Stewart, *The Housing Question in London*, p. 213; Beattie, *A Revolution in London Housing*, p. 53.
83. *Municipal Journal*, 2 March 1900, p. 159.
84. *Municipal Journal*, p. 153.
85. He claimed that the 'labouring class population displaced numbered 5,426 of whom 3,282 were adults and 2,144 children'. Curiously, this is a couple of hundred fewer than the 5,719 now generally cited.
86. *Municipal Journal*, 2 March 1900, p. 163.
87. *Municipal Journal*, p. 163.
88. *Municipal Journal*, p. 163.
89. Cleeve Buildings is eighteen windows wide and, for the most part, five storeys high (including an attic) above a basement; only the four-window-wide gabled centre is six storeys high.
90. This striking symmetry has been somewhat diluted because the east gable has been rebuilt, in distinctly reduced manner, after wartime bomb damage.
91. Stilwell, 'Housing for Workers', p. 8.
92. See Stilwell, 'Housing for Workers', table 2, p. 15. He states that Cleeve Buildings contained 103 rooms, that occupants numbered 143 at the time of the 1901 census, and that maximum occupancy was 206, so two people per room.
93. Stilwell, 'Housing for Workers', p. 13. Stilwell's interpretation of the 1901 census suggests that 78 per cent of Cleeve Buildings occupants were British-born, 16 per cent were 'foreign'-born (this seems too high) and 6 per cent were Jews born in Britain (p. 15). This relates closely to his analysis of the estate as a whole in 1901. Using census returns, he calculates that of its 4,499 residents (evidently a large number of apartments had yet to be occupied or were not occupied to maximum capacity), 76 per cent were British-born; 15 per cent were 'foreign'-born, and 8 per cent were British-born Jews (pp. 14–16). (He does not account for the missing 1 per cent.) See also Wise, *The Blackest Streets*, pp. 268–9.
94. Other apartments occupied by people from elsewhere in Europe were:

number 7, occupied by one woman – Hannah Borrison, aged 55, single and born in Russia; number 20, occupied by Herman Gordon, a 55-year-old foreman cap maker, who had been born in Russia, his wife, Naedwy, who had been born in Germany, as had his two daughters, and his youngest child, Aaron, aged 12, who had been born in London; and number 26, occupied by an Austrian-born couple – 26-year-old Benjamin Linker, a cabinetmaker, and his 22-year-old wife, Deborah.

95. Charles Booth, *Life and Labour of the People in London*, vol. 1: *Poverty* (London: Macmillan, 1902), pp. 66–7.

96. Booth, *Life and Labour of the People in London*, Religious Influences, vol. 2, *Religious Influences*, pp. 68 and 71; Beattie, *A Revolution in London Housing*, p. 54.

8. THE FIRST 'MODERN' HOUSE

New Ways, Northampton (1925–6)

1. *Evening Standard*, 8 December 1945.
2. *Small Houses: £500–£2500*, ed. H. Myles Wright (London: Architectural Press, 1937; 2nd edn, 1946); see p. 8.
3. *Small Houses*, p. 13.
4. Bassett-Lowke's new house is now numbered 508 Wellingborough Road.
5. J. M. Richards, *An Introduction to Modern Architecture* (Harmondsworth: Penguin, 1940), p. 66; see also Adrian Tinniswood, *The Art Deco House* (London: Mitchell Beazley, 2003), pp. 60–63.
6. The plans were submitted on 1 April 1916.
7. According to Thomas Howarth's 1952 biography of Mackintosh, Bassett-Lowke explained to Mackintosh when they met that structural alterations were already taking place at 78 Derngate and that – at the initial stage of the project at least –Anderson was playing a key role. See Howarth's *Charles Rennie Mackintosh and the Modern Movement* (London: Routledge & Kegan Paul, 1952); and copies of six letters from Bassett-Lowke to Mackintosh, dated 1916–19, in the museum now occupying 78 Derngate.
8. The Cloister Room was dismantled in 1971, along with the rest of the rooms, when the building in which it was housed was demolished. Elements survive in Glasgow in museum storage. The long-evolving art deco style secured the public's attention – and indeed its name – when it was displayed with dazzling success and great style at the 1925 Paris

Exposition Internationale des Arts Décoratifs et Industriels Modernes (see p. 331).

9. Track with a gauge of a quarter inch to the foot and models built to the scale of 1:43.5. 'o gauge' had been established by a pioneering German toy maker named Märklin.

10. The Deutscher Werkbund became an important factor in the growth of socially orientated modernism in Germany and in 1919 was involved in the foundation of the Bauhaus.

11. Tinniswood, *The Art Deco House*, pp. 60–63.

12. These details included some of the more prized Mackintosh interior fittings and fixtures and, it would seem, the idea of a bedroom balcony.

13. 'Ornament in Architecture', *Engineering Magazine* (August 1892), pp. 187–90.

14. The *Raumplan* concept would be further developed with Loos's split-level houses, notably the Müller House of 1930 in Prague.

15. Translated by Frederick Etchell.

16. The Russian constructivist movement promoted simple abstract design that rejected traditional decoration and reflected a modern industrial society. In architecture, methods and materials of construction were expressed in an almost cubist manner. Constructivism flourished in the USSR through the 1920s until replaced in the early 1930s by the crude and over-scaled classicism that Joseph Stalin favoured as the regime's socialist realist national style and that became a hallmark of totalitarianism.

17. Letter to H. P. Bremmer, 29 January 1914, cited in Carel Blotkamp, *Mondrian: The Art of Destruction* (London: Reaktion Books, 2001), p. 81.

18. Harry Holtzman and Martin S. James, *The New Art – The New Life: The Collected Writings of Piet Mondrian* (Boston: G. K. Hall, 1986), pp. 27–74).

19. *Architectural Review* (November 1926), pp. 175–9.

20. *Ideal Home: A Monthly Magazine for Home-Lovers* (January 1927).

21. Alan Windsor, *Peter Behrens: Architect and Designer* (London: Architectural Press, 1981), p. 162.

22. The Twentieth Century Society was founded by well-informed enthusiasts in 1979 – and initially called the Thirties Society – with the aim of explaining and promoting architecture of the mid to late twentieth century and fighting hard for its preservation from ignorant mutilation or destruction.

23. Some have traced art deco back to the decorative arts of Paris of the 1910s, or seen elements of it in cubism (which emerged in around 1908) or even in Vienna Secession design. But these connections are very general and

open to debate and interpretation. Arguably it was not until the early 1920s that most of the varied elements that define art deco coalesced to form a distinct style.

24. Quote recorded by the architect and architectural critic Kenneth Murchison. This quote appears in most accounts of Van Alen and the Chrysler Building, usually without a reference, but seems to have appeared first in a Murchison article in a 1930 edition of the weekly magazine *American Architect*, vol. 137.

25. Some critics see the plan in a different light. For Stanford Anderson, an authority on Behrens, the 'symmetrically organized' New Ways is 'spatially conservative' and 'a hopeless compromise between Behrens's recent handicraft ambitions and a felt need to move with his ascending younger colleagues'; see Anderson's *Peter Behrens and a New Architecture for the Twentieth Century* (Cambridge, MA: MIT Press, 2002), p. 237.

26. *Architectural Review* (November 1926), pp. 175–9.

27. *Architectural Review* (November 1926), pp. 175–9.

28. The maids' sitting room was not only supplied with hot and cold water but also, according to the *Architectural Review*, 'with a combination stove available for emergency cooking'.

29. Drawing in the RIBA Drawings Collection, RIBA 12385; library reference: PA9/2(1) (U18/28(1)).

30. See Sylvia Pinches, *The Friends of 78 Derngate Newsletter*, vol. 21 (December 2002).

31. RIBA Special Collection, 728.036.6.

32. Tinniswood, *The Art Deco House*, pp. 60–63.

33. *Small Houses*, p. 38.

34. Historic England, in its listed building description. Historic England adds that High & Over was 'one of only two buildings included (from Britain) in the exhibition "The International Style" held in the Museum of Modern Art, New York, under the curatorship of Henry-Russell Hitchcock and Philip Johnson in 1932'.

35. During the post-First World War house-building boom it became usual for developers of more economic new homes to construct them along existing roads, mostly those on the edge of built-up areas, because costs were reduced, particularly in the provision of services, and land was relatively cheap and sites accessible. This practice – known as 'bypass' or 'ribbon' development – soon became notorious because the neighbourhoods created could be both soulless and placeless. Myles Wright's *Small Houses* (p. 9) points out the problems in a most succinct manner. It observes that 'semi-detached houses' can be 'very good houses

indeed' – and in the 1930s many were designed in fashionable art deco of the moderne style – but the 'danger and harm of such houses is in their mechanically continuous development in ribbons, the greater distances imposed on residents walking to shops, railway stations or other social centres, the cutting down of trees and banishing of open spaces, and the consequent monotony of the whole neighbourhood's appearance'.

AFTERWORD

1. The Brunswick Centre – generally six storeys high – replaced terraces of late Georgian houses that had been long neglected, but the transformation of a long-marginal site into a mixed-use, high-value private housing enclave – as initially envisaged – proved a step too far and the plan failed commercially. In response, Camden leased the residential portion of the Centre to serve as council housing. This, ultimately, also did not work, and the Centre became increasingly run-down until the current approach was adopted in 2002 and has proved successful.

2. Clive Aslet, *King Charles III: 40 Years of Architecture* (London: Triglyph Books, 2025), p. 142.

Picture Acknowledgements

Black and white images are reproduced by kind permission of:

78 Derngate Northampton Trust: p. 312. Alamy: p. 210 (Chronicle). iStock: p. 366 (Blackbeck). The London Archives (City of London Corporation): p. 283. Richard Harris: p. xviii. Samuel C. Melnick: p. 65. Walthamstow Historical Society: p. 234. Wikimedia Commons: pp. xv, xx, xxv, 15, 81 above, 124, 143, 146 above, 146 below, 154 above, 154 below, 169, 185 above, 185 below, 191, 195, 199, 320, 327 above, 327 below, 334.

Colour section images are reproduced by kind permission of:

Alamy: James Gibbs, Richard Boyle (The Picture Art Collection), Charles Rennie Mackintosh (GL Archive), The Grange library (Goddard New Era), Cragside kitchen, Willow Road interior (The National Trust Photolibrary), Hopkins House (Anthony Weller-VIEW). Bridgeman Images: Mid-nineteenth century bedroom (© Geffrye Museum). Getty Images: Chiswick House interior, Kenwood House interior, Victorian bathroom (Heritage Images). Haddon Hall: great hall at Haddon Hall. Historic England Archive: Blenheim Palace corridor. © Iwan Baan: Parkside. The London Archives (City of London Corporation): Bedford Square interior. Sambourne House, Royal Borough Kensington and Chelsea: Sambourne House staircase, Sambourne House interior.

All other images from the author's collection.

The author and publisher gratefully acknowledge the permission granted to reproduce the copyright material in this book. Every effort has been made to trace copyright holders and to obtain their permission. The publisher apologises for any errors or omissions and, if notified of any corrections, will make suitable acknowledgement in future reprints or editions of this book.

Index

Page numbers in *italics* indicate illustrations

Abercromby Square, Liverpool, 150

Abergele, Conwy, 214

Abingdon Buildings, Shoreditch, 277

Acropolis, Athens, 348

Act of Union (1707), 28

Adam, James, 6, 123

Adam, Robert, 4, 6, 123

Adler, Dankmar, 322

Adler, Hermann, 55

Adler, Jacob, 57, 67

AEG Turbine Hall, Berlin, 318–19, *320*, 330, 338

Aesthetic Movement, 262

Africa trade, 131, 132, 149

Akkadian, 74

Alabama, CSS, 151

Albert, Prince Consort, 171, 205

Alberti, Leon Battista, 88

alcohol, 288

Alexandra Road Estate, Camden, 359

Aliens Act (1905), 298

All Saints, Derby, 93

Alnwick, Northumberland, 159

Alton West Estate, Roehampton, 354–6

American Civil War (1861–5), 150–51

American Revolutionary War (1775–83), 142

Amersham, Buckinghamshire, 344–5

Ancient Architecture of England (Carter), 163

Anderson, Alexander Ellis, 310, 313

Anderson, William James, 313

Andred, Glen, 187

Anglican Church, 40, 42

Anne, Queen of Great Britain, 28

Apollo, 101

Aramaic, 74

Arboretum, Derby, 242

Arboretum, Lincoln, 241

Archer, Thomas, 250–51

Architectura, De (Vitruvius), 164

Architectural Review, 328, 332, 335, 336, 337–8, *339*, 343

architectural schools, 156

Argand lamps, 142, 147

Arlington Street, London, 104–5

Armstrong, Margaret, 154, 159, 160, 161, 201

Armstrong, William, xii, 154, 159–61, 186–203

Arnold, Matthew, 262

Arnold Circus, Shoreditch, *246*, *264*, *265*, *269*, 271, 272, *273*, 282, 293, 301

Art Deco, 331, 336, 338, 352, 364

Art Nouveau, 307, 315, 322

Artillery Ground, London, 34

Arts and Crafts Exhibition Society, 307

Arts and Crafts Movement, xxii, 194, 201, 272, 281, 299, 317, 333, 344, 363

Arup, Ove, 347

Ashfield Street, Vauxhall, 248

Ashford Black Marble, xxi

Ashkenazim, 51–76

Ashmole, Bernard, 344–5

Ashmolean Museum, Oxford, 158

Assemble, 244

Association of Austrian Artists, 307

Assyria, 74

Atelier Primavera, 340

Atheneum, Liverpool, 140

Athens, Greece, 348

Attempt to Discriminate, An (Rickman), 163

Au Printemps, Paris, 340

Aubrey, John, 12

Austria, 306–7, 308–9, 321

Bacchus, 229

Bakewell, Robert, 93, 95, 102

Balfour Declaration (1917), 63

Baltic Sea, 83, 129

bandstands, 241, 268, 301

Bangladesh, 75, 300

Bank of England, 121, 141, *143*, 158

Bank of Liverpool, 151–2

Banks, Robert Richardson, 181

Banqueting House, Whitehall Palace, 182

Barbaro, Daniele, 88

Barber, Joseph, 137

Barbican Estate, London, 357–9, *358*

Barbon, Nicholas, 33–4

Barclays, 152

Barnack stone, xxi

Barnett, Samuel, 257

baroque, 4, 5, 10, 20–21, 84, 89, 98, 104, 166, 178, 197

Barrez, Alphonse, 343

Barry, Charles Jr, 181

Barry, Charles Sr, 168, 169, 179, 182

Barton-upon-Humber, Lincolnshire, 113

basements, 14, 95, 98, 118, 212

Bassae, Greece, 157

Bassett-Lowke, Wenman Joseph, xxii, 305–6, 310–17, 328–45, 367

Bath, Somerset, xxi, 12, 113, 123, 130

bathrooms, 225, 231–2

Battle of the Boyne (1690), 28

Battle of the Somme (1916), 314

Battle of the Styles, 182–6, 367

Battle of Worcester (1651), 12

Bauhaus School, 319

Baustein, Abraham, 236

Bawtree, Henry, 54

Bayleaf Farmstead, Kent, xiv, xvi, xvii, *xviii*

Beachcroft, Richard Middleton, 291–2

Beale, Mary, 3

Beattie, Susan, 266, 272, 282

Bebington, Wirral, 122

bedchambers, xvii, xxiii

Bedford, Walsham How, Bishop of, 258

Bedford Park, Chiswick, 263, 281

bedrooms
  Boundary Estate, 247, 277, 278, *294*
  Cragside, 192
  Great George Street, *146*
  New Ways, 340
  Pallant House, 17–20
  Princelet Street, 37, 45
  Toxteth, 223, 225, 231, 236, 240

Behrens, Peter, xxvii, 306, 317–21, 328–45, 367

Belgrave Road, Birmingham, 63

Bell, Isabella Finch, Lady, 105–7

Belle, Dido Elizabeth, 136

Bengalis, 75, 300

Benjamin Heywood Sons & Co., 128

Benson Buildings, Shoreditch, *273*, 277, 290

Berkeley Square, London, 103–4, 105–7, *106*

Berlin, Germany
  AEG Turbine Hall, 318–19, *320*, 330, 338
  Britz Horseshoe Estate, 352

Bethnal Green, London, 45, 60, 250, 296, 356

Bethnal Green Road, Shoreditch, 249, 252, 254, 258, *269*, 284, 287

béton brut, 319, 356, 360

Bill of Rights (1689), 135

Birkenhead, Merseyside, 241, 242

Birmingham, West Midlands, 62, 63, 168

Bishop Auckland, County Durham, 160

Blaides Staithe, Kingston-upon-Hull, 82

Blashill, Thomas, 261

Blaydes, Benjamin, 80

Blaydes House, Kingston-upon-Hull, 80–82, *81*, 113

Bloomsbury, London, 205, 207, 216

Blore, Edward, 182

Blue Anchor, Shoreditch, 285

Blue Coat School, Liverpool, 129

Board of Jewish Deputies, 69

board schools, 263–6, 267, 275, 285, 286, 299

Boer War (1899–1902), 281, 296–7

bolection, 25

Bolshevik Revolution (1917), 325

Bonny Island, Nigeria, 149

Book of Architecture (Gibbs), 92, 98

Book of Deuteronomy, 69

Book of Genesis, 134

Book of Leviticus, 134–5

Booker, John, 122

Booth, Charles, 57, 252–4, 258, 274, 284–7, 298

Boswell, James, 135, 137

Boundary Estate, Shoreditch, xxviii–xxix, *246*, 247–301
  board schools, 263–6, 267, 275, 285, 286, 299
  circus layout, 267–8, 274–5
  communal laundry block, 279
  construction (1890–1900), 260–77, *269*
  grid pattern plan, 260–61, 267
  Hynam's buildings, *273*, 277, 279, *280*
  inauguration (1900), 256, 289–90
  interior decoration, 281–2
  internal layouts, 277–80, 293–5, *294*
  Jewish community, 296–9
  lighting, 277, 282
  Minton Taylor's buildings, 271–2, *273*, *280*, 293, *294*
  Phillips' buildings, 271–2
  Plumbe's buildings, 270
  population density, 247, 278, 301
  press, reception in, 282–4
  relocations and, 287–92, 296–7
  sewage and services system, 276
  streets, 267–8, 274–5, 276
  'stripeland' moniker, 273, 282, 284
  Winmill's buildings, 268, 272, *273*
  workshops, 275

Boundary Street, Shoreditch, 248, *253*, 259, 276, 353

Bourdon, Peter, 46

Boyle, Dorothy, 105

Boynton Hall, East Yorkshire, 92

Bremmer, Hendricus Peter, 326

Brescia, Italy, 88

Breuer, Marcel, 352

Brick Lane, London, 34, 35, 52, 58, 59, 62–3, 287

brickwork, 95
  Boundary Estate, 271, 282
  Tayler & Green, 364
  Toxteth, 225, 226, 229, 230, 245

Bridelaw, William, 240

Bristol, England, 126, 136, 138, 145–7, 158

British Architect, 192, 281, 282, 284, 301

British Museum, London, 182, 344

Britz Horseshoe Estate, Berlin, 352

Broadbridge, John, 51

Brompton, Arthur Cayley, 3rd Baronet, 83

Brook Street, Mayfair, 45

Brown, Neave, 359

Brule, Samuel, 43

Brune Street, Spitalfields, 56

Brunel, Isambard Kingdom, 160

Brunelleschi, Filippo, 88

Brunswick Centre, Bloomsbury, 359

Buckingham and Chandos, Richard Temple, 3rd Duke, 255

Buckingham Palace, London, 170–71, 182

Buckland Street, Toxteth, 223–5, *224*, 230–31

Buffalo, New York, 322

Builder, The, 251

Builders' Magazine, 163

Building Acts, 8, 34, 225

Bundism, 56, 75

burgage plots, xxi

Burleigh, Bennet, 258

Burley-on-the-Hill, Rutland, 105

Burley, James, 19

Burlington, Richard Boyle, 3rd Earl, xxvii, 84, 85–119
 Burlington House, 87
 Kirby Hall, 89
 Londesborough Hall, 92, 118
 Maister House, 85–119
 Round Coppice, 96, *97*
 Wentworth Woodhouse, 90, *91*, 105, 112
 York Assembly Rooms, 90

Burlington House, London, 87

Burn, William, 157, 158

Burton, James, 6, 216

Butler Street, Spitalfields, 56

butteries, xvii, xix, 24

bye-law houses, 213, 266

Byker Wall, Newcastle upon Tyne, 359–60

Byrne, Catherine, 236

Cadet, Elizabeth, 44

Cairns Street, Toxteth, *219*, 237–8, *239*, 240, 244

Calvert Avenue, Shoreditch, *246*, 276, 289, 293, *294*, 300

Calvinism, 33, 37–51, 59, 214, 229

Cambridge University, 158

Campbell, Colen, 85, 87, 96

Campfield Estate, Everton, 216, 221

cannonballs, 83

Caribbean, 82, 126–7, 145–7, 148–9

Carlile, Joan, 3

Carlyle, Thomas, 173

Carnegie, Andrew, 233

Carr, Gareth, 217

Carter, Elizabeth, 51

Carter, John, 163

'Case for the Open Fire, The' (Orwell), 304

Case, Thomas, 132

Castle Street, Liverpool, 129

Catholicism, 27–8, 37–8, 84, 166

Cavendish, Mary, *see* Shrewsbury, Mary Talbot, Countess

Cavendish, William, 1st Earl of Devonshire, xxvi, xxvii

Cavendish Gardens, Toxteth, 243

cavity wall construction, 225

Cayley, Arthur, 3rd Baronet of Brompton, 83

Cayley, Mary, 83

cellars, 14, 95, 98, 118, 212

census
  1851: 51
  1861: 214, 251
  1881: 226, 227, 231
  1891: 58, 202, 237
  1901: 220, 235, 247, 295
central heating, 201, 303, 333
Ceres, 108–9
Cézanne, Paul, 30
Chadwick, Edwin, 209,
  212, 213
Chadwick, James, 129
chalk, xix
Chamberlin, Powell and Bon,
  354, 357
Chambers, William, 122–3
Chanell, John, 6, 16, 26
Charles II, King of England,
  Scotland and Ireland, 10, 39
Charles III, King of the United
  Kingdom, 365
Charles III, King/Jacobite
  Pretender, 44
Charles IX, King of France, 37
Chartist movement (1838–48),
  162, 171
Chassais l'Eglise, France, 43
Chatsworth House, Derbyshire,
  xxvii, 105, 172, 242
Cheadle, Staffordshire, 167
Cheere, Henry, 108, 116
Chelsea Embankment, London, 196
Chelsea Royal Hospital,
  London, 279
Chelsea, London, 309

Chertsey Buildings, Shoreditch, 271
cherubs, 12, *13*, 110, 197, *199*
Cheshire Street, Shoreditch, 284
Chesterfield, Philip Stanhope, 4th
  Earl, 26
Chevras Nidvat Chain, 51–2, 54, 62,
  65, 66
Chicago World's Fair (1893), 321
Chichester, West Sussex, xxviii,
  xxx, 1–30
Chichester Corporation, 2
Child of the Jago, A (Morrison), 288
Childers, Erskine, 309
Childs, Thomas, 214
chimneys, xi, *xii*, xiii, xiv, *xv*, xvii, xix
  Heywood's, 141
  Maister House, 108
  Toxteth bye-law houses, 225
chinoiserie, 48
Chiswick House, London, 90
cholera, 212
Christ Church, Spitalfields,
  40, 50
Christianity, 10, 27–8, 74, 84,
  87, 166
  Calvinism, 33, 37–51, 59,
    214, 229
  Catholicism, 27–8, 37–8, 84, 166
  Huguenots, xiv, 33, 37–51, 59, 129
  Protestantism, 27–8, 33, 37–51, 59,
    84, 87, 129, 166
  slavery and, 134–5, 139
Christie, Agatha, 350
Chrysler building, Manhattan,
  331–2

Church Street, Shoreditch, 252, 259, *269*, 285, 286

Church Street, Spitalfields, 34, 42, 44, 46, 57, 59

Citroën, 344

Citrohan House, Stuttgart, 328, 344

City Gardener, The (Fairchild), 49

City of London, 5, 8

  Bank of England, 121, 141, *143*

  Barbican Estate, 357–9, *358*

  Golden Lane Estate, 354, 357

  Spitalfields, xiv, xxvii, xxix, *32*, 33–51

  Threadneedle Street, 38

City of London Corporation, 248

City of Westminster, 8

Clapton, London, 49

Clarkson, Thomas, 139

clay, xx

Clayton Square, Liverpool, 130–31

Clayton, Richard, 6, 14

Clayton, Sarah, 130

Cleeve Buildings, Shoreditch, 276, 281, 293–5, *294*, 297, 299

Cloverley Hall, Shropshire, 192

Club Row, Shoreditch, 249, 250, *269*, 284

coal, 66, 144, 159, 195, 208, 225, 231, 232, 278, 293, 303

Coates, Wells, 350

cob, xxii

Cockerell, Charles Robert, 157–8, 184

Coggeshall, Essex, xvix, *xx*

Cohen, Barnet, 58

Coker, Frances, 145

Cole, Henry, 171, 172, 173, 176, 177, 187

Colebrooke, Edward Arthur, 255

collectivism, 347, 350

Collingwood, Luke, 138

Collingwood Street, Shoreditch, 275

colour schemes

  Derngate, *312*, 314–15

  Heywood's, 144, 147–8

  Maister House, 107

  New Ways, 337, 338

  Pallant House, 25–6

  Princelet Street, 46–8

  Toxteth bye-law houses, 235

Colquitt Street, Liverpool, 132, *133*

Colt, Samuel, 176

Columbus, Christopher, 321

columns, 10

  Heywood's, 142

  Maister House, 104

  Pallant House, 10

Colvin, Howard, 86, 155

Commercial Street, Spitalfields, 40, 44, 56

Common Colours, 25, 48

communism, 56–7, 161

Complete Body of Architecture, A (Ware), 16, 115

concinnitas, 88, 90

concrete, 360

  AEG Turbine Hall, 318–19

  Alexandra Road Estate, 359

concrete – *cont.*
  Barbican Estate, 357
  béton brut, 319, 356, 360
  Brunswick Centre, 359
  Dom-Ino House, 324
  High & Over, 344
  Highpoint I, 347–8
  Lawn Road Flats, *351*
  Millbank Estate, 300
  New Ways, 329, 330, 335
  Princelet Street, 64
  Southgate Estate, 350
  Unité d'Habitation, 354
Condition of the Working Class, The
  (Engels), 161
Confederate States of America
  (1861–5), 150–51
Connell, Amyas, 344–5
constructivism, 325, 350, 353
Contrasts (Pugin), 164
Cooke, Edward William, 187–8
Cookham Buildings, Shoreditch,
  272, *280*
cooking, 232, 303
Cooney, John, 58
coppers, 278
Corinthian order, 4, 10, 17, *22*, 145
Corn Exchange, Liverpool, 140
Cornhill, London, 49
cornices, 8
  Heywood's, 140
  Maister House, 94, 95, 96, 100,
    101, 108
  New Ways, 335–6
  Pallant House, 17

Princelet Street, 35, 70
  Toxteth, 229–30, 238, *239*, 245
cornucopia, 10
cotton, 150
Courbet, Gustave, 72
Court of Chancery, 2, 19
Courtauld, Samuel, 49
courtyards, xvii, 207–12, *210*, 216
Covent Garden, London, 94
Cragside, Northumberland, xiv,
    xxvii, xxviii, *154*, 159, 188–203, *191*
  central tower, 192
  corridor, 194
  dining room, 190–92
  drawing room, 192, 196–8, *199*
  fireplace, 190–92, 197–8, *199*
  Gilnockie tower, xxviii, 198–201
  kitchen, 192, *195*
  library, 192
  lighting, 190, *195*
  museum room, 192
  Owl Suite, 192, *193*
  panelling, 192
  pantries, 192
  picture gallery, 194, *195*
  sculleries, 192
Craig, James, 216
Cranbrook, Kent, 187
Crapper, Thomas, 201
Creswell Street, Liverpool, 214
crime, 57, 58, 249, 251, 252, 284, 286,
  290, 301
Crimean War (1853–6), 160–61
'Critic as Artist, The' (Wilde), 262
Crittall, Francis Henry, 343

Crosby, James, 125

Crowle, George, 90–91, 92

Crusades, The, xiii

Crystal Palace, London, 173–8, *174*, 189, 208, 242

Cuba, 147

Cubitt, Thomas, 6, 216

Cugoano, Ottobah, 139

Culham Buildings, Shoreditch, 270, *273*, 277, 284, 293

Culture and Anarchy (Arnold), 262

Custom House, Liverpool, 140

Cutter, Vincent, 1, 16

dado rails, 70, 107, 145, 190

Daily Mail, 256

Daily Telegraph, 258

Dale Street, Liverpool, 129, 215

Dalston, London, 157

Darwin, Charles, 150

Davidson, T. Raffles, *193*

De Stijl, 325–8

Dedham, Essex, 364

Defoe, Daniel, 41, 126, 129

Dekorative Kunst, 307

Derby, Derbyshire, 93, 166, 242

Derby Square, Liverpool, 129

Derngate, Northampton, 306, 310–15, *312*, 336, 341–3

Descartes, René, 110

Design and Industries Association, 316

Designs of Inigo Jones (Kent), 92

Dessau, Germany, 319

Deutscher Werkbund, 316, 317, 328, 344

Devey, George, 159

Devonport, Plymouth, 123

Devonshire, William Cavendish, 1st Earl, xxvi

Devonshire, William Cavendish, 6th Duke, 172

Dickens, Charles, 50–51, 176, 177, 217, 218, 289

Dictionary of the English Language (Johnson), 137

dining rooms
  Boundary Estate, 282
  Cragside, 190, 192, 197, 202
  Great George Street, 145
  New Ways, 332, 340
  Pallant House, 24–5
  Toxteth bye-law houses, 223, 237

Disraeli, Benjamin, 213

Dobson, John, 123, 132, 186

dog-tooth motifs, 220, 238

Dolben's Act (1788), 138

Dom-Ino House, 324, 330

Doric order, 4, 10, 35, 70, 98–100, 140, 340

Dorset Street, Spitalfields, 256

double pile, xxiii, 20

double-skin construction, 225

Doulting limestone, xxi

Doulton, Henry, 201

Downshire Hill, Hampstead, 361

Drinkwater, George, 136

Drive, Northampton, 315

Drogheda, County Louth, 125

Druids, 12, 229
Dubois, Esther, 44
Duchy of Cornwall, 365
Ducie Street, Toxteth, 244–5
Duckworth, George, 57
Dunbar, William Constable, 4th
    Viscount, 93
Duncan, Thomas, 243
Duncan, William, 209–13
Dundee, Scotland, 313
Dunglinson, Daniel, 220
Dutch architecture, 196, 263

East Elm, Essex, 51
East India Company, 180
East Pakistan (1955–71), 75
Easter, 10
Ebor Street, Shoreditch, 285–6
Eddowes, Catherine, 58
Edict of Nantes (1598), 38, 43
Edinburgh, Scotland, 156,
    157, 216
Edward I, King of England, 80
Edward VII, King of the United
    Kingdom, 255–6, 289–90
Egypt, 190
Ehn, Karl, 352
Eldon Square, Newcastle upon
    Tyne, 123
Eleanor Cross, Waltham
    Cross, 168
electricity, 303, 333
  lighting, xvi, 59, 190, 195
'Elegy in a Country Churchyard'
    (Gray), 135

Elementary Education Act (1870),
    263
Elizabeth Tower, Palace of
    Westminster, 168
Elizabethan architecture, xxiv, 167,
    179, 196
Elliot, Jane, 202
Elswick, Newcastle upon Tyne,
    160, 186
Elwy Street, Toxteth, 225, 229, 239
Emmerson, Henry
    Hetherington, 203
enfilade plan, xxiii
Engels, Friedrich, 161
Engineering Magazine, 321
Englische Haus, Das (Muthesius),
    272, 307
English bond, 225
English Garden Wall bond, 225
Eppenhausen, Germany, 332
Epstein, Jacob, 310
Erechtheion, Acropolis, 348
Erith, Raymond, 364
Erskine, Ralph, 360
Essay in Defence of Ancient
    Architecture (Morris), 89
Evans, David, 226, 235
Eve, Arthur, 296
Evening Standard, 304
Everton, Liverpool, 212, 216, 221
Exeter College, Oxford, 183
Exposition Internationale des Arts
    Décoratifs (1925), 331
Expressionism, 317–19, 320, 331,
    336, 338

Fabian Society, 316, 341

Fair Rents for Healthy Homes
    League, 258

Fairchild, Thomas, 49

Farmer and Brindley, 197

Farnsworth, Edith, 361

Farnsworth House, Plano,
    360–61, *362*

Farringdon Road, London, 248

Fashion Street, London, 52

Faustina, 116–17

Feather, Martha, 202

Federation of Synagogues, 54, 60

female architects, 3

femininity, 100, 116, 166

Fiennes, Celia, 129

Finch, Isabella, 105–7

fireplaces, xi–xvi, 303, 304
    Boundary Estate, 278, 282, 303
    Cragside, 190–92, 197–8, *199*
    Heywood's, 141, 144
    Maister House, 108, 115
    New Ways, 337, 338
    Princelet Street, 46, *47*, 48, 71, 76

First World War (1914–18), 197, 214,
    272, 308–9, 314

Fitzclarence Street, Liverpool, 214

flat roofs, 329–30

Fleet Street, Shoreditch, 285

Fleming, Owen, 261, 266, 268,
    271, 275

Flemish architecture, 196, 263, 264

Flemish bond, 225, 229, 245

flint, xxi

Flitcroft, Henry, 89, *91*

Flora, 108–9

Flower and Dean Street,
    Spitalfields, 58, 255, 256

flushing lavatories, xvi, 144, 201,
    207, 213, 223, 230, 278,
    293, 303

Fontana, Carlo, 4

food, 232

Foreign Office, London,
    180–86, *185*

Forsyth, James, 190

Foster, John Jr, 120, 140, 157

Foster, John Sr, 122, 140, 144

Fountains Abbey, North
    Yorkshire, 190

Four Per Cent Industrial Dwellings
    Company, 247

Fournier Street, Spitalfields, 34, 42,
    44, 46, 57, 59, 62–3

France, 183, 206, 244, 268, 317, 325,
    331, 340, 354

Freemasonry, 12, 28, 108

French Revolutionary Wars
    (1792–1802), 128

Friars Mount, London, 248

fridges, 303

Frost, William, 51

Fuller Street, Shoreditch, 254

Furlong Street, Liverpool, 216

gables
    Boundary Estate, 263, 264,
        268–74, 293, 299
    Brune Street, 56
    Cragside, 194, 196, 198

gables – *cont.*
  Glen Andred, 187
  Heywood's, 132
  Kingston-upon-Hull High Street,
    80, *81*
  Tayler & Green, 364
  Toxteth bye-law houses, 222,
    239, 244
Gallipoli campaign (1915–16),
  272, 314
Galsworthy, John, 309
Garden City Movement, 363
garderobe towers, xvii
gargoyles, 23, 194
Garthwaite, Anna Maria, 44–5
gas lamps, xvi, 66, *210*, 231, 277,
  282, 303
Gavin, Hector, 249–50, 288
Gebrüder Bing, 316
Geddes, Patrick, 308
general contractors, 6
general election (1900), 296–8
General Post Office,
  London, 182
Genizah, 61, 74
Gentileschi, Artemisia, 3
George I, King of Great Britain, 85
George II, King of Great
  Britain, 86
George IV, King of the United
  Kingdom, 242
George V, King of the United
  Kingdom, 341, 342
George, Saint, 190

Georgian period (1714–1837), xxix,
  352–3, 352
  Heywood's, xxi, xxix, *120*, 121–8,
    139–48, 151–2
  Maister House, xxi, xxvii, xxviii,
    79–119
Geraint Street, Toxteth, 221
Germantis, William, 58
Germany, 58, 59, 61, 75, 308–9,
  316–17, 331, 352
  AEG Turbine Hall, 318–19, *320*,
    330, 338
  Britz Horseshoe Estate, 352
  Villa Cuno, 332, *334*
  Weissenhof Estate, 328, 344
Gesamtkuntswerk, 317
Gestetner, Sigmund, 347–8
Gibbs, James, 3, 4, 92, 93, 98, 99
Gibraltar Walk, Shoreditch, 287
Gillow, Robert, 147
Ginzburg, Moisei, 353
Girouard, Mark, xxvii, 178, 194
Gittins, Samuel, 227
Giudecca, Venice, 104
Glasgow, Scotland, 310
Glasgow School of Art, 310, 313
Glebe Place, Chelsea, 309
Glen Andred, Groombridge, 187
Glorious Revolution (1688), 40
Goade, Charles, 58
Godin, David, 44
Godin and Ogier, 44
Golden Lane Estate, London,
  354, 357

Goldfinger, Erno, 352

Goldsmiths Row, Shoreditch, 260

Goodwood Park, West Sussex, 6

Gothic architecture, xxii, xxiii, xxviii, 157, 162–70, 175–203, 262, 318

Battle of the Styles, 180–86, 367

Boundary Estate, 264

Cragside, xiv, xxvii, xxviii, *154*, 159, 188–203

Crystal Palace, 173–8, *174*, 189, 208

Palace of Westminster, 167–8, *169*, 179–80, 181, 187

Toxteth, 220, 222, 240

Grafton Street, Liverpool, 215

Graham, Ann, 125

Grainger, Richard, 123

Grange, Ramsgate, 167

granite, xxii

Gray, Thomas, 135

great chambers, xvii, xix

Great Eastern Railway, 285

Great Exhibition (1851), 160, 170–78, 179, 180, 203, 205

Great Fire of London (1666), 5, 33–4

Great George Street, Bristol, 145–7, *146*

great halls, xvii, xix, xxiii, 190

Great House, Dedham, 364

Greece, ancient, 157, 162, 165, 178, 181, 313, 348

Green, Charles, 317

Green Men, 229

green spaces, 240–44

Greenwood, James, 251, 254

Gregson syndicate, 138

Grey Street, Newcastle upon Tyne, 123

Grey, Joseph, 202

Griffith, John, 236

Grimston, John, 108, 116

Groombridge, East Sussex, 187

Gropius, Walter, 319, 352

Guaranty Building, Buffalo, 322

Gwydir Street, Toxteth, 225

H-shaped plans, xxiii

Haiti, 149

Hall, Edward, 51

Hamley, William, 94

Hampstead Garden Suburb, London, 304, 363

Hampton Court Palace, Richmond, xxiii, 23

Hanbury Street, Spitalfields, 44, 46

Handel, George Frideric, 45, 89, 241

Hankey, Henry Alers, 267

Hanover Street, Liverpool, 126

Hanoverian dynasty, 28, 84, 86

Hansard, 182

Hanseatic League, 82, 83, 129

Harding, Arthur, 286

Hardman, John, 125

Hardwick Hall, Derbyshire, xxiii–xxvii, *xxx*

Hare Street, Shoreditch, 284

Harington, John, 201

Harnorsky, Joseph, 296

Hart, Thomas, 51
Haw, George, 288, 289
Hawksmoor, Nicholas, 5, 40
Hebrew, 66, 68, 74
Hedsor Buildings, Shoreditch, *273*, 289, 290
Heisar, Abraham, 62, 67
Henderson family, 255
Henley Buildings, Shoreditch, 270
Henry IV, King of France, 37–8
Henry V, King of England, 187
Henry VII, King of England, 167
Hepworth, Barbara, 352
Hera, 110
Herculaneum Dock, Liverpool, 215, 223
Heywood & Conway, 127
Heywood, Arthur, 121, 125–8, 139, 148, 192
Heywood, Benjamin Arthur, 127
Heywood, Benjamin the Elder, 123–5
Heywood, Benjamin the Younger, 125–6, 127–8, 148, 192
Heywood, Nathaniel, 128
Heywood, Richard, 121, 126, 127
Heywood's, Liverpool, xxi, xxix, *120*, 121–8, 139–48, 151–2
  Argand lamps, 142, 147
  banking hall, 141–2
  chimneys, 141
  colour scheme, 144, 147–8
  columns, 142
  cornices, 140
    fireplaces, 141, 144
    lavatories, 144
    mahogany, 147
    windows, 140, 141
High & Over, Amersham, 344–5
High Alumina Cement, 350
High Park Street, Toxteth, 243
high-rise buildings, 175, 266, 319, 322, 331–2, 347–52, 353
Highcliffe, Alton West Estate, 354–6
Highpoint I, London, 347–52, *349*, 353
Hill, Rowland, 171
Hiram, 214
Historic England, 331
Hodgkinson, Patrick, 359
Hoffman, Josef, 330
Hogarth House, Millbank, 282, *283*
Hollar, Wenceslaus, 80, 81
Holy Land, xiii, 10
Honduras, 147
Honeyman and Keppie, 307
Hopkins, Patty and Michael, 361
Hopwood Street, Everton, 216
Horsley, John, 187
hot water, 232, 303
Hotham family, 83
Houghton Hall, Norfolk, 117
Household Words, 50–51, 177, 289
Houses of Parliament, 167–8, *169*, 179–80
Housing of the Working Classes Act (1885), 257

Housing of the Working Classes
Committee, 261, 267, 289
Housing Question in London, The
(1900 report), 278, 281
How the Poor Live (Sims), 258
Howard, Ebenezer, 363
Hoxton, London, 48
Hughes, John, 352
Huguenots, xiv, 33, 37–51, 59, 129
Hull Minster, Kingston-upon-
Hull, 80
Hull, East Yorkshire, *see*
Kingston-upon-Hull
Hume, David, 137
hunky punks, 23
Hurley Buildings, Shoreditch,
271, *273*
Hussey, John, xix
Hussey, Walter, 30
Hynam, William, 261, 273, 277,
279, 280

Idea del tempio della pittura
(Lomazzo), 89
Ideal Home, 306, 329, 337
Iffley Buildings, Shoreditch, 271
igneous rock, xxii
Illustrated London News, 250–51
immigration, 296–9
Bengalis, 75, 300
Huguenots, xiv, 33, 37–51,
59, 129
Jews, xiii, xxix, 51–76, 285, 296–9
Immortal Seven, 27
India, 308

India Office, London, 180, 181,
185, 186
Industrial Revolution
(c.1760 – c.1840), 144,
159–60, 161
inglenooks, 190, 192, 197–8, *199*
Ingram Street Tea Rooms,
Glasgow, 310, 311
Ingram, M. Edward, 113
Institute of British Architects, 155
Institute of Engineering, 214
Institution of Civil Engineers, 155
International Style, 319, 323, 344
Ionic order, 4, 95, 98–100, 104, 197
Ireland, Samuel, 50
Irish famine (1845–52), 211
iron, 83, 159
Isokon Building, *see* Lawn Road
Flats
Israel, 62
Italianate architecture, *see*
Renaissance architecture
Italianate Travellers Club,
London, 168

Jack the Ripper, 58, 255
Jackman, Elizabeth, 202
Jacobean architecture, 80, 119, 187,
190, 197, *199*, 233, 281
Jacobites, 28, 86
Jacobs, Florence, 295
Jamaica, 135, 137–8, 147
James II, King of England,
Scotland and Ireland, 27, 28,
39, 86

James III, King/Jacobite Pretender, 44, 86
James of Compostela, Saint, 10
James Rogers & Company, 128
Japan, 272, 277, 307, 326
Jermyn Street, Toxteth, *219*, 238–40, *239*, 245
Jesmond Dene, Newcastle upon Tyne, 186–8
Jeune, Mary, 258
Jew's House, Lincoln, xi–xiv, *xii*
Jewish Labour Movement, 75
Jews, xiii, xxix, 51–76, 285, 296–9
John Foulston, 123
John, Augustus, 310
Johnson, Robert, 296
Johnson, Samuel, 135, 137–8
Johnson, Thomas, 127
Jones, Horace, 248
Jones, Inigo, 9, 85, 86, 182
Jones, John, 212, 226, 235
Jubilee Street, Spitalfields, 69

Kames, Henry Home, Lord, 137, 138
Karl-Marx Hof, Vienna, 352
Kauffman, Angelica, 3
Keay, Lancelot, 352
Keeling House, Bethnal Green, 356
Kelvin Grove, Toxteth, 220, 238
Kempster, Christopher, 5
Kennington Common, London, 171, 205
Kent, William, 89, 90, 92, 101, 102–7, 108
Kentish, Rolfe, 30

Kentish ragstone, xxi
Keppie, John, 308
Kilpeck Church, Herefordshire, 23
Kimber, John, 138
King Edward VI Grammar School, Birmingham, 168
King's Lynn, Norfolk, xxi, 82
Kingston-upon-Hull, East Yorkshire, xxi, xxvii, xxviii, *78*, 79–119, *81*
    Blaydes House, 80–82, *81*, 113
    Maister House, xxi, xxvii, xxviii, 79–119
    Patrington Manor, 83
    Prince Street, *114*
Kinloss, Mary Morgan-Grenville, 11th Baroness, 255
Kipling, Rudyard, 314
Kirby Hall, North Yorkshire, 89
kitchens, xiv, xvii, xix, 14, 23
    Cragside, 192
    Pallant House, 14–17, *15*
    Princelet Street, 45, 66
Klebensky family, 297–8
Kneesall, Nottinghamshire, xix
Knight, Joseph, 135, 137–8
Koch, Alexander, 307
Kook, Abraham Isaac, 62–4
Krier, Léon, 365
Krupp, Alfred, 176

La Roche, Raoul, 325
Labourer's Friend Society, 205
Laird, John, 151

Laleham Buildings, Shoreditch, 289

Lancaster, Lancashire, 127,
    136, 147

Land Tax, 44, 46

Landlordism (Lazarus), 255

landlords, 209, 255–8

Langley, Batty, 115

larders, 14

Lasdun, Denys, 356

lavatories, xvi, xvii, 58, 144, 201,
    207, 213, 223
  flushing, xvi, 144, 201, 207, 213,
    223, 230, 278, 293, 303
  privies, xvii, 58, 211, 230, 237

Lawn Road Flats, Hampstead,
    350–52, *351*, 353

Lazarus, Henry, 255

Le Corbusier, 319, 323, 324–5, 328,
    330, 344, 347, 348, 352, 354–6, 359

Leach family, 295

Leadenhall Street, London, 196

Lectures on Architecture (Morris),
    89, 98–9

Leonardo da Vinci, 88

Leoni, Giacomo, 85

Letchworth Garden City,
    Hertfordshire, 363

Lethaby, William Richard, 197

Levy, Harris, 59, 60, 62, 67, 71

Lewis, Wyndham, 310

Lichenstein, Leah, 59, 71

Lichtenstein, Rachel, 56

Life and Labour of the People
    (Booth), 57, 252–4, 258, 275,
    284, 298

lighting, xvi, 59, 66
  Argand lamps, 142, 147
  electric, xvi, 59, 190, *195*
  gas lamps, xvi, 66, *210*, 231, 277,
    282, 303
  oil lamps, xvi, 142, 147, 190, 231,
    234

Lily House, Chatsworth, 172

limestone, xxi

limewash, xxii, 72, 145

Lincoln, Lincolnshire, 241

Lincoln's Inn Fields, 142, 144

Lindsay, John, 136

linoleum, 233, *234*, 282

lintels, 12, 23, 27, 29, 190, 192,
    202–3, 211, 226, 229–30, 240, 336

Lithuania, 51, 59, 61, 75

Liverpool, Merseyside, xxi, xxviii,
    121–52, 205–45
  Abercromby Square, 150
  Atheneum, 140
  Bank of England offices, 158
  Blue Coat School, 129
  Castle, 129
  cholera epidemics, 212
  Corn Exchange, 140
  courtyard developments, 207–12,
    210, 216
  Custom House, 140
  Health of the Town Committee,
    213
  Herculaneum Dock, 215, 223
  Heywood's, xxi, xxix, *120*, 121–8,
    139–48, 151–2
  international port, 208

Liverpool, Merseyside – *cont.*
  Merchants' Exchange, 130, *131*
  New Exchange, 140
  Overhead Railway, 215
  Prince's Dock, 140
  slave trade, 126–9, 132–9, 148–52
  St Andrew's Gardens, 352
  Toxteth bye-law houses, *see*
    Toxteth bye-law houses
  Welsh community, 216–17, *219*,
    221–2, 226–7, 229, 235, 244–5
  Westminster Chambers, 215
  Wet Dock, 126–7, 129
Liverpool Chamber of
  Commerce, 132
Liverpool Corporation, 140,
  233, 248
Liverpool Guide, The (Moss), 132, 149
Liverpool Sanitary Act (1846), 213
Liverpool Sanitary Amendment
  Act (1864), 248
lobbies, xix, xxiii
Local Government Board, 257
Locke, John, 109–10
Lomazzo, Giovanni Paolo, 89
Londesborough Hall, East
  Yorkshire, 92, 118
London, England
  Alexandra Road Estate, 359
  Arlington Street, 104–5
  Bank of England, 121, 141, *143*
  Barbican Estate, 357–9, *358*
  Berkeley Square, 103–4, 105–7, *106*
  Boundary Estate, xxviii–xxix,
    246, 247–301, 304

British Museum, 182, 344
Brunswick Centre, 359
Buckingham Palace, 170–71, 182
Burlington House, 87
Chiswick House, 90
cholera epidemics, 212
Covent Garden, 94
Crystal Palace, 173–8, *174*, 189,
  208, 242
Downshire Hill, 361
Foreign Office, 180–86, *185*
General Post Office, 182
Golden Lane Estate, 354, 357
Great Exhibition (1851), 160,
  170–78, 179, 180, 203, 205
Great Fire (1666), 5, 33–4
Hampstead Garden Suburb, 363
Highpoint I, 347–52, *349*, 353
India Office, 180, 181, *185*, 186
Italianate Travellers Club, 168
Jack the Ripper murders (1888),
  58, 255
Keeling House, 356
Lawn Road Flats, 350–52, *351*, 353
Marlborough House, 176, 177
Millbank Estate, 248, 261, 274,
  282, *283*, 300
Museum of Manufactures, 176, 177
New Zealand Chambers, 196
Old Burlington Street, 87, 96
Old Nichol, 248–60, *253*, 263–4,
  268, 276, 285, 286–92
Palace of Westminster, 167–8,
  169, 179–80, 181, 187
Parkside, 361

Portland Place, 123

Pretoria Avenue, *234*

Princelet Street, xiv, xxvii, xxix, *32*, 33–76

Queen Anne's Mansions, 266–7

Regent Street, 123, *124*

Regent's Park, 123, 242–3

Royal Courts of Justice, 158

slave trade, 126, 136

Somerset House, 122–3, 177

St Paul's Cathedral, 5

Swan House, 196

Victoria and Albert Museum, 178

Victoria Park, 242–3

West Ham Jewish Cemetery, 56

Westminster Abbey, 108, 167

Whitehall Palace, 182

Willow Road, 352–3

London, Jack, 207, 288–9

London Building Act (1774), 208

London County Council (LCC), 247, 255, 258–9, 267, 274, 278, 288–92, 295, 297, 299, 354

London Hospital, Whitechapel, 270

London Labour and the London Poor (Mayhew), 206

London School Board (LSB), 264

Long, Mary Jane, 30

Longleat, Wiltshire, xxvi

Loos, Adolf, 321–4, 327, 328, 336, 348

Loudon, John Claudius, 184, 242

Louis XIV, King of France, 38, 39, 84

Louvre, Paris, 183

Low-life Deeps (Greenwood), 251

Loyal United Friends Friendly Society, 51–2, 54, 62, 65, 66

Lubetkin, Berthold, 347

Ludwig II, King of Bavaria, 198

Lutyens, Edwin, 304–5, 363

Lynn, Jack, 356

Lyon, France, 42

Lythwood Hall, Shropshire, 150

Macdonald, Margaret, 307, 315

Machzike Hadath, Spitalfields, 62–3

machzor, 74

Mackintosh, Charles Rennie, 306–15, 330, 333, 337, 343

magic lantern, 305

mahogany, 26, 48, 107, 127, 142, 147, 148

Maison d'habitations (Barrez), 343

Maister, Nathaniel, 83, 92, 94, 101, 102, 113–15, 116, 119

Maister the Elder, Henry, 82, 90–96, 100, 101, 107, 112, 113–15, 118

Maister the Younger, Henry, 108–9, 115–19

Maister House, Kingston-upon-Hull, xxi, xxvii, xxviii, 79–119, 367

brick construction, 95

busts, 108–10, 116

chimney, 108

colour scheme, 107

cornices, 94, 95, 96, 100, 101, 108

counting house, 108

doors, 95, 98–100, *99*, 107–8

Maister House – *cont.*
  fireplaces, 108, 115
  Locke, image of, 109–10
  oak leaves, 108, 109
  panelling, 107, 108, 119
  piano nobile, 96, 98
  plasterwork, 100–101,
    108–13, *111*
  staircase hall, 100–107,
    103, 115
  upper floors, 115–19
  windows, 95, 96–8
majolica, 190
Malton, Thomas Watson-
  Wentworth, Baron, 90, 105, 107
Manchester, England, 241
Manchester Institution of Fine
  Arts, 168
Mansfield, Katherine, 310
Mansfield, William Murray, 1st
  Earl, 135, 137
Margaret Morris Club, 309
Maritime Museum, Liverpool, 126
Marlborough, Sarah Churchill,
  Duchess, 3
Marlborough House, London,
  176, 177
Marlow Buildings, Shoreditch,
  246, 271, 293
Marseilles, France, 354–6, *355*
Martins Bank, 152
Martyrs' Memorial,
  Oxford, 168
Marx, Karl, 161

Mary II, Queen of England,
  Scotland and Ireland, 3, 28
masculinity, 24, 100, 118, 140
Mayhew, Henry, 206
McCarthy, Dennis, 295
McManus, Frederick, 343
Mearns, Andrew, 256–7
Mechanics' Institute, 156, 171
Melnick, Samuel, 52, 59–61, 63,
  67, 68
Merchants' Exchange, Liverpool,
  130, *131*
Merlin Street, Toxteth, 220
Mersey river, 127, 129
Metropolitan Board of
  Works, 289
Meyer, Edward, 240
mezuzahs, 69, 71
Michell, Simon, 34, 37
Midland Grand Hotel, London,
  185, 186
Midland Railway, 172
Mies van der Rohe, Ludwig, 319,
  328, 333, 360–61
Millbank Estate, London, 248, 261,
  274, 282, *283*, 300
Millbank Penitentiary, London,
  259, 274–5
Milton Keynes,
  Buckinghamshire, 360
Minton Taylor, Reginald, 261,
  271–3, 280, 293, 294
mirror plans, 225, 229
Mocatta, Frederick David, 69

Model Houses for Families, 205
modernism, 306, 309, 313, 315–45, 347–63
  AEG Turbine Hall, 318–19, *320*, 330, 338
  Alexandra Road Estate, 359
  Barbican Estate, 357–, *358*
  Brunswick Centre, 359
  Byker Wall, 359–60
  Citrohan House, 328, 344
  Dom-Ino House, 324, 330
  Downshire Hill, 361
  Farnsworth House, 360–61, *362*
  Golden Lane Estate, 354, 357
  High & Over, 344–5
  Highpoint I, 347–52, *349*, 353
  Keeling House, 356
  Lawn Road Flats, 350–52, *351*, 353
  New Ways, xxii, xxvii, xxviii, *302*, 306, 321, 325, 328–45, 347, 367
  Park Hill Estate, 356, *358*
  Parkside, 361
  Rufer House, 323–4
  Schröder House, 325–8, *327*
  Silver End, 343–4
  Starlock House, 343
  Steiner House, 321, 323, *327*
  Unité d'Habitation, 354–6, *355*, 357
  Villa La Roche, 325
  Willow Road, 352–3
Moffatt, William Bonython, 168
Monarch coffee house, Shoreditch, 258

Moncoutant, France, 43
Mondrian, Piet, 326, 336
Monkmoor Road, Shrewsbury, xxiii
Montagu, Samuel, 54, 55, 59, 69
Montclare Street, Shoreditch, 264, 270, 279
Montefiore, Moses Haim, 74
Moore, Henry, 352
Morley, Henry, 177
Morris, Margaret, 309
Morris, Robert, 89–90, 95, 98–9
Morris, Roger, 6, 89
Morris, William, 158, 170, 178, 189, 194, 266, 272, 344
Morrison, Arthur, 288, 289
Moscow, Russia, 353
Moss, William, 132–4, 149
Mount Street, Shoreditch, 259, 270
Municipal Journal, 282, *283*, 290
Museum of Manufactures, London, 176, 177
Musgrave, Henry, 93, 112, 115
Musgrave, Michael 93
Musgrave, Thomas, 93
Muthesius, Hermann, 272, 307

Narkomfin building, Moscow, 353–6
Nash, John, 123, 242
National Gallery of British Art, Millbank, 261
National Trust, 107, 201
Nazi Germany (1933–45), 59, 75

Nelson Street, Whitechapel, 56
neo-Georgian architecture,
    305, 364
neoclassicism, 132, 140, 144, 147
neoplasticism, 325–6
Nesfield, William Eden, 158,
    179, 192
Neuschwanstein Castle,
    Bavaria, 198
New Court, London, 52
New Exchange, Liverpool, 140
New Town Movement, 360
New Ways, Northampton, xxii,
    xxvii, xxviii, *302*, 306, 321, 325,
    328–45, 347, 367
  dining room, 332, 340
  entrance, 335–6
  interior decoration, 335, 338
  lounge, 337, *339*
  staircase hall, 336
  study, 337
  windows, 329, 330, 337, 338
New York, United States, 331–2
New Zealand Chambers,
    London, 196
Newberry, Francis, 310
Newcastle upon Tyne, 123, 157, 160,
    167, 186–8, 359–60
Newlands, John, 213
Newman, Isaac, 58
Nicholson, Ben, 352
night soil, 213
No Room to Live (Haw), 288
Norman period (1066–1135),
    xi–xiv, *xii*

Northampton, Northamptonshire,
    xxii, xxvii, xxviii, 305–6, 310–45
  Derngate, 306, 310–15, *312*, 336,
    341–3
  New Ways, xxii, xxvii, xxviii, *302*,
    306, 321, 325, 328–45, 347, 367
Nuremberg, Germany, 316

oak leaves, 10–12, 108, 109
Ogden, Sarah, 125
Ogier family, xiv, 37, 43–50, 66, 68,
    69, 70
Ogier, Abraham, 44
Ogier, Daniel, 43
Ogier, Esther, 44
Ogier, Jeanne, 43
Ogier, John, 44
Ogier, Louisa Perina, 49, 50
Ogier, Peter Abraham, 37, 43–50, 70
Ogier, Peter II, 43, 49
Ogier, Peter III, 49
Ogier, Peter IV, 44
Ogier, Pierre, 43
Ogier, Vansommer and Triquet, 44
oil lamps, xvi, 142, 190, 231, *234*
Okeover Hall, Staffordshire, 102
Old and New Hull (Wildridge), 116
Old Burlington Street, London,
    87, 96
Old English style, 158–9, 178, 187,
    190, 196, 197
Old Hall Farm, Kneesall, xix
Old Nichol, London, 248–60, *253*,
    263–4, 268, 276, 286–92
  relocation of residents, 286–92

Old Nichol Street, Shoreditch, 249, 251, *269*, 277, 287
Oldcotes Manor, Derbyshire, xxvi
onyx, 190
oolitic limestone, xxi
open hearths, xi–xii, xiv
Ordnance Survey, 217
Ormskirk, Lancashire, 125
'Ornament and Crime' (Loos), 322
Orwell, George, 304, 338
ostriches, 28–30, *29*
Ottoman Empire (*c.*1299–1922), 62
Ouse river, xxi
overcrowding, 57, 63, 212, 237–8, 248, 251, 256, 288–9
Overhead Railway, Liverpool, 215
Owens, Richard, 212, 214–17, 221–3, 226, 230, 238, 244
Oxford, Oxfordshire, 168, 183–4
Oxford University, 158, 183

Page, John, 6, 14
Page, Joseph, 92, 100, 109, 112, 114
Palace of Westminster, 167–8, *169*, 179–80, 181, 187
Palestine, 62
Pall Mall, London, 168
Pall Mall Gazette, 255
Palladian architecture, xxiv, xxviii, 84–119, 129
  Bath, 130
  Chiswick House, 90
  Cragside, 196–7
  Goodwood Park, 6
  Kirby Hall, 89

Maister House, xxi, xxvii, xxviii, 79–119
Wanstead House, 85
Wentworth Woodhouse, 90, *91*, 105, 112
York Assembly Rooms, 90
Palladio, Andrea, xxiv, 20, 84–92, 95, 100, 101, 102, 109, 129
Pallant House, Chichester, xxviii, *xxx*, 1–30, 79
  attic, 26, 37
  colour scheme, 25–6
  cornices, 17
  dining parlour, 24–5
  emblems, 27–8, *29*
  gate piers, 28–30, *29*
  keystone, 21, *22*
  kitchen, 14–17, *15*
  oak leaves, 10–12, 108
  outline plan, 20–21
  panelling, 24–5, 26
  private chambers, 17–20
  staircases, 8, 10, *11*, 17, 18
Pallant House (Flower et al.), 27
Palm House, Kew Gardens, 172
palm leaves, 10
Palmerston, Henry John Temple, 3rd Viscount, 181, 182–3, 184, 200
panelling
  Cragside, 192
  Maister House, 107, 108, 119
  Pallant House, 24–5, 26
  Princelet Street, 35, 37, *47*, 70
panopticon, 274–5

pantries, xvii, xix, 14, 24

Papworth, Wyatt, 243

parapets, 8, 12

Paris Commune (1871), 72

Paris, France, 183, 206, 244, 268, 317, 325, 331, 340

Park Hill Estate, Sheffield, 356, *358*

Parke & Heywood, 127

Parker Morris Committee, 359

Parker, Barry, 363

Parkside, Wimbledon, 361

Parliament Street, Toxteth, 244

parlours, xix, 24, 45, 108, 223, 233, 235, 237, 254

Parr Street, Liverpool, 132, *133*

Parr, Thomas, 132, 133, 149–50

Parthenon, Acropolis, 348

Pater, Walter, 262

Patrington Manor, Kingston-upon-Hull, 83

Paty, William, 145

Paxton, Joseph, 172–6, 242, 243

Paycocke's House, Coggeshall, xix, *xx*

Peacock, James, 147

Pease, Joseph, 82

pebbles, xxi

Peckham, Elizabeth, xxviii, *xxx*, 1–3, 6, 7–8, 14–21, 23, 26–7

Peckham, Henry, *xxx*, 1–3, 6, 7–8, 10, 12, 18–21, 26, 27, 28–30

Pedley Street, Shoreditch, 285

Peel Park, Salford, 241

Pelham, Henry, 104

Pembroke Place, Liverpool, 211

Pennethorne, James, 242

penny black stamps, 171

People of the Abyss, The (London), 288–9

Peter Behrens (Windsor), 330

philanthropic housing movement, 206

Philips Park, Manchester, 241

Phillips, Arthur Maxwell, 271

Phillips, Constantia, 94

Phillips, William Henry, 227

Phipps, Samuel, 34

piano nobile, 96, 98, 352

Piccadilly, London, 87

Pickersgill, Edward, 297

pilasters, 80
    Heywood's, 145
    Maister House, 98
    New Ways, 337, 340
    Pallant House, 17, *22*
    Wilberforce House, 80

Pinney, John Pretor, 145–7

pitched roofs, 305

Plano, Illinois, 360

plasterwork
    Cragside, 197
    Great George Street, 145
    Maister House, 100–101, 108–13, *111*
    Pallant House, 21
    Princelet Street, 60, 66, 72, 74

Plato, 88

Plumbe, Rowland, 270

Plymouth, Devon, 123

pointed architecture, 163–6

Poland, 51, 58, 61

porcelain, 10, 190

Porey, Thomas, 281, 296

Port-Vendres, France, 315

Portland Place, London, 123

Portland stone, xxi, 263

postal service, 171

Pound, Ezra, 310

Poundbury, Dorset, 365–7, *366*

poverty, 162, 203
  Liverpool, 208–12, 236–7
  London, 50, 57, 75, 249–60, 284–92

poverty maps, 57, 252–4, 275, 284–7

Pre-Raphaelites, 190

Pretoria Avenue, Walthamstow, *234*

Prince Street, Kingston-
  upon-Hull, *114*

Prince's Dock, Liverpool, 140

Prince's Park, Toxteth, 241–4

Princelet Street, Spitalfields, xiv,
  xxvii, xxix, *32*, 33–76, *65*, 129
  bedchambers, 37, 45
  Booth's survey (1886), 57–8
  colour scheme, 46–8
  cornices, 35, 70
  fireplaces, 46, *47*, 48, 71, 76
  gardens, 48–9
  kitchens, 45, 66
  lavatories, 58
  panelling, 35, 37, *47*, 70
  staircases, 34, 35–6, *36*
  synagogue, 52–6, *53*, 59–76, *65*
  weaving garrets, 50, *65*, 72

windows, 50, 55, 64, 71, 72, *73*
  Yiddish theatre, 57

Princes Avenue, Toxteth, 244

Princes Road, Toxteth, 217, *219*, 221, 244

Pritchard, Molly and Jack, 350

privies, xvii, 58, 211

Prollius, Henry, 58

Protestantism, 27–8, 84, 87, 166
  Huguenots, xiv, 33, 37–51, 59, 129

Pryor, John, 6, 17, 23, 25

Public Health Acts, 213, 257

public parks, 240–44

Public Record Office, 171

Pugin, Auguste, 163

Pugin, Augustus Welby
  Northmore, 163–70, 172, 175–7, 179–80, 181, 187, 318

Pythagoras, 88

Quadrant, Regent Street, *124*

Quaker Street, Shoreditch, 252

Quattro libri, I (Palladio), 20, 85, 86, 87, 92, 102, 109

Queen Anne Revival, 196, 262–4, 268, 299

Queen Anne's Gate, Westminster, 23

Queen Anne's Mansions, London, 266–7

Queen Square, Bath, 123, 130

Queen's House, Greenwich, *9*

Queen's Park, Manchester, 241

Rabaud, Catherine, 49

Rachel's Tomb, Bethlehem, 74

radiators, 303

railways, 172–3, 186

Ramsgate, Kent, 167, 179

Ramshaw, William, 160

Rationalism, 323, 350

Raumplan, 323

Re aedificatoria, De (Alberti), 88

Reback, Myer, 60

Recovery, 138

Red Lion Street, Spitalfields, 44

Redchurch Street, Shoreditch, 252, 259, *269*, 285, 286

Redentore, Giudecca, 104

Reform Act (1832), 151, 162

Regent Street, London, 123, *124*

Regent's Park, London, 123, 242–3

Renaissance architecture, xxii, xxiii, xxiv, 12, 21, 96, 104, 157, 162, 178, 233, 313

  Battle of the Styles, 180–86, 367

  Cragside, 197

  proportions, 331

Repton School, Derbyshire, 134

Revolution in London Housing, A (Beattie), 282

Rhiwlas Street, Toxteth, 227, 235, 236

Richards, James Maude, 306

Richmond, Charles Lennox, 2nd Duke, 6–7

Rickman, Thomas, 163

Riddle of the Sands, The (Childers), 309

Ridley, Samuel Forde, 296–8

Rietveld, Gerrit, 325–8

Rinkoff, Fanny, 69

River Mersey, 127, 129

River Ouse, xxi

Roberts, David, 214–17, 219, 221–3, 226

Roberts, Henry, 168, 205, 207, 208

Roberts, William, 235

Robinson, Richard, 136

Robinson and Heywood, 128

Robson, Edward Robert, 264, 266, 267

Rochelle School, Shoreditch, 263–6, 275, 299

Rockingham, Thomas Watson-Wentworth, 1st Marquess, 90, 105, 107

Rococo, xiv, 46, *47*, 48, 76, 101, 115, 116, *162*

Rocque, John, 249

Rodinsky, David, 60–61, 71–4

Roehampton, London, 354–6

Rogers, James, 128

Rogers, Richard and Su, 361

Rogerson, Joseph, 215

Romanesque architecture, xi–xiv, *xii*

Rome, ancient, xxii, 96, 104, 108–9, 116–17, 162, 164–5, 178, 197, 313

  bathhouses, 86, 90

  emperors, 110

  Faustina, 116–17

  gods, 108–9

  ostriches and, 28

pilasters, 80, 98
Vitruvius, 88, 164
rond-point, 267
roofs, 305, 329–30
rookeries, 248, 255
Roscoe, William, 150
Rosh Hashanah, 74
Rossetti, Dante Gabriel, 190
Rothbury, Northumberland, 159, 188
Rothschild, Evelina, 56
Rothschild, Ferdinand, Baron, 56
Rothschild, Leopold, 69
Rothschild, Lionel Walter, 2nd Baron, 63
Rothschild, Nathaniel, 1st Baron, 52, 55, 69
Rothschild Mausoleum, West Ham Jewish Cemetery, 56
Round Coppice, Buckinghamshire, 96, 97
Royal Academy of Arts, 156, 157
Royal Circus, Bath, 12
Royal Courts of Justice, London, 158
Royal Institute of British Architects, 156, 180
Ruabon brickworks, 220
Rufer House, Vienna, 323–4
Rufer, Josef, 324
Rumford, Benjamin Thompson, Count, 142–3
Runcorn New Town, Cheshire, 350
running water, 232, 303
Ruskin, John, 170, 173–4

Russian Empire (1721–1917), 51–2, 54, 58, 61, 62, 75, 325
Rye, East Sussex, 343

Saint-Domingue, 149
Saint, Andrew, 188, 197
Sainte-Chapelle, Paris, 183
Salford, Manchester, 241
Samuel, Stuart Montagu, 59
sandstone, 122, 229
Sandys Row synagogue, Spitalfields, 56
Sanitary Ramblings (Gavin), 249, 288
Santo Domingo, 149
Sassoon, Siegfried, 310
Scarlett, Frank, 343
schools, 263–6, 267, 275, 285, 286, 299
Schröder House, Utrecht, 325–8, 327
Schröder-Schräder, Truss, 325
Schwartz, Ahron Haim, 62, 63–4
Sclater Street, Shoreditch, 250, 254, 284
Scott, George Gilbert, 168–70, 180–86, 205
Scottish Baronial Revival, 157
sculleries, 14, 23, 45, 66, 225, 231, 278, 293
Seagram office tower, New York, 360
Seaward, George, 296
Second World War (1939–45), 59, 319, 341, 353, 354, 356, 364
sedimentary ironstone, xxi
seed-crushing industry, 83

Sefer Torah, 61

Sefton, William Molyneux, 4th
Earl, 215, 242

Self-Help (Smiles), 157, 241

Serlio, Sebastiano, xxiv

Settlement and Removal Act
(1662), 206

Seven Lamps of Architecture, The
(Ruskin), 175

Seven Years War (1756–63), 125

sewage; sewers, 144, 201, 209, *210,*
211–14

Shaftesbury, Anthony Ashley
Cooper, 3rd Earl, 84–5, 110

Shaftesbury, Anthony Ashley
Cooper, 7th Earl, 205

Sharp, Granville, 139

Shaw, George Bernard, 341–3

Shaw, Janet, 157

Shaw, Richard Norman, xxvii, 154,
156–61, 178–9, 182, 187–203,
263, 272

Shaw, Robert, 157

Shaw, Thomas, 130

Sheela-na-Gigs, 23

Sheffield, South Yorkshire, 356

Shelmerdine, Thomas, 233

Shenandoah, CSS, 151

Shinto shrines, *273*, 277

Shiplake Buildings, Shoreditch,
271, 277, 293

Shoreditch, London, xxviii–xxix,
45, 48

Shrewsbury, George Talbot, 6th
Earl, xxvii

Shrewsbury, John Talbot, 16th
Earl, 167

Shrewsbury, Mary Talbot,
Countess, xxiii, xxv, xxvi–xxvii, 3

Shrewsbury, Shropshire,
xxiii–xxvii, *xxx*

Sigournais, France, 43

silk, 10, 38–9, 41, 43, 50–51

Silver End, Essex, 343–4

Sims, George, 258

single pile, xxii, 34

skyscrapers, 175, 331

slate, xxii

slave trade, 82–3, 126–9, 132–9, 145,
148–52

Slave Trade Act (1788), 138

Slave Trade Act (1807), 139, 148

Slavery Abolition Act (1833), 150

slums, xxix, 59, 161, 205, 245, 247
Old Nichol, 248–60, *253*, 263–4,
268, 276, 285, 286–92

Small Houses, 305, 343

smallpox, 83, 256

Smart, Henry, 6, 7, 8, 12, 27, 79

Smiles, Samuel, 157, 241

Smirke, Robert, 182

Smith, Adam, 137

Smith, David, 57

Smith, Ivor, 356

Smith, Marmaduke, 34

Smithfield, London, 3

Smythson, Robert, xxv, xxvi

Snow, John, 212

Soane, John, 4, 106, 121, 141, 143,
144, 147

Society for Effecting the Abolition
of the Slave Trade, 139
Society for Improving the
Conditions of the Labouring
Classes (SICLC), 205–6,
207, 247
Society for the Encouragement of
Arts, 171
Society for the Protection of
Ancient Buildings, 170
Society of Civil Engineers, 155
Soho Square, London, 2
solars, xvi, xvii
Solomon, Lewis, 54, 55, 56
Solomon's Temple, Jerusalem, 10,
67, 214
Somerset, James, 135, 137
Somerset House, London, 122–3, 177
Sonning Building, Shoreditch, 270
Southgate Estate, Runcorn New
Town, 350
Soviet Union, 347, 350, 353
speculative builds, 6, 155, 208, 214,
245, 255
Kingston-upon-Hull, 113, 114
Liverpool, 217, 230, 231
London, 33–5, 37, 242
Spencer, Samuel, 92, 93, 115
Spiers, Kaufman, 227
spiral staircases, xv
Spitalfields, London, xiv, xxvii, xix,
32, 33–76, 250
Booth's survey (1886–98), 57–8
Flower and Dean Street rookery,
58, 255, 256

Huguenots in, xiv, 33, 37–51, 59,
129
Jack the Ripper murders (1888),
58, 255
Jews in, 51–76
Spitalfields Acts, 50
Spitalfields Great Synagogue, 59
Spitalfields Historic Buildings
Trust, 60, 74
Spraggs, Sarah Anne, 51
Springhead, East Yorkshire, 92
St Andrew's Gardens, Liverpool, 352
St Augustine's Church, Ramsgate,
167, 179
St Bartholomew's Day massacre
(1572), 37–8
St Bartholomew's Hospital,
Smithfield, 3
St Dunstan's, Stepney, 44
St George's Church, Liverpool, 129
St George's Church, Southwark,
167
St Giles slum, London, 205
St Giles' Church, Camberwell, 168
St Giles' Church, Cheadle, 167
St James's Park, London, 184, 185
St Jude's Church, Spitalfields, 257
St Leonard's Church, Shoreditch,
301
St Martin-in-the-Fields, Trafalgar
Square, 4
St Martin's Cottages, Vauxhall, 248
St Martin's Lane, Chichester, 2
St Mary's Cathedral, Newcastle
upon Tyne, 167

St Mary's Church, Derby, 166
St Oswulf Street, Shoreditch, 274
St Pancras Station, London, *185*, 186
St Paul's Cathedral, London, 5
St Peter's Church, Barton-upon-
    Humber, 113
staircases, xvii, xix
  Arlington Street, 104–5
  Berkeley Square, 103–4, 105–7, *106*
  Hardwick Hall, xxiv
  Maister House, 100–107,
    109, 115
  Pallant House, 8, 10, *11*, 17, 18
  Princelet Street, 34, 35–6, *36*
stamps, 171
Stanhope, James, 1st Earl, 85
Starlock House, Rye, 343
Steep Hill house, Lincoln, xi–xiv, *xii*
Steers, Thomas, 129
Steiner House, Vienna, 321, 323, *327*
Steiner, Lilly, 323
Stephenson, George, 160
Stevens, William Bagshaw, 134
Stilwell, Martin, 260, 276, 293–5
Stirling, James, 350
Stockholm, Sweden, 83
stone, xxi–xxii, 122
Stones of Venice, The (Ruskin), 170
Storeton sandstone, 122
Stowe House, Buckinghamshire, 255
Streatham Street, Bloomsbury,
    205, 207
Streatley Buildings, Shoreditch,
    260, 261, 268, 275
Street, George Edmund, 158, 170

Strickland, William, 92
Strutt, Joseph, 242
Strype, John, 41
Stuart dynasty, 85, 86
Stuart, James Francis Edward, 44,
    86
Studio, 307
Stuttgart, Germany, 328, 344
subletting, 291, 295
Sullivan, Louis, 175, 321–2, 323
Sunbury Buildings, Shoreditch,
    268, 270, 275
Sunderland, Charles Spencer, 3rd
    Earl, 85
Sunnyside, Toxteth, 243
*Survey of the Cities of London and
    Westminster* (Strype), 41
Surveyors' Club, 155
Swan Court, Shoreditch, 249
Swan House, Chelsea
    Embankment, 196
Swanfield Street, Shoreditch, 259,
    270
Swartz, Philip, 58
Sweden, 83
Swift, Jonathan, 49
Syers, Robert, 136
Sykes family, 83
synagogues, 52–6, *53*, 59–76

Tait, Thomas, 343
Taplow Building, Shoreditch, 270
tarmacadam, 276
Tate Britain, Millbank, 261
Taut, Bruno, 352

Tayler, William, 34
Tayler & Green, 364
Taylor Institution, Oxford, 158
Temple of Apollo Epicurius,
    Bassae, 157
Temples of Mammon (Booker), 122
Thompson, Benjamin, Count
    Rumford, 142–3
Threadneedle Street, London, 38
Timaeus (Plato), 88
Times, The, 161, 182, 297
Tite, William, 181
Torah, 61, 63, 67–8
Tours, France, 42
Tower Hamlets, London, 356
Towns, Henry, 92, 94
Townshend, Charles, 2nd
    Viscount, 85
Toxteth bye-law houses, Liverpool,
    xxviii–xxix, *204*, 215–45, *219*, *228*
  bathrooms, 225, 231–2
  brickwork, 225, 226, 229, 230,
    238, 245
  cornices, 220, 229–30, 238, *239*, 245
  demographics, 235–40
  green spaces, 240–44
  grid pattern, 216–19, *219*, 221
  households in, 236–7
  interior decoration, 233–5
  internal layouts, 225, 230
  kitchens, 223, 225, 232
  lavatories, 223, 230, 237
  lighting, 231
  linoleum, 233
  measurements, 230–31

mirror plans, 225, 229
  Prince's Park, 241–4
  sculleries, 225, 231
  street names, 217–18
  Welsh Streets, 216–17, *219*, 226,
    231–2, 238, *239*, 244
  windows, 221, 225–6, 229, 240
Toxteth Library, Liverpool, 233
Toxteth Park, Liverpool, 215, 216,
    220, 223, 225–7, 231, 243, 244
Toxteth Park sandstone, 122
Toynbee Hall, Spitalfields, 257
Treaty of Dover (1670), 39
Trevithick, Richard, 160
trompe l'œil, 37, 147
*True Principles of Pointed
    Architecture, The* (Pugin), 164
Truman, Joseph, 35
Tryquett, Thomas, 44
Tudor period (1485–1603), xvii,
    xxiii–xxvii, 167–8
Tudor style, 167–8
Tuileries, Paris, 183
Tunnicliffe, Ralph, 91
Turner Prize, 244
Turville Street, Shoreditch, 252,
    264, 270
Twentieth Century Society, 331
two-up two-down, xxviii, 214
Twyford, Thomas, 201
Tymperon, Mary, 83

Unité d'Habitation, Marseilles,
    354–6, *355*, 357
United Synagogue, 52

Unwin, Raymond, 363
Utrecht, Netherlands, 325

Valance Road, Spitalfields, 69
Van Alen, William, 332, 345
Vauxhall, London, 248
Veneto region, Italy, 21, 85, 86, 104, 170
Venice, Italy, 21, 86, 104, 170
Vers une Architecture (Le Corbusier), 324
Vicar's Close, Wells, xiv, *xv*
Victoria, Queen of the United Kingdom, 156
Victoria and Albert Museum, London, 178
Victoria Park, London, 242–3
Victoria Regia House, Chatsworth, 172
Victorian period (1837–1901), xxviii, xxix, 51–76, 155–203
  Boundary Estate, xxviii–xxix, *246*, 247–301
  Cragside, xiv, xxvii, xxviii, *154*, 159–203
  Princelet Street, 51–76
  Toxteth bye-law houses, xxviii–xxix, *204*, 205–45, *228*
Vienna, Austria, 321, 322
  Karl-Marx Hof, 352
  Rufer House, 323–4
  Steiner House, 321, 323, *327*
Vienna Secession (1897–1914), 306–7, 322, 331
Villa Cuno, Eppenhausen, 332, *334*

Villa La Roche, Paris, 325
Vilnius, Lithuania, 75
Virginia Road, Shoreditch, 259, 287
Virginia Road Primary School, Shoreditch, 263–4, *265*, 275, 299
Vitruvius Britannicus (Campbell), 85
Vitruvius, 88, 164
Voelas Street, Toxteth, 226–36, *228*, 240–41, 245

W & G Audsley, 222
W. G. Armstrong and Co., 160
Wagner, Martin, 352
Walberswick, Suffolk, 308
Walker, Thomas, 220
Walpole, Robert, 82, 104
Waltham Cross, Hertfordshire, 168
Walton Buildings, Shoreditch, 270
Walvin, James, 151
Wanstead House, Essex, 85
Ward, James, 296
Ware, Isaac, 16, 92, 115
Warton, Margaret, 115–16, 117
Warwick Street, Toxteth, 220
washrooms, 14, 24
water closets (WCs), 207, 223, 230, 277–8, 303
Water Street, Liverpool, 129
Waterlow, D. D., 289
Watkinson's Terrace, Liverpool, 211
Wealden hall houses, xiv, *xviii*
  Bayleaf Farmstead, xiv, xvi, xvii, *xviii*
Weavers' Company, 42, 43
weaving, 38–51

Webb, Philip, 158, 170, 272
Wedderburn, John, 135, 137
Weissenhof Estate, Stuttgart,
    328, 344
Welby, Reginald, 1st Baron, 289
Wellingborough Road,
    Northampton, 306
Wells, Somerset, xiv, *xv*
Welsh Presbyterian Church,
    Liverpool, 221–2, 244
Welsh Streets, Toxteth, 216–17, *219*,
    226, 231–2, 238, *239*, 244
Wentworth Woodhouse, South
    Yorkshire, 90, *91*, 105, 112
Werkbund Jahrbuch, 317
West Ham Jewish Cemetery, 56
West Indies, *see* Caribbean
Westminster Abbey, London,
    108, 167
Westminster Chambers,
    Liverpool, 215
Westminster City Council, 300
Whigs, 28, 82, 84, 85, 86, 87
white box architecture, 319, 323
Whitechapel, London, 270
Whitehall, Shrewsbury, xxiii
Whitehall Palace, London, 182
Wilberforce House, Kingston-
    upon-Hull, 80
Wilberforce, William, 139, 150
Wilbraham, Elizabeth, Lady, 3
Wilde, Oscar, 262
Wildridge, Tindall, 116
Willesley, Cranbrook, 187
William I, King of England, xiii

William III, King of England,
    Scotland and Ireland,
    27–8, 40
Williams, Montagu, 258
Williams and Jones, 214
*Williamson's Liverpool
    Advertiser*, 136
Willow Road, Hampstead, 315,
    352–3
Wilson, Colin St John, 30
Windermere Terrace, Toxteth, 243
windows
    Hardwick Hall, xxiv
    Heywood's, 140, 141
    Maister House, 95, 96–8
    New Ways, 329, 330, 337, 338
    Pallant House, 8, 10
    Princelet Street, 50, 55, 64, 71,
        72, *73*
    Steep Hill house, xi, *xi*
    Toxteth, 229
    Willow Road, 352–3
Windsor, Alan, 330
Winestead Old Hall, East
    Yorkshire, 83
Winmill, Charles Canning, 261,
    268, 272, 273, 284
Wise, Sarah, 254
witch bottles, 23
'Wohnung, Die' (1927
    exhibition), 328
Wollaton Hall, Nottinghamshire,
    xxvi
Womersley, J. L., 356
Wood, Charles, 34, 37

Wood the Elder, John, 12, 123, 130, 131

Wood the Younger, John, 130

workhouses, 206–7

World, The, 201

World's Columbian Exposition (1893), 321

Worrall, Samuel, xxvii, 34, 35–7, 79

Wren, Christopher, xxiii, 4, 5, 12, 23, 129, 279, 305

Wyatt, James, 140, 144

Wyatt, Matthew Digby, 55, 180

Yates, Richard Vaughan, 242

Yiddish, 51, 56, 57

York Assembly Rooms, 90

York Minster, York, 23

York Row, Shoreditch, 285

Zionism, 56, 62–4, 72

Zong, 138